P9-CCT-352

DISCARDED

THE ANCIENT NEAR EAST

TRANSLATORS AND ANNOTATORS

W. F. Albright, Johns Hopkins University
H. L. Ginsberg, Jewish Theological Seminary
Albrecht Goetze, Yale University
S. N. Kramer, University of Pennsylvania
Theophile J. Meek, University of Toronto
A. Leo Oppenheim, University of Chicago
Robert H. Pfeiffer, Harvard University
Franz Rosenthal, Yale University
E. A. Speiser, University of Pennsylvania
Ferris J. Stephens, Yale University
John A. Wilson, University of Chicago

Princeton University Press

THE

Ancient
Near
East

An Anthology
of Texts
and Pictures

220.93

221   Pritchard, James Bennet es B. Pritchard
.93   The ancient Near East;
P9612   an anthology of texts
         and pictures OHIO CHR

3053100024221

Copyright © 1958 by Princeton University Press

London: Oxford University Press

All rights reserved

L.C. Card 58-10052

ISBN 0-691-00200-2 (paperback edn.)

ISBN 0-691-03501-6 (hardcover edn.)

Printed in the United States of America
by Princeton University Press
Princeton, New Jersey

Fifth Princeton Paperback Printing, 1971

Fifth Hardcover Printing, 1971

This book is sold subject to the condition
that it shall not, by way of trade, be lent,
resold, hired out, or otherwise disposed of
without the publisher's consent, in any
form of binding or cover other than that
in which it is published.

Preface

THE aim of this volume is to make available in convenient form those ancient Near Eastern documents which are important for an understanding of biblical peoples and their writings. For many centuries the Old Testament and a few Greek sources provided the sole witness to life in the ancient Near East. In comparatively recent years, however, the sources for the history of the peoples of the biblical world have been greatly augmented by archaeological discovery. Writings of Egyptians, Syrians, Hittites, Assyrians, Babylonians and other contemporary peoples have been recovered, deciphered, and reliably understood. In addition to the words of the ancient Near Eastern people, there has been amassed a significant additional documentation in art, architecture, and artifacts of daily life.

The selection offered here has been made from the point of view of relevance to the Old Testament, the most widely studied and the most significant legacy from the ancient Near East. Some suggested points of contact with specific biblical passages have been entered beside the texts; the wide margins provide space for others which may occur to the user of the volume.

Most of the translations are taken from *Ancient Near Eastern Texts Relating to the Old Testament*, edited by James B. Pritchard, 2nd edition, Princeton University Press, 1955 (abbreviated *ANET*). In the side margins the reader may find references to the pages of *ANET*, where these translations are accompanied by full bibliographical references and footnotes.

The more pertinent information about the photographs has been given in the captions. A full documentation for most of them may be had by referring to the Catalogue of *The Ancient Near East in Pictures Relating to the Old Testament*, by James B. Pritchard, Princeton University Press, 1954 (abbreviated *ANEP*), where details of size, provenience, publication, and present location of the object can be found. An account of the discovery and of the significance of some of the most important extra-biblical materials from the ancient Near East is given in the editor's *Archaeology and the Old Testament*, Princeton University Press, 1958.

Italics have been used in the translations to designate a doubtful translation of a known text or for transliterations. Square brackets have been employed for restorations in the text; round brackets (parentheses) have been put around interpolations made for a better understanding of the translation; obvious scribal omissions have been placed between triangular brackets. In the translations from Ugaritic, half square brackets have been used to designate a text which has been partly restored. A lacuna has been indicated by three dots; in case the lacuna comes before a final sentence dot, four dots appear. References to the tablets, columns, lines of the text have been given usually in parentheses either within the translation, as in prose, or in the right-hand margin, when the form is poetry. Capital Roman numerals indicate the number of the tablet or some other well-recognized division; lowercase Roman numerals have been used for columns; Arabic numerals indicate the line or lines.

In the difficult task of making a choice of the most relevant texts and pictures the editor has benefited from earlier collections, such works as those of Barton, Rogers, Gressmann, and Galling. Twenty-five teachers of graduate courses in the fields of Near Eastern and Old Testament history have given helpful opinions as to the most essential material to be included. The editor's thanks are due to those predecessors and colleagues who have helped in a measure to check his own judgment in the choice of the most relevant material.

With pleasure the editor of this volume acknowledges his great debt to Herbert S. Bailey, Jr., director of the Princeton University Press, who first suggested the making of this anthology from the larger and more expensive collections of texts and pictures. Helen Van Zandt's skill in solving many of the technical problems connected with the making of this book has constituted no small part of the undertaking. In addition to the translators listed opposite the title page, Dr. Edmund I. Gordon, of the University Museum, University of Pennsylvania, participated by supplying translations of important Sumerian proverbs.

J. B. P.

Berkeley, California, February, 1958

Contents

IX. CANAANITE AND ARAMAIC INSCRIPTIONS

FRANZ ROSENTHAL

X. RITUALS AND HYMNS

XI. WISDOM, PROPHECY, AND SONGS

XII. LETTERS

List of Illustrations

A consolidated map will be found on the endpaper.

ACKNOWLEDGMENTS OF ILLUSTRATIONS

Albright, W. F.: 33. Allegro, J. M.: 173. American Schools of Oriental Research: 83. Archives Photographiques, Paris: 67, 68, 74, 96, 132, 134. Birnbaum, S. A.: 81. Bothmer, B. V.: 191. British Museum: p. x, 5, 16, 17, 28, 58, 69, 72, 97, 98, 100, 102, 114, 115, 118, 119, 122, 124, 142, 144, 146, 151, 155, 156, 157, 158, 161, 163, 164, 165, 167, 168. Brooklyn Museum: 70, 82, 160. Bulloz, J. E., Paris: 40. Cairo Museum: 4, 42, 84, 105, 106, 111, 129. Cameron, G. G.: 62. Department of Antiquities, Israel: 27. Dunand, M.: 103. Éditions "TEL," Paris: 86, 147. Felbermeyer, J.: 112. Foto Marburg: 6, 43, 93, 107, 108,

109, 110, 125, 127, 193. Gaddis, A.: 88, 94. Garber, P. L.: 182. Giraudon, Paris: 59, 117. Hessische Treuhandverwaltung des früheren preussischen Kunstgutes, Wiesbaden: 8, 87, 89, 91. Horn, S. H.: 73. Iraq Museum: 36, 169. Kenyon, K.: 49, 172. Mazar, B.: 38. Metropolitan Museum of Art, New York: 12, 19, 21, 26, 32, 41, 45, 46, 113, 159. Musées Royaux d'Art et d'Histoire, Brussels: 153. Museo di Antichità, Turin: 14, 120. Museum of the Ancient Orient, Istanbul: title page. Museum of Fine Arts, Boston: 104. Oriental Institute, Chicago: 3, 7, 10, 29, 30, 31, 48, 55, 92, 95, 123, 148, 149, 170, 175, 181, 185, 186, 196, 197. Palestine Archaeological Museum, Jerusalem: 9, 11, 22, 37, 39, 47, 49, 53, 80, 90, 135, 152, 166, 177, 178, 187. Palestine Institute, Pacific School of Religion: 23, 76, 176. Photo Rostemy, Teheran: 195. Porada, E.: 57. Pritchard, J. B.: p. i, 24, 78, 79, 116, 126, 128, 130, 136, 137, 139, 140, 143, 179, 180. Schaeffer, C. F. A.: 63, 133. Staatliche Museen, Berlin: 121, 189. Trans World Airline: 192. University Museum, University of Pennsylvania: p. iv, 1, 13, 15, 34, 35, 44, 60, 61, 66, 71, 85, 99, 131, 150, 154, 188, 194. Yadin, Y.: 174. Yale University News Bureau: 56.

ILLUSTRATIONS FROM BOOKS

2: C. R. Lepsius, *Denkmäler aus Ägypten und Äthiopien*, Berlin, 1848-1859, vol. 2, pl. 133.—18: N. de G. Davies, *The Tomb of Reḫ-mi-Rēʿ at Thebes*, New York, 1943, pl. 58.—20: A. Moortgat, *Vorderasiatische Rollsiegel*, Berlin, 1940, no. 526.—25, 138: *Syria*, XVIII, pl. 24, pl. 17.—50, 51: *Journal of the Palestine Oriental Society*, vol. 14, 1934, pl. 1, p. 180, fig. 2.—52: H. Junker, *Gîza*, vol. 2, Vienna and Leipzig, 1934, pl. 7b.—54, 101: A. H. Layard, *A Second Series of the Monuments of Nineveh*, London, 1853, pls. 35, 21.—64: H. Grimme, *Althebräische Inschriften vom Sinai*, Darmstadt, 1923, pl. 9, below.—65: D. Diringer, *Le iscrizioni antico-ebraiche palestinesi*, Florence, 1934, pl. 1.—75: A. Reifenberg, *Ancient Hebrew Seals*, London, 1950, p. 27.—77: W. F. Albright, *The Excavation of Tell Beit Mirsim*, vol. 1, *AASOR*, 12, New Haven, 1932, p. 78, fig. 13.—141: F. H. Weissbach, *Babylonische Miscellen, WVDOG*, 4, Leipzig, 1903, p. 16, fig. 1.—145: A. H. Layard, *The Monuments of Nineveh*, London, 1849, pl. 65.—162: A. J. Gayet, *Le temple de Louxor, Mémoires, Mission archéologique française au Caire*, vol. 15, Paris, 1894, pl. 63 (71).—171: H. Frankfort, *Cylinder Seals*, London, 1939, pl. 22k.—183: The Megiddo Expedition, *Megiddo II*, Text, Chicago, 1948, fig. 107.—184: *Bulletin of the American Schools of Oriental Research*, no. 52, 1933, fig. 1.—190: V. Place, *Ninive et l'Assyrie*, vol. 3, plates, Paris, 1867, pl. 18bis.

I. Egyptian Myths and Tales

TRANSLATOR: JOHN A. WILSON

The Memphite Theology of Creation

ANET, 4-5

When the First Dynasty established its capital at Memphis, it was necessary to justify the sudden emergence of this town to central importance. The Memphite god Ptah was therefore proclaimed to have been the First Principle, taking precedence over other recognized creator-gods. Mythological arguments were presented that the city of Memphis was the "place where the Two Lands are united" and that the Temple of Ptah was the "balance in which Upper and Lower Egypt have been weighed."

The extracts presented here are particularly interesting, because creation is treated in an intellectual sense, whereas other creation stories (like *ANET*, pp. 3-4) are given in purely physical terms. Here the god Ptah conceives the elements of the universe with his mind ("heart") and brings them into being by his commanding speech ("tongue"). Thus, at the beginning of Egyptian history, there was an approach to the Logos Doctrine.

The extant form of this document dates only to 700 B.C., but linguistic, philological, and geopolitical evidence is conclusive in support of its derivation from an original text more than two thousand years older.

(53) There came into being as the heart and there came into being as the tongue (something) in the form of Atum. The mighty Great One is Ptah, who transmitted [*life* to all gods], as well as (to) their *ka*'s, through this heart, by which Horus became Ptah, and through this tongue, by which Thoth became Ptah.[1]

(Thus) it happened that the heart and tongue gained control over [every] (other) member of the body, by teaching that he[2] is in every body and in every mouth of all gods, all men, [all] cattle, all creeping things, and (everything) that lives, by thinking and commanding everything that he wishes.

(55) His Ennead is before him in (the form of) teeth and lips. That is (the equivalent of) the semen and hands of Atum. Whereas the Ennead of Atum came into being by his semen and his fingers, the Ennead

---

[1] Ptah thought of and created by speech the creator-god Atum ("Totality"), thus transmitting the divine power of Ptah to all other gods. The gods Horus and Thoth, a commonly associated pair, are equated with the organs of thought and speech.   [2] Ptah, as heart and tongue.

Fig. 158

(of Ptah), however, is the teeth and lips in this mouth, which pronounced the name of everything, from which Shu and Tefnut came forth, and which was the fashioner of the Ennead.

The sight of the eyes, the hearing of the ears, and the smelling the air by the nose, they report to the heart. It is this which causes every completed (concept) to come forth, and it is the tongue which announces what the heart thinks.

Thus all the gods were formed and his Ennead was completed. Indeed, all the divine order   really came into being through what the heart thought and the tongue commanded. Thus the *ka*-spirits were made and the *hemsut*-spirits were appointed, they who make all provisions and all nourishment, by this speech. (*Thus justice was given to*) him who does what is liked, (*and injustice to*) him who does what is disliked.   Thus life was given to him who has peace and death was given to him who has sin. Thus were made all work and all crafts, the action of the arms, the movement of the legs, and the activity of every member, in conformance with (this) command which the heart thought, which came forth through the tongue, and which gives value to everything.

(Thus) it happened that it was said of Ptah: "He who made all and brought the gods into being." He is indeed Ta-tenen, who brought forth the gods, for everything came forth from him, nourishment and provisions, the offerings of the gods, and every good thing. Thus it was discovered and understood that his strength is greater than (that of the other) gods. And so Ptah

Gen. 2:2

was satisfied,[1] after he had made everything, as well as all the divine order.   He had formed the gods, he had made cities, he had founded nomes, he had put the gods in their shrines, (60) he had established their offerings, he had founded their shrines, he had made their bodies like that (with which) their hearts were satisfied. So the gods entered into their bodies of every (kind of) wood, of every (kind of) stone, of every (kind of) clay, or anything which might grow upon him,[2] in which they had taken form. So all the gods, as well as their *ka*'s gathered themselves to him, content and associated with the Lord of the Two Lands.

[1] Or, "so Ptah rested."
[2] Upon Ptah, in his form of the "rising land." Note that divine images were not the gods themselves, but only places.

Deliverance of Mankind from Destruction

The themes of this myth are the sin of mankind, the destructive disappointment of their creator, and the deliverance of mankind from annihilation. However, the setting of the present text shows that its purpose was magical protection rather than moral teaching. On the walls of three royal tombs of the Empire, it accompanies certain charms to protect the body of the dead ruler. This implies that the former deliverance of mankind from destruction will be valid also in this individual case.

ANET, 10-11

It happened that . . . Re, the god who came into being by himself, when he was king of men and gods all together. Then mankind plotted something in the (very) presence of Re. Now then, his majesty—life, prosperity, health!—was old. His bones were of silver, his flesh of gold, and his hair of genuine lapis lazuli.

Gen. 6:5-7

Then his majesty perceived the things which were being plotted against him by mankind. Then his majesty—life, prosperity, health! said to those who were in his retinue: "Pray, summon to me my Eye,[1] Shu, Tefnut, Geb, and Nut, as well as the fathers and mothers who were with me when I was in Nun,[2] as well as my god Nun also. He is to bring his court (5) with him. Thou shalt bring them *secretly*: let not mankind see; let not their hearts escape.[3] Thou shalt come with them to the Great House, that they may tell their plans, since *the* [*times*] *when* I came from Nun to the place in which I came into being."

Fig. 158

Then these gods were brought in, and these gods [*came*] beside him, putting their heads to the ground in the presence of his majesty, so that he might make his statement in the presence of the father of the eldest, he who made mankind, the king of people. Then they said in the presence of his majesty: "Speak to us, so that we may hear it."

Then Re said to Nun: "O eldest god, in whom I came into being, O ancestor gods, behold mankind, which came into being from my Eye[4]—they have plotted things against me. Tell me what ye would do about it. Behold, I am seeking; I would not slay them until I had heard

---

[1] The eye of the sun-god was an independent part of himself, with a complicated mythological history.

[2] The abysmal waters, in which creation took place.

[3] Was Re unwilling that mankind repent its rebellious purposes?

[4] Mankind originated as the tears of the creator-god.

what (10) ye might say about it." Then the majesty of Nun said: "My son Re, the god greater than he who made him and mightier than they who created him, sitting upon thy throne, the fear of thee is great when thy Eye is (directed) against them who scheme against thee!" Then the majesty of Re said: "Behold, they have fled into the desert, their hearts being afraid because I *might* speak to them." Then they said in the presence of his majesty: "May thy Eye be sent, that it may *catch* for thee them who scheme with evil things. (But) the Eye is not (*sufficiently*) prominent therein to smite

Fig. 162 them for thee. It should go down as Hat-Hor."

So then this goddess came and slew mankind in the desert. Then the majesty of this god said: "Welcome, Hat-Hor, who hast done for me *the deed for which I came*!" Then this goddess said: "As thou livest for me, I have prevailed over mankind, and it is pleasant in my heart!" Then the majesty of Re said: "I shall prevail over them *as a king* (15) by diminishing them!"[1] That is how Sekhmet came into being, the (beer)-mash of the night, to wade in their blood from Herakleopolis.[2]

Then Re said: "Pray, summon to me swift and speedy messengers, so that they may run like the shadow of a body." Then these messengers were brought immediately. Then the majesty of this god said: "Go ye to Elephantine and bring me red ochre very abundantly." Then this red ochre was brought to him. Then the majesty of this great god caused . . . , [and He-With]-the-Side-Lock who is in Heliopolis[3] ground up this red ochre. When further maidservants crushed barley to (make) beer, then this red ochre was added to this mash. Then (it) was like human blood. Then seven thousand jars of the beer were made. So then the majesty of the King of Upper and Lower Egypt: Re came, together with these gods, to see this beer.

Now when day broke for (20) the slaying of mankind by the goddess at their season of going upstream, then the majesty of Re said: "How good it is! I shall protect mankind with it!" Then Re said: "Pray, carry it to the place in which she expected to slay mankind." Then the majesty of the King of Upper and Lower

---

[1] It soon becomes clear that Re wishes the destruction to cease, whereas Hat-Hor is unwilling to halt her lustful annihilation.
[2] The formula by which the origin of a name was explained.
[3] An epithet of the High Priest of Re.

Egypt: Re went to work early in the depth of the night to have this sleep-maker poured out. Then the fields were filled with liquid *for* three palms, through the power of the majesty of this god.

Then this goddess went at dawn, and she found this (place) flooded. Then her face (looked) beautiful therein. Then she drank, and it was good in her heart. She came (back) drunken, without having perceived mankind.

(The remainder of this story has to do with the origin of certain names and customs, such as the use of strong drink at the Feast of Hat-Hor.)

The Story of Sinuhe

ANET, 18-22

A strong love of country was a dominant characteristic of the ancient Egyptian. Though he might feel the responsibilities of empire-building, he wished the assurance that he would close his days on the banks of the Nile. That sentiment made the following story one of the most popular classics of Egyptian literature. An Egyptian official of the Middle Kingdom went into voluntary exile in Asia. He was prosperous and well established there, but he continued to long for the land of his birth. Finally he received a royal invitation to return and join the court. This was his real success in life, and this was the popular point of the story. Much of the tale is pompous and over-styled in wording and phrasing, but the central narrative is a credible account, which fits the period as we know it. If this was fiction, it was based on realities and deserves a respected place in Egyptian literature.

The story opens with the death of Amen-em-het I (about 1960 B C.) and continues in the reign of his successor, Sen-Usert I (about 1971-1928 B.C.). Manuscripts are plentiful and run from the late Twelfth Dynasty (about 1800 B.C.) to the Twenty-First Dynasty (about 1000 B.C.). There are five papyri and at least seventeen ostraca. The most important papyri are in Berlin.

(R1) The Hereditary Prince and Count, Judge and District Overseer of the domains of the Sovereign in the lands of the Asiatics, real acquaintance of the king, his beloved, the Attendant Si-nuhe. He says:

I was an attendant who followed his lord, a servant of the royal harem (and of) the Hereditary Princess, the great of favor, the wife of King Sen-Usert in (the pyramid town) Khenem-sut, the daughter of King Amen-em-het (R5) in (the pyramid town) Qa-nefru, Nefru, the lady of reverence.

Year 30, third month of the first season, day 7.[1]

Fig. 105

---

[1] Around 1960 Amen-em-het I's death would have fallen early in March.

The god ascended to his horizon; the King of Upper and Lower Egypt: Sehetep-ib-Re was taken up to heaven and united with the sun disc. The body of the god merged with him who made him.[1] The Residence City was in silence, hearts were in mourning, the Great Double Doors were sealed shut. (R10) The courtiers (sat) head on lap, and the people were in grief.

Now his majesty had sent an army to the land of the Temeh-Libyans, with his eldest son as the commander thereof, the good god Sen-Usert, (R15) and even now he was returning and had carried off living captives of the Tehenu-Libyans and all (kinds of) cattle without number.

The courtiers of the palace sent to the western border to let the King's Son know the events which had taken place at the court. The messengers met him on the road, (R20) and they reached him in the evening time. He did not delay a moment; the falcon[2] flew away with his attendants, without letting his army know it. Now the royal children who had been following him in this army had been sent for, (B1) and one of them was summoned. While I was standing (near by) I heard his voice as he was speaking and I was a little way off. My heart was distraught, my arms spread out (in dismay), trembling fell upon all my limbs.[3] I removed myself *by leaps and bounds* to seek a hiding place for myself. I placed (5) myself between two bushes, in order to *cut (myself) off from* the road and its *travel*.

I set out southward, (but) I did not plan to reach this Residence City, (for) I thought that there would be civil disorder, and I did not expect to live after him. I crossed Lake Ma'aty near Sycamore, and I came to Snefru Island. I spent the day there on the *edge* of (10) the fields. I *came into the open* light, while it was (*still*) day, and I met a man standing near by. He stood in awe of me, for he was afraid. When the time of the evening meal came, I drew near to Ox-town. I crossed over in a barge without a rudder, by aid of the west

---

[1] The pharaoh was the "Son of Re," the sun-god. At death he was taken back into the body of his creator and father.

[2] The new king Sen-Usert I.

[3] We are never directly told the reason for Si-nuhe's sudden fright and voluntary exile. Later both he and the king protest his innocence. He may have been legally guiltless, but the transition between kings was a dangerous time for one who was not fully identified with the new king. Assume that Si-nuhe had adequate reason for his sudden and furtive departure and his long stay in Asia.

wind. I passed by the east of the quarry (15) above Mistress-of-the-Red-Mountain.[1] I gave (free) road to my feet going northward, and I came up to the Wall-of-the-Ruler, made to oppose the Asiatics and to crush the Sand-Crossers. I took a crouching position in a bush, for fear lest the watchmen upon the wall where their day's (duty) was might see me.

I set out (20) at evening time, and when day broke I reached Peten. I halted at the Island of Kem-wer. An attack of thirst overtook me. I was parched, and my throat was dusty. I said: "This is the taste of death!" (But then) I lifted up my heart and collected myself, for I had heard the sound of the lowing of cattle, (25) and I spied Asiatics. The sheikh among them, who had been in Egypt, recognized me. Then he gave me water while he boiled milk for me. I went with him to his tribe. What they did (for me) was good.

One foreign country gave me to another. I set off for Byblos and approached Qedem, and spent (30) a year and a half there. Ammi-enshi —he was a ruler of Upper Retenu —took me and said to me: "Thou wilt do well with me, and thou wilt hear the speech of Egypt." He said this, for he knew my character, he had heard of my wisdom, and the people of Egypt who were there with him[2] had borne witness for me. . . .

He set me at the head of his children. He married me to his eldest daughter. He let me choose for myself of his country, (80) of the choicest of that which was with him on his frontier with another country. It was a good land, named Yaa. Figs were in it, and grapes. It had more wine than water. Plentiful was its honey, abundant its olives. Every (kind of) fruit was on its trees. Barley was there, and emmer. There was no limit to any (kind of) cattle. (85) Moreover, great was that which accrued to me as a result of the love of me. He made me ruler of a tribe of the choicest of his country. Bread was made for me as daily fare, wine as daily provision, cooked meat and roast fowl, beside the wild beasts of the desert, for they hunted (90) for me and laid before me, beside the catch of my (own) hounds. Many . . . were made for me, and milk in every (kind of) cooking.

I spent many years, and my children grew up to be strong men, each man as the restrainer of his (own)

Num. 13:23, 27

---

[1] Gebel el-Ahmar, east of Cairo.
[2] Other exiles like Si-nuhe? He is in a land of refuge from Egypt.

tribe. The messenger who went north or who went south to the Residence City (95) stopped over with me, (for) I used to make everybody stop over. I gave water to the thirsty. I put him who had strayed (back) on the road. I rescued him who had been robbed. When the Asiatics became so bold as to oppose the rulers of foreign countries, I counseled their movements. This ruler of (100) (Re)tenu had me spend many years as commander of his army. Every foreign country against which I went forth, when I had made my attack on it, was driven away from its pasturage and its wells. I plundered its cattle, carried off its inhabitants, took away their food, and slew people in it (105) by my strong arm, by my bow, by my movements, and by my successful plans. I found favor in his heart, he loved me, he recognized my valor, and he placed me at the head of his children, when he saw how my arms flourished.

A mighty man of Retenu came, that he might challenge me (110) in my (own) camp. He was a hero without his peer, and he had repelled all of it.[1] He said that he would fight me, he intended to despoil me, and he planned to plunder my cattle, on the advice of his tribe. That prince discussed (it) with me, and I said: "I do not know him. Certainly I am no confederate of his, (115) so that I might move freely in his encampment. Is it the case that I have (ever) opened his *door* or overthrown his fences? (Rather), it is hostility because he sees me carrying out thy commissions. I am really like a stray bull in the midst of another herd, and a bull of (these) cattle attacks him. . . ."[2]

During the night I strung my bow and shot my arrows,[3] I gave free play to my dagger, and polished my weapons. When day broke, (Re)tenu was come. (130) It had *whipped up* its tribes and collected the countries of a (good) half of it. It had thought (only) of this fight. Then he came to me as I was waiting, (for) I had placed myself near him. Every heart burned for me; women and men groaned. Every heart was sick for me. They said: "Is there another strong man who could fight against him?" Then (*he took*) his shield, his battle-axe, (135) and his *armful of javelins*. *Now* after I had let his weapons issue forth, I made his arrows

[1] He had beaten every one of the land of Retenu.
[2] Si-nuhe goes on to state that he accepts the challenge, which has come to him because he is an outsider.   [3] In practice.

pass by me uselessly, one close to another. He charged me, and I shot him, my arrow sticking in his neck. He cried out and fell on his nose. (140) I felled him with his (own) battle-axe and raised my cry of victory over his back, while every Asiatic roared. I gave praise to Montu,[1] while his adherents were mourning for him. This ruler Ammi-enshi took me into his embrace. Then I carried off his goods and plundered his cattle. What he had planned to do (145) to me I did to him. I took what was in his tent and stripped his encampment. I became great thereby, I became extensive in my wealth, I became abundant in my cattle.

I Sam. 17:51

Thus did god to show mercy to him upon whom he had *laid blame*, whom he had led astray to another country. (But) today his heart is assuaged.[2] . . .

Now when the majesty of the King of Upper and Lower Egypt: Kheper-ka-Re, the justified,[3] was told about this situation in which I was, then his majesty kept sending (175) to me with presentations from the royal presence, that he might gladden the heart of this servant like the ruler of any foreign country. The royal children in his palace let me hear their commissions. [4]
. . . .

Then they came for this servant. . . . I was permitted to spend a day in Yaa handing over my property to my children, my eldest son being responsible for my tribe. (240) My tribe and all my property were in his charge: my serfs, all my cattle, my fruit, and every pleasant tree of mine.

Then this servant came southward. I halted at the "Ways of Horus."[5] The commander there who was responsible for the patrol sent a message to the Residence to make (it) known. Then his majesty sent a capable overseer of peasants of the palace, with loaded ships in his train, (245) carrying presentations from the royal presence FOR THE ASIATICS WHO HAD FOLLOWED ME, ESCORTING ME TO THE "WAYS OF HORUS." I called each of them by his name.[6] Every butler was (busy) at his duties. When I started and set sail, the kneading and straining (of beer) was carried on beside me, until I had reached the town of Lisht.

Gen. 45:21-23

[1] The Egyptian god of war.
[2] It is not clear how Si-nuhe expiated his sins, except by being a successful Egyptian in another country.   [3] Sen-Usert I.
[4] They also wrote to Si-nuhe.
[5] The Egyptian frontier station facing Sinai, probably near modern Kantarah.   [6] He introduced the Asiatics to the Egyptians.

When day had broken, very early, they came and summoned me, ten men coming and ten men going to usher me to the palace. I put my brow to the ground between the sphinxes, (250) while the royal children were waiting in a *recess* to meet me. The courtiers who usher into the audience hall set me on the way to the private chambers. I found his majesty upon the Great Throne in a *recess* of fine gold. When I was stretched out upon my belly, I knew not myself in his presence, (although) this god greeted me pleasantly. I was like a man caught in the dark: (255) my soul departed, my body was powerless, my heart was not in my body, that I might know life from death.

THEN HIS MAJESTY SAID TO ONE OF THESE COURTIERS: "Lift him up. Let him speak to me." Then his majesty said: "Behold, thou art come. Thou hast trodden the foreign countries *and made a flight.* (But now) elderliness has attacked thee; thou hast reached old age. It is no small matter that thy corpse be (properly) buried; thou shouldst not be interred by bowmen. Do not, do not act thus any longer: (for) thou dost not speak (260) when thy name is pronounced!" Yet (I) was afraid to respond, and I answered it with the answer of one afraid: "What is it that my lord says to me? I should answer it, (but) there is nothing that I can do: it is really the hand of a god. It is a terror that is in my belly like that which produced the fated flight. BEHOLD, I AM BEFORE THEE. THINE IS LIFE. MAY THY MAJESTY DO AS HE PLEASES."

THEREUPON the royal children WERE ushered in. Then his majesty said to the Queen: "Here is Si-nuhe, (265) come as a Bedu, (*in*) *the guise of* the Asiatics." She gave a very great cry, and the royal children clamored all together. Then they said to his majesty: "It is not really he, O Sovereign, my lord!" Then his majesty said: "It is really he!" Now when they had brought with them their bead-necklaces, their rattles, and their sistra, then they presented them to his majesty. ". . . Loose the horn of thy bow and relax thy arrow! (275) Give breath to him that was stifled! Give us our goodly gift in this sheikh Si-Mehit, a bowman born in Egypt. He made a flight through fear of thee; he left the land through terror of thee. (But) the face of him who beholds thy face shall not *blench*; the eye which looks at thee shall not be afraid!"

Exod. 15:20-21

Then his majesty said: "He shall not fear. (280) He has no *title* to be in dread. He shall be a courtier among the nobles. He shall be put in the ranks of the courtiers. Proceed ye to the inner chambers of the *morning* (*toilet*), in order to make his position." [1]

Gen. 41:42

So I went forth from the midst of the inner chambers, with the royal children giving me their hands. (285) Thereafter we went to the Great Double Door. I was put into the house of a royal son, in which were splendid things. A cool room was in it, and images of the horizon.[2] Costly things of the Treasury were in it. Clothing of royal linen, myrrh, and prime oil of the king and of the nobles whom he loves were in every room. (290) Every butler was (busy) at his duties. Years were made to pass away from my body. I was *plucked*, and my hair was combed. A load (of dirt) was given to the desert, and my clothes (to) the Sand-Crossers. I was clad in fine linen and anointed with prime oil. I slept on a bed. I gave up the sand to them who are in it, (295) and wood oil to him who is anointed with it. I was given a house *which had a garden*, which had been in the possession of a courtier. Many *craftsmen* built it, and all its wood(work) was newly restored. Meals were brought to me from the palace three or four times a day, apart from that which the royal children gave, without ceasing a moment.

Gen. 41:14

(300) There was constructed for me a pyramid-tomb of stone in the midst of the pyramid-tombs. The stonemasons who hew a pyramid-tomb took over its ground-area. The outline-draftsmen designed in it; the chief sculptors carved in it; and the overseers of works who are in the necropolis made it their concern. (305) Its necessary materials were made from all the outfittings which are placed at a tomb-shaft. Mortuary priests were given to me. There was made for me a necropolis garden, with fields in it *formerly (extending)* as far as the town, like that which is done for a chief courtier. My statue was overlaid with gold, and its skirt was of fine gold. It was his majesty who had it made. There is no poor man for whom the like has been done.

Fig. 192

(So) I was under (310) the favor of the king's presence until the day of mooring had come.[3]

---

[1] Si-nuhe's new rank is to be established by a change of dress in a properly designated place.

[2] Painted decorations. "Cool room" may have been either a bathroom or a cellar for preserving foods.   [3] Until the day of death.

The Story of Two Brothers

Gen. 39:1-20
This folk tale tells how a conscientious young man was falsely accused of a proposal of adultery by the wife of his elder brother, after he had actually rejected her advances. This part of the story has general similarity to the story of Joseph and Potiphar's wife. The two chief characters are brothers named Anubis and Bata. These were the names of Egyptian gods, and the tale probably does have a mythological setting. However, it served for entertainment, rather than ecclesiastical or moral purpose. The story is colloquial and is so translated.

Papyrus D'Orbiney is now British Museum 10183. Facsimiled in *Select Papyri in the Hieratic Character from the Collections of the British Museum*, II (London, 1860), Pls. IX-XIX, and in G. Möller, *Hieratische Lesestücke*, II (Leipzig, 1927), 1-20. The manuscript can be closely dated to about 1225 B.C. in the Nineteenth Dynasty. Transcription into hieroglyphic in A. H. Gardiner, *Late-Egyptian Stories* (*Bibliotheca Aegyptiaca*, I, Brussels, 1932), 9-29. Translation in Erman, *LAE*, 150-61.

Now THEY SAY THAT (ONCE) THERE WERE two brothers of one mother and one father. Anubis was the name of the elder, and Bata was the name of the younger. Now, as for Anubis, he [had] a house and had a wife, [and] his younger brother (lived) with him as a sort of minor. He was the one who made clothes for him and went to the fields driving his cattle. He was the one who did the plowing and who harvested for him. He was the one who did all (kinds of) work for him which are in the fields. Really, his younger [brother] was a good (grown) man. There was no one like him in the entire land. Why, the strength of a god was in him.

[Now] AFTER MANY DAYS AFTER THIS,[1] his younger brother (5) [was tending] his cattle in his custom of every [day], and he [left off] (to go) to his house every evening, loaded [with] all (kinds of) plants of the field, [with] milk, with wood, and [with] every [good thing of] the fields, and he laid them in front of his [elder brother], who was sitting with his wife. And he drank and he ate, and [he *went out to sleep* in] his stable among his cattle [*by himself*].

Now WHEN IT WAS DAWN AND A SECOND DAY HAD COME, [he *prepared food*], which was cooked, and laid it before his elder brother. [And he] gave him bread for the fields. And he drove his cattle out to let them feed in the fields. He went along after his cattle, [and] they

[1] The unthinking formula of a storyteller making a transition.

would say to him: "The grass [of] such-and-such a place is good," and he would understand whatever they said and would take them to the place (ii 1) of good grass which they wanted. So the cattle which were before him became very, very fine. They doubled their calving very, very much.

Now AT THE TIME OF plowing his [elder] brother said to him: "Get a yoke [of oxen] ready for us for plowing, for the fields have come out, and it is fine for plowing. Also come to the fields with seed, for we shall be busy (with) plowing [in] the morning." So he spoke to him. THEN [his] (5) younger brother did all the things which his elder brother had told him to [do].

Fig. 16

Now WHEN IT WAS DAWN [AND A SECOND] DAY HAD COME, they went to the fields with their [seed], and they were busy [with] plowing, and [their hearts] were very, very pleased with their activity at the beginning of [their] work.

Now [AFTER] MANY [DAYS] AFTER THIS, they were in the fields and ran short of seed. THEN HE sent his younger brother, saying: "Go and fetch us seed from the village." And his younger brother found the wife of his elder brother sitting and doing her hair. THEN HE said to her: "Get up and give me (some) seed, (iii 1) for my younger[1] brother is waiting for me. Don't delay!" THEN SHE said to him: "Go and open the bin and take what you want! Don't make me leave my combing unfinished!" THEN the lad went into his stable, and he took a big jar, for he wanted to carry off a lot of seed. So he loaded himself with barley and emmer and came out carrying them.

Fig. 10

THEN SHE said to him: "How much (is it) that is on your shoulder?" [And he] said to her: (5) "THREE sacks of emmer, two sacks of barley, FIVE IN ALL, is what is on your shoulder."[2] So he spoke to her. THEN SHE [talked with] him, saying "There is [great] strength in you! Now I see your energies every day!" And she wanted to know him as one knows a man.

THEN SHE stood up and took hold of him and said to him: "Come, let's spend an [hour] sleeping (together)! This will do you good, because I shall make fine clothes for you!" THEN the lad [became] like a leopard with [great] rage at the wicked suggestion which she had

---

[1] Read "elder."
[2] Read "my shoulder." He was carrying more than 11 bushels.

made to him, and she was very, very much frightened. THEN HE argued with her, saying: "See here—you are like a mother to me, and your husband is like a father to me! Because—being older than I—he was the one who brought me up. What (iv 1) is this great crime which you have said to me? Don't say it to me again! And I won't tell it to a single person, nor will I let it out of my mouth to any man!" And he lifted up his load, and he went to the fields. THEN HE reached his elder brother, and they were busy with activity (at) their work.

Now AT THE [TIME] OF EVENING, THEN his elder brother left off (to go) to his house. And his younger brother tended his cattle, and [he] loaded himself with everything of the fields, and he took his cattle (5) in front of him, to let them sleep (in) their stable which was in the village.

But the wife of his elder brother was afraid (because of) the suggestion which she had made. THEN SHE took fat and grease,[1] and she became like one who has been criminally beaten, wanting to tell her husband: "It was your younger brother who did the beating!" And her husband left off in the evening, after his custom of every day, and he reached his house, and he found his wife lying down, terribly sick. She did not put water on his hands, after his custom, nor had she lit a light before him, and his house was in darkness, and she lay (there) vomiting. So her husband said to her: "Who has been talking with you?" Then she said to him: "Not one person has been talking with me except your (v 1) younger brother. But when he came [to] take the seed to you he found me sitting alone, and he said to me: 'Come, let's spend an hour sleeping (together)! Put on your curls!'[2] So he spoke to me. But I wouldn't listen to him: 'Aren't I your mother?—for your elder brother is like a father to you!' So I spoke to him. But he was afraid, and he beat (me), so as not to let me tell you. Now, if you let him live, I'll kill myself! Look, when he comes, *don't* [*let him speak*], for, if I accuse (him of) this wicked suggestion, he will be ready to do it *tomorrow (again)*!"

THEN his elder brother became (5) like a leopard, and he made his lance sharp, and he put it in his hand. THEN his elder (brother) stood behind the door (of)

---

[1] Apparently to make her vomit.   [2] The wig of her festive attire.

his stable to kill his younger brother when he came back in the evening to put his cattle in the stable.

Now when the sun was setting, he loaded himself (with) all plants of the fields, according to his custom of every day, and he came back. When the first cow came into the stable, she said to her herdsman: "Here's your elder brother waiting before you, carrying his lance to kill you! Run away from him!" THEN HE understood what his first cow had said. And (vi 1) another went in, and she said the same. So he looked under the door of his stable, and he saw the feet of [his] elder brother, as he was waiting behind the door, with his lance in his hand. So he laid his load on the ground, and he started to run away and escape. And his elder brother went after him, carrying his lance.

THEN his younger brother prayed to the Re-Har-akhti, (5) saying: "O my good lord, thou art he who judges the wicked from the just!" Thereupon the Re heard all his pleas, and the Re made a great (body of) water appear between him and his elder (brother), and it was full of crocodiles. So one of them came to be on one side and the other on the other. And his elder brother struck his hand twice because of his not killing him. THEN his younger brother called to him from the (other) side, saying: "Wait here until dawn. When the sun disc rises, I shall (vii 1) be judged with you in his presence, and he will turn the wicked over to the just, for I won't be with you ever [again]; I won't be in a place where you are—I shall go to the Valley of the Cedar!"

NOW WHEN IT WAS DAWN AND A SECOND DAY HAD COME, the Re-Har-akhti arose, and one of them saw the other. THEN the lad argued with his elder brother, saying: "What do you (mean by) coming after me to kill (me) falsely, when you wouldn't listen to what I had to say? Now I am still your younger brother, and (5) you are like a father to me, and your wife is like a mother to me! Isn't it so? When I was sent to fetch us (some) seed, your wife said to me: 'Come, let's spend an hour sleeping (together)!' But, look, it is twisted for you into something else!" THEN HE let him know all that had happened to him and his wife. THEN HE swore to the Re-Har-akhti, saying "As for your killing (me) falsely, you carried your lance on the word of a filthy whore!" And he took a reed-knife, and he cut off his phallus, and he threw it into the water. And the shad swallowed (it).[1] And he (viii 1) was faint and became weak. And his elder brother's heart was very, very sad, and he stood weeping aloud for him. He could not cross over to where his younger brother was because of the crocodiles. . . .

THEN (the younger brother) went (7) off to the Valley of the Cedar, and his elder brother went off to his house, with his hand laid upon his head, and he was smeared with dust.[2] So he reached his house, and he killed his wife, and he threw her out (to) the dogs. And he sat in mourning for his younger brother. . . .

Josh. 7:6;
II Kings 9:33, 36

(The story continues with a number of episodes).

[1] The mutilation was a self-imposed ordeal to support his oath to the sun-god. There was a familiar element in the swallowing of the phallus by the fish. In the Plutarch account of the Osiris myths, it is related that Seth dismembered Osiris and scattered the pieces. Then Isis went about and buried each piece as she found it. However, she could not find the phallus, which had been thrown into the river and eaten by certain fishes, which thereby became forbidden food.
[2] Thus showing his grief.

The Journey of Wen-Amon to Phoenicia

ANET, 25-29

When the Egyptian Empire disintegrated, it left a vacuum in its place for a generation or two. Egyptians, Asiatics, and Africans continued to think in terms of an authority which was no longer real. In the following tale Egypt had already become a "bruised reed" but was continuing to assert traditional expressions of dominance. The Asiatics were beginning to express their scepticism and their independence of their great neighbor to the south.

Isa. 36:6

The story is almost picaresque in its atmosphere and must be classed as a narrative. Nevertheless, it deals at close range with actual individuals and situations and must have had a basis of fact, here exaggerated by the conscious and unconscious humor of the narrator. It does represent the situation in Hither Asia about 1100 B.C. more tellingly than a document of the historical-propagandistic category could do.

Wen-Amon, an official of the Temple of Amon at Karnak, tells how he was sent to Byblos on the Phœnician coast to procure lumber for the ceremonial barge of the god. Egypt had already split into small states and did not support his mission with adequate purchasing value, credentials, or armed force.

The papyrus, now in the Moscow Museum, comes from el-Hibeh in Middle Egypt and dates to the early Twenty-first Dynasty (11th century B.C.), shortly after the events it relates.

YEAR 5, 4TH MONTH OF THE 3RD SEASON, DAY 16: the day on which Wen-Amon, the Senior of the Forecourt of the House of Amon, [Lord of the Thrones] of the

Two Lands, set out to fetch the woodwork for the great
and august barque of Amon-Re, King of the Gods,
which is on [the River and which is named:] "User-het-
Amon." On the day when I reached Tanis, the place
[where Ne-su-Ba-neb]-Ded and Ta-net-Amon were,[1] I
gave them the letters of Amon-Re, King of the Gods,
and they (5) had them read in their presence. And they
said: "Yes, I will do as Amon-Re, King of the Gods,
our [lord], has said!" I SPENT UP TO THE 4TH MONTH OF
THE 3RD SEASON in Tanis. And Ne-su-Ba-neb-Ded and
Ta-net-Amon sent me off with the ship captain Menge-
bet, and I embarked on the great Syrian sea IN THE IST
MONTH OF THE 3RD SEASON, DAY I.

Fig. 99

I reached Dor, a town of the Tjeker, and Beder, its
prince, had 50 loaves of bread, one jug of wine, (10) and
one leg of beef brought to me. And a man of my ship
ran away and stole one [*vessel*] of gold, [amounting] to
5 *deben*, four jars of silver, amounting to 20 *deben*, and
a sack of 11 *deben* of silver. [Total of what] he [stole]:
5 *deben* of gold and 31 *deben* of silver.[2]

Judg. 1:27

I got up in the morning, and I went to the place where
the Prince was, and I said to him: "I have been robbed
in your harbor. Now you are the prince of this land,
and you are its investigator who should look for my
silver. Now about this silver—it belongs to Amon-Re,
(15) King of the Gods, the lord of the lands; it belongs
to Ne-su-Ba-neb-Ded; it belongs to Heri-Hor, my lord,
and the other great men of Egypt! It belongs to you; it
belongs to Weret; it belongs to Mekmer; it belongs to
Zakar-Baal, the Prince of Byblos!"[3]

And he said to me: "Whether you are important or
whether you are eminent—look here, I do not recognize
this accusation which you have made to me! Suppose it
had been a thief who belonged to my land who went
on your boat and stole your silver, I should have repaid
it to you from my treasury, until they had (20) found
this thief of yours—whoever he may be. Now about

[1] Ne-su-Ba-neb-Ded was the *de facto* ruler of the Delta, with Tanis as
his capital. Ta-net-Amon was apparently his wife. At Thebes in Upper
Egypt, the High Priest of Amon, Heri-Hor, was the *de facto* ruler.
Ne-su-Ba-neb-Ded and Heri-Hor were in working relations with each
other, and were shortly to become contemporary pharaohs.

[2] This value—about 450 grams (1.2 lb. troy) of gold and about 2.8
kilograms (7.5 lb. troy) of silver—was to pay for the lumber.

[3] On the one hand, the gold and silver belong to the Egyptians who
sent Wen-Amon. On the other hand, they belong to the Asiatics who
would receive it. Beder thus has double responsibilities to recover them.

the thief who robbed you—he belongs to you! He belongs to your ship! Spend a few days here visiting me,
so that I may look for him."

I spent nine days moored (in) his harbor, and I went
(to) call on him, and I said to him: "Look, you have
not found my silver. [*Just let*] me [*go*] with the ship
captains and with those who go (to) sea!" But he said

Fig. 98

to me: "Be quiet! . . ." . . . I went out of Tyre at the
break of dawn. . . . Zakar-Baal, the Prince of Byblos, . . .
(30) ship. I found 30 *deben* of silver in it, and I seized
upon it.[1] [And I said to *the Tjeker*: "*I have seized
upon*] your silver, and it will stay with me [until] you
find [my silver or the thief] who stole it! Even though
you have not *stolen*, I shall take it. But as for you, . . ."
So they went away, and I enjoyed my triumph [in] a
tent (on) the shore of the [sea], (in) the harbor of
Byblos. And [*I hid*] Amon-of-the-Road, and I put his
property inside *him*.[2]

And the [Prince] of Byblos sent to me, saying: "Get
[out of (35) my] harbor!" And I sent to him, saying:
"Where *should* [*I go to*]? . . . If [*you have a ship*] to
carry me, have me taken to Egypt again!" So I spent
twenty-nine days in his [harbor, while] he [spent] the
time sending to me every day to say: "Get out (of) my
harbor!"

Now WHILE HE WAS MAKING OFFERING to his gods, the

I Sam. 19:24

god seized one of his youths and made him possessed.[3]
And he said to him: "Bring up [*the*] god! Bring the
messenger who is carrying him! (40) Amon is the one
who sent him out! He is the one who made him come!"
And while the possessed (youth) was having his frenzy
on this night, I had (already) found a ship headed for
Egypt and had loaded everything that I had into it.
While I was watching for the darkness, thinking that
when it descended I would load the god (also), so that
no other eye might see him, the harbor master came to
me, saying: "Wait until morning—so says the Prince."
So I said to him: "Aren't you the one who spend the
time coming to me every day to say: 'Get out (of) my
harbor'? Aren't you saying 'Wait' tonight (45) in order

---

[1] Nearly the same amount as the silver which had been stolen from
him, without account of the gold.

[2] The divine image would have its daily cult and therefore its cultic
apparatus would be stored within the hollow image.

[3] Perhaps a court page was seized with a prophetic frenzy.

to let the ship which I have found get away—and (then)
you will come again (to) say: 'Go away!'?" So he went
and told it to the Prince. And the Prince sent to the
captain of the ship to say: " Wait until morning—so says
the Prince!"

When MORNING CAME, he sent and brought me up,
but the god stayed in the tent where he was, (on) the
shore of the sea. And I found him sitting (in) his upper
room, with his back turned to a window, so that the
waves of the great Syrian sea broke against the back (50)
of his head.[1]

So I said to him: *"May* Amon *favor you!"* But he said
to me "How long, up to today, since you came from the
place where Amon is?" So I said to him: "Five months
and one day up to now." And he said to me: "Well,
you're truthful! Where is the letter of Amon which
(should be) in your hand? Where is the dispatch of
the High Priest of Amon which (should be) in your
hand?" And I told him: "I gave them to Ne-su-Ba-neb-
Ded and Ta-net-Amon." And he was very, very angry,
and he said to me: "Now see—neither letters nor dispatches are in your hand! Where is the cedar ship which
Ne-su-Ba-neb-Ded gave to you? Where is (55) its Syrian
crew? Didn't he turn you over to this foreign ship captain to have him kill you and throw you into the sea?
(Then) with whom would they have looked for the
god? And you too—with whom would they have looked
for you too?" So he spoke to me.

BUT I SAID TO HIM: "Wasn't it an Egyptian ship? Now
it is Egyptian crews which sail under Ne-su-Ba-neb-
Ded! He has no Syrian crews." And he said to me:
"Aren't there twenty ships here in my harbor which are   Ezek. 27:8-9
in commercial relations with Ne-su-Ba-neb-Ded? As to
this Sidon, (ii 1) the other (place) which you have
passed, aren't there fifty more ships there which are in
commercial relations with Werket-El, and which are
drawn up to his house?" And I was silent in this great
time.

And he answered and said to me: "On what business
have you come?" So I told him: "I have come after the
woodwork for the great and august barque of Amon-
Re, King of the Gods. Your father did (it), (5) your

---

[1] Pictorially, not literally. Wen-Amon gives his vivid first view of
Zakar-Baal, framed in an upper window overlooking the surf of the
Mediterranean.

grandfather did (it), and you will do it too!" So I spoke to him. But he said to me: "To be sure, they did it! And if you give me (something) for doing it, I will do it! Why, when my people carried out this commission, Pharaoh—life, prosperity, health!—sent six ships loaded with Egyptian goods, and they unloaded them into their storehouses! You—what is it that you're bringing me—me also?" And he had the journal rolls of his fathers brought, and he had them read out in my presence, and they found a thousand *deben* of silver and all kinds of things in his scrolls.

(10) So he said to me: "If the ruler of Egypt were the lord of mine, and I were his servant also, he would not have to send silver and gold, saying: 'Carry out the commission of Amon!' There would be no carrying of a royal-gift, such as they used to do for my father. As for me—me also—I am not your servant! I am not the servant of him who sent you either! If I cry out to the Lebanon, the heavens open up, and the logs are here lying (on) the shore of the sea! Give (15) me the sails which you have brought to carry your ships which would hold the logs for (Egypt)! Give me the ropes [which] you have brought [*to lash the cedar*] logs which I am to cut down to make you ... which I shall make for you (as) the sails of your boats, and the *spars* will be (too) heavy and will break, and you will die in the middle of the sea! See, Amon made thunder in the sky when he put Seth near him![1] Now when Amon (20) founded all lands, in founding them he founded first the land of Egypt, from which you come; for craftsmanship came out of it, to reach the place where I am, and learning came out of it, to reach the place where I am. What are these silly trips which they have had you make?"

And I said to him: "(That's) not true! What I am on are no 'silly trips' at all! There is no ship upon the River which does not belong to Amon! The sea is his, and the Lebanon is his, of which you say: 'It is mine!' It forms (25) the *nursery* for User-het-Amon, the lord of [every] ship! Why, he spoke—Amon-Re, King of the Gods—and said to Heri-Hor, my master: 'Send me forth!' So he had me come, carrying this great god. But see, you have made this great god spend these twenty-nine days moored (in) your harbor, although

[1] As god of thunder. Thus Amon and Seth were gods of all lands, not of Egypt alone.

you did not know (it). Isn't he here? Isn't he the (same) as he was? You are stationed (here) to carry on the commerce of the Lebanon with Amon, its lord. As for your saying that the former kings sent silver and gold— suppose that they had life and health; (then) they would not have had such things sent! (30) (But) they had such things sent to your fathers in place of life and health![1] Now as for Amon-Re, King of the Gods—he is the lord of this life and health, and he was the lord of your fathers. They spent their lifetimes making offering to Amon. And you also—you are the servant of Amon! If you say to Amon: 'Yes, I will do (it)!' and you carry out his commission, you will live, you will be prosperous, you will be healthy, and you will be good to your entire land and your people! (But) don't wish for yourself anything belonging to Amon-Re, (King of) the Gods. Why, a lion wants his own property! Have your secretary brought to me, so that (35) I may send him to Ne-su-Ba-neb-Ded and Ta-net-Amon, the *officers* whom Amon put in the north of his land, and they will have all kinds of things sent. I shall send him to them to say: 'Let it be brought until I shall go (back again) to the south, and I shall (then) have every bit of the debt still (due to you) brought to you.'" So I spoke to him.

So he entrusted my letter to his messenger, and he loaded in the *keel*, the bow-post, the stern-post, along with four other hewn timbers—seven in all—and he had them taken to Egypt. And in the first month of the second season his messenger who had gone to Egypt came back to me in Syria. And Ne-su-Ba-neb-Ded and Ta-net-Amon sent: (40) 4 jars and 1 *kak-men* of gold; 5 jars of silver; 10 pieces of clothing in royal linen; 10 *kherd* of good Upper Egyptian linen; 500 (rolls of) finished papyrus; 500 cowhides; 500 ropes; 20 sacks of lentils; and 30 baskets of fish. And she sent to me (personally): 5 pieces of clothing in good Upper Egyptian linen; 5 *kherd* of good Upper Egyptian linen; 1 sack of lentils; and 5 baskets of fish.

And the Prince was glad, and he detailed three hundred men and three hundred cattle, and he put supervisors at their head, to have them cut down the timber. *Fig. 89*

[1] In contrast with the past, Wen-Amon has brought an actual god in "Amon-of-the-Road," so that there may be spiritual rather than material advantages for Zakar-Baal.

So they cut them down, and they spent the second season lying there. [1]

In the third month of the third season they dragged them (to) the shore of the sea, and the Prince came out and stood by them. And he sent to me, (45) saying: "Come!" Now when I presented myself near him, the shadow of his lotus-blossom fell upon me. And Pen-Amon, a butler who belonged to him, cut me off, saying: "The shadow of Pharaoh— life, prosperity, health!— your lord, has fallen on you!" But he was angry at him, saying: "Let him alone!" [2]

So I presented myself near him, and he answered and said to me: "See, the commission which my fathers carried out formerly, I have carried it out (also), even though you have not done for me what your fathers would have done for me, and you too (should have done)! See, the last of your woodwork has arrived and is lying (here). Do as I wish, and come to load it in— for aren't they going to give it to you? (50) Don't come to look at the terror of the sea! If you look at the terror of the sea, you will see my own (too)![3] Why, I have not done to you what was done to the messengers of Kha-em-Waset, when they spent seventeen years in this land—they died (where) they were!" And he said to his butler: "Take him and show him their *tomb* in which they are lying."

But I said to him: "Don't show it to me! As for Kha-em-Waset—they were men whom he sent to you as messengers, and he was a man himself. You do not have one of his messengers (here in me), when you say: 'Go and see your companions!' Now, shouldn't you rejoice (55) and have a stela [made] for yourself and say on it: 'Amon-Re, King of the Gods, sent to me Amon-of-the-Road, his messenger—[life], prosperity, health!—and Wen-Amon, his human messenger, after the woodwork for the great and august barque of Amon-Re, King of the Gods. I cut it down. I loaded it in. I provided it (with) my ships and my crews. I caused them to reach Egypt, in order to ask fifty years of life from Amon for myself, over and above my fate.'

[1] Seasoning in the mountains.

[2] Perhaps we have to do with the blight of majesty. The butler's jest has point if the shadow of pharaoh was too intimate and holy to fall upon a commoner.

[3] If you use wind or weather as excuses for delay, you will find me just as dangerous.

And it shall come to pass that, after another time, a messenger may come from the land of Egypt who knows writing, and he may read your name on the stela. And you will receive water (in) the West, like the gods who are (60) here!"[1]

And he said to me: "This which you have said to me is a great testimony of words!"[2] So I said to him: "As for the many things which you have said to me, if I reach the place where the High Priest of Amon is and he sees how you have (carried out this) commission, it is your (carrying out of this) commission (which) will *draw out* something for you."

And I went (to) the shore of the sea, to the place where the timber was lying, and I spied eleven ships belonging to the Tjeker coming in from the sea, in order to say: " Arrest him! Don't let a ship of his (go) to the land of Egypt!" Then I sat down and wept. And the letter scribe of the Prince came out to me, (65) and he said to me: "What's the matter with you?" And I said to him: "Haven't you seen the birds go down to Egypt a second time?[3] Look at them— how they travel to the cool pools! (But) how long shall I be left here! Now don't you see those who are coming again to arrest me?"

So he went and told it to the Prince. And the Prince began to weep because of the words which were said to him, for they were painful. And he sent out to me his letter scribe, and he brought to me two jugs of wine and one ram. And he sent to me Ta-net-Not, an Egyptian singer who was with him,[4] saying: "Sing to him! Don't let his heart take on cares!" And he sent to me, (70) to say: "Eat and drink! Don't let your heart take on cares, for tomorrow you shall hear whatever I have to say."

When morning came, he had his assembly summoned, and he stood in their midst, and he said to the Tjeker: "What have you come (for)?" And they said to him: "We have come after the *blasted* ships which you are sending to Egypt with our opponents!" But he said to them: "I cannot arrest the messenger of Amon inside my land. Let me send him away, and you go after him to arrest him."

[1] A libation to help maintain the dead.

[2] We cannot be sure whether the irony was conscious or unconscious.

[3] Wen-Amon had been away from Egypt for more than a year, seeing two flights of birds southward.

[4] Egyptian women who entertained or participated in cult ceremonies in Asia are known in the inscriptions on the Megiddo ivories.

So he loaded me in, and he sent me away from there at the harbor of the sea. And the wind cast me on the land of (75) Alashiya. And they of the town came out against me to kill me, but I *forced my way* through them to the place where Heteb, the princess of the town, was. I met her as she was going out of one house of hers and going into another of hers.

So I greeted her, and I said to the people who were standing near her: "Isn't there one of you who understands Egyptian?" And one of them said: "I understand (it)." So I said to him: "Tell my lady that I have heard, as far away as Thebes, the place where Amon is, that injustice is done in every town but justice is done in the land of Alashiya. Yet injustice is done here every day!" And she said: "Why, what do you (mean) (80) by saying it?" So I told her: "If the sea is stormy and the wind casts me on the land where you are, you should not let them take me *in charge* to kill me. For I am a messenger of Amon. Look here—as for me, they will search for me all the time! As to this crew of the Prince of Byblos which they are bent on killing, won't its lord find ten crews of yours, and he also kill them?"

So she had the people summoned, and they stood (there). And she said to me: "Spend the night . . ."

(At this point the papyrus breaks off. Since the tale is told in the first person, it is fair to assume that Wen-Amon returned to Egypt to tell his story, in some measure of safety or success.)

The Tradition of Seven Lean Years in Egypt

ANET, 31-32

The prosperity of Egypt depends upon the satisfactory flow of the Nile, particularly upon its annual inundation, and that river is antic and unpredictable. Ancient Egyptian texts have frequent references to hunger, "years of misery," "a year of low Nile," and so on.[1] The text which follows tells of seven years of low Niles and famine. In its present form the text derives from the Ptolemaic period (perhaps around the end of the 2nd century B.C.). However, its stated setting is the reign of Djoser

[1] Vandier gives a previously unpublished text from the First Intermediate Period (23rd-21st century B.C.), from a tomb some distance south of Thebes. "When the entire Upper Egypt was dying because of hunger, with every man eating his (own) children, I never allowed death to occur from hunger in this nome. I gave a loan of grain to Upper Egypt. . . . Moreover, I kept alive the domain of Elephantine and kept alive Iat-negen in these years, after the towns of Hefat and Hor-mer had been satisfied." He took care of his home districts first.

of the Third Dynasty (about 28th century B.C.). It states the reasons why a stretch of Nile land south of Elephantine had been devoted to Khnum, god of Elephantine. It is a question whether *Fig. 162* it is a priestly forgery of some late period, justifying their claim to territorial privileges, or whether it correctly recounts an actual grant of land more than 2,500 years earlier. This question cannot be answered in final terms. We can only affirm that Egypt had a tradition of seven lean years, which, by a contractual arrangement between pharaoh and a god, were to be followed by years of plenty.

Year 18 of the Horus: Netjer-er-khet; the King of Upper and Lower Egypt: Netjer-er-khet; the Two Goddesses: Netjer-er-khet; the Horus of Gold: Djoser, *and under* the Count, Mayor, *Royal Acquaintance*, and Overseer of Nubians in Elephantine, Madir. There was brought to him[1] this royal decree:

To let thee know. I was in distress on the Great Throne, and those who are in the palace were in heart's affliction from a very great evil, since the Nile had not come in my time for a space of seven years. Grain was *Gen. 41:27* scant, fruits were dried up, and everything which they eat was short. Every man *robbed* his companion. They moved without going (*ahead*). The infant was wailing; the youth was *waiting*; the heart of the old men was in sorrow, their legs were bent, crouching on the ground, their arms were *folded*. The courtiers were in need. The temples were shut up; the sanctuaries held [*nothing but*] *air*. Every[*thing*] was found empty.

I extended my heart back to the beginnings, and I asked him who was the *Chamberlain*, the Ibis, the Chief Lector Priest Ii-em-(ho)tep,[2] the son of Ptah, South-of-His-Wall: "What is the birthplace of the Nile? *Who is . . .* the god there? Who is the god?"

Then he answered (5) me: "I need the guidance of Him Who Presides over the House of the Fowling Net,[3] *. . . for the heart's confidence* of all men about what they should do. I shall enter into the House of Life and spread out the Souls of Re,[4] (to see) if some guidance be in them."

So he went, and he returned to me immediately, that he might *instruct* me on the inundation of the Nile, . . .

[1] To Madir, the Governor at Elephantine. [2] The famed minister of Djoser, whose reputation for wisdom later brought him deification.
[3] Thoth of Hermopolis, the god of wisdom and of priestly lore.
[4] The scriptorium in which the sacred and magic books "The Souls of Re," were kept.

and everything about which they had written. He uncovered for me the hidden spells thereof, to which the ancestors had taken (their) way, without their equal among kings since the limits *of time. He said* to me:

"There is a city in the midst of the waters [*from which*] the Nile *rises*, named Elephantine. It is the Beginning of the Beginning, the Beginning Nome, (*facing*) *toward* Wawat.[9] It is the *joining* of the land, the primeval hillock[10] *of earth, the throne* of Re, when he *reckons to cast* life beside everybody. 'Pleasant of Life' is the name of its dwelling. 'The Two Caverns' is the name of the water; they are the two breasts which pour forth all good things. It is the couch of the Nile, in which he becomes young (again). . . . He fecundates (the land) by mounting as the male, the bull, to the female; he renews (his) virility, assuaging his desire. He rushes twenty-eight cubits (high at Elephantine); he hastens at Diospolis seven cubits (high). Khnum is there as a god. . . ." . . .

I Kings 3:5

(18) . . . As I slept in life and satisfaction, I discovered the god standing over against me. I propitiated him with praise; I prayed to him in his presence. He *revealed* himself to me, *his face* being fresh. His words were:

"I am Khnum, thy fashioner. . . . I know the Nile. When he is introduced into the fields, his introduction gives life to every nostril, like the introduction (of life) to the fields . . . The Nile will pour forth for thee, without a year of cessation or laxness for any land. Plants will grow, bowing down under the *fruit*. Renenut[1] will be at the head of everything. . . . Dependents *will fulfill* the purposes in their hearts, (22) as well as the master. The starvation year will have gone, and (people's) *borrowing* from their granaries will have departed. Egypt will come into the fields, the banks will sparkle, . . . and contentment will be in their hearts more than that which was formerly."

Gen. 41:56

Then I awoke *quickly*, my heart cutting off weariness. I made this decree beside my father Khnum:[2]

"An offering which the King gives to Khnum, the Lord of the Cataract Region, Who Presides over Nubia, in recompense for these things which thou wilt do for me:

"I offer to thee thy west in Manu and thy east (in)

---

[1] The goddess of the harvest.   [2] That is, in the temple of Khnum.

Bakhu,[1] from Elephantine as far as [Takompso], for twelve *iters*[2] on the east and west, whether arable land or desert or river in every part of these *iters* . . .".

(The remainder of the text continues Djoser's promise to Khnum, the essence of which is that the land presented to the god shall be tithed for his temple. It is finally provided that the decree shall be inscribed on a stela in the temple of Khnum.)

[1] Manu was the western and Bakhu the eastern mountain range bordering the Nile. [2] The *Dodekaschoinos* known from the Greek writers.

II. Myths and Epics from Mesopotamia

A Sumerian Myth

TRANSLATOR: S. N. KRAMER

ANET, 42-44

THE DELUGE

This Sumerian myth concerning the flood, with its Sumerian counterpart of the antediluvian Noah, offers the closest and most striking parallel to biblical material as yet uncovered in Sumerian literature. Moreover, its introductory passages are of considerable significance for Mesopotamian cosmogony; they include a number of important statements concerning the creation of man, the origin of kingship, and the existence of at least five antediluvian cities.

(approximately first 37 lines destroyed)

"My mankind, *in* its destruction I will . . . ,[1]
To Nintu [2] I will *return the* . . . *of* my creatures,
I will *return* the people *to* their *settlements,*   (40)
Of the cities, verily they   will build their *places of
    (divine) ordinances,*   I   will make peaceful their
    shade,
Of *our*[3] houses, verily they will lay their bricks in pure
    places,
The places of our decisions verily they will found in pure
    places."
He   directed   the . . . *of the temenos,*
Perfected the rites (and) the exalted (divine)
    ordinances,
On the earth he . . . d, placed the . . . there.
After Anu, Enlil, Enki, and Ninhursag
Had fashioned the black-headed (people),[4]
Vegetation luxuriated from the earth,
Animals, four-legged (creatures) of the plain, were
    brought artfully into existence.   (50)

(approximately 37 lines destroyed)

After the . . . of kingship had been lowered from heaven,

---

[1] There is some possibility that it is more than one deity who is speaking. Our interpretation of the text assumes that the speaking deity (or deities) plans to save mankind from destruction, but this is uncertain.

[2] Nintu is the Sumerian mother goddess known also under the names Ninhursag and Ninmah.

[3] Perhaps "of the houses of the (divine) ordinances."

[4] The word "black-headed" usually refers to inhabitants of Sumer and Babylon; in the present context, it seems to refer to mankind as a whole.

After the exalted [*tiara*] (and) the throne of kingship
    had been lowered from heaven,
He[1] [pe]rfected the [rites (and) the ex]alted
    [(divine) ordinances] ...,   (90)
Founded the [*five*] *ci*[*ties*] in ... p[ure places],
Cal[led] their names, [appor]tioned them *as* [*cu*]*lt-*
    centers.
The *first* of these cities, Eridu, he gave to Nudimmud, [2]
    the leader,
The second, Badtibira, he gave to ... ,
The third, Larak, he gave to Endurbilhursag,
The fourth, Sippar, he gave to the hero Utu,[3]
The fifth, Shuruppak, he gave to Sud.[4]
When he had called the names of these cities, apportioned
    them *as cult-centers,*
He *brought* ...,[5]
Established the *cleaning* of the small
    rivers *as* ...   (100)
        (approximately 37 lines destroyed)
The flood ...   Gen. 6
...
Thu[s w]as treated ...
Then did Nin[tu *weep*] like a ...,
The pure Inanna [set up] a lament for *its*[6] people,
Enki took coun[sel] with himself,
Anu, Enlil, Enki, (and) Ninhursag ...,
The gods of heaven and earth [uttered] the name of [7]
    Anu (and) Enlil.
Then did Ziusudra, the king, the *pašišu* [of] ...,
Build giant ... ;
Humbly obedient, reverent*ly* [he] ...,
Attending daily, constantly [he] ...,
Bringing forth all kinds of dreams, [he] ...,
Uttering the name of heaven (and) earth,
    [he] ...   (150)
... the gods a *wall* ...,
Ziusudra, standing at *its* side, list[ened].
"Stand *by the wall* at my left side ...,[8]
By the wall I will say a word to thee, [take my word],

---

[1] Identity of deity or deities uncertain; perhaps it is Anu Enlil.
[2] Nudimmud is a name for the water-god Enki.
[3] The sun-god, known as the tutelary deity of both Sippar and Larsa.
[4] The tutelary goddess of Shuruppak identified by the later Babylonian
theologians with the goddess Ninlil, the wife of Enlil.
[5] It may deal with rain and water supply.
[6] That is "the earth's" or "the land's." [7] "Conjured by Anu (and) Enlil."
[8] The name of the speaking deity is not given, no doubt, Enki.

[Give] ear to my instruction:
By our ... a flood [*will sweep*] over the cult-centers;
To destroy the seed of mankind ... ,
Is the decision, the word of the assembly [of the gods].
By the word commanded by Anu (and) Enlil ... ,
Its kingship, its rule [*will be put to an end*]."   (160)
          (approximately 40 lines destroyed)
All the windstorms, exceedingly powerful,
          attacked as one,   (201)
At the same time, the flood sweeps *over the cult-centers.*
After, for seven days (and) seven nights,
The flood had *swept over* the land,
(And) the huge boat had been tossed about by the
          windstorms on the great waters,
Utu came forth, who sheds light on heaven (and)
          earth.
Ziusudra opened a *window of* the huge boat,
The hero Utu *brought his rays into* the giant boat.
Ziusudra, the king,
Prostrated himself before Utu,   (210)
The king kills an ox, *slaughters* a sheep.
          (approximately 39 lines destroyed)
"Ye will utter 'breath of heaven,' 'breath of earth,' verily
          it will *stretch* itself by *your*. . . ."   (251)
Anu (and) Enlil *uttered* "breath of heaven," "breath of
          earth," *by their* . . . , it stretched itself.
Vegetation, coming up out of the earth, rises up.
Ziusudra, the king,
Prostrated himself before Anu (and) Enlil.
Anu (and) Enlil cherished Ziusudra,
Life like (that of) a god they give him,
Breath eternal like (that of) a god they *bring down* for
          him.
Then, Ziusudra the king,
The *preserver of the name* of vegetation (and)
          of the seed of mankind.   (260)
In the land[1] *of crossing,*[2] the land of Dilmun, the place
          where the sun rises, they[3] caused to dwell.
          (Remainder of the tablet,
          about 39 lines of text, destroyed.)

[1] The Sumerian word twice rendered by "land" in this line may also
be translated as "mountain" or "mountain-land."
[2] Perhaps the crossing of the sun immediately upon his rising in the
east; the Sumerian word used may also mean "of rule."
[3] That is, probably Anu and Enlil.

Akkadian Myths and Epics

TRANSLATOR: E. A. SPEISER

THE CREATION EPIC

ANET, 60, 66-69,
514

The struggle between cosmic order and chaos was to the ancient Mesopotamians a fateful drama that was renewed at the turn of each new year. The epic which deals with these events was therefore the most significant expression of the religious literature of Mesopotamia. The work, consisting of seven tablets, was known in Akkadian as *Enūma eliš* "When on high," after its opening words. It was recited with due solemnity on the fourth day of the New Year's festival.

There is as yet no general agreement as regards the date of composition. None of the extant texts antedates the first millennium B.C. On the internal evidence, however, of the context and the linguistic criteria, the majority of the scholars would assign the epic to the Old Babylonian period, i.e. the early part of the second millennium B.C. There does not appear to be any convincing reason against this earlier dating.

(Tablets I-III recount the birth of the gods, who spring from the primordial Apsu and Tiamat, and the choice of Marduk as the champion of the younger gods in the battle against Tiamat.)

Tablet IV

They erected for him a princely throne.
Facing his fathers, he sat down, presiding.
"Thou art the most honored of the great gods,
Thy decree is unrivaled, thy command is Anu.[1]
Thou, Marduk, art the most honored of the great gods,   *Fig. 141*
Thy decree is unrivaled, thy word is Anu.
From this day unchangeable shall be thy pronounce-
    ment.
To raise or bring low—these shall be (in) thy hand.   I Sam. 2:7
Thy utterance shall be true, thy command shall be un-
    impeachable.
No one among the gods shall transgress
    thy bounds!   (10)
Adornment being wanted for the seats of the gods,
Let the place of their shrines ever be in thy place.
O Marduk, thou art indeed our avenger.
We have granted thee kingship over the universe entire.

---

[1] i.e. it has the authority of the sky-god Anu.

When in Assembly thou sittest, thy word shall be
    supreme.
Thy weapons shall not fail; they shall smash thy foes!
O lord, spare the life of him who trusts thee,
But pour out the life of the god who seized evil."

Judg. 6:36-40

Having placed in their midst a piece of cloth,
They addressed themselves to Marduk, their
    first-born: (20)
"Lord, truly thy decree is first among gods.
Say but to wreck or create; it shall be.
Open thy mouth: the cloth will vanish!
Speak again, and the cloth shall be whole!"
At the word of his mouth the cloth vanished.
He spoke again, and the cloth was restored.
When the gods, his fathers, saw the fruit of his word,
Joyfully they did homage: "Marduk is king!"
They conferred on him scepter, throne, and *vestment*;
They gave him matchless weapons that ward off
    the foes: (30)
"Go and cut off the life of Tiamat.
May the winds bear her blood to places undisclosed."
Bel's destiny thus fixed, the gods, his fathers,
Caused him to go the way of success and attainment.
He constructed a bow, marked it as his weapon,
Attached thereto the arrow, fixed its bow-cord.
He raised the mace, made his right hand grasp it;
Bow and quiver he hung at his side.
In front of him he set the lightning,
With a blazing flame he filled his body.   (40)
He then made a net to enfold Tiamat therein.
The four winds he stationed that nothing of her might
    escape,
The South Wind, the North Wind, the East Wind, the
    West Wind.
Close to his side he held the net, the gift of his father,
    Anu.
He brought forth Imhullu "the Evil Wind," the Whirl-
    wind, the Hurricane,
The Fourfold Wind, the Sevenfold Wind, the Cyclone,
    the Matchless Wind;
Then he sent forth the winds he had brought forth, the
    seven of them.
To stir up the inside of Tiamat they rose up behind him.
Then the lord raised up the flood-storm, his mighty
    weapon.

He mounted the storm-chariot irresistible
    [and] terrifying. (50)
He harnessed (and) yoked to it a team-of-four,
The Killer, the Relentless, the Trampler, the Swift.
Sharp were their teeth, bearing poison.
They were versed in ravage, in destruction skilled.
On his right he posted the *Smiter*, fearsome in battle,
On the left the Combat, which repels all the zealous.
For a cloak he was wrapped in an armor of terror;
With his fearsome halo his head was turbaned.
The lord went forth and followed his course,
Towards the raging Tiamat he set his face. (60)
In his lips he held a spell;
A plant to put out poison was grasped in his hand.
Then they milled about him, the gods milled about him,
The gods, his fathers, milled about him, the gods milled
    about him.
The lord approached to scan the inside of Tiamat,
(And) of Kingu, her consort, the scheme to perceive.
As he looks on, his course becomes upset,
His will is distracted and his doings are confused.
And when the gods, his helpers, who marched at his
    side,
Saw the valiant hero, blurred became
    their vision. (70)
Tiamat emitted [a cry], without turning her neck,
Framing   savage[1] defiance in her lips:[2]
"Too [imp]ortant art thou [for] the lord of the gods
    to rise up against thee!   Judg. 12:6
Is it in their place that they have gathered, (or) in thy
    place?"
Thereupon the lord, having [raised] the flood-storm, his
    mighty weapon,
[To] enraged [Tiamat] he sent word as follows:
"*Why* art thou risen, art haughtily exalted,
Thou hast charged thine own heart to stir up conflict,
. . . sons reject their own fathers,
Whilst thou, who hast born them,
    hast foresworn love! (80)
Thou hast appointed Kingu as thy consort,
Conferring upon him the rank of Anu, not rightfully
    his.

1 "her incantation" is not impossible.
2 Tiamat's taunt, as recorded in the next two lines, is not clear.

Against Anshar, king of the gods, thou seekest evil;
[Against] the gods, my fathers, thou hast confirmed thy
    wickedness.
[Though] drawn up be thy forces, girded on thy
    weapons,
Stand thou up, that I and thou meet in single combat!"
When Tiamat heard this,
She was like one possessed; she took leave of her senses.
In fury Tiamat cried out aloud.
To the roots her legs shook both together.   (90)
She recites a charm, keeps casting her spell,
While the gods of battle sharpen their weapons.
Then joined issue Tiamat and Marduk, wisest of gods.
They strove   in single combat, locked in battle.
The lord spread out his net to enfold her,
The Evil Wind, which followed behind, he let loose in
    her face.
When Tiamat opened her mouth to consume him,
He drove in the Evil Wind that she close not her lips.
As the fierce winds charged her belly,
Her body was distended   and her mouth
    was wide open.   (100)
He released the arrow, it tore her belly,
It cut through her insides, splitting the heart.
Having thus subdued her, he extinguished her life.
He cast down her carcass to stand upon it.
After he had slain Tiamat, the leader,
Her band was shattered, her troupe broken up;
And the gods, her helpers who marched at her side,
Trembling with terror, turned their backs about,
In order to save and preserve their lives.
Tightly encircled, they could not escape.   (110)
He made them captives and he smashed their weapons.
Thrown into the net, they found themselves ensnared;
Placed in cells, they were filled with wailing;
Bearing his wrath, they were held imprisoned.
And the eleven creatures which she had charged with
    awe,
The band of demons that marched . [..] before her,
He cast into fetters, their hands [...].
For all their resistance, he trampled (them) underfoot.
And Kingu, who had been made chief among them,
He bound and accounted him to Uggae.[1]   (120)

---
[1] God of death.

He took from him the Tablets of Fate, not rightfully
    his,
Sealed (them) with a seal[1] and fastened (them) on his
    breast.
When he had vanquished and subdued his adversaries,
Had . . . the vainglorious foe,
Had wholly established Anshar's triumph over the foe,
Nudimmud's desire had achieved, valiant Marduk
Strengthened his hold on the vanquished gods,
And turned back to Tiamat whom he had bound.
The lord trod on the legs of Tiamat,
With his unsparing mace he crushed her skull.   (130)
When the arteries of her blood he had severed,
The North Wind bore (it) to places undisclosed.
On seeing this, his fathers were joyful and jubilant,
They brought gifts of homage, they to him.
Then the lord paused to view her dead body,
That he might divide the monster and do artful works.
He split her like a shellfish into two parts:
Half of her he set up and ceiled it as sky,
Pulled down the bar and posted guards.
He bade them to allow not her waters
    to escape.   (140)
He crossed the heavens and surveyed the regions.
He squared Apsu's quarter,   the abode of Nudimmud,
As the lord measured the dimensions of Apsu.
The Great Abode, its likeness, he fixed as Esharra,
The Great Abode, Esharra, which he made as the firma-
    ment.
Anu, Enlil, and Ea he made occupy their places.   *Figs. 167, 168*

Tablet V

He constructed stations for the great gods,
Fixing their astral likenesses as constellations.
He determined the year by designating the zones:
He set up three constellations for each of the twelve
    months.
After defining the days of the year [by means] of
    (heavenly) figures,
He founded the station of Nebiru[2] to determine their
    (heavenly) bands,
That none might transgress or fall short.

---

[1] This was an essential act of attestation in Mesopotamian society.

[2] i.e. the planet Jupiter. This station was taken to lie between the band of the north, which belonged to Enlil, and the band of the south, which belonged to Ea.

Alongside it he set up the stations of Enlil and Ea.
Having opened up the gates on both sides,
He strengthened the locks to the left
    and the right. (10)
In her[1] belly he established the zenith.
The Moon he caused to shine, the night (to him) en-
    trusting.
He appointed him a creature of the night to signify the
    days:
"Monthly, without cease, form designs with a crown.
At the month's very start, rising over the land,
Thou shalt have luminous horns to signify six days,
On the seventh day reaching a [half]-crown.
At full moon[2] stand in opposition[3] in mid-month.
When the sun [overtakes] thee at the base of heaven,
Diminish [thy crown] and retrogress in light. (20)
[At the time of disappearance] approach thou the course
    of the sun,
And [on the twenty-ninth] thou shalt again stand in
    opposition to the sun."

(The remainder of this tablet is broken away or too
fragmentary for translation.)

Tablet VI

When Marduk hears the words of the gods,
His heart prompts (him) to fashion artful works.
Opening his mouth, he addresses Ea
To impart the plan he had conceived in his heart:
Gen. 1:26   "Blood I will mass and cause bones to be.
I will establish a savage, 'man' shall be his name.
Verily, savage-man I will create.
He shall be charged with the service of the gods
    That they might be at ease!
The ways of the gods I will artfully alter.
Though alike revered, into two (groups) they
    shall be divided." (10)
Ea answered him, speaking a word to him,
Giving him another plan for the relief of the gods:
"Let but one of their brothers be handed over;
He alone shall perish that mankind may be fashioned.[4]
Let the great gods be here in Assembly,

---

[1] Tiamat's.
[2] Akkadian *šapattu*, the prototype of the "Sabbath" in so far as the injunctions against all types of activity are concerned.
[3] i.e. with regard to the sun. This verb was a technical term in Babylonian astronomy.   [4] Out of his blood.

Let the guilty be handed over that they may endure."
Marduk summoned the great gods to Assembly;
Presiding graciously, he issues instructions.
To his utterance the gods pay heed.
The king addresses a word to the Anunnaki: (20)
"If your former statement was true,
Do (now) the truth on oath by me declare!
Who was it that contrived the uprising,
And made Tiamat rebel, and joined battle?
Let him be handed over who contrived the uprising.
His guilt I will make him bear. You shall dwell in
      peace!"
The Igigi, the great gods, replied to him,
To Lugaldimmerankia, [1] counselor of the gods, their
      lord:
"It was Kingu who contrived the uprising,
And made Tiamat rebel, and joined battle." (30)
They bound him, holding him before Ea.
They imposed on him his guilt and severed his blood
      (vessels).
Out of his blood they fashioned mankind.
He [2] imposed the service and let free the gods.
After Ea, the wise, had created mankind,
Had imposed upon it the service of the gods—
That work was beyond comprehension;
As artfully planned by Marduk, did Nudimmud create
      it—
Marduk, the king of the gods divided
All the Anunnaki above and below. [3] (40)
He assigned (them) to Anu to guard his instructions.
Three hundred in the heavens he stationed as a guard.
In like manner the ways of the earth he defined.
In heaven and on earth six hundred (thus) he settled.
After he had ordered all the instructions,
To the Anunnaki of heaven and earth had allotted their
      portions,
The Anunnaki opened their mouths
And said to Marduk, their lord:
"Now,[4] O lord, thou who hast caused our deliverance,
What shall be our homage to thee? (50)
Let us build a shrine whose name shall be called

[1] "The king of the gods of heaven and earth."   [2] Ea.
[3] Here and elsewhere in this epic the Anunnaki are understood to be the
celestial gods (normally Igigi) as well as those of the lower regions.
[4] Not "O Nannar," as translated by some.

'Lo, a chamber for our nightly rest'; let us repose in it!
Let us build a throne, a recess for his abode!
On the day that we arrive[1] we shall repose in it."
When Marduk heard this,
Brightly glowed his features, like the day:
"Like that of *lofty* Babylon, whose building you have
    requested,
Let its brickwork be fashioned. You shall name it 'The
    Sanctuary.'"
The Anunnaki applied the implement;
For one whole year they molded bricks. (60)
When the second year arrived,

Fig. 189 They raised high the head of Esagila equaling Apsu.[2]
Having built a stage-tower *as high as* Apsu,
They set up *in it* an abode for Marduk, Enlil, (and) Ea
In their presence he *adorned* (it) in grandeur.
To the base of Esharra its horns look down.
After they had achieved the building of Esagila,
The Anunnaki *themselves* erected their shrines.
[...] all of them gathered,
[...] they had built as his dwelling. (70)
The gods, his fathers, at his banquet he seated:
"This is Babylon, the place that is your home!
Make merry in its precincts, occupy its broad [places]."
The great gods took their seats,
They set up festive drink, sat down to a banquet.
After they had made merry within it,
In Esagila, the *splendid*, had performed their rites,
The norms had been fixed (and) *all* [their] portents,
All the gods apportioned the stations of heaven and
    earth.
The fifty great gods took their seats. (80)
The seven gods of destiny set up the three hundred [in
    heaven].
Enlil raised the bo[w, his wea]pon, and laid (it)
    before them.
The gods, his fathers, saw the net he had made.
When they beheld the bow, how skillful its shape,
His fathers praised the work he had wrought.
Raising (it), Anu spoke up in the Assembly of the gods,
As he kissed the bow: "This is my daughter!"
He named the names of the bow as follows:

[1] For the New Year's festival.
[2] Meaning apparently that the height of Esagila corresponded to the
depth of Apsu's waters.

"Longwood is the first, the second is [. . .];
Its third name is Bow-Star, in heaven I have made   (90)
    it shine."
He fixed a place which the gods, its[1] brothers, [. . .].
After Anu had decreed the fate of the Bow,
And had placed the *exalted* royal throne before the
    gods,
Anu seated it in the Assembly of the gods.
When the great gods had assembled,   (95)
And had [. . .] the fate which Marduk had exalted,
They pronounced among themselves a curse,
Swearing by water and oil to place life in jeopardy.
When they had granted him the exercise of kingship of
    the gods,
They confirmed him in dominion over the gods of
    heaven and earth.   (100)
Anshar pronounced supreme his name Asar(u)luhi:
"Let us make humble obeisance at the mention of his
    name;
When he speaks, the gods shall pay heed to him.
Let his utterance be supreme above and below!"
"Most exalted be the Son, our avenger;
Let his sovereignty be surpassing, having no rival.
May he shepherd the black-headed ones,[2] his creatures.
To the end of days, without forgetting, let them acclaim
    his ways.
May he establish for his fathers the great
    food-offerings;   (110)
Their support they shall furnish, shall tend their sanc-
    tuaries.
May he cause incense to be smelled, . . . their spells,
A likeness on earth of what he has wrought in heaven.
May he order the black-headed to re[*vere him*],
May the subjects ever bear in mind their god,
And may they at his word pay heed   to the goddess.
May food-offerings be borne for their gods and god-
    desses.
Without fail let them support their gods!
Their lands let them improve, build their shrines,
Let the black-headed wait on their gods.   (120)
As for us, by however many names we pronounce, he is
    our god!
Let us then proclaim his fifty names. . . .

[1] Referring to the Bow.
[2] A common Akkadian metaphor for "the human race."

The Epic of Gilgamesh

ANET, 72-79, 83-90, 92-97, 514-515

The theme of this epic is essentially a secular one. The poem deals with such earthy things as man and nature, love and adventure, friendship and combat—all masterfully blended into a background for the stark reality of death. The climactic struggle of the protagonist to change his eventual fate, by learning the secret of immortality from the hero of the Great Flood of long ago, ends in failure; but with the failure comes a sense of quiet resignation. For the first time in the history of the world a profound experience on such a heroic scale has found expression in a noble style. The scope and sweep of the epic, and its sheer poetic power, give it a timeless appeal. All but a few of the Akkadian texts come from the library of Ashurbanipal at Nineveh. Unlike the Creation Epic, however, the Gilgamesh Epic is known also from versions which antedate the first millennium B.C. From the middle of the second millennium have come down fragments of an Akkadian recension current in the Hittite Empire, and the same Boğazköy archives have yielded also important fragments of a Hittite translation, as well as a fragment of a Hurrian rendering of the epic. From the first half of the second millennium we possess representative portions of the Old Babylonian version of the epic, which pertain to Tablets I-III, and X. That this version was itself a copy of an earlier text is suggested by the internal evidence of the material. The original date of composition of the Akkadian work has to be placed at the turn of the second millennium, if not slightly earlier.

Fig. 69

Tablet I (i)

He who saw everything [to the end]s of the land,
[Who all thing]s experienced, [conside]red all!
[...] together [...],
[...] of wisdom, who all things . [..].
The [hi]dden he saw, [laid bare] the undisclosed.
He brought report of before the Flood,
Achieved a long journey, weary and [w]orn.
All his toil he engraved on a stone stela.
Of ramparted Uruk the wall he built,
Of hallowed Eanna,[1] the pure sanctuary.   (10)
Behold its outer wall, whose cornice is like copper,
Peer at the inner wall, which none can equal!
Seize upon the threshold, which is from of old!
Draw near to Eanna, the dwelling of Ishtar,
Which no future king, no man, can equal.
Go up and walk on the walls of Uruk,
Inspect the base terrace, examine the brickwork:
Is not its brickwork of burnt brick?
Did not the Seven [Sages][2] lay its foundations?

[1] The temple of Anu and Ishtar in Uruk.
[2] The seven sages, who brought civilization to seven of the oldest cities.

(Remainder of the column broken away. A Hittite fragment [cf. J. Friedrich, *ZA*, xxxix (1929), 2-5] corresponds in part with the damaged initial portion of our column ii, and hence appears to contain some of the material from the end of the first column. We gather from this fragment that several gods had a hand in fashioning Gilgamesh, whom they endowed with superhuman size. At length, Gilgamesh arrives in Uruk.)

(ii)

Two-thirds of him is god, [one-third of him is human].
The form of his body [...]
                    (mutilated or missing)   (3-7)
[...] like a wild ox lofty [...];   (8)
The onslaught of his weapons verily has no equal.
By the *drum*[1] are aroused [his] companions.   (10)
The nobles of Uruk *are gloo[my]* in [their chamb]ers:
"Gilgamesh leaves not the son to [his] father;
[Day] and [night] is unbridled his arro[gance].
[Is this Gilga]mesh, [the shepherd of ramparted]
       Uruk?
Is this [our] shepherd, [bold, stately, wise]?
[Gilgamesh] leaves not [the maid to her mother],
The warrior's daughter, [the noble's spouse]!"
The [gods hearkened] to their plaint,
The gods of heaven Uruk's lord [they ...]:
"Did not [*Aruru*][2] bring forth this strong
       wild ox?   (20)
[The onslaught of his weapons] verily has no equal.
By the *drum* are aroused his [companions].
Gilgamesh leaves not the son to his father;
       Day and night [is unbridled his arrogance].
Is this the shepherd of [ramparted] Uruk?
Is this their [...] shepherd,
Bold, stately, (and) wise? ...
Gilgamesh leaves not the maid to [her mother],
The warrior's daughter, the noble's spouse!"
When [Anu] had heard out their plaint,
The great Aruru they called: (30)
       "Thou, Aruru, didst create [the man];
Create now his double;
       His stormy heart   let him match.
Let them contend, that Uruk may have peace!"
When Aruru heard this,

---

[1] Here perhaps the reference is to the abuse for personal purposes of an instrument intended for civic or religious use.
[2] A goddess.

A double of Anu she conceived within her.
Aruru washed her hands,
    Pinched off clay and cast it on the steppe.
[On the step]pe she created valiant Enkidu,
    Offspring of . . . , essence   of Ninurta.
[Sha]ggy   with hair is his whole body,
    He is endowed with head hair like a woman.
The locks of his hair sprout like Nisaba.[1]
He knows neither people nor land;
    Garbed is he like Sumuqan.[2]
With the gazelles he feeds on grass,
With the wild beasts he jostles   at the
        watering-place,   (40)
With the teeming creatures his heart delights in water.
(Now) a hunter, a trapping-man,
Faced him at the watering-place.
[One] day, a second, and a third
    He faced him at the watering-place.
When the hunter saw him, his face became motionless.
He and his beasts went into his house,
[Sore a]fraid, still, without a sound,
(While) his heart [was disturbed], overclouded his face.
For woe had [entered] his belly;
His face was like that [of a wayfarer]
    from   afar.   (50)

(iii)

The hunter opened [his mouth] to speak,
    Saying to [his father]:
"My father, there is [a] fellow who [has come from the
    hills],
He is the might[iest in the land]; strength he has.
[Like the essence] of Anu, so mighty his strength!
[Ever] he ranges over the hills,
[Ever] with the beasts [he feeds on grass].
[Ever sets he] his feet at the watering-place.
[I am so frightened that] I dare not approach him!
[He filled in] the pits that I had dug,
[He tore up] my *traps* which I had [set],   (10)
The beasts and creatures of the steppe
    [He has made slip through my hands].[3]
[He does not allow] me to engage in fieldcraft!

[His father opened his mouth to speak],

---

[1] Goddess of grain. [2] God of cattle. [3] Perhaps "he has made me forfeit."

Saying to the hunter:
"[My son], in Uruk [there lives] Gilgamesh.
[No one is there more mighty] than he.
[Like the essence of Anu, so mi]ghty is his strength!
[Go, then, toward Uruk set] thy face,
[Speak to him of] the power of the man.
[Let him give thee a harlot-lass]. Take (her) [with
    thee];
[Let her prevail against him] by dint of
    [greater] might.   (20)
[When he waters the beasts at] the watering-place,
[She shall pull off] her cloth[ing, laying bare] her ripe-
    ness.
[As soon as he sees] her, he will draw near to her.
Reject him[1] will his beasts [that grew up on] his
    steppe!"
[Giving heed to] the advice of his father,
The hunter went forth [to Gilgamesh].
He took the road, in Uruk he set [his foot]:
"[...] Gilga[mesh ...],
There is a fellow [who has come from the hills],
He is the might[iest in the land; strength
    he has].   (30)
Like the essence of Anu, so mighty [his strength]!
[Ever] he ranges over the hills,
Ever with the beasts [he feeds on grass],
Ever [sets] he his feet at the watering-place.
I am so frightened that I dare not approach [him]!
He filled in the pits that [I] had dug,
He tore up my *traps* [which I had set],
The beasts and creatures [of the steppe]
    He has made slip through my hands.
He does not allow me to engage in fieldcraft!"
Gilgamesh says to him, [to] the hunter: (40)
"Go, my hunter, take with thee a harlot-lass.
When he waters the beasts at the watering-place,
She shall pull off her clothing, laying bare her ripeness.
As soon as he sees her, he will draw near to her.
Reject him will his beasts that grew up on his steppe!"
Forth went the hunter, taking with him a harlot-lass.
They took the road, going straight on the(ir) way.
On the third day at the appointed spot they arrived.
The hunter and the harlot sat down in their places.

[1] Lit. "regard as stranger, deny."

One day, a second day, they sat by the
    watering-place. (50)
The wild beasts came to the watering-place to drink.

(iv)

The creeping creatures came, their heart delighting in
    water.
But as for him, Enkidu, born in the hills—
With the gazelles he feeds on grass,
With the wild beasts he drinks at the watering-place,
With the creeping creatures his heart delights in water—
The lass beheld him, the savage-man,
The barbarous fellow from the depths of the steppe:
"There he is, O lass! Free thy breasts,
Bare thy bosom that he may possess thy ripeness!
Be not bashful! Welcome his ardor! (10)
As soon as he sees thee, he will draw near to thee.
Lay aside   thy cloth that he may rest upon thee.
Treat him, the savage, to a woman's task!
Reject him will his wild beasts that grew up on his
    steppe,
As his love is drawn unto thee."
The lass freed her breasts, bared her bosom,
    And he possessed her ripeness.
She was not bashful as she welcomed his ardor.
She laid aside her cloth and he rested upon her.
She treated him, the savage, to a woman's task,
As his love was drawn unto her. (20)
For six days and seven nights Enkidu comes forth,
    Mating with the lass.
After he had had (his) fill of her charms,
He set his face toward his wild beasts.
On seeing him, Enkidu, the gazelles ran off,
The wild beasts of the steppe drew away from his body.
Startled was Enkidu, as his body became taut,
His knees were motionless—for his wild beasts had gone.
Enkidu had to slacken his pace—it was not as before;
But he now had [wi]sdom, [br]oader understanding.
Returning, he sits at the feet of the harlot. (30)
He looks up at the face of the harlot,
His ears attentive, as the harlot speaks;
[The harlot] says to him, to Enkidu:
"Thou art [wi]se,   Enkidu, art become like a god!
Why with the wild creatures dost thou roam over the
    steppe?

Come, let me lead thee ⌊to⌋ ramparted Uruk,
To the holy temple, abode of Anu and Ishtar,
Where lives Gilgamesh, accomplished in strength,
And like a wild ox lords it over the folk."
As she speaks to him, her words find favor,   (40)
His heart enlightened,   he yearns for   a friend.
Enkidu says to her, to the harlot:
"Up, lass, escort thou me,
To the pure sacred temple, abode of Anu and Ishtar,
Where lives Gilgamesh, accomplished in strength,
And like a wild ox lords it over the folk.
I will challenge him [and will bo]ldly address him,

(v)

[I will] shout in Uruk: 'I am he who is mighty!
[I am the] one who can alter destinies,
[(He) who] was born on the steppe is mighty; strength
      he has.' "
"[Up then, let us go, that he may see] thy face.
⌊I will show thee Gilgamesh; where] he is I know well.
Come then, O Enkidu, to ramparted [Uruk],
Where people are re[splend]ent in festal attire,
(Where) each day is made a holiday,
Where [...] lads ... ,
And la[ss]es [..] . of figure.   (10)
Their ripeness [...] full of perfume.
They drive the great ones from their couches!
To thee, O Enkidu, who rejoicest in living,
I will show Gilgamesh, the joyful man!
Look thou at him, regard his face;
He is radiant with manhood, vigor he has.
With ripeness gorgeous is the whole of his body,
Mightier strength has he than thou,
Never resting by day or by night.
O Enkidu, renounce thy presumption!   (20)
Gilgamesh—of him Shamash is fond;   *Fig. 144*
Anu, Enlil, and Ea have broadened his wisdom.
Before thou comest down from the hills,
Gilgamesh will see thee in (his) dreams in Uruk: ...

(Remaining lines of the Assyrian Version of Tablet I
are here omitted since the Old Babylonian Version of
Tablet II takes up at this point.)

Tablet II

OLD BABYLONIAN VERSION

(ii)

Gilgamesh arose to reveal the dream,
Saying to his mother:
"My mother, in the time of night
I felt joyful and I walked about
In the midst of the nobles.
The stars appeared in the heavens.
The essence of Anu descended towards me.
I sought to lift it; it was too heavy for me!
I sought to move it; move it I could not! (10)
Uruk-land was gathered about it,
While the nobles kissed its feet.
As I set my forehead,[1]
They gave me support.
I raised it and brought it to thee."
The mother of Gilgamesh, who knows all,
Says to Gilgamesh:
"Forsooth, Gilgamesh, one like thee
Was born on the steppe,
And the hills have reared him.
When thou seest him, [as (over) a woman]
    thou wilt rejoice. (20)
The nobles will kiss his feet;
Thou wilt embrace him and [..] . him;
Thou wilt lead him to me."
He lay down and saw another
[Dream]: he says to his mother:
[My mother], I saw another
[...] in the confusion.   In the street
[Of] broad-marted Uruk
There lay an axe, and
They were gathered round it. (30)
That axe, strange was its shape.
As soon as I saw it, I rejoiced.
I loved it, and as though to a woman,
I was drawn   to it.
I took it and placed it
At my side."
The mother of Gilgamesh, who knows all,
[Says to Gilgamesh]:
                                      (small break)

Fig. 97   [1] To press the carrying strap against it; this method, which is wit-
nessed on the Ur Standard, is still practiced in modern Iraq.

(ii)

"Because I made it vie with thee."
While Gilgamesh reveals his dream,
Enkidu sits before the harlot.
[...] *the two of them.*
[Enki]du forgot where he was born.
For six days and seven nights Enkidu came forth
Mating with the l[ass].
Then the harlot opened her mouth,
Saying to Enkidu: (10)
"As I look at thee, Enkidu, thou art become like a god;
Wherefore with the wild creatures
Dost thou range over the steppe?
Up, I will lead thee
To broad-marted Uruk,
To the holy temple, the abode of Anu,
Enkidu, arise, I will lead thee
To Eanna, the abode of Anu,
Where lives [Gilgamesh, accomplished] in deeds,
And thou, li[ke ...],   (20)
Wilt love [him like] thyself.
Up, arise from the ground,
The shepherd's bed!"
He hearkened to her words, approved   her speech;
The woman's counsel
Fell upon his heart.
She pulled off (her) clothing;
With one (piece) she clothed him,
With the other garment
She clothed herself.   (30)
Holding on to his hand,
She leads him like a mother
To the board   of shepherds,
The place of the sheepfold.
Round him the shepherds gathered.
                              (several lines missing)
(iii)

The milk of wild creatures
He was wont to suck.
Food they placed before him;
He gagged, he gaped
And he stared.
Nothing does Enkidu know
Of eating food;
To drink strong drink

He has not been taught.
The harlot opened her mouth,   (10)
Saying to Enkidu:
"Eat the food, Enkidu,
As is life's due;
Drink the strong drink, as is the custom of the land."
Enkidu ate the food,
Until he was sated;
Of strong drink he drank
Seven goblets.
Carefree became his mood (and) cheerful,
His heart exulted   (20)
And his face glowed.
He rubbed [the *shaggy growth*],
The hair of his body,
Anointed himself with oil,
Became human.
He put on clothing,
He is like a groom!
He took his weapon
To chase the lions,
That shepherds might rest at night.   (30)
He caught wolves,
He captured lions,
The chief cattlemen could lie down;
Enkidu is their watchman,
The bold man,
The unique hero!
To [. . .] he said: (several lines missing)

(iv)   (some eight lines missing)

He made merry.
When he lifted his eyes,   (10)
He beheld a man.
He says to the harlot:
"Lass, fetch the man!
Why has he come hither?
His name let me hear."
The harlot called the man,
Going up to him and saying to him:
"Sir, whither hastenest thou?
What is this thy toilsome course?"
The man opened his mouth,   (20)
Saying to En[kidu]:
"Into the meeting-house he has [*intruded*],
Which is set aside   for the people,

... for *wedlock*.
On the city he has heaped *defilement*,
Imposing strange things on the *hapless* city.
For the king of broad-marted Uruk
The *drum*[1] of the people is free for
  nuptial choice.   (30)
For Gilgamesh, king of broad-marted Uruk,
The *drum* of the people is free
For nuptial choice,
That with lawful   wives he might mate!
He is the first,
The *husband*   comes after.
By the counsel of the gods it has (so) been ordained.
With the cutting of his umbilical cord
It was decreed for him!"
At the words of the man
His face grew pale.
     (some three lines missing)

    (v)
      (some six lines missing)
[Enkidu] walks [in front]
And the lass behind him.
When he entered broad-marted Uruk,
The populace gathered about him.   (10)
As he stopped in the street
Of broad-marted Uruk,
The people were gathered,
Saying about him:
"He is like Gilgamesh *to a hair*!
Though shorter in stature,
He is stronger of bone.
[...] ...
[He is the strongest in the land]; strength he has.
The milk of wild creatures   (20)
He was wont to suck.
In Uruk (there will be) a constant (*clatter of*) *arms*."
The nobles rejoiced:
"A hero has appeared
For the man of proper mien!
For Gilgamesh, the godlike,
His equal has come forth."
For Ishhara[2] the bed
Is laid out.
Gilgamesh. [..],
At night .. [.],

---

[1] Instrument to summon the listeners. [2] A form of Ishtar, as goddess of love.

As he approaches,
[Enkidu] stands in the street
To bar the way
To Gilgamesh
[...] in his might.   (some three lines missing)

(vi)

                                        (some five lines missing)
Gilgamesh [...]
On the steppe [...]
Sprouts [...].
He rose up and [...]
Before him.   (10)
They met in the Market-of-the-Land.
Enkidu barred the gate
With his foot,
Not allowing Gilgamesh to enter.
They grappled each other,
Holding fast like bulls.
They shattered the doorpost,
As the wall shook.
Gilgamesh and Enkidu
Grappled each other,   (20)
Holding fast like bulls;
They shattered the doorpost,
As the wall shook.
As Gilgamesh bent the knee—
His foot on the ground—
His fury abated
And he turned away.
When he had turned away,
Enkidu to him
Speaks up, to Gilgamesh:
"As one alone thy mother
Bore thee,
The wild cow of the steer-folds,
Ninsunna!
Raised up above men is thy head.
Kingship over the people
Enlil has granted thee!"

Tablet III

OLD BABYLONIAN VERSION

(From fragments of text it is clear that Gilgamesh
has decided on an expedition against monstrous Ḫuwa-

wa [Assyrian Ḫumbaba], who lives in the Cedar Forest. Enkidu tries to dissuade him, but Gilgamesh's determination is apparent from the following lines of the Old Babylonian Version:)

Gilgamesh opened his mouth, (3)
Saying to [Enkidu]:
"Who, my friend can scale he[aven]?
Only the gods [live] forever under the sun.
As for mankind, numbered are their days;   Eccles. 1:2-4
Whatever they achieve is but the wind!
Even here thou art afraid of death.
What of thy heroic might? (10)
Let me go then before thee,
Let thy mouth call to me, 'Advance, fear not!'
Should I fall, I shall have made me a name:
'Gilgamesh'—they will say—against fierce Huwawa
Has fallen!' (Long) after
My offspring has been born in my house,"

(From the fragmentary text of Tablets IV and V it is clear that the hazardous expedition of the two heroes against Ḫuwawa is successful.)

Tablet VI

He[1] washed his grimy hair, polished his weapons,
The braid of his hair he shook out against his back.
He cast off his soiled (things), put on his clean ones,
Wrapped a fringed cloak about and fastened a sash.
When Gilgamesh had put on his tiara,
Glorious Ishtar raised an eye at the beauty of Gilgamesh:
"Come, Gilgamesh, be thou (my) lover!
Do but grant me of thy fruit.
Thou shalt be my husband and I will be thy wife.
I will harness for thee a chariot of lapis
    and gold, (10)
Whose wheels are gold and whose horns are brass.
Thou shalt have storm-demons to hitch on for mighty
    mules.
In the fragrance of cedars thou shalt enter our house.
When our house thou enterest,
Threshold (and) dais shall kiss thy feet!
Humbled before thee shall be kings, lords, and princes!
The *yield* of hills and plain they shall bring thee as
    tribute.
Thy goats shall cast triplets, thy sheep twins,

[1] Gilgamesh.

Thy he-ass in lading shall surpass thy mule.
Thy chariot horses shall be famed for racing,   (20)
[Thine ox] under yoke shall not have a rival!"

[Gilgamesh] opened his mouth to speak,
[Saying] to glorious Ishtar:
["What am I to give] thee, that I may take thee in
    marriage?
[Should I give oil] for the body, and clothing?
[Should I give] bread and victuals?
[...] food fit for divinity,
[...] drink fit for royalty.

                    (mutilated)   (29-31)

[... if I] take thee in marriage?
[Thou art but a brazier which goes out   ] in the cold;
A back door [which does not] keep out blast and wind-
    storm;
A palace which crushes the valiant [...];
A *turban* whose cover [...];
Pitch which [soils] its bearers;
A waterskin which [soaks through] its bearer;
Limestone which [*springs*] the stone rampart;
Jasper [which ...] enemy land;   (40)
A shoe which [pinches the foot   ] of its owner!
Which lover didst thou love forever?
Which of thy shepherds   pleased   [thee for all time]?
Come, and I will na[me for thee] thy lovers:

Of ... [...] ...
For Tammuz, the lover of thy youth,
Thou hast ordained wailing year after year.
Having loved the dappled shepherd-bird,
Thou smotest him, breaking his wing.
In the groves he sits,   crying 'My wing!"[1]   (50)
Then thou lovedst a lion, perfect in strength;
Seven pits and seven thou didst dig for him.
Then a stallion thou lovedst, famed in battle;
The whip, the spur, and the lash thou ordainedst fo
    him.
Thou decreedst for him to gallop seven leagues,
Thou decreedst for him the muddied to drink;
For his mother, Silili, thou ordainedst wailing!
Then thou lovedst the keeper of the herd,

[1] Akk. *ḳappi*, plainly a word play on the cry of the bird

Who ash-cakes ever did heap up for thee,
Daily slaughtered kids for thee;   (60)
Yet thou smotest him, turning him into a wolf,
So that his own herd boys drive him off,
And his dogs bite his thighs.
Then thou lovedst Ishullanu, thy father's gardener,
Who baskets of dates ever did bring to thee,
And daily did brighten thy table.
Thine eyes raised at him, thou didst go to him:
'O my Ishullanu, let us taste of thy vigor!
Put forth thy "hand" and touch our "modesty!"'
Ishullanu said to thee: (70)
'What dost thou want with me?
Has my mother not baked, have I not eaten,
That I should taste the food of stench and foulness?
Does reed-work afford cover against the cold?"[1]
As thou didst hear this [his talk],
Thou smotest him and turn[edst] him into a *mole*.
Thou placedst him in the midst of .. [.] ;
He cannot go up ... nor can he come down ...
If thou shouldst love me, thou wouldst [treat me] like
        them."

When Ishtar heard this,
Ishtar was enraged and [mounted] to heaven.   (80)
Forth went Ishtar before Anu, her father,
To Antum, her mother, she went and [said]:
"My father, Gilgamesh has heaped insults upon me!
Gilgamesh has recounted my stinking deeds,
My stench and my foulness."
Anu opened his mouth to speak,
Saying to glorious Ishtar:
"But surely, thou didst invite . [..],
And so Gilgamesh has recounted thy stinking deeds,
Thy stench and [thy] foulness."   (91)

Ishtar opened her mouth to speak,
Saying to [Anu, her father]:
"My father, make me the Bull of Heaven [that he smite
        Gilgamesh],
[And] fill Gil[gamesh ...]!
If thou [dost not make] me [the Bull of Heaven],
I will smash [the doors of the nether world],
I will [...],

---

[1]   This appears to be a proverbial expression.

I will [raise up the dead eating (and) alive],
So that the dead shall outnumber the living!"   (100)

Anu [opened his mouth to speak],
Saying [to glorious Ishtar]:
"[If I do what] thou askest [of me],
[There will be] seven years of (barren) husks.
Hast thou gathered [grain for the people]?
Hast thou grown grass [for the beasts]?"

[Ishtar opened her mouth] to speak,
[Saying to A]nu, her father:
"[Grain for the people] I have stored,
[Grass for the beasts] I have provided.   (110)
[If there should be seven] years of husks,
[I have ga]thered [grain for the people],
[I have grown] grass [for the beasts]."

(Lines 114-28 are too fragmentary for translation. It
is plain, however, that Anu did Ishtar's bidding, for the
Bull comes down and kills hundreds of men with his
first two snorts.)

With [his] third snort [*he sprang*] at Enkidu.
Enkidu *parried*   his onslaught.   (130)
Up leaped Enkidu, seizing the Bull of Heaven by the
    horns.
The Bull of Heaven hurled [his] foam in [his] face,
Brushed   him with the thick of his tail.

Enkidu opened his mouth to speak,
Saying [to Gilgamesh]:
"My friend, we have gloried [...]."

(Lines 137-51 mutilated, but the course of the battle is
made plain by the following:)

Between neck and horns [he thrust]
    his sword.   (152)
When they had slain the Bull, they tore out his heart,
Placing it before Shamash.
They drew back and did homage before Shamash.
The two brothers sat down.

Then Ishtar mounted the wall of ramparted Uruk,
Sprang on the battlements, uttering a curse:
"Woe unto Gilgamesh because he insulted me
    By slaying the Bull of Heaven!"

When Enkidu heard this speech of Ishtar,   (160)
He *tore loose* the right thigh of the Bull of Heaven
          And tossed it in her face:
"Could I but get thee, like unto him
I would do unto thee.
His entrails I would hang at thy side!"
(Thereupon) Ishtar assembled the votaries,
The (pleasure-)lasses and the (temple-)harlots.
Over the right thigh of the Bull of Heaven she set up a
          wail.
But Gilgamesh called the craftsmen, the armorers,
All (of them).
The artisans admire the thickness of his horns: (170)
Each is cast from thirty minas of lapis;
The coating   on each is two fingers (thick);
Six measures   of oil, the capacity of the two,
He offered as ointment to his god, Lugalbanda.
He brought (them) and hung them in his princely bed-
          chamber.

In the Euphrates they washed their hands,
They embraced each other as they went on,
Riding through the market-street of Uruk.
The people of Uruk are gathered to gaze [upon them].
Gilgamesh to the *lyre maids*[1] [of Uruk]   (180)   I Sam. 18:7
Says (these) words:
"Who is most splendid among the heroes?
Who is most glorious among men?"
"Gilgamesh is most splendid among the heroes,
[Gilgamesh is most glori]ous among men."

                    (mutilated)   (186-188)

Gilgamesh in his palace holds a celebration.
Down lie the heroes on their beds of night.   (190)
Also Enkidu lies down, a dream beholding.
Up rose Enkidu to relate his dream,
Saying to his friend:
"My friend, why are the great gods in council?"

Tablet VII

   The first two columns of this tablet, Enkidu's dream, are miss-
ing in the Assyrian Version
"[...] ... Then daylight came."
[And] Enkidu answered Gilgamesh:

[1] The context calls clearly for musicians or singers, not servant girls.

"[*He*]*ar* the dream which I had last night:
Anu, Enlil, Ea, and heavenly Shamash
　　[Were in council].
And Anu said to Enlil:
'Because the Bull of Heaven they have slain, and
　　Huwawa
They have slain, therefore'—said Anu—'the one of them
Who stripped the mountains of the cedar
　　[Must die!]'
But Enlil said: 'Enkidu must die;
Gilgamesh, however, shall not die!'　　　　　　　　(10)

Then heavenly Shamash answered valiant Enlil:
'Was it not at my　command
That they slew the Bull of Heaven and Huwawa?
　　Should now innocent
Enkidu die?' But Enlil turned
In anger to heavenly Shamash: 'Because, *much like*
One of their　comrades, thou didst daily go down to
　　them.'"
Enkidu lay down (ill) before Gilgamesh.
And as his [1] tears were streaming down, (he said):
"O my brother, my dear brother! Me they would
Clear at the expense of my brother!"
　　Furthermore:　　　　　　　　　　　　　　　(20)
"Must I by the spirit (of the dead)
Sit down, at the spirit's door,
Never again [to behold] my dear brother with (mine)
　　eyes?"
　　(The remainder is lost. In a deathbed review of his
life, Enkidu seems to bemoan the events that had led up
to this sorry state, cursing the successive steps in his
fated life. One of his curses, preserved in an Assyrian
fragment,　is directed against the gate that lamed his
hand.)
Enkidu [...] lifted up [his eyes],　　　　　　　(36)
Speaking with the door as though [it were human]:
"Thou door of the woods, uncom[prehending],
Not endowed with understanding!
At twenty leagues away I found choice
　　thy wood,　　　　　　　　　　　　　　　　(40)
(Long) before I beheld the lofty cedar.
There is no counterpart of thy wood [*in the land*].
Six dozen cubits is thy height, two dozen thy breadth
　　[...].　　　　　　　　　　　[1] Referring to Gilgamesh.

Thy pole, thy pole-ferrule, and thy pole-knob   [...].
A *master-craftsman* in Nippur built thee [...].   *Fig. 61*
Had I known, O door, that this [*would come to pass*]
And that this [thy] beauty [...],
I would have lifted the axe, would have [...],
I would have *set* a reed frame *upon* [*thee*]!"

(A long gap follows. When the text sets in again,
Enkidu—continuing his bitter survey—invokes the curse
of Shamash upon the hunter.)

(iii)

"[...] destroy his wealth,   diminish his power!
May his [*way be repugnant*] before thee.
May [*the beasts he would trap*] escape from before him.
[Let not] the hunter at[tain] the fullness of his heart!"
[Then his heart] prompted (him) to curse [the harlo]t-
        lass:
"Come, lass, I will decree (thy) [fa]te,
[A fa]te that shall not end for all eternity!
[I will] curse thee with a great curse,
[*An oath*], whose curses shall soon overtake thee.
[...] surfeit of thy charms.   (10)
            (mutilated)   (11-17)
[...] shall cast into thy house.
[...] the road shall be thy dwelling place,
[The shadow of the wall] shall be
        thy station,   (20)
[...] thy feet,
[The besotted and the thirsty shall smite] thy cheek!
            (mutilated)   (23-30)
Because me [thou hast ...]
And because [...] upon me."
When Shamash heard [these words] of his mouth,
Forthwith he called down to him [from] heaven:
"Why, O Enkidu, cursest thou the harlot-lass,
Who made thee eat food fit for divinity,
And gave thee to drink wine fit for royalty,
Who clothed thee with noble garments,
And made thee have fair Gilgamesh for a comrade?
And has (not) now Gilgamesh, thy bosom
        friend,   (40)
Made thee lie on a noble couch?
He has made thee lie on a couch of honor,
Has placed thee on the seat of ease, the seat at the left,

That [the prin]ces of the earth may kiss thy feet!
He will make Uruk's people weep over thee (and)
    lament,
Will fill [joyful] people with woe over thee.
And, when thou art gone,
    He will his body with uncut hair invest,
Will don a lion skin and roam over the steppe."

[When] Enkidu [heard] the words of valiant Shamash,
[. . .] his vexed heart grew quiet.

(Short break. Relenting, Enkidu changes his curse into a blessing. He addresses himself once again to the
girl:)   (iv)

"May [. . .] return to thy pl[ace . . .].
[Kings, prin]ces, and nobles shall love [thee].
[None shall on account of thee] smite his thigh.[1]
[Over thee shall the old man] shake his beard.
[. . . *the young*] shall unloose his girdle.
[. . .] *carnelian*, lapis, and gold.
[May he be paid] back who defiled thee,
[*May his home be emptied*], his heaped-up storehouse.
[To the presence of] the gods [the priest] shall let
    thee enter,
[On thy account] shall be forsaken the wife,
    (though) a mother of seven."   (10)
[. . . Enki]du, whose mood is bitter,
[. . .] lies down all alone.
That night [he pours out] his feelings to his friend:
"[My friend], I saw a dream last night:
The heavens [moaned], the earth responded;[2]
[. . .] I stood [alo]ne.
[. . .] his face was darkened.
Like unto [. . .] was his face.
[. . . like] the talons of an eagle were his claws.
[. . .] he *overpowered* me.   (20)
[. . .] he leaps.
[. . .] he submerged me.

                (mutilated or missing)   (23-30)
[. . .] . . . he transformed me,
So that my arms were [. . .] like those of a bird.
Looking at me, he leads me to the House of Darkness,
    The abode of Irkalla,
To the house which none leave who have entered it,

---
[1] In derision or embarrassment.   [2] A portent of death.

On the road from which there is no way back,
To the house wherein the dwellers are bereft of light,
Where dust is their fare and clay their food.
They are clothed like birds, with wings for garments,
And see no light, residing in darkness.
In the House of Dust, which I entered, (40)
I looked at [rulers], their crowns put away;
I [saw princes], those (born to) the crown,
     Who had ruled the land from the days of yore.
[These *doubl*]es of Anu and Enlil were serving meat
    roasts;
They were serving bake[meats] and pouring
    Cool water from the waterskins.
In the House of Dust, which I entered,
Reside High Priest and acolyte,
Reside incantatory and ecstatic,
Reside the laver-anointers of the great gods,
Resides Etana,[1] resides Sumuqan.[2]
Ereshkigal [lives there], Queen of the nether world, (50)
[And Belit-]Seri, recorder of the nether world, kneels
    before her.
[She holds a tablet] and reads out to her.
[Lifting] up her head, she beheld me:
[Saying: 'Who] has brought this one hither?' "
    (The remainder of the tablet in the Assyrian Version
is missing. The following fragment may be relevant.)
"Remember all my travels [with him]! (4)
My friend saw a dream whose [*portents*] were un[favor-
    able]:
The day on which he saw the dream was ended.
Stricken is Enkidu, one day, [a second day].
Enkidu's [suffering], on his bed, [increases].
A third day, a fourth day [. . .].
A fifth day, a sixth, and a seventh; (10)
    An eighth, a ninth, [and a tenth day],
Enkidu's suffering, on his bed, [increases].
    An eleventh and a twelfth day [. . .].
[Stricken] is Enkidu on his bed [*of pain*]!
At length he called Gilgamesh [and said to him]:
'My friend, [. . .] has cursed me!
[Not] like one [fallen] in battle [shall I die],
For I feared the battle [. . .].
My friend, he who [is slain] in battle [is blessed].
But as for me, [. . .].' "

1 King of Kish who was carried to heaven by an eagle.   2 God of cattle.

220.93 Circleville Bible College Library 12753
PR

Tablet VIII (obverse, i)

With the first glow of dawn Gilgamesh said to his
   friend:
"Enkidu, thy [moth]er a gazelle, a wild ass thy father,
   [produce]d thee.
They whose *mark* is their tails reared thee, and the
   cattle
Of the steppe and of all the pastures.
   May the tracks of Enkidu in the Cedar Forest
Weep for thee, may they not *hush* night and day.
May the elders of wide, ramparted Uruk weep for thee.
   [May weep for thee]
The finger that is extended behind us in blessing.
   May weep for thee
And echo the countryside as though it were thy mother.
   May weep for thee [. . .]
In whose midst we . . . May weep for thee
   bear, hyena, [panther],
Tiger, hart, *leopard*, lion; oxen, deer, [ibex],   (10)
And the wild creatures of the steppe.
   May weep for thee the river Ula [. . .]
By whose banks we used to walk.
   May weep for thee the pure Euphrates, [*where we
   drew*]
Water for the skin. May weep for thee
   The warriors of wide, [ramparted] Uruk
[. . .] we slew the Bull . . . May weep for thee [. . .]
[Who] in Eridu extolled thy name. May weep for thee
   [. . .]
[Who . . .] extolled thy name. May weep for thee
   [. . .]
[Who] provided . . . grain for thy mouth. May weep
   for thee [. . .]
[Who] put salve on thy back. May weep for thee [. . .]
[Who] put ale in thy mouth. May weep for thee the
   [*harlot*]
[Who] anointed thee with fragrant oil.
   May we[ep for thee . . .]   (20)
[Of the h]arem who [*brought to thee*]
   The wife and the ring *of* thy choice.[1]
May brothers weep for thee like sisters [. . .
   and may they let grow long]
Their head-hair over thee [. . .]!"

---

[1] Or perhaps, "a wife, a ring, thy counsel."

(ii)

"Hear me, O elders [and give ear] unto me!
It is for Enkidu, my [friend], that I weep,
Moaning bitterly like a wailing woman.
The axe at my side, my hand's trust,
The dirk in my belt, [the shield] in front of me,
My festal robe, my richest trimming—
An evil [*demon*] rose up and robbed me!
[O my younger   friend], thou chasedst
      The wild ass   of the hills, the panther of the steppe!
Enkidu, my younger friend, thou who chasedst
      The wild ass of the hills, the panther of the steppe!
We who [have conquered] all things, scaled
      [the mountains],   (10)
Who seized the Bull [and slew him],
Brought affliction   on Hubaba,[1] who [dwelled in the
      Cedar Forest]!
What, now, is this sleep that has laid hold [on thee]?
Thou art benighted and canst not hear [me]!"
But he lifts not up [his eyes];
He touched his heart, but it does not beat.
Then he veiled (his) friend like a bride [. . .],
Storming over him like a lion,
Like a lioness deprived of [her] whelps.
He paces back and forth before [*the couch*],   (20)
Pulling out (his hair) and strewing [it . . .],   Jer. 16:6; 48:37
Tearing off and flinging down (his) finery,
      [As though] unc[lean]!
With the first glow [of dawn], Gil[gamesh . . .].
Then Gilgamesh issued a call to the land: "O smith,
      [. . .],
Coppersmith, goldsmith, lapidary! Make my friend
      [. . .]!"
[Then] he fashioned a statue for his friend,
      The friend whose stature [. . .]:
"[. . .], of lapis is thy breast, of gold thy body, [. . .]."

(iii)

"On a couch [of honor I made thee lie],
I placed thee [on the seat of ease, the seat at the left],
That the princes of the earth [might kiss thy feet]!
Over thee I will make [Uruk's] people weep (and)
      [lament],
Joyful people [I will fill with woe over thee].
And, when thou art gone,

---

[1]   Variant of Ḥumbaba, Ḥuwawa

[I shall invest my body with uncut hair],
And, clad in a [lion] skin, [I shall roam over the
    steppe]!"

With the first glow of dawn, [Gilgamesh]
Loosened his band [...].

(The remainder of the tablet is missing or too fragmentary for translation, with the exception of the following lines:)

(v)

With the first glow of dawn, Gilgamesh
    fashioned [...],   (45)
Brought out a large table of *elammaqu* wood,
Filled with honey a bowl of *carnelian*,
Filled with curds a bowl of lapis,
[...] he decorated and exposed to the sun.

Tablet IX

(i)

For Enkidu, his friend, Gilgamesh
Weeps bitterly, as he ranges over the steppe:
"When I die, shall I not be like Enkidu?
Woe has entered my belly.
Fearing death, I roam over the steppe.
To Utnapishtim,[1] Ubar-Tutu's son,
I have taken the road to proceed in all haste.
When arriving by night at mountain passes,
I saw lions and grew afraid,
I lifted my head to Sin[2] to pray.   (10)
To [...] of the gods went out my orisons.
[...] preserve thou me!"
[As at night] he lay, he awoke from a dream.
[There were ...], rejoicing in life.
He raised his axe in his hand,
He drew [the dirk] from his belt.
Like an ar[row] he descended among them.
He smote [them] and hacked away at them.

(The remainder of Tablet IX gives the adventures
of Gilgamesh as he passes successfully the darkness of
the mountain range of Mashu guarded by scorpion-
men.)

---

[1] Mesopotamian hero of the Flood—Sumerian Z i u s u d r a and Greek
Xisouthros.   [2] The moon-god.

Tablet X

This tablet, which traces further the successive stages in Gilgamesh's quest of immortality, happens to be represented by as many as four separate versions. Two of these, however, the Hittite and Hurrian, are extant only in fragments that are too slight for connected translation. Substantial portions are available, on the other hand, in the Old Babylonian and Assyrian recensions.

OLD BABYLONIAN VERSION

(i)

(top broken away)

"[...] ...
With their skins [he clothes himself],   as he eats flesh.
[.] .., O Gilgamesh, which has not happened
As long as my wind drives the waters."
Shamash was distraught, as he betook himself to him;
He says to Gilgamesh:
"Gilgamesh, whither rovest thou?
The life thou pursuest thou shalt not find."
Gilgamesh says to him, to valiant Shamash:
"After marching (and) roving over the steppe,   (10)
Must I lay my head in the heart of the earth
That I may sleep through all the years?
Let mine eyes behold the sun
    That I may have my fill of the light!
Darkness withdraws when there is enough light.
May one who indeed is dead behold yet the radiance of
    the sun!"

(ii)

(Beginning lost. Gilgamesh is addressing Siduri, the ale-wife:)

"He who with me underwent all hard[ships]—
Enkidu, whom I loved dearly,
Who with me underwent all hardships—
Has now gone to the fate of mankind!
Day and night I have wept over him.
I would not give him up for burial—
In case   my friend should rise at my plaint—
Seven days and seven nights,
Until   a worm fell out of his nose.
Since his passing I have not found life,   (10)
I have roamed like a hunter in the midst of the steppe.
O ale-wife, now that I have seen thy face,
Let me not see the death which I ever dread."

The ale-wife said to him, to Gilgamesh:

(iii)

"Gilgamesh, whither rovest thou?
The life thou pursuest thou shalt not find.

Ps. 115:17

When the gods created mankind,
Death for mankind they set aside,
Life in their own hands retaining.
Thou, Gilgamesh, let full be thy belly,

Eccles. 5:18

Make thou merry   by day and by night.
Of each day make thou a feast of rejoicing,

Eccles. 8:15
Eccles. 9:8-9

Day and night dance thou and play!
Let thy garments be sparkling fresh,   (10)
Thy head be washed; bathe thou in water.
Pay heed to the little one that holds on to thy hand,
Let thy spouse delight in thy bosom!
For this is the task of [mankind]!"

(remainder of the column broken away)

(iv)

In his wrath he shatters them. [1]
When he returned, he goes up to him. [2]
Sursunabu [3] his eyes behold.
Sursunabu says to him, to Gilgamesh:
"Tell me, thou, what is thy name?
I am Sursunabu, (he) of Utanapishtim [4] the Faraway."
Gilgamesh said to him, to Sursunabu:
"As for me, Gilgamesh is my name,
Who have come from Uruk-Eanna,
Who have traversed   the mountains,   (10)
A distant journey, as the sun *rises*.
O Sursunabu, now that I have seen thy face,
Show me Utanapishtim the Faraway."
Sursunabu [says] to him, to Gilgamesh.

(remainder broken away)

(The Assyrian Version of Tablet X gives the episodes
of the meetings with Siduri and with Sursunabu [Ursha-
nabi in the Assyrian Version] and an account of the
crossing of the Waters of Death to the abode of Utnapishtim. The concluding part of Tablet X follows:)

---

[1] Apparently the mysterious "Stone Things."   [2] To the boatman.
[3] The Urshanabi of the Assyrian Version.   [4] Assyrian Utnapishtim.

(v)

Gilgamesh also said to him, to Utnapishtim: (23)
"That now I might come and behold Utnapishtim,
    Whom they call the Faraway,
I ranged and wandered over all the lands,
I traversed difficult mountains,
I crossed all the seas!
My face was not sated with sweet sleep,
I fretted myself with wakefulness;
    I filled my joints with misery.
I had not reached the ale-wife's house,
    When my clothing was used up.   (30)
[I sl]ew bear,   hyena, lion, panther,
    Tiger, stag, (and) ibex—
    The wild beasts and creeping things of the steppe.
Their [flesh] I ate and their skins I *wr[apped about
    me]*."

(The remainder of this column is too mutilated for
translation. The beginning of the last column is broken
away, except for the conclusion of the sage observations
of Utnapishtim:)

(vi)

"Do we build a house for ever?   (26)
    Do we seal (contracts) for ever?
Do brothers divide shares for ever?
Does hatred persist for ever in [the land]?   Eccles. 9:6
Does the river for ever raise up (and) bring on floods?
The dragon-fly [leaves] (its) shell   (30)
That its face might (but) glance at the face of the sun.
Since the days of yore there has been no [permanence];   Eccles. 1:11; 1:4;
The *resting* and the dead, how alike [they are]!   2:16; 9:5; 3:19
Do they not compose   a picture of death,
The commoner and the noble,
    Once they are near to [their fate]?
The Anunnaki, the great gods, foregather;
Mammetum, maker of fate, with them the fate decrees:
Death and life they determine.   Deut. 30:19
(But) of death, its days are not revealed."

Tablet XI

Gilgamesh said to him, to Utnapishtim the Faraway:
"As I look upon thee, Utnapishtim,
Thy features are not strange; even as I art thou.
Thou art not strange at all; even as I art thou.
My heart had regarded thee as resolved   to do battle,

[Yet] thou liest indolent upon thy back!
[Tell me,] how joinedst thou the Assembly of the gods,
    In thy quest of life?"

Utnapishtim said to him, to Gilgamesh:
"I will reveal to thee, Gilgamesh, a hidden matter
And a secret of the gods will I tell thee: (10)
Shurippak—a city which thou knowest,
[(And) which on Euphrates' [banks] is situate—
That city was ancient, (as were) the gods within it,
When their heart led the great gods to produce the flood.
[There] were Anu, their father,
Valiant Enlil, their counselor,
Ninurta, their assistant,
Ennuge, their irrigator.[1]
Ninigiku-Ea was also present with them;
Their words he repeats to the reed-hut:[2]   (20)
'Reed-hut, reed-hut! Wall, wall!
Reed-hut, hearken! Wall, reflect!
Man of Shuruppak,   son of Ubar-Tutu,

Gen. 6:14   Tear down (this) house, build a ship!
Give up possessions, seek thou life.
Forswear (worldly) goods and keep the soul alive!

Gen. 6:19-20   Aboard the ship take thou the seed of all living things.
The ship that thou shalt build,
Her   dimensions shall be to measure.

Gen. 6:15   Equal shall be her width and her length.   (30)
Like the Apsu thou shalt ceil her.'
I understood, and I said to Ea, my lord:
'[Behold], my lord, what thou hast thus ordered,
I will be honored to carry out.
[But what] shall I answer the city, the people and
    elders?'
Ea opened his mouth to speak,
Saying to me, his servant:
'Thou shalt then thus speak unto them:
"I have learned that Enlil is hostile to me,
So that I cannot reside in your city,
Nor set my f[oo]t in Enlil's territory.   (40)
To the Deep I will therefore go down,
    To dwell with my lord Ea.
[But upon] you he will shower down abundance,
[The choicest] birds, the rarest fishes.

---

[1] More specifically, "inspector of canals."
[2] Presumably, the dwelling place of Utnapishtim. Ea addresses him
through the barrier of the wall.

[*The land shall have its fill*] of harvest riches.
[He who at dusk orders] the husk-greens,
Will shower down upon you a rain of wheat."[1]

With the first glow of dawn,
The land was gathered [about me].
      (too fragmentary for translation)   (50-53)
The little ones [carr]ied bitumen,
While the grown ones brought [all else] that was need-
    ful.
On the fifth day I laid her framework.
One (whole) acre   was her floor space,
    Ten dozen cubits the height of each of her walls,   Gen. 6:15
Ten dozen cubits each edge of the square deck.[2]
I laid out the contours (and) joined her together.
I provided her with six decks,   (60)   Gen. 6:16
Dividing her (thus) into seven parts.
Her floor plan I divided into nine parts.
I hammered water-plugs into her.
I saw to the punting-poles and laid in supplies.
Six 'sar'[3]   (measures) of bitumen I poured into the   Gen. 6:14
    furnace,
Three sar of asphalt [I also] poured inside.
Three sar of oil the basket-bearers carried,
Aside from the one sar of oil which the *calking*   con-
    sumed,
And the two sar of oil [which] the boatman stowed
    away.
Bullocks I slaughtered for the [people],   (70)   Gen. 6:21
And I killed sheep every day.
Must, red wine, oil, and white wine
[I gave the] workmen [to drink], as though river water,
That they might feast as on New Year's Day.
I op[ened ...] ointment, applying (it) to my hand.
[On the sev]enth [day] the ship was completed.
[*The launching*] was very difficult,
So that they had to shift the floor planks   above and
    below,
[*Until*] two-thirds of [*the structure*]   [*had g*]one [*into
    the water*].

---

  [1] As has long been recognized, these lines feature word plays in that both
kukku and *kibâti* may designate either food or misfortune; Wily Ea plays
on this ambiguity: To the populace, the statement would be a promise of
prosperity; to Utnapishtim it would signalize the impending deluge.
  [2] The ship was thus an exact cube.
  [3] The number 3,600. If the measure understood with it was the *sutu*
(seah), each *sar* designated about 8,000 gallons.

[Whatever I had] I laded upon her: (80)
Whatever I had of silver I laded upon her;
Whatever I [had] of gold I laded upon her;

Gen. 7:7-8   Whatever I had of all the living beings I [laded] upon her.

All my family and kin I made go aboard the ship.

Gen. 7:13-16   The beasts of the field, the wild creatures of the field,
All the craftsmen I made go aboard.
Shamash had set for me a stated time:
'When he who orders unease at night,
    Will shower down a rain of blight,
Board thou the ship and batten up the entrance!'
That stated time had arrived:
'He who orders unease at night, showers down
    a rain of blight.' (90)
I watched the appearance of the weather.
The weather was awesome to behold.
I boarded the ship and battened up the entrance.
To batten down   the (whole) ship, to Puzur-Amurri,
    the boatman,
I handed over the structure together with its contents.

With the first glow of dawn,

Gen. 7:11   A black cloud rose up from the horizon.
Inside it Adad thunders,
While Shullat and Hanish[1]   go in front,
Moving as heralds over hill and plain. (100)
Erragal[2]   tears out the posts;[3]
Forth comes Ninurta and causes the dikes to follow.
The Anunnaki lift up the torches,
Setting the land ablaze with their glare.
Consternation   over Adad reaches to the heavens,
Who turned to blackness all that had been light.
[The wide] land was shattered like [a pot]!
For one day the south-storm [blew],

Gen. 7:20-22   Gathering speed as it blew, [submerging the mountains],
Overtaking the [people] like a battle. (110)
No one can see his fellow,
Nor can the people be recognized from heaven.
The gods were frightened by the deluge,
And, shrinking back, they ascended to the heaven of
    Anu.[4]

---

[1] Two heralds.   [2] Nergal, god of the nether world.   [3] Of the world dam.
[4] The highest heaven in the Mesopotamian conception of the cosmos.

The gods cowered like dogs
    Crouched against the outer wall.
Ishtar cried out like a woman in travail,
The sweet-voiced mistress of the [gods] moans aloud:
'The olden days are alas turned to clay,   Gen. 7:23
Because I bespoke evil in the Assembly of the gods.
How could I bespeak evil in the Assembly
    of the gods,   (120)
Ordering battle for the destruction of my people,   Gen. 8:21
When it is I myself who give birth to my people!
Like the spawn of the fishes they fill the sea!'
The Anunnaki gods weep with her,
The gods, all humbled, sit and weep,
Their lips *drawn tight*,   [...] one and all.
Six days and [six] nights
Blows the flood wind, as the south-storm sweeps the
    land.
When the seventh day arrived,
    The flood(-carrying) south-storm subsided in the
    battle,
Which it had fought like an army.   (130)
The sea grew quiet, the tempest was still, the flood   Gen. 8:1-2
    ceased.
I looked at the weather: stillness had set in,
And all of mankind had returned to clay.
The landscape was as level as a flat roof.
I opened a hatch, and light fell upon my face.   Gen. 8:6
Bowing low, I sat and wept,
Tears running down on my face.
I looked about for coast lines in the expanse of the sea:
In each of fourteen   (regions)
    There emerged a region(-mountain).
On Mount Nisir   the ship came to a halt.   (140)   Gen. 8:4
Mount Nisir held the ship fast,
    Allowing no motion.
One day, a second day, Mount Nisir held the ship fast,
    Allowing no motion.
A third day, a fourth day, Mount Nisir held the ship
    fast,
    Allowing no motion.
A fifth, and a sixth (day), Mount Nisir held the ship
    fast,
    Allowing no motion.
When the seventh day arrived,
I sent forth and set free a dove.

Gen. 8:8-10	The dove went forth, but came back;
	Since no resting-place for it was visible, she turned round.
	Then I sent forth and set free a swallow.
	The swallow went forth, but came back; (150)
	Since no resting-place for it was visible, she turned round.
Gen. 8:7	Then I sent forth and set free a raven.
	The raven went forth and, seeing that the waters had diminished,
	He eats, circles, caws, and turns not round.
	Then I let out (all) to the four winds
	And offered a sacrifice.
Gen. 8:19-20	I poured out a libation on the top of the mountain.
	Seven and seven cult-vessels I set up,
	Upon their pot-stands I heaped cane, cedarwood, and myrtle.
Gen. 8:21	The gods smelled the savor,
	The gods smelled the sweet savor, (160)
	The gods crowded like flies about the sacrificer.

When at length as the great goddess [1] arrived,
She lifted up the great jewels which Anu had fashioned
    to her liking:
'Ye gods here, as surely as this lapis
    Upon my neck I shall not forget,
I shall be mindful of these days, forgetting (them) never.
Let the gods come to the offering;
(But) let not Enlil come to the offering,
For he, unreasoning, brought on the deluge
And my people consigned to destruction.'
When at length as Enlil arrived,   (170)
And saw the ship, Enlil was wroth,
He was filled with wrath over the Igigi gods:[2]
'Has some living soul escaped?
    No man was to survive the destruction!'
Ninurta opened his mouth to speak,
    Saying to valiant Enlil:
'Who, other than Ea, can devise plans?[3]
It is Ea alone who knows every matter.'
Ea opened his mouth to speak,
    Saying to valiant Enlil:
'Thou wisest of gods, thou hero,
How couldst thou, unreasoning, bring on the deluge?

---

[1] Ishtar.   [2] The heavenly gods.
[3] An allusion to one of the common epithets of Ea.

On the sinner impose his sin, (180)
    On the transgressor impose his transgression!
(Yet) be lenient, lest he be cut off,
Be patient,   lest he be dis[lodged]!
Instead of thy bringing on the deluge,
    Would that a lion had risen up to diminish man-
    kind!
Instead of thy bringing on the deluge,
    Would that a wolf had risen up to diminish man-
    kind!
Instead of thy bringing on the deluge,
    Would that a famine had risen up to l[ay low] man-
    kind!
Instead of thy bringing on the deluge,
    Would that pestilence   had risen up to smi[te
    down] mankind!
It was not I who disclosed the secret of the great gods.
I let Atrahasis [1] see a dream,
    And he perceived the secret of the gods.
Now then take counsel in regard to him!'
Thereupon Enlil went aboard the ship.
Holding me by the hand, he took me aboard. (190)
He took my wife aboard and made (her) kneel by my
    side.
Standing between us, he touched our foreheads to bless
    us:
'Hitherto Utnapishtim has been but human.
Henceforth Utnapishtim and his wife shall be like unto
    us gods.
Utnapishtim shall reside far away, at the mouth of the
    rivers!'
Thus they took me and made me reside far away,
    At the mouth of the rivers.
But now, who will for thy sake call the gods to Assembly
That the life which thou seekest thou mayest find?
Up, lie not down to sleep
    For six days and seven nights."
As he sits there on his haunches, (200)
Sleep fans him like the whirlwind.
Utnapishtim says to her, to his spouse:
"Behold this hero who seeks life!
Sleep fans him like a mist."
His spouse says to him, to Utnapishtim the Faraway:
"Touch him that the man may awake,

Ezek. 14:13-21

---

[1] "Exceeding Wise," an epithet of Utnapishtim.

That he may return safe on the way whence he came,
That through the gate by which he left he may return to
    his land."
Utnapishtim says to her, to his spouse:

Gen. 8:21 "Since to deceive is human, he will seek
    to deceive thee.   (210)
Up, bake for him wafers, put (them) at his head,
And mark on the wall the days he sleeps."
She baked for him wafers, put (them) at his head,
And marked on the wall the days he slept.
His first wafer is dried out
The second is gone bad,   the third is soggy;
    The crust   of the fourth has turned white;
The fifth has a moldy cast,
    The sixth (still) is fresh-colored;
The seventh—just as he touched him the man awoke.

Gilgamesh says to him, to Utnapishtim the Faraway:
"Scarcely   had sleep surged over me,   (220)
When straightway thou dost touch and rouse me!"
Utnapishtim [says to him], to Gilgamesh:
"[Go], Gilgamesh, count thy wafers,
[That the days thou hast slept] may become known to
    thee:
Thy [first] wafer is dried out,
[The second is gone] bad, the third is soggy;
    The crust of the fourth has turned white;
[The fifth] has a moldy cast,
    The sixth (still) is fresh-colored.
[The seventh]—at this instant thou hast awakened."
Gilgamesh says to him, to Utnapishtim the Faraway:
"[What then] shall I do, Utnapishtim,   (230)
    Whither shall I go,
[Now] that the Bereaver has laid hold on my [mem-
    bers]?
In my bedchamber lurks death,
And wherever I se[t my foot], there is death!"

Utnapishtim [says to him], to Urshanabi, the boatman:
"Urshanabi, may the landing-pl[ace not rejoice in thee],
    May the place of crossing renounce thee!
To him who wanders on its shore, deny thou its shore!
The man thou hast led (hither), whose body is covered
    with grime,
The grace of whose members skins have distorted,

---

[1] By asserting that he had not slept at all.

Take him, Urshanabi, and bring him to the washing-
    place.
Let him wash off his grime in water
    clean as snow,   (240)
Let him cast off his skins, let the sea carry (them)
    away,
    That the fairness of his body may be seen.
Let him renew the band round his head,
Let him put on a cloak to clothe his nakedness,
That he may arrive in his city,
That he may achieve his journey.
Let not (his) cloak have a moldy cast,
    Let it be wholly new."
Urshanabi took him and brought him to the washing-
    place.
He washed off his grime in water clean as snow.
He cast off his skins, the sea carried (them) away,
That the fairness of his body might be seen.   (250)
He renewed [the band] round his head,
He put on a cloak to clothe his nakedness,
That he might ar[rive in his city],
That he might achieve his journey.
[The cloak had not a moldy cast, but] was [wholly]
    new.
Gilgamesh and Urshanabi boarded the boat,
[They launch]ed the boat on the waves (and) they
    sailed away.

His spouse says to him, to Utnapishtim the Faraway:
"Gilgamesh has come hither, toiling and straining.
What wilt thou give (him) that he may return
    to his land?"   (260)
At that he, Gilgamesh, raised up (his) pole,
To bring the boat nigh to the shore.
Utnapishtim [says] to him, [to] Gilgamesh:
"Gilgamesh, thou hast come hither, toiling and straining.
What shall I give thee that thou mayest return to thy
    land?
I will disclose, O Gilgamesh, a hidden thing,
And [*a secret of the gods* I will] tell thee:
This plant, like the buckthorn is [its . . .].
Its thorns will pr[ick thy hands] just as does the *rose*.
If thy hands obtain the plant, [thou wilt
    find new life]."   (270)
No sooner had Gilgamesh heard this,

Than he opened the *wa*[*ter-pipe*],
He tied heavy stones [to his feet].
They pulled him down into the deep [and he saw the
    plant].
He took the plant, though it pr[icked his hands].
He cut the heavy stones [from his feet].
The [s]ea   cast him up upon its shore.

Gilgamesh says to him, to Urshanabi, the boatman:
"Urshanabi, this plant is a plant *apart*,
Whereby a man may regain his *life's breath*.
I will take it to ramparted Uruk,   (280)
    Will cause [...] to eat the plant ... !
Its name shall be 'Man Becomes Young in Old Age.' [1]
I myself shall eat (it)
    And thus return to the state of my youth."
After twenty leagues they broke off a morsel,
After thirty (further) leagues they prepared for the
    night.
Gilgamesh saw a well whose water was cool.
He went down into it to bathe in the water.
A serpent snuffed the fragrance of the plant;
It came up [from the water] and carried off the plant.
Going back it shed [its] slough.

Thereupon Gilgamesh sits down and weeps,   (290)
His tears running down over his face.
[He took the hand]   of Urshanabi, the boatman:
"[For] whom,   Urshanabi, have my hands toiled?
For whom is being spent the blood of my heart?
I have not obtained a boon for myself.
For the earth-lion[2]   have I effected a boon!
And now the tide   will bear (it) twenty leagues away!
When I opened the *water-pipe* and [. . .] the year,[3]
I found that which has been placed as a sign for me:
    I shall withdraw,
And leave the boat on the shore!"   (300)
    After twenty leagues they broke off a morsel,
After thirty (further) leagues they prepared for the
    night.

---

[1] Note that the process is one of rejuvenation, not immortality.

[2] An allusion to the serpent?

[3] The opening of the *râṭu* (normally "pipe, tube," apparently took
place in connection with Gilgamesh's dive (cf. also l. 271). But the details remain obscure. In the *Eridu Creation Story*, II, the same term is
used, perhaps for a pipe connecting with a source of sweet waters which
would nourish the miraculous plant.

When they arrived in ramparted Uruk,
Gilgamesh says to him, to Urshanabi, the boatman:
"Go up, Urshanabi, walk on the ramparts of Uruk.
Inspect the base terrace, examine its brickwork,
    If its brickwork is not of burnt brick,
And if the Seven Wise Ones laid not its foundation!
One 'sar' is city, one sar orchards,
    One sar margin land; (further) the *precinct* of the
    Temple of Ishtar.
Three sar and the *precinct* comprise Uruk."

(Tablet XII has been omitted from this abridgment, since it is an inorganic appendage to the epic proper.)

A COSMOLOGICAL INCANTATION: THE WORM AND THE TOOTHACHE

ANET, 100-101

Among the incantations which contain cosmological material, one of the best-known attributes toothache to a worm that had obtained the permission of the gods to dwell among the teeth and gums. The present text, which is designated ideographically as an "Incantation against Toothache," dates from Neo-Babylonian times and was published by R. Campbell Thompson in *CT*, xvii (1903), Pl. 50. But the colophon indicates that the copy had been made from an ancient text. And indeed, the Mari documents of the Old Babylonian period include a tablet with the Akkadian label *ši-pa-at tu-ul-tim* "Toothache Incantation." The text itself, however, is in Hurrian. But although it cites various deities of the Hurrian pantheon—and is thus clearly religious in nature—the context does not correspond to the Neo-Babylonian legend, to judge from the intelligible portions.

After Anu [had created heaven],
Heaven had created [the earth],
The earth had created the rivers,
The rivers had created the canals,
The canals had created the marsh,
(And) the marsh had created the worm—
The worm went, weeping, before Shamash,
His tears flowing before Ea:
"What wilt thou give for my food?
What wilt thou give me for my sucking?" (10)
"I shall give thee the ripe fig,
(And) the apricot."
"Of what use are they to me, the ripe fig
And the apricot?
Lift me up and among the teeth
And the gums cause me to dwell!
The blood of the tooth I will suck,

And of the gum I will gnaw
Its *roots*!"

Fix the pin and seize its foot.[1]   (20)
Because thou hast said this, O worm,
May Ea smite thee with the might
Of his hand!

[1] This is the instruction to the dentist.

ANET, 101-103   ADAPA

The story of Adapa shares with the Epic of Gilgamesh the *motif* of man's squandered opportunity for gaining immortality. It is extant in four fragmentary accounts. The oldest and longest of these (B) comes from the El-Amarna archives (fourteenth century B.C.), whereas the other three (A, C, and D) derive from the library of Ashurbanipal. The order of presentation is contextual, except that C is roughly parallel to parts of B.

A

[Wis]dom ... [...].
His command was indeed ... [...] like the command
of [Ea].
Wide understanding he had perfected for him to disclose[1] the designs of the land.
To him he had given wisdom; eternal life he had not given him.
In those days, in those years, the sage from Eridu,
Ea, created him as the *model* of men.
The sage—his command no one can vitiate—
The capable, the most wise among the Anunnaki is he;
Ps. 24:4   The blameless, the clean of hands, the ointment priest, the observer of rites.
With the bakers he does the baking   (10)
With the bakers of Eridu he does the baking;
Bread and water for Eridu daily he provides,
With his clean hand(s) he arranges the (offering) table,
Without him the table cannot be cleared.
He steers the ship, he does the prescribed fishing for Eridu.
In those days Adapa, the one of Eridu,
While [...] Ea ... upon the couch,
Daily did attend to the sanctuary of Eridu.
At the holy quay, the Quay of the New Moon, he boarded the sailboat;
Then a wind blew thither and his boat drifted;   (20)
[With the o]ar he steers his boat
[...] upon the wide sea.   (remainder destroyed)

B⁴

... [...]

The south wind b[lew and submerged him],

[causing him to go down] to the home [of the *fish*]:

"South wind, [. .]. me all thy *venom* . . . [. . .].

I will break thy wi[ng]!" Just as he had said (this) with
his mouth,

The wing of the sou[th wi]nd was broken. For seven
days

The [south win]d blew not upon the land. Anu

Calls [to] Ilabrat, his vizier:

"Why has the south wind not blown over the land these
seven days?"

His vizier, Ilabrat, answered him: "My lord,   (10)

Adapa, the son of Ea,¹ the wing of the south wind

Has broken." When Anu heard this speech,

He cried, "Mercy!" Rising from his throne: "[Let]
them fetch him hither!"

At that, Ea, he who knows what pertains to heaven,
took hold of him,

[Adapa], caused him to wear (his) [hai]r unkempt, a
mourning garb

[He made him put on], and gave him (this) [ad]vice:

"[Adapa], thou art going [before Anu], the king;

[The road to heaven thou wilt take. When to] heaven

[Thou hast] go[ne up and] hast [approached the gate
of Anu],

[Tammuz and Gizzida] at the gate of Anu   (20)

Will be standing. When they see thee, they will [as]k
thee: 'Man,

For whom dost thou look thus? Adapa, for whom

Art thou clad with mourning garb?'

'From our land two gods have disappeared,

Hence I am thus.' 'Who are the two gods who from the
land

Have disappeared?' 'Tammuz and Gizzida.' They will
glance at each other

And will smile. A good word they

Will speak to Anu, (and) Anu's benign face

They will cause to be shown thee. As thou standest
before Anu,

When they offer thee bread of death,

¹ It should be added that Adapa's purpose was plainly to catch fish for
Ea's temple, hence that god's primary interest in Adapa. For the importance of fishing to the temple economy cf. the so-called Weidner
Chronicle, which employs this *motif* as a reason for the rise and fall of
dynasties (and, incidentally, mentions Adapa).

Thou shalt not eat (it). When they offer thee
　　water of death,　　　　　　　　　　　　　　(30)
Thou shalt not drink (it). When they offer thee a gar-
　　ment,
Put (it) on. When they offer thee oil, anoint thyself
　　(therewith).
(This) advice that I have given thee, neglect not; the
　　words
That I have spoken to thee, hold fast!" The messenger
Of Anu arrived there (saying as follows): "Adapa the
　　south wind's
Wing has broken, bring him before me!"

He made him take the road to heaven, and to heaven
　　he went up.
When he had ascended to heaven and approached the
　　gate of Anu,
Tammuz and Gizzida were standing at the gate of Anu.
When they saw Adapa, they cried, "Mercy!　　　(40)
Man, for whom dost thou look thus? Adapa,
For whom art thou clad with mourning garb?"
"Two gods have disappeared from the land, therefore
　　with mourning garb
I am clad." "Who are the two gods who from the land
　　have disappeared?"
"Tammuz and Gizzida." They glanced at each other
And smiled.[1] As Adapa before Anu, the king,
Drew near and Anu saw him, he called:
"Come now, Adapa, wherefore the south wind's wing
Didst thou break?" Adapa replied to Anu: "My lord,
For the household of my master, in the midst
　　of the sea　　　　　　　　　　　　　　　(50)
I was catching fish. The sea was like a mirror.
But the south wind came blowing and submerged me,
Causing (me) to go down to the home of the *fish*. In
　　the wrath of my heart
I cursed the [south wind]." Speaking up at [his] side,
　　Tammuz
[And] Gizzida to Anu [a g]ood word
Addressed. His heart quieted as he was . . .
"Why did Ea to a *worthless* human of the heaven
And of the earth the plan　disclose,
Rendering him *distinguished* and making a name for
　　him?

---

[1] Apparently pleased because Adapa mourned their loss.

As for us, what shall we do about him? Bread
    of life   (60)
Fetch for him and he shall eat (it)." When the bread of
    life
They brought him, he did not eat; when the water of
    life
They brought him, he did not drink. When a garment
They brought him, he put (it) on; when oil
They brought him, he anointed himself (therewith).
As Anu looked at him, he laughed at him:
"Come now, Adapa! Why didst thou neither eat nor
    drink?
Thou shalt not have (eternal) life! Ah, per[ver]se man-
    kind!"
    "Ea, my master,
Commanded me: 'Thou shalt not eat, thou shalt not
    drink'"
"Take him away and return him to his earth."
                             (remainder destroyed)

C

When [Anu] heard th[is],
[... in the wr]ath of his heart
[...] he dispatches a messenger,
[..., who] knows the heart of the great gods,
That he [...] ...
To reach [... of Ea], the king.
[...] he discussed the matter.
[...] to Ea, the king.
[...] ...   (10)
[...], the wise, who knows the heart of the great gods
[...] heaven ...
[...] unkempt hair he caused him to wear,
[...] ... and clad him with a mourning garb,
[He gave him advice], saying to him (these) [wor]ds:
["Adapa,] thou art going [before Anu], the king;
[Neglect not my advice], my words hold fast!
[When thou hast gone up to heaven and] hast ap-
    proached the gate of Anu,
[Tammuz and Gizzida] will be standing [at the gate of
    Anu]."   (remainder missing)

D

[...] he [...]
[Oil] he commanded for him, and he an[ointed him-
    self],

[A ga]rment he commanded for him, and he was
clothed.

Anu laughed aloud   at the doing of Ea, [saying]:

"Of the gods of heaven and earth, as many as there be,
   Who [ever] gave such a command,
So as to make his own command exceed the command
   of Anu?"

As Adapa from the horizon of heaven to the zenith of
   heaven
Cast a glance, he saw its awesomeness.

[Th]en Anu imposed on Adapa [...];

For [the city] of Ea   he decreed release,   (10)

His [pri]esthood to glorify in the future he [*decreed*]
   as destiny.

[...] ... as for Adapa, the human offspring,

[Who ...], lord-like, broke the south wind's wing,

Went up to heaven—and so forth—

[...] what ill he has brought upon mankind,

[And] the disease that he brought upon the bodies of
   men,

These Ninkarrak[1] will allay.

[Let] malady be lifted,   let disease turn aside.

[Upon] this [...] let horror fall,

Let him [*in*] sweet sleep not lie down,

[...] ... joy of human heart(s).

[1] Goddess of healing.   (remainder broken off)

DESCENT OF ISHTAR TO THE NETHER WORLD

ANET, 106-109   This myth has as its central theme the detention of the goddess
of fertility—Sumerian Inanna, Akkadian Ishtar—in the realm
of the dead and her eventual return to the land of the living.
The cuneiform material is extant in Sumerian and Akkadian
formulations. The Sumerian version is obviously primary. But
although the Semitic version has various points of contact with
the older source, it is by no means a mere translation from the
Sumerian.

(obverse)

To the Land of no Return, the realm of [*Ereshkigal*],
Ishtar, the daughter of Sin, [set] her mind.
Yea, the daughter of Sin set [her] mind
To the dark house, the abode of Irkal[la],[2]
To the house which none leave who have entered it,
To the road from which there is no way back,

[2] Ereshkigal, Queen of the Nether World.

To the house wherein the entrants are bereft of li[ght],
Where dust is their fare and clay their food,
(Where) they see no light, residing in darkness,
(Where) they are clothed like birds, with wings
  for garments,   (10)
(And where) over door and bolt is spread dust.
When Ishtar reached the gate of the Land of no Return,
She said (these) words to the gatekeeper:
"O gatekeeper, open thy gate,
Open thy gate that I may enter!
If thou openest not the gate so that I cannot enter,
I will smash the door, I will shatter the bolt,
I will smash the doorpost, I will move the doors,
I will raise up the dead, eating the living,
So that the dead will outnumber the living."   (20)
The gatekeeper opened his mouth to speak,
Saying to exalted Ishtar:
"Stop, my lady, do not throw it[1] down!
I will go to announce thy name to Queen E[reshk]igal."
The gatekeeper entered, saying [to] Eresh[kigal]:
"Behold, thy sister Ishtar is waiting at [the gate],
She who upholds the great festivals,
  Who stirs up the deep before Ea, the k[ing]."
When Ereshkigal heard this,
Her face turned pale like a cut-down tamarisk,
While her lips turned dark like a bruised
  kunīnu-reed.[2]   (30)
"What drove her heart to me? What impelled her spirit
  hither?
Lo, should I drink water with the Anunnaki?
Should I eat clay for bread, drink muddied water for
  beer?
Should I bemoan the men who left their wives behind?
Should I bemoan the maidens who were wrenched from
  the laps of their lovers?
(Or) should I bemoan the tender little one who was sent
  off before his time?[3]
Go, gatekeeper, open the gate for her,
Treat her in accordance with the ancient rules."
Forth went the gatekeeper (to) open the door for
  her:
"Enter, my lady, that Cutha[4] may rejoice over thee, (40)

---

[1] The door.   [2] Word play šabaṭ "bruised": šapat-š[a] "her lips."
[3] i.e. Ereshkigal would have cause for weeping if all these occupants of
the nether world should be liberated by Ishtar.
[4] A name of the nether world, the Akkadian city-name Kutu.

That the palace of the Land of no Return may be glad
at thy presence."

When the first door he had made her enter,
He stripped[14] and took away the great crown
on her head.

"Why, O gatekeeper, didst thou take the great crown on
my head?"

"Enter, my lady, thus are the rules of the Mistress of the
Nether World."

When the second gate he had made her enter,
He stripped and took away the pendants on her
ears.

"Why, O gatekeeper, didst thou take the pendants on
my ears?"

"Enter, my lady, thus are the rules of the Mistress of the
Nether World."

When the third gate he had made her enter,
He stripped and took away the chains round her
neck.

"Why, O gatekeeper, didst thou take the chains round
my neck?"

"Enter, my lady, thus are the rules of the Mistress
of the Nether World." (50)

When the fourth gate he had made her enter,
He stripped and took away the ornaments on
her breast.

"Why, O gatekeeper, didst thou take the ornaments on
my breast?"

"Enter, my lady, thus are the rules of the Mistress of the
Nether World."

When the fifth gate he had made her enter,
He stripped and took away the girdle of birth-
stones on her hips.

"Why, O gatekeeper, didst thou take the girdle of birth-
stones on my hips?"

"Enter, my lady, thus are the rules of the Mistress of the
Nether World."

When the sixth gate he had made her enter,
He stripped and took away the clasps round
her hands and feet.

"Why, O gatekeeper, didst thou take the clasps round
my hands and feet?"

"Enter, my lady, thus are the rules of the Mistress of the
Nether World."

When the seventh gate he had made her enter, (60)

He stripped and took away the breechcloth round
her body.

"Why, O gatekeeper, didst thou take the breechcloth on
my body?"

"Enter, my lady, thus are the rules of the Mistress of the
Nether World."

As soon as Ishtar had descended to the Land of no
Return,

Ereshkigal saw her and burst out at her presence.

Ishtar, unreflecting, flew at her.

Ereshkigal opened her mouth to speak,

Saying (these) words to Namtar, her vizier:

"Go, Namtar, lock [her] up [in] my [palace]!

Release against her, [against] Ishtar, the sixty mis[eries]:

Misery of the eyes [against] her [eyes],   (70)

Misery of the sides ag[ainst] her [sides],

Misery of the heart ag[ainst her heart],

Misery of the feet ag[ainst] her [feet],

Misery of the head ag[ainst her head]—

Against every part of her, against [her whole body]!"

After Lady Ishtar [had descended to the nether world],

The bull springs not upon the cow, [the ass impregnates
not the jenny],

In the street [the man impregnates not] the maiden.

The man lies [in his (own) chamber, the maiden lies
on her side],

[. . . l]ies [. . .].   (80)

(reverse)

The countenance of Papsukkal, the vizier of the great
gods,

    Was fallen, his face was [clouded].

He was clad in mourning, long hair he wore.

Forth went Papsukkal before Sin his father, weeping,

[His] tears flowing before Ea, the king:

"Ishtar has gone down to the nether world, she has not
come up.

Since Ishtar has gone down to the Land of no Return,

The bull springs not upon the cow, the ass impregnates
not the jenny,

In the street the man impregnates not the maiden.

The man lies down in his (own) chamber,

The maiden lies down on her side."   (10)

Ea in his wise heart conceived an image,

And created Asushunamir, a eunuch:

"Up, Asushunamir, set thy face to the gate of the Land
of no Return;

The seven gates of the Land of no Return shall be
　　opened for thee.
Ereshkigal shall see thee and rejoice at thy presence.
When her heart has calmed, her mood is happy,
Let her utter the oath　of the great gods.
(Then) lift up thy head, paying mind to the life-water
　　bag:
"Pray, Lady, let them give me the life-water bag
　　That water therefrom I may drink." [1]
As soon as Ereshkigal heard this,
She smote her thigh, [2] bit her finger:
"Thou didst request of me a thing that should not be
　　requested.
Come, Asushunamir, I will curse thee with a mighty
　　curse! [3]
The food of the city's *gutters* shall be thy food,
The *sewers* of the city shall be thy drink.
The shadow of the wall shall be thy station,
The threshold shall be thy habitation,
The besotted and the thirsty shall smite thy cheek!"
Ereshkigal opened her mouth to speak,
Saying (these) words to Namtar, her vizier:　　　　　(30)
"Up, Namtar, knock at Egalgina, [4]
Adorn the thresholds with *coral*-stone,
Bring forth the Anunnaki and seat (them) on thrones
　　of gold,
Sprinkle Ishtar with the water of life and take her from
　　my presence!"
Forth went Namtar, knocked at Egalgina,
Adorned the thresholds with *coral*-stone,
Brought forth the Anunnaki, seated (them) on thrones
　　of gold,
Sprinkled Ishtar with the water of life and took her from
　　her presence.
When through the first gate he had made her go out,
　　He returned to her the breechcloth for her body.
When through the second gate he had made
　　her go out,　　　　　　　　　　　　　　　　(40)
　　He returned to her the clasps for her hands and feet.

---

[1] The scheme evidently succeeds as Ereshkigal, distracted by the beauty of
Aṣūšunamir "His Appearance is Brilliant," does not recover until too late.
[2] A gesture of annoyance, or derision.
[1] Or read "I will decree for thee a fate not to be forgotten,
　　　　A fate will I decree for thee,
　　　　　　Not to be forgotten throughout eternity."
[4] "Palace of Justice."

When through the third gate he had made her go out,
    He returned to her the birthstone girdle for her hips.
When through the fourth gate he had made her go out,
    He returned to her the ornaments for her breasts.
When through the fifth gate he had made her go out,
    He returned to her the chains for her neck.
When through the sixth gate he had made her go out,
    He returned to her the pendants for her ears.
When through the seventh gate he had made her go out,
    He returned to her the great crown for her head.
"If she does not give thee her ransom price, bring her
    back.[1]
As for Tammuz, the lover of her youth,
Wash him with pure water, anoint him with sweet oil;
Clothe him with a red garment, let him *play* on a flute of
    lapis.
Let courtesans *turn* [*his*] mood."
[When]Belili was string[ing] her jewelry,
[And her] lap was filled with "eye-stones,"
On hearing the sound of her brother, Belili struck the
    jewelry on [. . .]
So that the "eye-stones" filled the [. . .]. . . .
"My only brother, bring no harm to me!
On the day when Tammuz comes up to me,
    When with him the lapis flute (and) the carnelian
    ring come up to me,
When with him the wailing men and the wailing   Ezek. 8:14
    women come up to me,
May the dead rise and smell the incense."

[1] This continuation of Ereshkigal's instructions appears to be out of place here, as regards the N version. A speaks of the ransom before Ishtar is led away. The mention of Tammuz is likewise startling in this context. There is no indication in the Sumerian version—contrary to earlier assumptions—that Tammuz had gone down to the nether world. The concluding part of the myth, therefore, will remain obscure in its allusions so long as additional material is not available.

THE LEGEND OF SARGON   ANET, 119

Sargon, the mighty king, king of Agade, am I.
My mother was a *changeling*,[1] my father I knew not.
The brother(s) of my father *loved* the hills.
My city is Azupiranu, which is situated on the banks of
    the Euphrates.
My *changeling* mother conceived me, in secret she bore   Exod. 2:3
    me.

[1] There is no indication as to whether the term refers to a change in the social, religious, or national status.

She set me in a basket of rushes, with bitumen she sealed
  my lid.
She cast me into the river which rose not (over) me.
The river bore me up and carried me to Akki, the
  drawer of water.
Akki, the drawer of water lifted me out as he dipped his
  e[w]er.
Akki, the drawer of water, [took me] as his son
  (and) reared me.   (10)
Akki, the drawer of water, appointed me as his gardener.
While I was a gardener, Ishtar granted me (her) love,
And for four and [...] years I exercised kingship.
The black-headed [people] I ruled, I gov[erned];
Mighty [moun]tains with chip-axes of bronze I con-
  quered,
The upper ranges I scaled,
The lower ranges I [trav]ersed,
The sea [lan]ds three times I circled.
Dilmun my [hand] cap[tured],
[To] the great Der I [went up], I [...],   (20)
[...] I altered and [...].
Whatever king may come up after me,
[...],
Let him r[ule, let him govern] the black-headed
  [peo]ple;
[Let him conquer] mighty [mountains] with chip-axe[s
  of bronze],
[Let] him scale the upper ranges,
[Let him traverse the lower ranges],
Let him circle the sea [lan]ds three times!
[Dilmun let his hand capture],
Let him go up [to] the great Der and [...]!   (30)
[...] from my city, Aga[de ...]
[...] ... [...].

                              (Remainder broken away.)

III. A Hittite Myth

TRANSLATOR: ALBRECHT GOETZE

The Telepinus Myth

ANET, 126-128

a. The God's Anger, His Disappearance and Its Consequences

(The upper third of the tablet, about 20 lines, is broken off. It probably told the reasons for the god's anger.)

(i) Telepinus [flew into a rage and shouted:] "There must be no inter[ference!]" In his agitation] he tried to put [his right shoe] on his left foot and his left [shoe on his right foot]. ... [...].

(5) *Mist* seized the windows, *vapor* seized the house. In the fireplace the logs were stifled, at the altars the gods were stifled, in the fold the sheep were stifled, in the stable the cattle were stifled. The sheep neglected its lamb, the cow neglected its calf.

(10) Telepinus walked away and took grain, (fertile) breeze, ... , ... and satiation to the country, the meadow, the *steppes*. Telepinus went and lost himself in the *steppe; fatigue* overcame him. So grain (and) spelt thrive no longer. So cattle, sheep and man no longer (15) breed. And even those with young cannot bring them forth.

The *vegetation* dried up; the trees dried up and would bring forth no fresh shoots. The pastures dried up, the springs dried up. In the land famine arose so that man and gods perished from hunger. The great Sun-god arranged for a feast and invited the thousand gods. They ate, (20) but they did not satisfy their hunger; they drank, but they did not quench their thirst.

b. The Search for the Vanished God

The Storm-god became anxious about Telepinus, his son: "Telepinus, my son, (he said) is not here. He has flown into a rage and taken (with him) every good thing." The great gods and the lesser gods began to search for Telepinus. The Sun-god sent out the swift Eagle (saying): "Go! Search every high (25) mountain!"

"Search the deep valleys! Search the watery depth!" The Eagle went, but he could not find him. Back to the Sun-god he brought his message: "I could not find him,

him, Telepinus, the noble god." The Storm-god said to
Hannahannas[1]: "What shall we do? (30) We shall die
of hunger." Hannahannas said to the Storm-god: "Do
something, O Storm-god! Go! Search for Telepinus thyself!"

The Storm-god began to search for Telepinus. In his
city he [knock]s at the gate, but he is not there and
opens not. He broke open his bolt and his lock, [but he
has no luck], the Storm-god. So he gave up and sat
down to rest. Hannahannas (35) sent [out the Bee]:
"Go! Search thou for Telepinus!"

[The Storm-god s]aid [to Hannahannas]: "The great
gods (and) the lesser gods have searched for him, but
[did not find] him. Shall then this [Bee] go out [and
find him]? Its wings are small, it is small itself. Shall
they admit that it is greater than they?"

Hannahannas said to the Storm-god: "Enough! It
will go (and) find him." Hannahannas sent out the little
Bee: "Go! Search thou for Telepinus! When thou findest him, sting him on his hands (and) his feet! Bring
him to his feet! Take wax and wipe his eyes and his feet,
purify him and bring him before me!"

The Bee went away and searched . . . the streaming
rivers, and searched the murmuring springs. The honey
within it gave out, [the wax within it] gave out. Then
[it found] him in a meadow in the grove at Lihzina.
It stung him on his hands and his feet. It brought him
to his feet, it took wax and wiped his eyes (and) his
feet, [it purified him] and [. . .].

[Telepinus . . .] declares: "For my part I had flown
into a rage [and walked away. How dare] ye a[rouse
me] from my sleep? How dare ye force me to talk
when enraged?" He grew [still more infu]riated. [He
stopped] the murmuring springs, he diverted the flowing rivers and made them flow over their banks. He
[*blocked off*] the clay pits, he shattered [the windo]ws,
he shattered the houses.

He had men perish, he had sheep and cattle perish.
[It came to] pass that the gods [*despaire*]d (asking):
"Wh[y has Te]lepinus become [so infur]iated? [Wh]at
shall we do? [What] shall we do?"

[The great Sun-god(??) decl]ares: "[Fetch ye] man!
Let him [t]ake the spring Hattara on mount Ammuna

---

[1] The name is ideographically written NIN.TU or MAH; mother of the gods.

[as . . .]! Let him (man) make him move! With the
eagle's wing let him make him move! Let man make
him move! With the eagle's wing [let man make him
move]![1]

(A gap follows in which Kamrusepas, the goddess
of magic and healing, is commissioned to pacify Telepinus and to bring him back.)

c. The Ritual

ENTREATY

(The beginning is mutilated.)

(ii) "O Telepinus! [Here lies] sweet and soothing
[cedar essence. Just as it is . . .], [even so let] the stifled
[be set right] again!

"Here [I have] *upthrusting sap* [with which to purify
thee]. (10) Let it [invigorate] thy heart and thy soul, O
Telepinus! Toward the king [turn] in favor!

"Here lies *chaff*. [Let his heart (and) soul] be *segre-
gated* [like it]! Here lies an ear [of grain]. Let it attract
his heart [(and) his soul]!

"(15) Here lies sesame. [Let his heart (and) his soul]
be *comforted* by it. Here [lie] figs. Just as [figs] are
sweet, even so let Te[lepinus' heart (and) soul] become
sweet!

"Just as the olive [holds] oil within it, [as the grape]
(20) holds wine within it, so hold thou, Telepinus, in
(thy) heart (and thy) soul good feelings [toward the
king]!

"Here lies *ointment*. Let it anoint Telepin[us' heart
(and) soul]! Just as malt (and) malt-loaves are harmo-
niously fused, even so let thy soul be in harmony with
the affairs of mankind! [Just as spelt] (25) is clean,
even so let Telepinus' soul become clean! J[ust as] honey
is sweet, as cream is smooth, even so let Telepinus' soul
become sweet and even so let him become smooth!

"See, O Telepinus! I have now sprinkled thy ways
with fine oil. So walk thou, Telepinus, over these ways
that are sprinkled with fine oil! (30) Let *šaḫiš* wood
and *ḫappuriašaš* wood be at hand! Let us set thee right,
O Telepinus, into whatever state of mind is the right
one!"

Telepinus came in his fury. Lightning flashed, it
thundered while the dark earth was in turmoil. (35)
Kamrusepas saw him. The eagle's wing made him move

[1] A certain ritual.

out there. It took off him (iii) the rage, it took off him the anger, it took off him [the ire], it took off him the fury.

KAMRUSEPAS' RITUAL OF PURIFICATION

Kamrusepas tells the gods: "Come ye, O gods! See! Hapantallis is shepherding the Sun-god's sheep. (5) Select ye twelve rams! I want to fix long days for Telepinus. I have taken death, one thousand eyes. I have strewn about the selected sheep of Kamrusepas.

"Over Telepinus I have swung them this way and that. (10) From Telepinus' body I have taken the evil, I have taken the malice. I have taken the rage, I have taken the anger, I have taken the ire, I have taken the fury.

"When Telepinus was angry, his heart (and) his soul were stifled (like) firebrands. (15) Just as they burned these brands, even so let Telepinus' rage, anger, malice (and) fury burn themselves out! Just as [malt] is barren, (as) people do not bring it to the field to use it for seed, (as) people do not make it into bread (or) put it in the storehouse, even so let Telepinus' rage, [anger], (20) malice (and) fury become barren!

"When Telepinus was angry, [his heart (and) his soul] were a burning fire. Just as this fire [is quenched], even so let (his) rage, anger (and) fury [be quenched] too!

"O Telepinus, give up thy rage, [give up] thine anger, (25) give up thy fury! Just as (water in) a pipe flows not upward, even so let Telepinus' [rage, anger (and)] fury not [come] back!

"The gods [were gathered] in assembly under the *ḫatalkešnaš* tree. For the *ḫatalkešnaš* tree I have fixed long [years]. (30) All gods are now present, (including) the [*Is*]*tustayas*, the Good-women (and) the Mother-goddesses, the Grain-god, Miyatanzipas, Telepinus, the Patron-god, Hapantaliyas (and) the Patron of the field. For these gods I have fixed long years; I have purified him, [O Telepinus]!

(35) "[. . .] I have taken the evil [from] Telepinus' body, I have taken away his [rage], [I have taken away] his an[ger], I have taken away his [ire], [I have taken away] his fury, I have taken away his malice, [I have taken away his] ev[il]."

(small gap)

MAN'S RITUAL

(The beginning is lost, but Telepinus is addressed:)

". . . (When) thou [departedst] from the *ḫatalkešnaš* tree on a summer day, the crop got *smutted*. (When) the ox departed [with thee], (iv) thou *wastedst* its *shape*. (When) the sheep departed with thee, thou *wastedst* its form. O Telepinus, stop rage, anger, malice (and) fury!

"(When) the Storm-god comes in his wrath, the Storm-god's priest (5) stops him. (When) a pot of food boils over, the (stirring) *spoon* stops it. Even so let the word of me, the mortal, stop Telepinus' rage, anger, and fury!

"Let Telepinus' rage, anger, malice, (and) fury depart! Let the house let them go, let the interior . . . let them go, (10) let the window let them go! In the . . . let the interior courtyard let them go, let the gate let them go, let the gateway let them go, let the road of the king let them go! Let it not go to the thriving field, garden (or) grove! Let it go the way of the Sun-god of the nether world!

"The doorkeeper has opened the seven doors, has unlocked the seven bolts. (15) Down in the dark earth there stand bronze cauldrons, their lids are of *abaru*-metal, their *handles* of iron. Whatever goes in there comes not out again; it perishes therein. Let them also receive Telepinus' rage, anger, malice (and) fury! Let them not come back!"

d. The God's Home-Coming

(20) Telepinus came home to his house and cared (again) for his land. The *mist* let go of the windows, the *vapor* let go of the house. The altars were set right for the gods, the hearth let go of the log. He let the sheep go to the fold, he let the cattle go to the pen. The mother tended her child, the ewe tended her lamb, (25) the cow tended her calf. Also Telepinus tended the king and the queen and provided them with enduring life and vigor.

Telepinus cared for the king. A pole was erected before Telepinus and from this pole the fleece of a sheep was suspended. It signifies fat of the sheep, it signifies grains of corn (and) (30) wine, it signifies cattle (and) sheep, it signifies long years and progeny.

It signifies the lamb's favorable message.[1] It signifies . . . . . . It signifies *fruitful* breeze. It signifies . . . satiation. . . .   (end of the text lost)

---

[1] Favorable omens when intestines of the sacrificial lamb are inspected.

IV. Ugaritic Myths and Epics

TRANSLATOR: H. L. GINSBERG

ANET, 129-135, 138-142

Poems about Baal and Anath

Both large and small fragments of tablets containing poetic mythological texts in which the leading role is played by the rain- and fertility-god Baal and the next in importance by the warrior-goddess Anath came to light in the French excavations of Ras Shamra-Ugarit in the years 1930, 1931, and 1933, and at least one small fragment (which may be a duplicate of one of the others) in 1929. Because so many letters, words, lines, columns, and probably some whole tablets are missing, not all of the tablets can be declared, with certainty, to be parts of the great epic of Baal and arranged in their proper order within it. However, in the following translations, even small fragments whose pertinence to the larger epic is probable have, for the most part, been included (if only, in a few desperate cases, in the form of sketchy summaries) and assigned tentative positions within it. Tablets whose pertinence to the larger poem is doubtful have been added at the end by way of an appendix.

a. VI AB

Editions: Ch. Virolleaud, *La déesse 'Anat* (Paris, 1938), pp. 91-102 and the last photograph; C. H. Gordon, *Ugaritic Handbook*, II, pp. 189-190, 'nt, pls. ix-x (transliteration only). Studies: A. Herdner, *Syria*, XXIII (1942-43), 283-285. Owing to the very poor state of preservation, connected translation is possible only for groups of lines which, because they are stereotyped, can be completed with the help of parallels; while just the crucial passages are very doubtful. It seems, however, that El, the head of the pantheon, (1) instructs the craftsman-god Kothar wa-Khasis to build a palace on his (El's) grounds, the name of the latter being Khurshan-zur-kas (col. iii), (2) announces that his (eldest? favorite?) son is to be known as El's Beloved Yamm (= Sea) and as Master (cf. iv 15, 20 with II AB ii 34-35, and iv 17 with III AB B 17, 33-34), and (3) perhaps authorizes Yamm to banish Baal from his throne (iii 22-25).

b. III AB C

Editions: Ch. Virolleaud, *Syria*, XXIV (1944-45), 1-12; C. H. Gordon, *Ugaritic Handbook*, II, Text 129. This fragment comprises 24 very mutilated lines from the right-hand column on one of the sides of a tablet with two very broad columns on each side. Such a tablet is the one of whose col. i, III AB B is the lower part, and of whose col. iv, III AB A is the upper part; Virolleaud therefore surmises that III AB C is part of (the lower half of) col. iii of the same tablet. For its content, however, a position between III AB B and III AB A seems strange; so, perhaps, it belongs to a tablet which preceded, and in outward disposition resembled, the tablet of which III AB B-A is a remnant.

In it, El instructs Kothar to build a palace for Yamm. Ashtar complains of not being accorded the like favor.

[. . . There] he is off on his way   (3)
    To El of the Sources [of the Floods,
    In the midst of the headwaters of the Two Oceans.
He penetrates] E[l]'s *field* and *enters*
    The [pa]vilion of King [Father Shunem.[1]
At El's feet he bows] and falls down,
    Prostrates himself, doing [him] *homage.*
(. . . " . . . O) Kothar wa-Kha[sis!
Quic]*kly* bu(ild the h)ouse of Yamm,
    [Ere]ct the palace of Judge Nahar.
. . .

Fig. 138

    . . .
Build the house of Prince Yamm,
    [Ere]ct the pala[ce *of Judge*] Nahar,
    In the midst of [. . . .
Quickly] his [hou]se shalt thou build,   (10)
    Quickly erec[t his palace].
. . . "

    (All that can be made out is that Ashtar is displeased.)
Quoth the Gods' Torch Shapsh,[2]
    Raising her voice and [crying:
"Heark]en, I pray thee!
Thy father Bull El *favors*
    Prince Yamm . . . [. . .] . . .
[Sh]ould thy father Bull [E]l hear thee,
    He will pull out [the *pillars* of thy dwelling!
Yea, overt]urn [the throne of thy] kingship!
    Yea, break the sce[pter] of thy dominion!"
Quoth [Ashtar] of the [. . .] . . . :
    "*Oh*, my father Bull El!
I have no house [like] the gods,
    [Nor] court like [*the holy on*]*es.*   (20)
. . . "
                  (the rest obscure)

---

[1] One of El's epithets; vocalization uncertain. Some render "Father of Years."   [2] The sun-goddess.

c. III AB B-A

Editions: (1) Of III AB B: *Ugaritic Handbook,* II, Text 137. (2) Of III AB A: Ch. Virolleaud, *Syria,* XVI (1935), 29-45, with Pl. XI; H. L. Ginsberg, *JPOS,* XV (1935), 327-331; *Kitbe Ugarit,* 73-76; H. Bauer, *AKTRSch.,* Ca. Studies: W. F. Albright, *JPOS,* XVI (1936), 17-20; T. H. Gaster, *Iraq,* 4 (1937), 21-23; J. Obermann, *JAOS,* LXVII (1947), 195-208. See the paragraph preceding the translation of III AB C.

(1) III AB B

Fig. 136 ... [... Quoth] Puissant Baal: (3)
"[May'st thou be driven from the throne of thy kingship,
      From the seat of thy do]minion!
... [...]
Ayamur[3] upon thy head, [O Yamm;
      Upon thy back Yagrush,[4]][5] Judge Nahar.
May [Horon] break, [O Yamm,
      May Horon break] thy head,
      Ashtoreth [Name of Baal thy pate.
...] down may'st thou fall in ... [...]   (10)
      ... [...]."
[Me]ssengers Yamm doth send.

       (Two lines defective and unintelligible.)

"Depart ye, lad[s, don't tarry.
      There now, be off] on your way
Towards the Assembled Body[6]
      In the m[idst of the Mount of Lala.
At the feet of El] fall not down,
      Prostrate you not to the Assembled [Body.
Proudly standing] say ye your speech.
And say unto Bull [my] father [El,
      Declare unto the Assembled] Body:
'Message of Yamm your lord,
      Of your master Ju[dge Nahar].
Surrender the god with a following,
      Him whom the multitudes worship:
Give Baal [to me to lord over],
      Dagon's son whose spoil I'll possess.' "—
The lads depart, they delay not.
[There, they are off] on their way   (20)
      To the midst of the Mount of Lala,
      Towards the Assembled Body.
Now, the gods were sitting to e[at],
      The holy ones for to dine,
      Baal attending upon El.
As soon as the gods espy them,
      Espy the messengers of Yamm,
      The envoys of Judge Nahar,
The gods do drop their heads
      Down upon their knees

[3] Name of a bludgeon, meaning something like "Driver"; see episode (2).
[4] Name of a bludgeon, meaning "Chaser"; see episode (2).
[5] Evidently Kothar has already promised Baal the two cudgels which he
wields so effectively in episode (2).   [6] The assembly of the gods.

And on the thrones of their princeship.
Them doth Baal rebuke:
"Why, O gods, have ye dropt
    Your head[s] down upon your knees
    And on your thrones of princeship?
I see the gods are cowed
    With terror of the messengers of Yamm,
    Of the envoys of Judge Naha[r].
Lift up, O gods, your heads
    From upon your knees,
    From upon the thrones of your princeship,
And I'll answer[1] the messengers of Yamm,
    The envoys of Judge Nahar."
The gods lift up their heads
    From upon their knees,
    From upon [their] thrones of prin[ceship].
Then come the messengers of Yamm,   (30)
    The envoys of Judge Nahar.
At El's feet they do [not] fall down,
    Prostrate them not to the Assembled Body.
Prou[dly] standing, [they] say their speech.
    Fire, burning fire, *doth flash*;
    A whetted sword [are their e]yes.
They say to Bull his father El:
"Message of Yamm your lord,
    Of your master Judge Nahar.
Surrender the god *with* a following,
    etc." (see 18-19)
[Quoth] Bull, his father, El: (36)
"Thy slave is Baal, O Yamm,
    Thy slave is Baal [for eve]r,
Dagon's Son is thy captive;
    He shall be brought as thy tribute.
For the gods bring [thy gift],
    The holy ones are thy tributaries."—
Now, Prince Baa[l] *was wroth*.
[Sei]zing [*a cudgel*] in his hand,
    A *bludgeon* in his right hand,
    He r[*eached*] to strike the lads.
[His right hand Ashtore]th seizes,   (40)
    Ashtoreth seizes his left hand.
"How [canst thou strike the messengers of Yamm,
    The en]voys of Judge Nahar?
A messenger ... [...

                              [1] Or, perhaps, humble.

...] a messenger [bears];
Upon his shoulders the words of his lord,
And ... [...]."
But Prince Baal was wroth.
The *cudgel* in ha[nd he ...
He con]*fronts* the messengers of Yamm,
The [en]voys of Judge Naha[r.
...] ... "I say unto Yamm your lord,
[Your] ma[ster Judge Nahar]:
..."   (lines 46-47 too defective for understanding)

(2) III AB A
                                   (1-4 defective and obscure)
"... [ho]uses.
To the earth shall fall the strong,
    To the dust the mighty."—
Scarce had the word lef[t] her mouth,
    Her speech left her lips,
As she uttered her ... voice
    Under the throne of Prince Yamm,
    Quoth Kothar wa-Khasis:
"I tell thee, O Prince Baal,
    I declare, O Rider of the Clouds.

Ps. 92:9 Now thine enemy, O Baal,
    Now thine enemy wilt thou smite,
    Now wilt thou cut off thine adversary.

Ps. 145:13 Thou'lt take thine eternal kingdom,   (10)
    Thine everlasting dominion."
Kothar brings down two clubs
    And gives them names.
"Thou, thy name is Yagrush ('Chaser').
    Yagrush, chase Yamm!
Chase Yamm from his throne,
    [Na]har from his seat of dominion.
Do thou swoop in the hand of Baal,
    Like an eagle between his fingers;
Strike the back of Prince Yamm,
    Between the arms[1] of [J]udge Nahar."

II Kings 9:24 The club swoops in the hand of Baal,
    Like an eagle between his [fi]ngers;
It strikes the back of Prince Yamm,
    Between the arms of Judge Nahar.
Yamm is firm, he is not bowed;
    His joints bend not,
    Nor breaks his frame.—   [1] i.e. on the back.

Kothar brings down two clubs
    And gives them names.
"Thou, thy name is Ayamur ('Driver'?).
    Ayamur, drive Yamm!
Drive Yamm from his throne,   (20)
    Nahar from his seat of dominion.
Do thou swoop in the hand of Baal,
    Like an eagle between his fingers;
Strike the pate of Prince Yamm,
    Between the eyes[1] of Judge Nahar.   Exod. 13:9, 16;
Yamm shall collapse   Deut. 6:8; 11:18;
    And fall to the ground."   Dan. 8:5
The club swoops in the hand of Baal,
    [Like] an eagle between his fingers;
It strikes the pate of Prince [Yamm],
    Between the eyes of Judge Nahar.
Yamm collapses,
    He falls to the ground;
His joints bend,
    His frame breaks.
Baal would rend, would smash Yamm,
    Would annihilate Judge Nahar.
By name Ashtoreth rebukes [him].
"For shame, O Puissant [Baal];
    For shame, O Rider of the Clouds!
For our captive is Prin[ce Yamm],
    Our captive is Judge Nahar."   (30)
As [the word] left [her mouth],
    Puissant Baal was ashamed ...

(The rest is too defective for any meaning to be ex-
tracted, except that Yamm seems to say twice "I am
dying, Baal will reign." But apparently Yamm does not
die, but is only confined to his proper sphere, the seas.
Hence there is still talk of him, e.g. at the end of col. ii
of episode e.)

d. Fragment b

"... Homage to Lady Asherah of [the Sea],
    Obeisance to the Progenitress of the Gods,
(So) [she] will give a house to Baal like the [g]ods',
    And a court like [A]sherah's sons'."—
Loudly to his lads Baal cries:
"Look ye, Gapn and Ugar sons of Ghulumat,[2]
    Amamis twain, *sons* of Zulumat (*Zlmt*)[2]

---

[1] On the front of the head.
[2] Means "darkness." Ghulumat is also known as the name of a goddess.

OHIO CHRISTIAN UNIVERSITY

> The stately, win[g]-spreading, ... ;
Winged ones twain, flock of clouds,   (10)
> 'Neath [...];
Birdlike ones twain, fl[ock of ... snow].
> ..."
>   (obscure beginnings of 5 more lines)

e. II AB

At the beginning, Baal's messengers explain to Anath why a démarche before Asherah is indicated.

...   (some 20 lines missing, 3 obliterated)
But alas!
He cri]es unto Bull El [his father,   (5)
> To E]l the King [his begetter;
He cries] unto Ashe[rah and her children],
> To [E]lath [and the band of] her [kindred:
Look, no house has Baal like the gods,   (10)
> Nor court like the children of Ashe]r[ah].
The abode of El is the shelter of his son.
> The abode of Lady Asherah of the Sea
> Is the abode of the perfect brides:
'Tis the dwelling of Padriya daughter of Ar,
> The shelter of Talliya(tly) the daughter of Rabb,
> (And) the abode of Arsiya ($arṣy$) the daughter of
> Ya'abdar.[1]

And here's something more I would tell thee: (20)
Just try doing homage to Lady Asherah of the Sea,
> Obeisance to the Progenitress of the Gods.
Hayyin[2] would go up to the bellows,
> In Khasis' hands would be the tongs,
To melt silver,
> To beat out gold.
He'd melt silver by the thousands (of shekels),
> Gold he'd melt by the myriads.
He'd melt ... and ... :   (30)
A gorgeous dais weighing twice ten thousand (shekels),
> A gorgeous dais cast in silver,
> Coated with a film of gold;
A gorgeous throne resting above
> A gorgeous footstool o'erspread with a mat;
A gorgeous couch having a ... ,
> He pours it over with gold;
A gorgeous table which is filled

Fig. 126

---

[1] The three names mean "Flashie (or, Lightningette) daughter of Light, Dewie daughter of Distillation, Earthie daughter of . . ." They are Baal's wives or daughters, and Baal is the god of rain and dew and "the Prince, Lord of the Earth."   [2] "Deft," another name of the craftsman-god.

With all manner of game[1] from the foundations of
the earth; (40)
Gorgeous bowls shaped like small beasts like those of
Amurru,
Stelae shaped like the wild beasts of Yam'an,
Wherein are wild oxen by the myriads.

(The first lines of the following scene perhaps show
Asherah, "Lady Asherah of the Sea," presenting an
offering of fish to El.) (ii)

(Some 16 lines entirely missing, then 4 defective and
obscure.)
Its[2] *skin*, the covering of its flesh.
She[3] *flings* its vestment into the sea,
Both its *skins* into the deeps.
She puts fire on the brazier,
A pot upon the coals,
(And) *propitiates* Bull El Benign, (10)
Does obeisance to the Creator of Creatures.—
Lifting up her eyes she beholds.
The advance of Baal Asherah doth espy,
The advance of the Maiden Anath,
The onrush of Yabamat [Liimmim].
Thereat her feet [do stumble];
Her loins [do crack be]hind her,
Her [face breaks out in s]weat [above her].
Bent are the [joints of her loins],
Weakened those of [her] back.[4] (20)
She lifts up her voice and cries:
"*Why* is Puissant [Ba]al come?
And why the Ma[id]en Anath?
Have my children slain [each other],
O[r the b]and of my kinsmen [destroyed one an-
other]?"
[The *work*] of silver Asherah doth espy,
The *work* of silver and [. . .] of gold.
Lady A[sherah] of the Sea rejoices;
Loudly unto her lad [she] doth [cry]:
"Look thou, Deft One, yea [give heed], (30)
O fisherman of Lady Asher[ah of the Sea].

---

[1] If the translation is correct: rhytons, or vessels having the shape of
animals.   [2] Of some beast or fish.
[3] Apparently, Lady Asherah of the Sea.
[4] Because she fears the unexpected visitors bring bad news (cf. Ezek.
21:11-12). This is the standard reaction of a female character to an unexpected visit.

Take a net in thy hand,
> A large [*seine*] *on thy two hands.*
[*Cast it*] into El's Beloved [Yamm][1]
> Into the Sea of El *Be*[*nign,*
> Into the De]ep of El ... [...]. ..."

(Only the beginnings of 37-47 preserved, and no connected sense recoverable.)

(iii)

(about 12 lines missing, 9 lines defective)
C[ome]s Puissant Baal,   (10)
> *Advances* the Rider of the Clouds.
Lo, he takes his stand and *cries defiance,*
> He stands erect and spits
> In the midst of the *as*[*sem*]*bly* of the divine beings:
"*Ab*[*omination*] has been placed upon my table,
> Filth in the cup I drink.
For two [kinds of] banquets Baal hates,
> Three the Rider of the Clouds:
A banquet of shamefulness,
> A banquet {banquet} of baseness,   (20)
> And a banquet of handmaids' *lewdness.*
Yet herein is flagrant shamefulness,
> And herein is handmaids' *lewdness.*"—
After this goes Puissant Baal,
> Also goes the Maiden Anath.
As they do homage to Lady Asherah of the Sea,
> Obeisance to the Progenitress of the Gods,
> Quoth Lady Asherah of the Sea:
"Why do ye homage to Lady Asherah of the Sea,
> Obeisance to the Progenitress of the Gods?   (30)
Have ye done homage to Bull El Benign,
> Or obeisance to the Creator of Creatures?"
Quoth the Maiden Anath:
"We do homage to [*th*]*ee*, Lady Asherah of the Sea,
> [Obei]sance to the Progenitress of the Gods. ..."

(Rest of column badly damaged. It is clear that Asherah makes a feast for her visitors, and it may be inferred
that they urge her to intercede for Baal with El, as she
does in the next column.)

(iv-v)

(Some 10 lines missing; lines 1-2a too fragmentary to
be restored.)

[Loudly unto her lad] Ashe[rah doth cry:

---

[1] Yamm (= Sea) is apparently still El's Beloved, despite what he went
through above, in episode III AB A.

"Look thou, Qadesh wa-Amrur,
     Fisherman of Lady] Asherah of the Sea!
[Saddle a donkey],
     Harness a jackass.
[Attach trappings of] silver,
     [A housing] of gol[d],
     Put on the trappings of [thy] she-asses."
Qad[esh] wa-Amrur obeys.
He saddles a donkey,
     Harnesses a jackass.
He attaches trappings of silver,   (10)
          A *housing* of gold,
     Puts on the trappings of his she-asses.
Qadesh wa-Amrur embraces
     And places Asherah on the donkey's back,
     On the beautiful back of the jackass.
Qadesh proceeds to lead,
     Amrur is like a star in front;
The Maiden Anath follows,
     While Baal leaves for Zaphon's summit.—
There, she [1] is off on her way   (20)
          Towards El of the Sources of the Two Floods
     In the midst of the headwaters of the Two Oceans.
She penetrates El's field and enters
     The pavilion of King Father Shunem.
At El's feet she bows and falls down,
     Prostrates her and does him reverence.
As soon as El espies her,
     He *parts his jaws* and laughs.
His feet upon the footstool he puts
     And doth twiddle his fingers.   (30)
He lifts up his voice and [cri]es:
"Why is come Lady Asher[ah of the S]ea?
     Why hither the Progenitress of the G[ods]?
Art thou become hungry and *fa[int]*,
     Or art become thirsty and *pa[rched]*?
Eat, pray, yea drink.
Ea[t] thou from the tables bread;
     Drink from the flagons wine,
     From the golden gob⟨lets⟩ blood of vines.
See, El the King's love stirs thee,
     Bull's affection arouses thee."
Quoth Lady Asherah of the Sea: (40)
"Thy decree, O El, is wise:
     Wisdom with ever-life thy portion.   [1] Asherah.

Thy decree is: our king's Puissant Baal,
  Our sovereign second to none;
All of us must bear his gi[ft],
  All of us [must b]ear his purse.[1]
[But alas!]
He cries unto Bull El his father,
  To [El] the King his begetter;
He cries unto *Asherah* and her children,
  Elath and the band of her kin[dred]:
Look, no house has Baal like the gods,   (50)
  Nor court like the children of Asherah.
The abode of El is the shelter of his son.
The abode of Lady Asherah of the Sea
  Is the abode of the perfect brides:
The abode of Padriya daughter of Ar,
  The shelter of Talliya daughter of Rabb,
  (And) the abode of Arsiya daughter of Ya'abdar."
Quoth the Kindly One El Ben[ign]:
"Am I a slave, an attendant of Asherah?
  Am I a slave, to handle . . . ?   (60)
Or is Asherah a handmaid, to make bricks?

                         (v)

Let a house be built for Baal like the gods',
  And a court like the children of Asherah's!"
Quoth Lady Asherah of the Sea:
"Art great indeed, O El, and wise,
  Thy beard's gray hair instructs thee,
  . . . , [. . .] to thy breast.
Now, too, the *seasons* of his rains will Baal *observe*,
  The *seasons* of . . . with *snow*;
And (he will) peal his thunder in the clouds,   (70)
  Flashing his lightnings to the earth.
The house of cedar—*let him burn it*;
  Yea, the house of brick—*remove it*.
Be it told to Puissant Baal:
Summon *weeds* into thy house,
  Herbs into the midst of thy palace.[2]
The mountains shall bring thee much silver,
  The hills a treasure of gold;
  They'll bring thee *god's grandeur aplenty*.
So build thou a silver and gold house,   (80)
  A house of most pure lapis lazuli."

---

[1] Must be tributary to him. But the translation is uncertain.

[2] This seems—if the sense is correctly guessed—to imply that Baal had some sort of habitation before, but that it was not one worthy of a "ranking" god, such as Baal had become by vanquishing Yamm.

The Maiden Anath rejoices,
Stamps with her foot so the earth *quakes*.
There, she is off on her way
Unto Baal upon Zaphon's summit,
O'er a thousand fields, ten thousand acres.
Laughing, the Maiden Anath
Lifts up her voice and cries:
"Receive, Baal, the glad tidings I bring thee.
They will build thee a house like thy brethren's   (90)
And a court like unto thy kindred's.
Summon *weeds* into thy house,
Herbs into the midst of thy palace.
The mountains shall bring thee much silver,
The hills a treasure of gold;
They'll bring thee *god's grandeur aplenty*.
So build thou a silver and gold house,
A house of most pure lapis lazuli."
Puissant Baal rejoiced.
He summoned *weeds* into his house,
Herbs into the midst of his palace.
The mountains did bring him much silver,   (100)
The hills a treasure of gold;
They brought him *god's grandeur aplenty*.
Then he ⟨se⟩nt unto Kothar wa-Khasis.
(Direction to the reciter):
Now turn to the account of the sending of the lads.[1]

After this comes Kothar wa-Khasis.
Before him an ox is set,
A fatted one at his disposal.
A throne is placed and he's seated
To the right of Puissant Baal.   (110)
So ate [the gods] and drank.
Then answered *Puiss[ant Baal,*
Responded the Ri]d[er of the Clouds]:
"Quickly, a house, O K[othar],
Quickly raise up a pal[ace].
Quickly the house shalt thou build,
Quickly shalt raise up the pa[lace]
In the midst of the fastness of Zaphon.
A thousand fields the house shall cover,
A myriad of acres the palace."
Quoth Kothar wa-Khasis: (120)

[1] No doubt refers to an earlier passage, lost to us, in which Baal dispatched Gapn and Ugar to Kothar. The reciter is directed simply to repeat that passage verbatim here.

"Hearken, O Puissant Baal:
  Give heed, O rider of the Clouds.
A window I'll make in the house,
  A casement within the palace."
But Puissant Baal replied:
"Make not a window in [the house],
  [A casement] within the pal[ace]."

                    (2 or 3 lines missing?)

(vi)

Quoth Ko[thar wa-Khas]is:
  "Thou'lt heed [my words], O Baal."
Again spake Ko[thar wa]-Khasis:
  "Hark, pray, Pu[is]sant Baal!
A wi[nd]ow I'll make in the house,
  A casement withi[n the pa]lace."
But Puissa[nt] Baal replied:
"Make not a w[ind]ow in the house,
  A casement with[in the pa]lace.
Let not [Padriya] daughter of Ar [*be seen*]   (10)
  Or T[alliya] daughter of Rabb *be espied*
  By [...] El's Beloved Yamm!"
[...] *cried defiance*
  And spat [...].
Quoth Kothar [wa-Khasis]:
  "Thou'lt heed my words, O Baal."
[*As for Baal*] his house is built,
  [*As for Hadd*][1] his palace is raised.
They [...] from Lebanon and its trees,
  From [Siri]on its precious cedars.
... [... Le]banon and its trees,   (20)
  Si[r]ion its precious cedars.
Fire is set to the house,
  Flame to the palace.
Lo, a [d]ay and a second,
  Fire feeds on the house,
  Flame upon the palace:
A third, a fourth day,
  [Fi]re feeds on the house,
  Flam[e] upon the palace.
A fifth, a s[ix]th day,
  Fire feeds [on] the house,
  Flame u[pon] the palace.   (30)
There, on the seventh d[ay],

[1] Another name of Baal.

The fire *dies down* in the house,
   The f[la]me in the palace.
The silver turns into blocks,
   The gold is turned into bricks.
Puissant Baal exults:
"My h⟨ouse⟩ have I builded of silver;
   My palace, indeed, of gold."
For ⟨his⟩ house preparations [Baa]l makes,
   [Prepa]rations makes Hadd for his palace.   (40)
He slaughters both neat [and] small cattle,
   Fells bulls [*together with*] fatlings;
   Rams ⟨and⟩ one-year-ol[d] calves;
   Lambs ... k[i]ds.
He summons his brethren to his house,
   His ki[nd]red within his palace:
   Summons Asherah's seventy children.
He sates the he-lamb gods with *w[ine]*,
   He sates the ewe-lamb goddesses [... ?]
He sates the bull-gods with *w[ine]*,
   He sates the cow-goddesses [... ?]   (50)
He sates the throne-gods with *wi[ne]*,
   He sates the chair-goddesses [... ?]
He sates the gods with jars of wine,
   He sates the goddesses with pitchers.
So eat the gods and drink.
They sate them with fatness abundant,
   With tender [fat]ling by bounteous knife;[1]   Isa. 60:16; 66:11
While drinking the [wine] from flag[ons,
   From gold cups the blood of vines].
                              (some 9-10 lines missing)

(vii)

(The first 8 lines are very defective. El's Beloved
Yamm—see above vi 12—figures in lines 3-4. Since Baal's
misgivings about a window are thereupon dispelled—15
ff.—perhaps Yamm is here given his quietus.)

Sixty-six towns he took,
   Seventy-seven hamlets;   (10)
Eighty ⟨took⟩ Baal of [Zaphon's] s[ummit],
   Ninety Baal of the *sum[mit.*
Baal] *dwells in his house,*
   Baal in the midst of the house.
Quoth Puissant Baal:

---

[1] Literally: They were sated with sucking of breast; by milch knife, with
fatling's teat.

"I will make (one), Kothar, this day;
    Kothar, this very hour.
A casement shall be opened in the house,
    A window within the palace.
Yea, *I'll open rifts in* the clouds
    At *thy word*, O Kothar wa-Khasis!"   (20)
Kothar wa-Khasis laughs,
    He lifts up his voice and cries:
"Said I not to thee, Puissant Baal,
    'Thou'lt heed my words, O Baal'?"—
He opens a casement in the house,
    A window within the pa[lace].
Baal op[ens] *rifts in* [the cloud]s.
Ba[al gives] forth his holy voice,
    Baal discharges the *ut[terance of his li]ps.*   (30)
His h[oly] voice [convulses] the earth, . . . the mountains quake,
    A-tremble are . . .
East and west, earth's high places reel.
Baal's enemies take to the woods,
    Hadd's foes to the sides of the mountain.
Quoth Puissant Baal:
"Baal's enemies, why do you quake?
    Why do you quake . . . ?"
Baal's eye seeks out for his hand   (40)
    When the yew-club swings in his right hand.
So Baal dwells in his house.
    "Nor king nor commoner
    The earth my dominion shall . . .
Tribute I'll send not to Divine Mot,[1]
    Not dispatch to El's Darling Ghazir.
Mot calls out in his soul,
    The Beloved thinks in his heart,
'I alone will have sway o'er the gods   (50)
    So that gods and men may feed,
    Who satisfies the multitudes of the earth.' "
Aloud unto [his l]ads Baal doth cry:
"Look ye, [Gapn and] Ugar so⟨ns⟩ of Ghulumat,
    ['*Amami*]s twain, sons of Zulumat
    [The stately, wing]-spreading, . . . ;
Winged ones twain, flock of clouds,
    ['Neath . . . ;
Birdlike ones twain, *flock* of . . . snow].
             (some 5 lines missing)

---

[1] God of the rainless season and, apparently, of the nether world.

(viii)

There now, be off on your way
　　Unto the Mount of Targhuzizza,
Unto the Mount of Tharumegi,
　　Unto the Ridge of the Loam of the Earth.
Lift the mount on your hands,
　　The elevation upon your palms,
And descend to the depth of the earth,
　　Be of those who descend into earth.
There now, be off on your way　　　　　　(10)
　　Into his city *Pit*,
Low the throne that he sits on,
　　Filth the land of his inheritance.
Yet beware, divine messengers.
　　Approach not Divine Mot,
Lest he make you like a lamb in his mouth,
　　Ye be crushed like a kid in his *gullet*.　　(20)
Even the Gods' Torch Shapsh,
　　Who wings over heaven's expanse,
Is in Mot El's Beloved's hand![1]
From a thousand fields, ten thousand acres,[2]
　　To Mot's feet bow and fall down,
　　Prostrate you and show him honor.
And say unto Divine Mot,　　　　　　　　(30)
　　Declare unto El's Darling Ghazir:
Message of Puissant Baal,
　　Work of the Mighty Wa[rrior]:
'My house I have builded [of silver,
　　My palace, indeed, of gold.]
. . .'"

(Ten lines of which only the ends are preserved, and
approximately another 15 lines missing altogether.)
(Broken colophon in margin:)

[Written by Elimelech(?) Do]nated by Niqmadd,
King of Ugarit.

---

[1] After Yamm, this is the next favorite-and-bully of El that Baal has to
vanquish. That is logical: first the earth—Baal's domain—must be made
safe from the encroachments of the sea, then from the blight of sterility.
[2] From a safe distance.

f. V AB

(For the provisional assignment of V AB to this position in the epic and for a translation of the preserved
portions of the text, see *ANET*, pp. 135-138.)

g. I* AB

(i)   " . . .

Ps. 74:14; Isa. 27:1 If thou smite Lotan, the serpent slant,
Destroy the serpent tortuous,
Shalyat (*šlyṭ*) of the seven heads,
. . ."

(two couplets very obscure)

From the *tomb* of the Godly Mot,
From the pit of El's Belov'd Ghazir,
The gods twain[1] depart, tarry not.
There, they are off on their way   (10)
To Baal of the Summit of Zaphon.
Then Gapn and Ugar declare:
"Message of Godly Mot,
Word of the God-Belov'd Ghazir:

(even the gist of 14-27 still eludes savants)

If thou smite Lotan, the serpent slant,
Destroy the serpent tortuous,
Shalyat of the seven heads,
. . ."

(Traces of the two obscure couplets mentioned above.
Some 30 lines missing.)

(ii)   (12 lines missing at the top)

One lip to earth and one to heaven,[2]
[He stretches his to]ngue to the stars.
Baal enters his mouth,
Descends into him like an olive-cake,[3]
Like the yield of the earth and trees' fruit.
Sore afraid is Puissant Baal,
Filled with dread is the Rider of Clouds:
"Begone![4] Say unto Godly Mot,
Repeat unto El's Belov'd Ghazir:
'Message of Puissant Baal,   (10)
Word of the Powerful Hero:
Be gracious, O Godly Mot;
Thy slave I, thy bondman for ever.' "—
The gods depart, tarry not.
There, they are off on their way
Unto Godly Mot,

[1] Gapn and Ugar.
[2] Also occurs elsewhere in describing some ravenous creature opening its mouth.
[3] Apparently a flat loaf of bread with olives, a common meal in ancient and modern times.
[4] Said by Baal to Gapn and Ugar. A quotation without an introduction.

Into his city Hamriya,
>Down to the throne that ⌐he⌐ sits on
>His ⌐filthy⌐ land of inher'tance.
They lift up their voice and cry:
"Message of Puissant Son Baal,
>Word of the Powerful Hero:
Be gracious, O Godly Mot;
>Thy slave I, thy bondman for ever."—
The Godly Mot rejoices (20)
>[And lifting] his [vo]ice he cries:
"How *humbled is* [...]."

(Several ends of lines, then about 20-25 lines missing. Cols. iii-iv too damaged for connected sense.)

(v)

(About 25 lines missing at the top. Then 1-5 defective.)

". . .[1]

But thou, take thy cloud, thy wind,
>Thy ..., thy rains;
With thee thy seven lads,
>Thine eight *boars*.
With thee Padriya, daughter of Ar; (10)
>With thee Tatalliya (*Ṭṭly*), daughter of Rabb.
There now, be off on thy way
>Unto the Mount of Kankaniya.
Lift the mount upon thy hands,
>The elevation upon thy palms,
And descend to the depth of the earth,
>Be of those who descend into earth,
>And ..."—
Puissant Baal complies.
He desires a cow-calf in Dubr,
>A heifer in Shihlmemat-field (*šd šḥlmmt*);
Lies with her times seventy-seven, (20)
>[...] ... times eighty-eight.
She [conc]eives and gives birth to Math.

(fragments of 3 more lines; another 11 missing)

(vi)

(about 30 lines missing at the top)

[They[2] penetrate El's Field and enter
>The pavilion of King El Father] Shunem.
[And lifting their voice they cr]y:

---

[1] Addressed (by Mot?) to Baal.   [2] Probably Gapn and Ugar.

"We went [. . .],
   . . .
We [ca]me to the pleasance of Dabr-land,
  To the beauty of Shihlmemat-field.
We came upon Baal
  Fallen on the ground:
Puissant Baal is dead,
  The Prince, Lord of Earth, is perished."   (10)
Straightway Kindly El Benign
  Descends from the throne,
  Sits on the footstool;
From the footstool,
  And sits on the ground;
Pours dust of mourning on his head,
  Earth of mortification on his pate;
  And puts on *sackcloth and loincloth.*
He *cuts a gash* with a stone,
  Incisions with . . .
He *gashes* his cheeks and his chin,
  He *harrows* the *roll* of his *arm.*   (20)
He plows his chest like a garden,
  Harrows his back like a plain.
He lifts up his voice and cries:
"Baal's dead!—What becomes of the people?
  Dagon's Son!—What of the masses?
  After Baal I'll descend into earth."
Anath also goes and wanders
  Every mount to the heart of the earth,
  Every hill to the earth's very bo[we]lls.
She comes to the pleasance of Dabr-[land],
  To the beauty of Shihlmemat-field.   (30)
She [comes] upon Baal
  Fal[len] on the ground:
  She puts on [*sackcloth*] *and loincloth.*

h. I AB

(Pertaining to "Baal.")
She *cuts a gash* with a stone,
  Incisions with . . . etc.   (See g, col. vi.)

Ps. 42:3 Then weeps she her fill of weeping;
Ps. 80:5   Deep she drinks tears, like wine. (10)
Loudly she calls
  Unto the Gods' Torch Shapsh.
"Lift Puissant Baal, I pray,
  Onto me."

Hearkening, Gods' Torch Shapsh
    Picks up Puissant Baal,
    Sets him on Anath's shoulder.
Up to Zaphon's *Fastness* she brings him,
    Bewails him and buries him too,
    Lays him in the hollows of the earth-ghosts.
She slaughters seventy buffaloes
    As tribute to Puissant Baal;
She slaughters seventy neat   (20)
    [As tr]ibute to Puissant Baal;
[She slaugh]ters seventy small cattle
    [As tribu]te to Puissant Baal;
[She slaugh]ters seventy deer
    [As tribute to] Puissant Baal;
[She slaughters] seventy mountain-goats
    [As tribute to Pu]issant Baal;
[She slaughters seventy ro]ebucks
    [As tribu]te to Puissant Baal.
    ...] ... A[nath],   (30)
    [...] Yabama[t] Liimmim.—
[The]re, she is off on her way
    To [E]l of the Sources of the Floods,
    In the midst of [the Hea]dwaters of the Two Deeps.
She penetrates El's Field and enters
    The pavilion of King Father Shunem.
At El's feet she bows and falls down,
    Prostrates her and does him honor.
She lifts up her voice and cries:
"Now let Asherah rejoice and her sons,   (40)
    Elath and the band of her kinsmen;
For dead is Puissant Baal,
    Perished the Prince, Lord of Earth."[1]
Loudly El doth cry
    To Lady Asherah of the Sea:
"Hark, Lady A[sherah of the S]ea,
    Give one of thy s[ons] I'll make king."
Quoth Lady Asherah of the Sea:
    "Why, let's make Yadi' Yalhan (*yd' ylḥn*) king."
Answered Kindly One El Benign:
"Too weakly. He can't race with Baal,   (50)
    Throw jav'lin with Dagon's Son *Glory-Crown!*"
Replied Lady Asherah of the Sea:
    "Well, let's make it Ashtar the Tyrant;

[1] Now a son of Asherah can rule the earth. In col. v Asherah's sons are Baal's enemies. His epithet "Dagon's Son" may echo a stage of tradition in which he was not a son of El, either.

Let Ashtar the Tyrant be king."—
Straightway Ashtar the Tyrant
    Goes up to the *Fastness* of Zaphon
    (And) sits on Baal Puissant's throne.
(But) his feet reach not down to the footstool,
    Nor his head reaches up to the top.   (60)
So Ashtar the Tyrant declares:
    "I'll not reign in Zaphon's *Fastness*!"
Down goes Ashtar the Tyrant,
    Down from the throne of Baal Puissant,
    And reigns in El's Earth, all of it.   [...] ...

(ii)

(some 30 lines missing on top)

[...]. A day, days go by,   (4)
    [And Anath the Lass] draws nigh him.
Like the heart of a c[ow] for her calf,
    Like the heart of a ew[e] for her lamb,
    So's the heart of Ana[th] for Baal.
She grabs Mot by the fold of his garment,
    Seizes [him] by the hem of his robe.   (10)
She lifts up her voice and [cries]:
    "Now, Mot! Deliver my brother."
Responds the Godly Mot:
    "What wouldst thou, O Maiden Anath?
I indeed have gone and have wander'd
    Every mount to the heart of the earth,
    Every hill to the earth's very bowels.
Lifebreath was wanting 'mong men,
    Lifebreath among earth's masses.
I came to the pleasance of Dabr-land,
    The beauty of Shihlmemat-field.   (20)
I did *masticate* Puissant Baal.
I made him like a lamb in my mouth;
    Like a kid in my gullet he's crushed.
Even the Gods' Torch Shapsh,
    Who wings over heaven's expanse,
    Is in Mot the Godly's hand."
A day, even days pass by,
    From days unto months.
    Then Anath the Lass draws nigh him.
Like the heart of a cow for her calf,
    Like the heart of a ewe for her lamb,
    So's the heart of Anath for Baal.   (30)
She seizes the Godly Mot—

With sword she doth cleave him.
With fan she doth winnow him—
    With fire she doth burn him.[1]
With hand-mill she grinds him—
    In the field she doth sow him.
Birds eat his *remnants,*
    Consuming his *portions,*
    Flitting from remnant to remnant.[2]

(iii-iv)

". . . [3](some 40 lines missing on top of col. iii)
[That Puissant Baal had died],
    That the Prince [Lord of Earth] had perished.
And behold, alive is [Puissant Baal]!
    And behold, existent the Prince, Lo[rd of Earth]!
In a dream, O Kindly El Benign,
    In a vision, Creator of Creatures,
The heavens fat did rain,
    The wadies flow with honey.
So I knew
That alive was Puissant Baal!
    Existent the Prince, Lord of Earth!
In a dream, Kindly El Benign,   (10)
    In a vision, Creator of Creatures,
The heavens fat did rain,
    The wadies flow with honey!"—
The Kindly One El Benign's glad.
    His feet on the footstool he sets,
    And parts his *jaws* and laughs.
He lifts up his voice and cries:
    "Now will I sit and rest
    And my soul be at ease in my breast.
For alive is Puissant Baal,   (20)
    Existent the Prince, Lord of Earth!"   (edge)
Loudly El doth cry
    Unto the Maiden Anath.
"Hearken, O Maiden Anath!
    Say to the Gods' Torch Shapsh:

(iv)

'Parch'd is the furrow of Soil, O Shapsh;
    Parched is El's Soil's furrow:
    Baal neglects the furrow of his tillage.

---

[1] That is to say, the parts of him corresponding to chaff and straw.
[2] But somehow Mot comes to life entire in col. vi, and Baal even earlier.
[3] Who the speaker is is not known.

Where is Puissant Baal?
Where is the Prince, Lord of Earth?' "—
The Maiden Anath departs. (30)
There, she is off on her way
Unto the Gods' Torch Shapsh.
She lifts up her voice and cries:
"Message of Bull El thy father,
Word of the Kindly, thy begetter:
Parch'd is the furrow of Soil, O [Shapsh];
Parched is El's Soil's furrow:
Baal ne[glects] the furrow of his tillage.
Where is Puissant Baal?
Where is the Prince, Lord of Earth?"— (40)
Answer'd the Gods' Torch Sha[psh]:
". . . in the . . . [of thy brother],
In the . . . of thy sibling,
And I'll look for Puissant Baal."—
Quoth the Maiden Anath:
". . . . . ., O Shapsh;
   . . .
May . . .[. . .] guard thee,
   . . . [. . .]."(?) (some 35 lines missing)

(v)

Baal seizes the sons of Asherah.
Rabbim[1] he strikes in the back.
Dokyamm he strikes with a bludgeon,
   . . . he fells to the earth.
Baal [mounts] his throne of kingship,
   [Dagon's Son] his seat of dominion.
[From] days to months, from months to years.
   Lo, after seven years,
The Godly Mot [. . .]
   Unto Puissant Baal. (10)
He lifts up his voice and says:
"Upon thee . . . may I see,
   Downfall upon thee may I see.
Winnowing ⟨with fan
   Upon thee may I see.
Cleaving⟩ with sword
   Upon thee may I see.
Burning with fire
   Upon thee [may I see.
Gri]nding with hand-mill

---

[1] According to f (between lines 30 and 40), Anath has already destroyed Rabbim once.

Up[on thee] may I s[ee
Siftin]*g* with *sieve*
Upon thee [may I] see.
[...] . [...] in the soil
Upon thee may I see.
Sowing on the sea
[...] .. [...]."

(Lines 20-28 defective and obscure. Some further 35
lines missing.)

(vi)

Returning to Baal of Zaphon's *Fastness*,   (12)
   He lifts *up* his voice and cries:
"My brothers hast thou given, Baal, my ... [s?];
   My mother's sons, my ..."
They ... like *camels*:
   Mot's firm, Baal's firm.
They gore like buffaloes:
   Mot's firm. Baal's firm.
They bite like snakes:
   Mot's firm. Baal's firm.   (20)
They *kick* like *chargers*:
   Mot falls. Baal falls.
Above Shapsh cries to Mot:
"Hearken, now, Godly Mot!
   Why striv'st thou with Puissant Baal? Why?
Should Bull El thy father hear thee,
   He'll pull out thy dwelling's *pillars*.
Overturn thy throne of kingship,
   Break thy staff of dominion!"
Sore afraid was Godly Mot,   (30)
   Filled with dread El's Belovèd Ghazir.
Mot ...
  .. [....]
Baal seats him [on] his kingdom's [throne],
   Upon his dominion's [seat].

(36-42 missing, defective, or unintelligible)
" ... ¹

Thou'lt² eat the bread of honor,   (46)
   Thou'lt drink the wine of favor.
Shapsh *shall govern* the *gathered ones*,³
   Shapsh *shall govern* the divine ones.
... gods ... mortals,
   ... Kothar thy fellow,
   Even Khasis thine intimate."

¹ Apparently Baal is handing out rewards to his allies.
² Or, "she'll."   ³ The *rephaim*, or shades?

On the sea of *monster* and dragon, (50)
    Proceedeth Kothar wa-Khasis,
    Kothar wa-Khasis doth journey.[1]

[1] Perhaps the quotation should be closed here.

(colophon)   Written by Elimelech the Shabnite.
Dictated by Attani-puruleni, Chief of Priests, Chief of (Temple)-herdsmen.
Donated by Niqmadd, King of Ugarit, Master of Yargub, Lord of Tharumeni.

APPENDIX. IV AB+RŠ 319

There exist a large (IV AB) and a very small piece (RŠ 319) of a tablet with three columns of writing on only one side. That they both belong to the same tablet is not certain but very probable. That only one side of the tablet is written on is probably due to the fact that it contained the whole of the composition in question, which was quite short. It has no colophon. It is distinct from the Baal epic which we have been following in the preceding pieces. RŠ 319, which is apparently the missing top right-hand corner of IV AB, contains a graphic account of sexual intercourse between Baal and Anath; and IV AB itself is suggestive of something more than platonic relations between the two. This is entirely at variance with the epic, as everyone will realize who has read the former

        (col. i too fragmentary for use)

        (ii)

        (some 20 lines missing on top?)

". . . Baal in his house,
    The God Hadd in the midst of his palace?"[1]
The lads of Baal make answer:
"Baal *is not* in his house,
    [The God] Hadd in the midst of his palace.
His bow he has ta'en in his hand,
    Also his *darts* in his right hand.
There he is off on his way
    To Shimak Canebrake,[2] the [buf]falo-*filled*."—
The Maiden Ana[th] lifts her wing, (10)
    Lifts her wing and speeds in flight,
    To Shimak Canebrake, the [buf]falo-*filled*.—
Puissant Baal lifts up his eyes,
    Lifts up his eyes and beholds,
Beholds the Maiden Anath,
    Fairest *among* Baal's sisters.
Before her he rises, he stands,

[1] The inquirer is evidently Anath.
[2] Semachonitis, the modern Lake Ḥûleh in Galilee?

At her feet he kneels and falls down.
And he lifts up his voice and cries:
"Hail, sister, and . . . ! (20)
The horns of thy . . . , O Maiden Anath,
    The horns of thy . . . Baal will anoint,
    Baal will *anoint* them in flight.
We'll thrust my foes into the earth,
    To the ground them that rise 'gainst thy brother!"—
The Maiden Anath lifts up her eyes,
    Lifts up her eyes and beholds,
Beholds a cow and proceeds a-walking,
    Proceeds a-walking and proceeds *a-dancing*,
    In the pleasant spots, in the lovely places. (30)

(RŠ 319)

(8 or 9 badly damaged lines at the bottom)

He seizes and holds [her] womb;
    [She] seizes and holds [his] stones.
Baal . . . *to an ox.*
[. . . the Mai]den Anath
    [. . .] to conceive and bear.

(another 14 lines very fragmentary)

(IV AB iii)

[Calve]s the cows dr[op]:
    An ox for Maiden Anath
    And a heifer for Yahamat Liimmim.
Quoth Puissant [Baal]:
". . . that our progenitor is eternal,
    To all generations our begetter."
Baal scoops [his hands] full,
    ⁱThe Godⁱ Hadd [his] fin[gers] full.
. . . the mouth of Maiden An[ath], (10)
    E'en the mouth of [his] fairest sister.
Baal goes up in the mou[ntain],
    Dagon's Son in the s[ky].
Baal sits upon [his th]rone,
    Dagon's Son upon [his se]at.
(In lines 16-29, which are poorly preserved, there is again talk of a buffalo being born to Baal, it being still not absolutely clear that his bovine mother was Anath herself.)
And so she goes up to Arar, (30)
    Up to Arar and Zaphon.
In the pleasance, the Mount of Possession,
    She cries aloud to Baal:

"Receive, Baal, godly tidings,
        Yea receive, O Son of Dagon:
A wild-ox is [born] to Baal,
        A buffalo to Rider of Clouds."
Puissant Baal rejoices.

The Tale of Aqhat

ANET, 149-155

The rich epigraphic harvests of the French excavations of 1930 and 1931 at the site of ancient Ugarit included large portions of three tablets, and a possible fragment of a fourth, belonging to an epic about a youth whose name is spelled *a-q-h-t* and conventionally vocalized *Aqhat*. The text was at first called the Epic of Daniel, or Danel, for Aqhat's father; but on the one tablet of which the first line, containing the title of the composition to which the tablet belongs, is preserved, it reads "Pertaining to 'Aqhat,'" and closer study reveals that the text really tells about Daniel only what concerns Aqhat.

Fig. 68

AQHT A
(i)

(about 10 lines missing at top)

II Sam. 21:16, 18, 20, 22; Gen. 14:5; Deut. 2:11, 20; 3:11, 13

[... Straightway Daniel[1] the Raph]a[2]-man,   (1)
        Forthwith [Ghazir[3] the Harnamiyy[4]-man],
Gives oblation to the gods to eat,
        Gives oblation to drink to the holy ones.
A couch of sackcloth he mounts and lies,
        A couch of [loincloth] and ⌜passes the night⌝.
Behold a day and a second,
        Oblation to the gods gives Daniel,
Oblation to the gods to eat,
        Oblation to drink to the holy ones.
A third, a fourth day,
        Oblation to the gods gives Daniel,   (10)
Oblation to the gods to eat,
        Oblation to drink to the holy ones.
A fifth, a sixth, a seventh day,
        Oblation to the gods gives Daniel,
Oblation to the gods to eat,
        Oblation to drink to the holy ones.
A sackcloth couch doth Daniel,
        A sackcloth couch mount and lie,

---

[1] The name means "God judges." Judging the cause of the widow and the fatherless is Daniel's special concern; see v 4-8 etc. His wife's name, Danatiya (v 16, 22), is from the same root.

[2] This Rapha is perhaps identical with the aboriginal giant race of Canaan.   [3] As a common noun, *gzr* means "boy."

[4] Perhaps connected with *Hrnm*, a Syrian locality named in an early Egyptian source (Harnaim).

A couch of loincloth and pass the night.
But lo, on the seventh day,
    Baal approaches with his plea:
"Unhappy is Daniel the Rapha-man,
    A-sighing is Ghazir the Harnamiyy-man;
Who hath no son like his brethren,   (20)
    Nor scion hath like his kindred.
Surely there's a son for him ⌜like⌝ his brethren's,
    And a scion like unto his kindred's!
He gives oblation to the gods to eat,
    Oblation to drink to the holy ones.
Wilt thou not bless him, O Bull El, my father,
    Beatify him, O Creator of Creatures?
So shall there be a son in his house,
    A scion in the midst of his palace:
Who sets up the stelae of his ancestral spirits,
    In the holy place the protectors of his clan;
Who frees his spirit from the earth,
    From the dust guards his footsteps;
Who smothers the life-force of his detractor,   (30)
    Drives off who attacks his abode;
Who takes him by the hand when he's drunk,
    Carries him when he's sated with wine;   Isa. 51:17-18
Consumes his funerary offering in Baal's house,
    (Even) his *portion in* El's house;
Who plasters his roof when it leaks,
    Washes his clothes when they're soiled."—
[*By the hand*] El takes his servant,
    Blessing Daniel the Rapha-man,
    Beatifying Ghazir the Harnamiyy-man:
"With life-breath shall be quickened Daniel the Rapha-man,
    With spirit Ghazir the Harnamiyy-man.
[*With life-breath*] he is *invigorated.*[1]
    Let him mount his bed [. . .].   (40)
In the kissing of his wife [she'll conceive],
    In her embracing become pregnant.
[By conception] (and) pregnancy she'll bear
    [A man-child to Daniel the Ra]pha-[man].
So shall there be a son [in his house,
    A scion] in the midst of his palace:
[Who sets up the stelae of his ances]tral spirits,
    In the holy place [the protectors of his clan];
Who frees [his spirit from the e]arth,

---

[1] This does not imply that Daniel's vigor was previously below average.

[From the dust gu]ards his footsteps;
[Who smothers the life-force of his detractor],
    Drives off who attacks [his abode;
Etc.]"

(After line 48 some 10 lines are missing, but the first 4 of these were obviously identical with lines 31-34 above. After that it was related that somebody was instructed to tell the good news to Daniel.)

(ii)

(Another 10 lines, approximately, missing here. The messenger obeyed instructions and addressed Daniel as follows: ". . . A son shall be borne thee like thy brethren's,
    A scion like unto thy kindred's:
Who sets up the stelae of thine ancestral spirits,
    In the holy place)
                                    the pro[tectors of thy clan;
Who frees thy spirit from the earth],   (1)
    From the dust etc., etc."   (2-8c)
        (see above, i 25 ff.)
Daniel's face lights up,   (8d)
    While above his forehead shines.
He *parts his jaws* and laughs,   (10)
    Places his foot on the footstool,
    And lifts up his voice and cries:
Now will I sit and rest
    And my soul be at ease in my breast.
For a son's born to me like my brethren's
    A scion like unto my kindred's
Etc., etc.
Daniel goes to his house,
    To his palace Daniel betakes him.   (25)
Into his house come skillful ones,[1]
    Daughters of joyful noise, *swallows*.
Straightway Daniel the Rapha-man,
    Forthwith Ghazir the Harnamiyy-man,
Prepares an ox for the skillful ones,   (30)
    Gives food to the [ski]llful ones and gives drink
    To the daughters of joy[ful noise], the *swallows*.
Behold a day and a second,
    He give[s f]ood to the skillful ones and dr[in]k
    To the daughters of joyful noise, the *swallows*;
A third, a fo[urth] day,
    He gives food to the skillful ones and drink

---

[1] "Artistes."

To the daughters of joyful noise, the *swallows*;
A fifth, a sixth day,
 He gives food to the skill[ful] ones and d[rink
 To the d]aughters of joyful noise, the *swallows*.
Lo, on the seventh day,
 Away from his house go the skillful ones,   (40)
 The daughters of joyful noise, the *swallows*.—
[...] the fairness of the bed [*of conception*],
 The beauty of the bed of *childbirth*.
Daniel sits [and cou]nts her months.
A month follows a month;
 A third, a fou[rth (a fifth?) month.
But in the fifth (sixth?)] month,
 He goes [*to the shrine of* ...].
        (ten lines of col. ii and all of cols. iii-iv missing)

(v)

 (Some 13 lines missing at the top. The preserved por-
tion begins in the middle of a speech of the craftsman-
god addressed to Daniel:)
 "...   (abraded except for traces) (1)
I myself will bring the bow,
 Even I will convey the *darts*."
And behold, on the seventh day—
Straightway Daniel the Rapha-man,
 Forthwith Ghazir the Harnam[iyy]-man,
Is upright, sitting before the gate,
 Beneath *a mighty tree* on the threshing floor,
Judging the cause of the widow,
 Adjudicating the case of the fatherless.
Lifting up his eyes, he beholds:
 From a thousand fields, ten thousand acres,[1]   (10)
The march of Kothar[2] he espies,
 He espies the onrush of Khasis,[3]
See, he bringeth a bow;
 Lo, he conveyeth *darts*.
Straightway Daniel the Rapha-man,
 Forthwith Daniel the Harnamiyy-man,
Loudly unto his wife doth call:
"Hearken, Lady Danatiya,
 Prepare a lamb from the flock
For the desire of Ko[th]ar wa-Khasis,[4]
 For the appetite of Hayyin[5] of the Handicrafts.

---

[1] i.e. in the distance. [2] "Skillful," a common name of the craftsman-god.
[3] "Clever," another of his names. [4] "Skillful and Clever." [5] "Deft."

Give food, give drink to the godhead;   (20)
  Serve, honor him,
  The Lord of Hikpat-El,[1] all of it.
Lady Danatiya obeys,
  She prepares a lamb from the flock
For the desire of Kothar wa-Khasis,
  For the appetite of Hayyin of the Handicrafts.
Afterwards, Kothar wa-Khasis comes.
The bow he delivers into Daniel's hand;
  The *darts* he places upon his knees.
Straightway Lady Danatiya
  Gives food, gives drink to the godhead;
She serves, honors him,   (30)
  The Lord of Hikpat-El, all of it.
Kothar departs for[2] his tent,
  Hayyin departs for[2] his tabernacle.
Straightway Daniel the Rapha-man,
  Forthwith Ghazir the Harnamiyy-man,
The bow doth [...] ... , upon Aqhat he doth ...
  [...]:
"*The choicest* of thy game, O my son,
  The choicest of thy game ... [...],
  The game of thy ... [...]."[3]
                          (some 12 lines missing)

                    (vi)

(Some 19 lines missing. Then come 15 broken lines
which tell about a feast and about the warrior-goddess
Anath coveting Aqhat's bow: Aqhat will have been
entertaining her tête-à-tête.)
[She lifts up her voice and] cries: (16)
  "Hearken, I pray thee, [Aqhat the Youth!
A]sk for silver, and I'll give it thee;
  [For gold, and I'll be]stow't on thee;
But give thou thy bow [to me;
  Let] Yabamat-Liimmim[4] *take* thy *darts*."
But Aqhat the Youth answers: (20)
"*I vow yew trees* of Lebanon,
  I vow sinews from wild oxen;
I vow horns from mountain goats,
  Tendons from the hocks of a bull;
I vow from a *cane-forest* reeds:
  Give (these) to Kothar wa-Khasis.

---

[1] *hkpt il*, the name of the craftsman-god's "estate."
[2] Or "from," if Daniel's tent is meant rather than Kothar's.
[3] Perhaps Daniel here impresses upon his son the duty of offering some
of his game to the gods.   [4] Alternative designation of the Maiden Anath.

He'll make a bow for thee,
>   *Darts* for Yabamat-Liimmim."[1]
Then quoth the Maiden Anath:
"Ask for life, O Aqhat the Youth.
Ask for life and I'll give it thee,
>   For deathlessness, and I'll bestow't on thee.
I'll make thee count years with Baal,
>   With the sons of El shalt thou count months.[2]
And Baal when he gives life gives a feast,   (30)
>   Gives a feast to the life-given and bids him drink;
Sings and chants over him,
>   Sweetly serenad[es] him:
So give I life to Aqhat the Youth."
But Aqhat the Youth answers:
"Fib not to me, O Maiden;
>   For to a Youth thy fibbing is *loathsome*.
Further life—how can mortal attain it?
>   How can mortal attain life enduring?
Glaze will be poured [on] my head,
>   *Plaster* upon my pate;[3]
And I'll die as everyone dies,
>   I too shall assuredly die.
Moreover, this will I say:
My bow is [*a weapon for*] warriors.   (40)
>   Shall now females [*with it*] to the chase?"
—[Loud]ly Anath doth laugh,
>   While forging [a plot] in her heart:
"Give heed *to* me, Aqhat the Youth,
>   Give heed to me for thine own good.
[. . .] I'll meet thee in the path of arrogance,
>   [Encounter thee] in the path of presumption,
Hurl thee down at [my feet *and trample*] thee,
>   My darling great big he-man!"—
[She *stamps* with her fe]et and *traverses* the earth.
There, [she is off on her w]ay
>   Towards El of the Source of the Floods
>   [In the midst of the headwaters] of the Two
>   Oceans.
She penetrates El's field [and enters
>   The pavili]on of King Father Shunem.[4]
[At El's feet she] bows and falls down,   (50)
>   Prostr[ates herself, doing him rever]ence.

---

[1] Yew-wood, horn, sinew, and tendon go into the making of a composite bow; reed into that of arrows.   [2] i.e. shalt be immortal like them.
[3] My hair will turn white.   [4] One of El's names.

She denounces Aqhat the Youth,
   [Damns the child of Dani]el the Rapha-man.
Quoth [the Maiden Anath,
   Lifting up] her [voice] and crying:
   (In 54-55 only the word "Aqhat" can be made out. A
further 10 lines or so are missing. In them Anath may
well have told a cock-and-bull story about the unaccom-
modating youth. In any case, El declared he could, or
would, do nothing against Aqhat.)
         (colophon on edge of tablet)
[Dictated by Attani]-puruleni. [1]

> [1] Known from the colophon at the end of the Baal epic to have been
> chief of priests in the reign of Niqmadd, king of Ugarit, second quarter
> of the 14th century B.C.

AQHT B

   (The preserved fragment of this four-column tablet
bears the top of col. i on the obverse and the bottom of
col. iv on the reverse, the surface of the obverse being
largely abraded.)
         (i)

[. . . But the Maiden Anath] [replied]:
"[. . .], O El!
   [. . . rejoice not.
Re]joice not [. . . ,
   Exult] not [. . . .   (10)
With] the *might* [of my] *lon*[*g hand*,
   I'll verily smash] thy [pa]te,
Make [thy gray hair] flow [with blood,
   The gray hair of] thy [beard] with gore.
And [call] Aqhat and let him save thee,
   The son [of Daniel] and let him deliver thee,
   From the hand of the Maiden [Anath]!"—
Answered the Kindly One El Be[nign]:
"I ween'd, daughter mine, thou wast *gentle*,
   And goddesses fr[ee from] *contumely*.
On, then, *perverse* daughter;
   [Thou'lt ta]ke whatsoever thou wilt.
Thou'lt compass [whatever thou] list:
   Who hinders thee will be crushed."—
[The Maid]en Anath [rejoices].   (20)
There, she is off [on her way
   Towards A]qhat the Youth,
   O'er thousand fi[elds, ten thousand a]cres.
Now laughs the Maiden [Anath,
   And lifts up] her voice and cries:

"Oh, hearken bu[t, Aqhat the Youth],
    Thou'rt my brother, and I [*thy sister*]...."

(Lines 25-35 too damaged to yield anything but the probable general sense that Anath offers to show Aqhat a particularly good place to hunt in, namely, the environs of the home-town of Yatpan [*yṭpn*], on whom see further on. Probably in the additional 20 lines of this column and in the whole of cols. ii-iii, which are missing altogether, the twain betook them thither; Aqhat had good luck, and Anath left him for a while.)

(iv)

(some 20 lines missing, 4 lines fragmentary)

The Maiden Anath [depar]ts.   (5)
[There, she is off on her way]
    Towards Yatpan [*the Drunken*] *Soldier.*
[She lifts up her voice] and cries:
(The sense of her imperfectly preserved utterance has not yet been determined, except that it shows that Yatpan dwelt in "the city of Abelim, Abelim the city of Prince Yarikh [= Moon].")

Quoth Yatpan [*the Drunken Soldier*]:   (11)
    "Hearken, O Maiden Anath.
Wouldst thou slay him[1] fo[r his bow],
    Slay him for his *darts*,
    Him ma[ke live again]?
The darling Youth has set meat and [*drink*].
    He is left in the fields and ... [...]."
Quoth the Maiden Anath:
    "Give heed, Yatp,[2] and [I'll tell] thee.
I'll make thee like a vulture in my girdle,
    Like a swift flier in my pouch.
[As] Aqhat [sits] to eat,
    The son of Daniel to [dine],
[Over him] vultures will soar,   (20)
    [A flock of sw]ift fliers will *coast.*
'Mong the vultures will I be soaring;
    Above Aqhat will I pose thee.
Strike him twice on the crown,
    Thrice above the ear;
Pour out his blood like *sap*,
    Like *juice* to his knees.
Let his breath escape like wind,
    His soul like vapor,

---

[1] Aqhat.   [2] Hypocoristicon of, or mistake for, Yatpan.

Like smoke from his nostrils {from nostrils}.[30]
⌈His vigor⌉ I will revive."
—She takes Yatpan *the Drunken Soldier,*
　　Makes him like a vulture in her girdle,
　　Like a swift flier in her pouch.
As Aqhat sits to e[at],
　　The son of Daniel to dine,　　　　　　　　　　　　(30)
Over him vulture[s] soar,
　　A flock of swift flier[s] coasts.
[Among] the vultures soars Anath;
　　Above [Aqhat] she poses him.
He smites him twice [on the crown],
　　Thrice above the ear;
Pou[rs out] his blood [like] *sap,*
　　Like *ju*[*ice* to his knees.
His] breath escapes like wind,
　　His soul [like vapor],
　　Like smoke [from his nostrils].
Anath, [seeing] his vigor extinguished—
　　[The vigor of] Aqhat—doth weep.
"*Woe!* [Would] I could heal [thy corse]!　　　　　　　(40)
'Twas but for [thy bow I slew thee,
　　'Twas but for] thy *darts.*
　　But thou, would thou didst l[ive.
. . .] and perished . . . [. . .]."

AQHT C

(i)

(In the first 13 lines, defective in various degrees, it is only clear that Anath figures there. She is apparently speaking; it is not known to whom.)

　　　　　　　　　　　　　　　　　　　　　　　" . . .
I smote him *but* for his bow,
　　I smote him for his *darts.*
　　So his bow has been given to me.
But *through his death . . . ,*
　　The [*fr*]*uits* of summer *are withered,*
　　The ear [*in*] its husk."—
Straightway Daniel the Rapha-man,　　　　　　　　　　(20)
　　Forthwith Gha*zir* [the Harna]miyy-[man],
*Is up*right, [sitting before the g]at[e,
　　Un]der [a mighty tree on the threshing floor,
Judging] the cause [of the widow,
　　Adjudicating] the case [of the fatherless.
. . .]　　　　　　　　　　(lines 25-28 almost entirely missing)

[Lift]ing her eyes she [1] beholds:
[. . .] on the threshing floors *dries up*;   (30)
   [. . .] *droops*;
   Blasted are the buds [. . .].
O'er her father's house vultures are soaring
   A flock of swift fliers is coasting.
Paghat weeps in her heart,
   Cries in her inward parts.
She rends the garment of Daniel the Rapha-man,
   The vest⟨ment⟩ of Ghazir the Harnamiyy-man. [2]
Straightway Daniel the Rapha-man,
. . . s a cloud in the heat of the *season*;   (40)
   . . . s a cloud raining upon the figs,
   Dew distilling upon the grapes.[3]
"Seven years shall Baal fail,
   Eight the Rider of the Clouds.
No dew,   II Sam. 1:21
   No rain;
No welling-up of the deep, [4]   Gen. 7:11
   No sweetness of Baal's voice. [5]
For rent
Is the garment of Daniel the Rapha-man,
   The vestment of Ghazir [the Harnamiyy-man]."—
Loudly to h[is] daughter he doth cry:

(ii)

"Hearken, Paghat who observes the wat[er],   (50)
   Who studies the dew from the drip,
   Who knows the course of the stars. [6]
Saddle a donkey, harness a jackass.
   Attach my trappings of silver,
   My golden housing."—
She obeys, Paghat who observes the water,
   Who studies the ⌈dew [from the drip]⌉,
   Who knows the course of the stars. ⌈ . . . ⌉
See, she saddles a donkey;
   See, she harnesses a ja⌈ck⌉ass.
See, she lifts up her father,
   Places him on the donkey's back,

[1] Daniel's daughter Paghat.
[2] Because she realizes the blight upon the land must be due to the murder of some innocent person. She has the gift of divination; see below.
[3] In Syria rain sometimes falls in September.
[4] Through springs; What Daniel here either predicts or wishes, David wishes for Gilboa, the scene of Saul and Jonathan's death in battle.
[5] Baal is the god of rain and thunder.
[6] Apparently forms of weather-wisdom bordering on divination.

On the comely back of the jackass.— (60)
Yadinel[1] turns to the *vegetable-patch*;
He sees a *stalk* in the *vegetable-patch*;
Seeing a *stalk* in the *seedbeds*,
H[e embraces] the *stalk* and kisses it:
"Ah, if it may be, *stalk,*
Let the *stalk* grow in the *vegetable-patch*;
Let it grow in the *beds* of the *plants.*
May the hand of Aqhat the Youth gather thee,
Deposit thee in the granary."—
Yadin⌜el⌝⟨l⟩ turns to the *grainfields*;
In the *grainfi[el]ds* he sees a corn-ear;
Seeing an ear in the unwatered land, (70)
He em[braces] the ear and kisses it:
"Ah, if it may be, co[rn-ear],
Let the corn-ear grow in the unwatered land;
Let it grow in the [*beds*] of the *plants.*
May the hand of Aqhat the You[th] gather thee,
Deposit thee in the granary."—
Scarce hath the word left his mouth,
His speech left his lips,
When he lifts up his eyes and they behold:[2]

(Lines 77-89 rather mutilated and obscure. The gist
of them is that somebody finds out what has happened
to Aqhat; either because Paghat sees two supernatural
beings act it out in dumb show, or because two attend-
ants of Daniel hear the tale from the dying boy.)
[. . .] they come.
They lift up [their] voice, [and cry]:
"Hearken, O Daniel the [Rapha]-man! (90)
Aqhat the Youth is dead.
The Maiden Anath [has caused
His breath to escape] like [wind],
His soul like vapor."
[Daniel's legs] tremble.
Abo[ve, his face sweats;
Behind, he is broken] in the loins.
[The joints of his loins are bent],
Weakened [those of his back.[3]
He lifts up his voice] and cri[es:
"*Cursed be*] the slayer [of my son].

(lines 100-104 missing)

---

[1] Apparently variant of "Daniel."
[2] Or "as she (Paghat) lifts up her eyes, she beholds."
[3] He is overcome with dismay.

Lift[ing up his eyes he beholds:
    ... vultures .... .

(iii)

He lifts up his voice] and cries: (107)
"The vultures' wings may Baal bre⟨ak⟩,
    May Ba[a]l br[eak the pinions of them].
Let them fall down at my feet.
    I'll spl[it their bellies and] gaze.   (110)
An there be fat,
    An the[re be] bone,
I'll w⌈ee⌉p and inter it,
    Lay't in the hollows of the ear⌈th⌉-ghosts."
Scarce hath the word left his mouth,
    [His] speech left his lips,
The vultures' wings Baal doth break,
    Baal doth break the pinions of them.
They do fall down at his feet,
    He splits their bellies a[nd gazes]:
No fat is there,
    No bone.
He lifts up his voice and cries:
"The vultures' wings may Baal mend,
    May ⟨Baal⟩ mend the pinions of them.
    Vultures, flutter and fly."   (120)
Lifting his eyes, he s[ees];
    Beholds Hargab, the *vul*tures' father.
He lifts up his voice and cries:
    "The *wi*ngs of Har[ga]b may Baal bre⟨ak⟩,
    May Baal b[re]ak the pinions of [him].
And let him fall down at my feet.
    I'll split [his] b[elly] and gaze.
An there be fat,
    An there be [bone],
I'll weep and inter it,
    Lay't in the *ho*[llo]*ws* of [the earth-ghosts]."
[Scarce hath the word left his mouth],
    His speech [left] his [li]ps,
Hargab's wings Baal doth [br]eak,
    Baal doth break the pinions of him.
He doth fall down at his feet.   (130)
    So he splits his belly and gazes:
No fat is there,
    No bone.

He lifts up [his] voice *and* cries:
"The wings of Hargab may Baal [mend,
　　May Ba]al mend the pinions of him.
　　Hargab, may'st flutter and fly."—
Lifting his eyes he sees,
　　Beholds Samal (*ṣml*), the vultures' mother.
He lifts up his voice and cries:
"The wings of Samal may Baal break,
　　May Baal break the [pi]nions of her.
Let her fall down at my feet.
　　I'll split her belly and gaze.
An there be fat,
　　An there be bone, 　　　　　　　　　　　　(140)
I'll weep and inter it,
　　Lay't in the hollows of the earth-ghosts."
Scarce hath the word [left] his mouth,
　　His speech left his lips,
Samal's wings [Ba]a[l doth break],
　　Baal doth break the pinions of her.
She doth fa[ll down at] his feet.
　　So he splits her belly and gazes.
There is fat,
　　There is bone.
Taking them for Aqhat he ⟨we⟩eps,
　　Weeps and inters him.
He inters him in . . . , in . . . ,
　　Then lifts up his voice and cries:
"The wings of the vultures may Baal break,
　　May Baal break the pinions of them, 　　　(150)
An they fly over the grave of my son,
　　Rousing him from his sleep."—
Qiru-mayim[1] the king doth *curse*:
　　"Woe to thee, O Qiru-mayim,
O[n] which rests the blood-guilt of Aqhat the Youth!
　　. . . the dwellers of the house of El;
Now, *tomorrow*, and for evermore,
　　From now unto all generations!"
Again he waves the staff of his hand,
　　And comes to Marurat-taghullal-banir.[2]
He lifts up his voice and cries:
"Woe to thee, Marurat-taghullal-banir,
　　On which rests the blood-guilt of Aqhat the Youth!

---

[1] Perhaps "Water-Sources." In any case a locality near the scene of the
murder. 　　　　　[2] Perhaps "Blessed One Harnessed with a Yoke."

Thy root grow not in the earth;
    In uprooter's hand droop thy head—   (160)
Now, *tomorrow*, and for evermore,
    From now unto all generations!"
Again he waves the staff of his hand,

(iv)

    And comes to the city of Abelim,
    Abelim the city of Prince Yàrikh.[1]
He lifts up his voice and cries:
"Woe to thee, city of Abelim,
    On which rests the blood-guilt of Aqhat the Youth!
May Baal make thee blind
    From now for evermore,
    From now unto all generations!"
Again he waves the staff of his hand.
    Daniel goes to his house,   (170)
    To his palace Daniel betakes him.
Into his palace come weeping-women,
    Wailing-women into his court *Pẓġm ġr.*[2]
He weeps for Aqhat the Youth,
    Cries for the child, does Daniel the Rapha-man.
From days to months, from months to years,
    Until seven years,
He weeps for Aqhat the Youth,
    Cr[ie]s for the child, does Daniel the [Rapha]-man.
But after seven years,   (180)
    [Daniel] the Rapha-[man] speaks up,
    Ghazir [the Harnamiyy-m]an makes answer.
[He] lifts up his voice and cries:
"De[part], weeping-women, from my pala[ce];
    Wailing-women, from my court *Pẓġm ġr.*"—
He ta[kes] a sacrifice for the gods,
    Offers up a *clan-offering* to heaven,
    The *clan-offering* of Harnamiyy to the stars.
        (three and one-half lines mutilated)
Quoth Paghat who observes the *flowing* water: (190)
"Father has sacrificed to the gods,
    Has offered up a *clan-offering* to heaven,
    The *clan-offering* of Harnamiyy to the stars.
Do thou bless me, so I'll go blessed;
    Beatify me, so I'll go beatified.
I'll slay the slayer of my brother,
    [Destroy] the [de]stroyer of my [si]bling."—

---

[1] The actual home of the murderer; see B i end and B iv.
[2] It has been suggested that this is the proper name of Daniel's court.

[Dani]e[l] the Ra[p]ha-man makes answer:
"With life-breath shall be quickened [Paghat],
    She who observes the water,
Who studies the dew from the drip,   (200)
    Who knows the courses of the stars.
With life-breath she is *invigorated*.
She'll slay the slayer [of her brother],
    Destroy the destroyer of [her] sibling."
... in the sea she bat[hes],
    And stains herself red with murex,   ...
She emerges, dons a youth's raiment,
    Puts a *k*[*nife*] in her sheath,
A sword she puts in her scabbard,
    And o'er all dons woman's garb.
At the rising of Gods' Torch Shapsh,[1]
    Paghat ...   (210)
At the set[ting] of Gods' Torch Shapsh,
    Paghat arriv[es] at the tents.
Word [is b]rought to Yat[pan]:
"*Our hired woman* has entered thy fields,
    [...] has entered the *t⟨e⟩nts*."
And Yatpan *the Drunken Soldier* makes answer:
    "Take her and let her give me wine to drink.
[Let her place] the cup in my hand,
    The goblet in my right hand."
Paghat [t]akes and gives him drink:
    Pl[aces the cup] in his hand,
    The goblet in his right hand.
Then spake Yat[pa]n *the Drunken* [*Sold*]*ier*:
    (one and one-half lines partly defective and obscure)
"The hand that slew [Aqha]t the Youth   (220b)
    Can slay thousands of foes."
    (Two and one-half lines obscure, except that Paghat's
"heart is like a serpent's," i.e. filled with fury.)
A second time she gives the mixture to him to drink,
    Gives the [mi]xt[ure] to drink   (224)
(Direction to the reciter, along the edge to the left of
172-186:) Here one proceeds to tell about the daughter.
    (The story, continuing on one or more missing tab-
lets, no doubt went on to relate that [a] Paghat killed
Yatpan while he lay unconscious in the arms of Bacchus,
and [b] between El's pity and Anath's remorse some
modus was found for restoring Aqhat to his father,
perhaps only for half—the fertile half—of the year.
The familiar Adonis-Tammuz theme.)   [1] The sun-goddess.

V. Legal Texts

Collections of Laws from Mesopotamia

THE LAWS OF ESHNUNNA ANET, 161-163

TRANSLATOR: ALBRECHT GOETZE

Texts: Iraq Museum 51059 and 52614 excavated at Tell Abu Harmal[1] near Baghdad by the Iraq Directorate of Antiquities in Pre-Hammurabi layers.

1: 1 kor of barley is (priced) at 1 shekel of silver; 3 *qa* of "best oil" are (priced) at 1 shekel of silver; 1 seah (and) 2 *qa* of sesame oil are (priced) at 1 shekel of silver; 1 seah (and) 5 *qa* of lard are (priced) at 1 shekel of silver; 4 seah of "river oil" are (priced) at 1 shekel of silver; 6 minas of wool are (priced) at 1 shekel of silver; 2 kor of salt are (priced) at 1 shekel of silver; 1 kor . . . is (priced) at 1 shekel of silver; 3 minas of copper are (priced) at 1 shekel of silver; 2 minas of refined copper are (priced) at 1 shekel of silver.

2: 1 *qa* of sesame oil *ša nishātim*—its (value in) barley is 3 seah; 1 *qa* of lard *ša nishātim*—its (value in) barley is 2 seah and 5 *qa*; 1 *qa* of "river oil" *ša nishātim*—its (value in) barley is 8 *qa*.

3: The hire for a wagon together with its oxen and its driver is 1 pan (and) 4 seah of barley. If it is (paid in) silver, the hire is one third of a shekel. He shall drive it the whole day.

4: The hire for a boat is 2 *qa* per kor (of capacity), 1 seah 1 *qa* is the hire for the boatman. He shall drive it the whole day.

5: If the boatman is negligent and causes the sinking of the boat, he shall pay in full for everything the sinking of which he caused.

6: If a man . . .[2] takes possession of a boat (which is) not his, he shall pay 10 shekels of silver.

7: The wages of a harvester are 2 seah of barley; if they are (paid in) silver, his wages are 12 grain.

8: The wages of winnowers are 1 seah of barley.

---

[1] Abu Harmal formed part of the kingdom of Eshnunna—the Diyala region east of Baghdad—which flourished between the downfall of the Third Dynasty of Ur (about 2000 B.C.) and the creation of Hammurabi's empire. Eshnunna was one of the numerous Amurrite-controlled states of the period. The city of Eshnunna itself is located at Tell Asmar which was excavated by the Oriental Institute of the University of Chicago.

[2] Possibly "(who finds himself) in *great peril*."

9: Should a man pay 1 shekel of silver to a hired man for harvesting—if he (the hired man) does not place himself at his disposal and does not complete for him the harvest work everywhere, he [shall p]ay 10 shekels of silver. Should he have received 1 seah (and) 5 *qa* (of barley) as wages and leave the rations of [barley], oil (and) cloth shall also be refunded.

10: The hire for a donkey is 1 seah of barley, and the wages for its driver are 1 seah of barley. He shall drive it the whole day.

11: The wages of a hired man are 1 shekel of silver; his provender is 1 pan of barley. He shall work for one month.

12: A man who is caught in the field of a *muškēnum*[1] in the *crop* during daytime, shall pay 10 shekels of silver. He who is caught in the *crop* [at ni]ght, shall die, he shall not get away alive.

13: A man who is caught in the house of a *muškēnum*, in the house, during daytime, shall pay 10 shekels of silver. He who is caught in the house at night, shall die, he shall not get away alive.

14: The fee of a . . .[2]—should he bring 5 shekels of silver the fee is 1 shekel of silver; should he bring 10 shekels of silver the fee is 2 shekels of silver.

15: The *tamkarrum*[3] and the *sabītum*[4] shall not receive silver, barley, wool (or) sesame oil from a slave or a slave-girl *as an investment*.

16: To a coparcener or a slave a mortgage cannot be furnished.

17: Should the son of a man bring bride-money to the house of (his) father-in-law—, if one of the two deceases, the money shall revert to its owner.

18: If he takes her (the girl) and she enters his house, but *afterward* the young woman should decease, he (the husband) can not obtain refunded that which he brought (to his father-in-law), but will retain the excess (in) his (hand).

18A: Per 1 shekel (of silver) there will accrue ⅙ shekel and 6 grain as interest; per 1 kor (of barley) there will accrue 1 pan and 4 seah as interest.

---

[1] The *muškēnum* is a member of a social class which at Eshnunna seems to be closely connected with the palace or the temple.
[2] The word must denote some kind of "money-lender" or "merchant."
[3] The official "finance officer" who has a state monopoly on certain commercial transactions. [4] The woman to whom trade in liquor is entrusted.

19: The man who gives (a loan) in terms of his retake shall make (the debtor) pay on the threshing floor.

20: If a man gives a loan ... expressing the value of the silver in barley, he shall at harvest time receive the barley and its interest, 1 pan (and) 4(?) seah per kor.

21: If a man gives silver (as a loan) *at face value*, he shall receive the silver and its interest, one sixth (of a shekel) and [6 grain] per shekel.

22: If a man has no claim against a(nother) man, but (nevertheless) distrains the (other) man's slave-girl, the owner of the slave-girl shall [decla]re under oath: "Thou hast no claim against me" and he shall pay (him) silver in full compensation for the slave-girl.

23: If a man has no claim against a(nother) man, but (nevertheless) distrains the (other) man's slave-girl, detains the distrainee in his house and causes (her) death, he shall give two slave-girls to the owner of the slave-girl as a replacement.

24: If he has no claim against him, but (nevertheless) distrains the wife of a *muškēnum* (or) the child of a *muškēnum* and causes (their) death, it is a capital offence. The distrainer who distrained shall die.

25: If a man calls at the house of (his) father-in-law, and his father-in-law *accepts* him *in servitude*, but (nevertheless) gives his daughter to [another man], the father of the girl shall refund the bride-money which he received twofold.

26: If a man gives bride-money for a(nother) man's daughter, but another man seizes her forcibly without asking the permission of her father and her mother and deprives her of her virginity, it is a capital offence and he shall die.

27: If a man takes a(nother) man's daughter without asking the permission of her father and her mother and concludes no formal marriage contract with her father and her mother, even though she may live in his house for a year, she is not a housewife.

28: *On the other hand*, if he concludes a formal contract with her father and her mother and cohabits with her, she is a housewife. When she is caught with a(nother) man, she shall die, she shall not get away alive.

29: If a man has been made prisoner during a raid or an invasion or (if) he has been carried off forcibly and [stayed in] a foreign [count]ry for a [long] time, (and if) another man has taken his wife and she has born him a son—when he returns, he shall [get] his wife back.

30: If a man hates his town and his lord and becomes a fugitive, (and if) another man takes his wife—when he returns, he shall have no right to claim his wife.

31: If a man deprives another man's slave-girl of her virginity, he shall pay one-third of a mina of silver; the slave-girl remains the property of her owner.

32: If a man gives his son (away) for having (him) nursed and brought up, but does not give (the nurse) rations of barley, oil (and) wool for three years, he shall pay (her) 10 minas (of silver) for bringing up his son and shall take back his son.

33: If a slave-girl by subterfuge gives her child to a(nother) man's daughter, (if) its lord sees it when it has become older, he may seize it and take it back.

34: If a slave-girl of the palace gives her son or her daughter to a *muškēnum* for bringing (him/her) up, the palace may take back the son or the daughter whom she gave.

35: Also the adoptant of the child of a slave-girl of the palace shall recompense the palace with its equivalent.

36: If a man gives property of his as a deposit to . . . and if the property he gives disappears without that the house was burglarized, the *sippu*[1] broken down (or) the window forced, he (the depositary) will replace his (the depositor's) property.

37: If the man's (the depositary's) house either collapses or is burglarized and together with the (property of the) deposit(or) which he gave him loss on the part of the owner of the house is incurred, the owner of the house shall swear him an oath in the gate of Tishpak[2] (saying): "Together with your property my property was lost; I have done nothing *improper* or fraudulent." If he swears him (such an oath), he shall have no claim against him.

38: If one of several brothers wants to sell his share (in a property common to them) and his brother wants to buy it, he shall pay. . . .[3]

39: If a man is hard up and sells his house, the owner of the house shall (be entitled to) redeem (it) whenever the purchaser (re)sells it.

---

[1] Part of the house at or near the door. [2] The main god of Eshnunna.
[3] This expression seems to imply a preferential treatment.

40: If a man buys a slave, a slave-girl, an ox or any other valuable good but cannot (legally) establish the seller, he is a thief.

41: If an *ubarum*, a *naptarum* or a *mudūm*[1] wants to sell his beer, the *sabītum* shall sell the beer for him at the current price.

42: If a man bites the nose of a(nother) man and severs it, he shall pay 1 mina of silver. (For) an eye (he shall pay) 1 mina of silver; (for) a tooth ½ mina; (for) an ear ½ mina; (for) a slap in the face 10 shekels of silver.

43: If a man severs a(nother) man's finger, he shall pay two-thirds of a mina of silver.

44: If a man throws a(nother) man to the floor in an *altercation* and breaks his *hand*, he shall pay ½ mina of silver.

45: If he breaks his foot, he shall pay ½ mina of silver.

46: If a man assaults a(nother) man and breaks his ..., he shall pay two-thirds of a mina of silver.

47: If a man *hits* a(nother) man *accidentally*, he shall pay 10 shekels of silver.

48: And in *addition*, (in cases involving penalties) from two-thirds of a mina to 1 mina, they shall formally try the man. A capital offence comes before the king.

49: If a man is caught with a stolen slave (or) a stolen slave-girl, he shall surrender slave by slave (and) slave-girl by slave-girl.

50: If the governor, the river commissioner (or) an-(other) official whoever it may be seizes a lost slave, a lost slave-girl, a lost ox, a lost donkey belonging to the palace or a *muškēnum* and does not surrender it to Eshnunna but keeps it in his house, even though he may let pass only seven days, the palace shall prosecute him for theft.

51: A slave or a slave-girl of Eshnunna which is marked with a *kannum*, a *maškanum* or an *abbuttum* [2] shall not leave the gate of Eshnunna without its owner's permission.

52: A slave or a slave-girl which has entered the gate of Eshnunna in the custody of a (foreign) envoy shall be marked with a *kannum*, a *maškanum* or an *abbuttum* but remains in the custody of its master.

---

[1] Social classes who seem to be entitled to a ration of beer.
[2] Markings that can easily be removed.

53: If an ox gores an(other) ox and causes (its) death, both ox owners shall divide (among themselves) the price of the live ox and also the equivalent of the dead ox.

54: If an ox is known to gore habitually and the authorities have brought the fact to the knowledge of its owner, but he does not have his ox *dehorned*, it gores a man and causes (his) death, then the owner of the ox shall pay two-thirds of a mina of silver.

55: If it gores a slave and causes (his) death, he shall pay 15 shekels of silver.

56: If a dog is vicious and the authorities have brought the fact to the knowledge of its owner, (if nevertheless) he does not keep it in, it bites a man and causes (his) death, then the owner of the dog shall pay two-thirds of a mina of silver.

57: If it bites a slave and causes (its) death, he shall pay 15 shekels of silver.

58: If a wall is threatening to fall and the authorities have brought the fact to the knowledge of its owner, (if nevertheless) he does not strengthen his wall, the wall collapses and causes a free man's death, then it is a capital offence; jurisdiction of the king.

59: If a man divorces his wife after having made her bear children and takes [ano]ther wife, he shall be driven from his house and from whatever he owns and may go after him who will accept him.

(60 and 61 badly mutilated and therefore incomprehensible)

The Code of Hammurabi

ANET, 163-164, 166-177

TRANSLATOR: THEOPHILE J. MEEK

Hammurabi (also spelled Hammurapi) was the sixth of eleven kings in the Old Babylonian (Amorite) Dynasty. He ruled for 43 years, from 1728 to 1686 according to the most recent calculations. The date-formula for his second year, "The year he enacted the law of the land," indicates that he promulgated his famous lawcode at the very beginning of his reign, but the copy which we have could not have been written so early because the Prologue refers to events much later than this. Our copy was *Fig. 59* written on a diorite stela, topped by a bas-relief showing Hammurabi in the act of receiving the commission to write the lawbook from the god of justice, the sun-god Shamash. The stela was carried off to the old Elamite capital, Susa (the Shushan of Esther and Daniel), by some Elamite raider (apparently Shutruk-Nahhunte, about 1207-1171 B.C.) as a trophy of war.

It was discovered there by French archaeologists in the winter of 1901-1902 and was carried off by them to the Louvre in Paris as a trophy of archaeology. All the laws from col. xvi 77 to the end of the obverse (from the end of §65 to the beginning of §100) were chiseled off by the Elamites, but these have been preserved in large part on other copies of the Code.

The Laws

1: If a seignior[1] accused a(nother) seignior and brought a charge of murder against him, but has not proved it, his accuser shall be put to death.

Deut. 5:20; 19:16-21; Exod. 23:1-3

2: If a seignior brought a charge of sorcery against a(nother) seignior, but has not proved it, the one against whom the charge of sorcery was brought, upon going to the river,[2] shall throw himself into the river, and if the river has then overpowered him, his accuser shall take over his estate; if the river has shown that seignior to be innocent and he has accordingly come forth safe, the one who brought the charge of sorcery against him shall be put to death, while the one who threw himself into the river shall take over the estate of his accuser.

3: If a seignior came forward with false testimony in a case, and has not proved the word which he spoke, if that case was a case involving life, that seignior shall be put to death.

4: If he came forward with (false) testimony concerning grain or money, he shall bear the penalty of that case.

5: If a judge gave a judgment, rendered a decision, deposited a sealed document, but later has altered his judgment, they shall prove that that judge altered the judgment which he gave and he shall pay twelvefold the claim which holds in that case; furthermore, they shall expel him in the assembly from his seat of judgment and he shall never again sit with the judges in a case.

Fig. 57

6: If a seignior stole the property of church or state, that seignior shall be put to death; also the one who received the stolen goods from his hand shall be put to death.

---

[1] *awēlum* seems to be used in at least three senses: (1) sometimes to indicate a man of the higher class, a noble; (2) sometimes a free man of any class, high or low; and (3) occasionally a man of any class, from king to slave I follow the ambiguity of the original and use the rather general term "seignior," as employed in Italian and Spanish, to indicate any free man of standing.

[2] The river (the Euphrates) as judge in the case was regarded as god.

7: If a seignior has purchased or he received for safe-keeping either silver or gold or a male slave or a female slave or an ox or a sheep or an ass or any sort of thing from the hand of a seignior's son or a seignior's slave without witnesses and contracts, since that seignior is a thief, he shall be put to death.

8: If a seignior stole either an ox or a sheep or an ass or a pig or a boat, if it belonged to the church (or) if it belonged to the state, he shall make thirtyfold restitution; if it belonged to a private citizen,[1] he shall make good tenfold. If the thief does not have sufficient to make restitution, he shall be put to death.

Exod. 20:15; Deut. 5:19; 22:1-4; Lev. 19:11, 13

9: When a seignior, (some of) whose property was lost, has found his lost property in the possession of a(nother) seignior, if the seignior in whose possession the lost (property) was found has declared, "A seller sold (it) to me; I made the purchase in the presence of witnesses," and the owner of the lost (property) in turn has declared, "I will produce witnesses attesting to my lost (property)"; the purchaser having then produced the seller who made the sale to him and the witnesses in whose presence he made the purchase, and the owner of the lost (property) having also produced the witnesses attesting to his lost (property), the judges shall consider their evidence, and the witnesses in whose presence the purchase was made, along with the witnesses attesting to the lost (property), shall declare what they know in the presence of god, and since the seller was the thief, he shall be put to death, while the owner of the lost (property) shall take his lost (property), with the purchaser obtaining from the estate of the seller the money that he paid out.[2]

10: If the (professed) purchaser has not produced the seller who made the sale to him and the witnesses in whose presence he made the purchase, but the owner of the lost property has produced witnesses attesting to his lost property, since the (professed) purchaser was the thief, he shall be put to death, while the owner of the lost property shall take his lost property.

11: If the (professed) owner of the lost property has not produced witnesses attesting to his lost property,

---

[1] Ordinarily indicates a man of the middle class, a commoner, but here it manifestly refers to a private citizen as distinct from the church and state.

[2] In the time of Hammurabi coinage had of course not yet been invented and the money (usually silver, as here) was weighed out in bars.

since he was a cheat and started a false report, he shall be put to death.

12: If the seller has gone to (his) fate, the purchaser shall take from the estate of the seller fivefold the claim for that case.

13: If the witnesses of that seignior were not at hand, the judges shall set a time-limit of six months for him, and if he did not produce his witnesses within six months, since that seignior was a cheat, he shall bear the penalty of that case.

14: If a seignior has stolen the young son of a(nother) seignior, he shall be put to death.

Exod. 21:16; Deut. 24:7

15: If a seignior has helped either a male slave of the state or a female slave of the state or a male slave of a private citizen or a female slave of a private citizen to escape through the city-gate, he shall be put to death.

16: If a seignior has harbored in his house either a fugitive male or female slave belonging to the state or to a private citizen and has not brought him forth at the summons of the police, that householder shall be put to death.

17: If a seignior caught a fugitive male or female slave in the open and has taken him to his owner, the owner of the slave shall pay him two shekels[1] of silver.

18: If that slave has not named his owner, he shall take him to the palace in order that his record may be investigated, and they shall return him to his owner.

19: If he has kept that slave in his house (and) later the slave has been found in his possession, that seignior shall be put to death.

20: If the slave has escaped from the hand of his captor, that seignior shall (so) affirm by god to the owner of the slave and he shall then go free.

21: If a seignior made a breach in a house, they shall put him to death in front of that breach and wall him in.

Exod. 22:2-3

22: If a seignior committed robbery and has been caught, that seignior shall be put to death.

23: If the robber has not been caught, the robbed seignior shall set forth the particulars regarding his lost property in the presence of god, and the city and governor, in whose territory and district the robbery was committed, shall make good to him his lost property.

---

[1] A weight of about 8 gr.

Deut. 21:1 ff.

24: If it was a life (that was lost), the city and governor shall pay one mina[1] of silver to his people.

25: If fire broke out in a seignior's house and a seignior, who went to extinguish (it), cast his eye on the goods of the owner of the house and has appropriated the goods of the owner of the house, that seignior shall be thrown into that fire.

26: If either a private soldier or a commissary,[2] whose despatch on a campaign of the king was ordered, did not go or he hired a substitute and has sent (him) in his place, that soldier or commissary shall be put to death, while the one who was hired by him shall take over his estate.

27: In the case of either a private soldier or a commissary who was carried off while in the armed service of the king, if after his (disappearance) they gave his field and orchard to another and he has looked after his feudal obligations—if he has returned and reached his city, they shall restore his field and orchard to him and he shall himself look after his feudal obligations.

28: In the case of either a private soldier or a commissary, who was carried off while in the armed service of the king, if his son is able to look after the feudal obligations, the field and orchard shall be given to him and he shall look after the feudal obligations of his father.

29: If his son is so young that he is not able to look after the feudal obligations of his father, one-third of the field and orchard shall be given to his mother in order that his mother may rear him.

30: If either a private soldier or a commissary gave up his field, orchard and house on account of the feudal obligations and has then absented himself, (and) after his (departure) another took over his field, orchard and house and has looked after the feudal obligations for three years—if he has returned and demands his field, orchard and house, they shall not be given to him; the one who has taken over and looked after his feudal obligations shall himself become the feudatory.

31: If he has absented himself for only one year and has returned, his field, orchard and house shall be

---

[1] About 500 gr., divided into 60 shekels.

[2] The exact meaning of the two military terms used here, *redum* and *ba'irum*, is uncertain. The former means literally "follower" and is regularly used for the ordinary foot-soldier; the latter means literally "fisher, hunter," hence "commissary" here.

given back to him and he shall look after his feudal obligations himself.

32: If a merchant has ransomed either a private soldier or a commissary, who was carried off in a campaign of the king, and has enabled him to reach his city, if there is sufficient to ransom (him) in his house, he himself shall ransom himself; if there is not sufficient to ransom him in his house, he shall be ransomed from the estate of his city-god; if there is not sufficient to ransom him in the estate of his city-god, the state shall ransom him, since his own field, orchard and house may not be ceded for his ransom.

33: If either a sergeant or a captain has obtained a soldier by conscription or he accepted and has sent a hired substitute for a campaign of the king, that sergeant or captain shall be put to death.

34: If either a sergeant or a captain has appropriated the household goods of a soldier, has wronged a soldier, has let a soldier for hire, has abandoned a soldier to a superior in a lawsuit, has appropriated the grant which the king gave to a soldier, that sergeant or captain shall be put to death.

35: If a seignior has bought from the hand of a soldier the cattle or sheep which the king gave to the soldier, he shall forfeit his money.

36: In no case is the field, orchard, or house belonging to a soldier, a commissary, or a feudatory[1] salable.

37: If a seignior has purchased the field, orchard, or house belonging to a soldier, a commissary, or a feudatory, his contract-tablet shall be broken and he shall also forfeit his money, with the field, orchard, or house reverting to its owner.

38: In no case may a soldier, a commissary, or a feudatory deed any of his field, orchard, or house belonging to his fief to his wife or daughter, and in no case may he assign (them) for an obligation of his.

39: He may deed to his wife or daughter any of the field, orchard, or house which he purchases and accordingly owns,[2] and he may assign (them) for an obligation of his.

40: A hierodule,[3] a merchant, and a feudatory extraordinary may sell his field, orchard and house, with

---

[1] Or, officers of some sort.   [2] i.e. in fee simple and not as a fief.
[3] The exact meaning of the term used here, *naditum*, is unknown, but it ᐧdicates some kind of religious functionary.

the purchaser assuming the feudal obligations of the field, orchard and house which he purchases.

41: If a seignior acquired by barter the field, orchard, or house belonging to a soldier, a commissary, or a feudatory, and also made an additional payment, the soldier, commissary, or feudatory shall repossess his field, orchard, or house, and he shall also keep the additional payment that was made to him.

42: If a seignior rented a field for cultivation, but has not produced grain in the field, they shall prove that he did no work on the field and he shall give grain to the owner of the field on the basis of those adjoining it.

43: If he did not cultivate the field, but has neglected (it), he shall give grain to the owner of the field on the basis of those adjoining it; furthermore, the field which he neglected he shall break up with mattocks, harrow and return to the owner of the field.

44: If a seignior rented a fallow field for three years for development, but became so lazy that he has not developed the field, in the fourth year he shall break up the field with mattocks, plow and harrow (it), and he shall return (it) to the owner of the field; furthermore, he shall measure out ten *kur*[1] of grain per eighteen *iku*.[2]

45: If a seignior let his field to a tenant and has already received the rent of his field, (and) later Adad has inundated the field or a flood has ravaged (it), the loss shall be the tenant's.

46: If he has not received the rent of the field, whether he let the field for one-half or one-third (the crop), the tenant and the owner of the field shall divide proportionately the grain which is produced in the field.

47: If the tenant has asked (another) to cultivate the field because he did not get back his investment in the previous year, the owner of the field shall not object; his (new) tenant shall cultivate his field and at harvest-time he shall take grain in accordance with his contracts.

48: If a debt is outstanding against a seignior and Adad has inundated his field or a flood has ravaged (it) or through lack of water grain has not been produced in the field, he shall not make any return of

---

[1] A measure equal to a little more than 7 bushels, divided into 300 *qu*.
[2] A land measure equal to about ⅞ of an acre.

grain to his creditor   in that year; he shall cancel[1] his contract-tablet and he shall pay no interest for that year.

49: When a seignior borrowed money from a merchant and pledged to the merchant a field prepared for grain or sesame, if he said to him, "Cultivate the field, then harvest (and) take the grain or sesame that is produced," if the tenant has produced grain or sesame in the field, the owner of the field at harvest-time shall himself take the grain or sesame that was produced in the field and he shall give to the merchant grain for his money, which he borrowed from the merchant, together with its interest, and also for the cost of cultivation.

50: If he pledged a field planted with ⟨grain⟩ or a field planted with sesame, the owner of the field shall himself take the grain or sesame that was produced in the field and he shall pay back the money with its interest to the merchant.

51: If he does not have the money to pay back, ⟨grain or⟩ sesame at their market value in accordance with the ratio fixed by the king[2] he shall give to the merchant for his money, which he borrowed from the merchant, together with its interest.

52: If the tenant has not produced grain or sesame in the field, he may not change his contract.

53: If a seignior was too lazy to make [the dike of] his field strong and did not make his dike strong and a break has opened up in his dike and he has accordingly let the water ravage the farmland, the seignior in whose dike the break was opened shall make good the grain that he let get destroyed.

54: If he is not able to make good the grain, they shall sell him and his goods, and the farmers whose grain the water carried off shall divide (the proceeds).

55: If a seignior, upon opening his canal for irrigation, became so lazy that he has let the water ravage a field adjoining his, he shall measure out grain on the basis of those adjoining his.

56: If a seignior opened up the water and then has let the water carry off the work done on a field adjoining his, he shall measure out ten *kur* of grain per eighteen *iku*.

---

[1] Lit., "he shall wash off."
[2] In ancient Mesopotamia the ratio between silver (the money of the time) and various commodities was fixed by the state.

57: If a shepherd has not come to an agreement with the owner of a field to pasture sheep on the grass, but has pastured sheep on the field without the consent of the owner of the field, when the owner of the field harvests his field, the shepherd who pastured the sheep on the field without the consent of the owner of the field shall give in addition twenty *kur* of grain per eighteen *iku* to the owner of the field.

58: If after the sheep have gone up from the meadow, when the whole flock has been shut up within the city-gate,[1] the shepherd drove the sheep into a field and has then pastured the sheep on the field, the shepherd shall look after the field on which he pastured and at harvest-time he shall measure out sixty *kur* of grain per eighteen *iku* to the owner of the field.

59: If a seignior cut down a tree in a(nother) seignior's orchard without the consent of the owner of the orchard, he shall pay one-half mina of silver.

60: If, when a seignior gave a field to a gardener to set out an orchard, the gardener set out the orchard, he shall develop the orchard for four years; in the fifth year the owner of the orchard and the gardener shall divide equally, with the owner of the orchard receiving his preferential share.

Lev. 19:23-25

61: If the gardener did not set out the whole field, but left a portion bare, they shall assign the bare portion to him as his share.

62: If he did not set out, the field that was given to him as an orchard, if it was a cultivated field, the gardener shall pay [2] to the owner of the field rent for the field for the years that it was neglected on the basis of those adjoining it; also he shall do the (necessary) work on the field and return (it) to the owner of the field.

63: If it was fallow land, he shall do the (necessary) work on the field and return (it) to the owner of the field; also he shall measure out ten *kur* of grain per eighteen *iku* for each year.

64: If a seignior gave his orchard to a gardener to pollinate,[3] the gardener shall give to the owner of the orchard two-thirds of the produce of the orchard as rent

---

[1] The reference to the city-gate evidently reflects the Near Eastern custom in both ancient and modern times of bringing the sheep into the shelter of the town or village at night.

[2] Lit., "measure out," indicating that the rent was to be paid in grain.

[3] The orchard was a date orchard (see §66) and hence had to be artificially fertilized.

of the orchard as long as the orchard is held, with himself taking one-third.

65: If the gardener did not pollinate the orchard and so has let the yield decline, the gardener [shall measure out] rent for the orchard on the basis of those adjoining it.

66: When a seignior borrowed money from a merchant and his merchant foreclosed on him and he has nothing to pay (it) back, if he gave his orchard after pollination to the merchant and said to him, "Take for your money as many dates as there are produced in the orchard," that merchant shall not be allowed; the owner of the orchard shall himself take the dates that were produced in the orchard and repay the merchant for the money and its interest in accordance with the wording of his tablet and the owner of the orchard shall in turn take the remaining dates that were produced in the orchard.

67: If a seignior built a house, his neighbor. . . .

68: f.: (not preserved)

70: . . . he shall give to him.

71: If he is giving grain, money, or goods for a fief estate belonging to an estate adjoining his, which he wishes to purchase, he shall forfeit whatever he paid, while the estate shall revert to its [owner]. If that estate does not carry feudal obligations, he may purchase (it), since he may give grain, money, or goods for such an estate.

72-77: (Only a few words preserved, having to do with house building.)

78: [If a seignior let a house to a(nother) seignior and] the seignior (who was) the tenant paid his rental money in full for the year to the owner of [the house] and the owner of the house has then said to the [tenant] while his term was (still) incomplete, "Move out," the owner of the house [shall forfeit] the money which the tenant paid to him [because] he made the tenant [move out] of his house while his term was (still) incomplete.

79-87: (not preserved)

88: If a merchant [lent] grain at interest, he shall receive sixty *qu* of grain per *kur* as interest.[1] If he lent money at interest, he shall receive one-sixth (shekel)

---

[1] Since there were 300 *qu* in a *kur*, the interest rate was 20%.

six *še* (i.e. one-fifth shekel) per shekel of silver as interest.[1]

89: If a seignior, who [incurred] a debt, does not have the money to pay (it) back, but has the grain, [the merchant] shall take grain for his money [with its interest] in accordance with the ratio fixed by the king.

90: If the merchant increased the interest beyond [sixty *qu*] per *kur* [of grain] (or) one-sixth (shekel) six *še* [per shekel of money] and has collected (it), he shall forfeit whatever he lent.

91: If a merchant [lent] grain at interest and has collected money [for the full interest] on the grain, the grain along with the money may not [*be charged to the account*].

92: (not preserved)

93: [If the merchant] . . . or he has not had the full amount of grain [which he received] deducted and did not write a new contract, or he has added the interest to the principal, that merchant shall pay back double the full amount of grain that he received.

94: If a merchant lent grain or money at interest and when he lent (it) at interest he paid out the money by the small weight and the grain by the small measure, but when he got (it) back he got the money by the [large] weight (and) the grain by the large measure, [that merchant shall forfeit] whatever he lent.

95: If a [merchant lent grain or money] at interest and gave . . . , he shall forfeit whatever he lent.

96: If a seignior borrowed grain or money from a merchant and does not have the grain or money to pay (it) back, but has (other) goods, he shall give to his merchant whatever there is in his possession, (affirming) before witnesses that he will bring (it), while the merchant shall accept (it) without making any objections.

97: . . . , he shall be put to death.

98: If a seignior gave money to a(nother) seignior for a partnership, they shall divide equally in the presence of god the profit or loss which was incurred.

99: If a merchant lent money at interest to a trader [2] for the purpose of trading [and making purchases] and sent him out on the road, the trader shall . . . on the road [the money which was entrusted] to him.

---

[1] Since there were 180 *še* in a shekel, the interest rate was again 20%.
[2] i.e. a traveling salesman peddling his wares.

100: If he has realized a profit where he went, he shall write down the interest on the full amount of money that he borrowed and they shall count up the days against him and he shall repay his merchant.

101: If he has not realized a profit where he went, the trader shall repay to the merchant double the money that he borrowed.

102: If a merchant has lent money to a trader as a favor[1] and he has experienced a loss where he went, he shall pay back the principal of the money to the merchant.

103: If, when he went on the road, an enemy has made him give up whatever he was carrying, the trader shall (so) affirm by god and then he shall go free.

104: If a merchant lent grain, wool, oil, or any goods at all to a trader to retail, the trader shall write down the value and pay (it) back to the merchant, with the trader obtaining a sealed receipt for the money which he pays to the merchant.

105: If the trader has been careless and so has not obtained a sealed receipt for the money which he paid to the merchant, the money with no sealed receipt may not be credited to the account.

106: If a trader borrowed money from a merchant and has then disputed (the fact) with his merchant, that merchant in the presence of god and witnesses shall prove that the trader borrowed the money and the trader shall pay to the merchant threefold the full amount of money that he borrowed.

107: When a merchant entrusted (something) to a trader and the trader has returned to his merchant whatever the merchant gave him, if the merchant has then disputed with him whatever the trader gave him, that trader shall prove it against the merchant in the presence of god and witnesses and the merchant shall pay to the trader sixfold whatever he received because he had a dispute with his trader.

108: If a woman wine seller, instead of receiving grain for the price of a drink, has received money by the large weight and so has made the value of the drink less than the value of the grain, they shall prove it against that wine seller and throw her into the water.

109: If outlaws have congregated in the establishment of a woman wine seller and she has not arrested those

---

[1] i.e. without interest.

outlaws and did not take them to the palace, that wine seller shall be put to death.

110: If a hierodule, a nun,[1] who is not living in a convent, has opened (the door of) a wineshop or has entered a wineshop for a drink, they shall burn that woman.

111: If a woman wine seller gave one (flask) of *pīḫum*-drink on credit, she shall receive fifty *qu*[2] of grain at harvest-time.

112: When a seignior was engaged in a (trading) journey and gave silver, gold, (precious) stones, or (other) goods in his possession to a(nother) seignior and consigned (them) to him for transport, if that seignior did not deliver whatever was to be transported where it was to be transported, but has appropriated (it), the owner of the goods to be transported shall prove the charge against that seignior in the matter of whatever was to be transported, but which he did not deliver, and that seignior shall pay to the owner of the goods to be transported fivefold whatever was given to him.

113: If a seignior held (a debt of) grain or money against a(nother) seignior and he has then taken grain from the granary or threshing floor without the consent of the owner of the grain, they shall prove that that seignior took grain from the granary or threshing floor without the consent of the owner of the grain and he shall return the full amount of grain that he took and he shall also forfeit everything else that he lent.

114: If a seignior did not hold (a debt of) grain or money against a(nother) seignior, but has distrained (someone as) his pledge, he shall pay one-third mina of silver for each distraint.

115: If a seignior held (a debt of) grain or money against a(nother) seignior and distrained (someone as) his pledge and the pledge has then died a natural death in the house of his distrainer, that case is not subject to claim.

116: If the pledge has died from beating or abuse in the house of his distrainer, the owner of the pledge shall prove it against his merchant, and if it was the seignior's son, they shall put his son to death; if it was the seignior's slave, he shall pay one-third mina of silver and also forfeit everything else that he lent.

[1] The ideogram means literally "lady of a god."
[2] A measure equal to a little more than ¾ of a quart, dry measure.

117: If an obligation came due against a seignior and he sold (the services of) his wife, his son, or his daughter, or he has been bound over to service, they shall work (in) the house of their purchaser or obligee for three years, with their freedom reestablished in the fourth year.

Exod. 21:2-11; Deut. 15:12-18

118: When a male slave or a female slave has been bound over to service, if the merchant foreclosed, he may sell (him), with no possibility of his being reclaimed.

119: If an obligation came due against a seignior and he has accordingly sold (the services of) his female slave who bore him children, the owner of the female slave may repay the money which the merchant paid out and thus redeem his female slave.

120: If a seignior deposited his grain in a(nother) seignior's house for storage and a loss has then occurred at the granary or the owner of the house opened the storage-room and took grain or he has denied completely (the receipt of) the grain which was stored in his house, the owner of the grain shall set forth the particulars regarding his grain in the presence of god and the owner of the house shall give to the owner of the grain double the grain that he took.

Exod. 22:7-9

121: If a seignior stored grain in a(nother) seignior's house, he shall pay five *qu* of grain per *kur* of grain[1] as the storage-charge per year.

122: If a seignior wishes to give silver, gold, or any sort of thing to a(nother) seignior for safekeeping, he shall show to witnesses the full amount that he wishes to give, arrange the contracts, and then commit (it) to safekeeping.

123: If he gave (it) for safekeeping without witnesses and contracts and they have denied (its receipt) to him at the place where he made the deposit, that case is not subject to claim.

124: If a seignior gave silver, gold, or any sort of thing for safekeeping to a(nother) seignior in the presence of witnesses and he has denied (the fact) to him, they shall prove it against that seignior and he shall pay double whatever he denied.

125: If a seignior deposited property of his for safekeeping and at the place where he made the deposit his

[1] 1 2/3% since there were 300 *qu* in a *kur*.

property has disappeared along with the property of the owner of the house, either through breaking in or through scaling (the wall), the owner of the house, who was so careless that he let whatever was given to him for safekeeping get lost, shall make (it) good and make restitution to the owner of the goods, while the owner of the house shall make a thorough search for his lost property and take (it) from its thief.

126: If the seignior's property was not lost, but he has declared, "My property is lost," thus deceiving his city council, his city council shall set forth the facts regarding him in the presence of god, that his property was not lost, and he shall give to his city council double whatever he laid claim to.

Ruth 3:11; 4:10

127: If a seignior pointed the finger at a nun or the wife of a(nother) seignior, but has proved nothing, they shall drag that seignior into the presence of the judges and also cut off half his (hair).

128: If a seignior acquired a wife, but did not draw up the contracts for her, that woman is no wife.

Deut. 22:22

129: If the wife of a seignior has been caught while lying with another man, they shall bind them and throw them into the water. If the husband of the woman wishes to spare his wife, then the king in turn may spare his subject.

Deut. 22:23-27

130: If a seignior bound the (betrothed) wife of a(nother) seignior, who had had no intercourse with a male and was still living in her father's house, and he has lain in her bosom and they have caught him, that seignior shall be put to death, while that woman shall go free.

131: If a seignior's wife was accused by her husband, but she was not caught while lying with another man, she shall make affirmation by god and return to her house.

132: If the finger was pointed at the wife of a seignior because of another man, but she has not been caught while lying with the other man, she shall throw herself into the river[1] for the sake of her husband.

Num. 5:11-31

133: If a seignior was taken captive, but there was sufficient to live on in his house, his wife [shall not leave her house, but she shall take care of her person by not] entering [the house of another].[2]

---

[1] i.e. submit to the water ordeal, with the river as divine judge.
[2] i.e. in order to live there as another man's wife.

133a: If that woman did not take care of her person, but has entered the house of another, they shall prove it against that woman and throw her into the water.[1]

134: If the seignior was taken captive and there was not sufficient to live on in his house, his wife may enter the house of another, with that woman incurring no blame at all.

135: If, when a seignior was taken captive and there was not sufficient to live on in his house, his wife has then entered the house of another before his (return) and has borne children, (and) later her husband has returned and has reached his city, that woman shall return to her first husband, while the children shall go with their father.

136: If, when a seignior deserted his city and then ran away, his wife has entered the house of another after his (departure), if that seignior has returned and wishes to take back his wife, the wife of the fugitive shall not return to her husband because he scorned his city and ran away.

137: If a seignior has made up his mind to divorce a lay priestess,[2] who bore him children, or a hierodule who provided him with children, they shall return her dowry to that woman and also give her half of the field, orchard and goods in order that she may rear her children; after she has brought up her children, from whatever was given to her children they shall give her a portion corresponding to (that of) an individual heir in order that the man of her choice   may marry her.

138: If a seignior wishes to divorce his wife who did not bear him children, he shall give her money to the full amount of her marriage-price and he shall also make good to her the dowry which she brought from her father's house and then he may divorce her.

139: If there was no marriage-price, he shall give her one mina of silver as the divorce-settlement.

140: If he is a peasant,   he shall give her one-third mina of silver.

141: If a seignior's wife, who was living in the house of the seignior, has made up her mind to leave in order that she may engage in business, thus neglecting her house (and) humiliating her husband, they shall prove

---

[1] i.e. to be drowned.
[2] The exact meaning of the word used here, šu.ge₄-tum, is unknown, but it indicates some kind of priestess.

it against her; and if her husband has then decided on her divorce, he may divorce her, with nothing to be given her as her divorce-settlement upon her departure. If her husband has not decided on her divorce, her husband may marry another woman, with the former woman   living in the house of her husband like a maidservant.

142: If a woman so hated her husband that she has declared, "You may not have me," her record shall be investigated at her city council, and if she was careful and was not at fault, even though her husband has been going out and disparaging her greatly, that woman, without incurring any blame at all, may take her dowry and go off to her father's house.

143: If she was not careful, but was a gadabout, thus neglecting her house (and) humiliating her husband, they shall throw that woman into the water.

144: When a seignior married a hierodule and that hierodule gave a female slave to her husband and she has then produced children, if that seignior has made up his mind to marry a lay priestess, they may not allow that seignior, since he may not marry the lay priestess.

145: If a seignior married a hierodule and she did not provide him with children and he has made up his mind to marry a lay priestess, that seignior may marry the lay priestess, thus bringing her into his house, (but) with that lay priestess ranking in no way with the hierodule.

146: When a seignior married a hierodule and she gave a female slave to her husband and she has then borne children, if later that female slave has claimed equality with her mistress because she bore children, her mistress may not sell her; she may mark her with the slave-mark and count her among the slaves.

147:.If she did not bear children, her mistress may sell her.

148: When a seignior married a woman and a fever has then seized her, if he has made up his mind to marry another, he may marry (her), without divorcing his wife whom the fever seized; she shall live in the house which he built and he shall continue to support her as long as she lives.

149: If that woman has refused to live in her husband's house, he shall make good her dowry to her which she brought from her father's house and then she may leave.

150: If a seignior, upon presenting a field, orchard, house, or goods to his wife, left a sealed document with her, her children may not enter a claim against her after (the death of) her husband, since the mother may give her inheritance to that son of hers whom she likes, (but) she may not give (it) to an outsider.

151: If a woman, who was living in a seignior's house, having made a contract with her husband that a creditor of her husband may not distrain her, has then had (him) deliver a written statement;[1] if there was a debt against that seignior before he married that woman, his creditors may not distrain his wife; also, if there was a debt against that woman before she entered the seignior's house, her creditors may not distrain her husband.

152: If a debt has developed against them after that woman entered the seignior's house, both of them shall be answerable to the merchant.[2]

153: If a seignior's wife has brought about the death of her husband because of another man, they shall impale that woman on stakes.

154: If a seignior has had intercourse with his daughter, they shall make that seignior leave the city.

155: If a seignior chose a bride for his son and his son had intercourse with her, but later he himself has lain in her bosom and they have caught him, they shall bind that seignior and throw him into the water.

156: If a seignior chose a bride for his son and his son did not have intercourse with her, but he himself has lain in her bosom, he shall pay to her one-half mina of silver and he shall also make good to her whatever she brought from her father's house in order that the man of her choice may marry her.

157: If a seignior has lain in the bosom of his mother after (the death of) his father, they shall burn both of them.

158: If a seignior after (the death of) his father has been caught in the bosom of his foster mother who was the bearer of children, that seignior shall be cut off from the parental home.

159: If a seignior, who had the betrothal-gift brought to the house of his (prospective) father-in-law (and) paid the marriage-price, has then fallen in love with another woman and has said to his (prospective) father-

Lev. 18:6-18; 20:10-21; Deut. 27:20, 22-23

---

[1] Lit. "a tablet."   [2] i.e. the money-lender who made the loan.

in-law, "I will not marry your daughter," the father of the daughter shall keep whatever was brought to him.

160: If a seignior had the betrothal-gift brought to the house of the (prospective) father-in-law (and) paid the marriage-price, and the father of the daughter has then said, "I will not give my daughter to you," he shall pay back double the full amount that was brought to him.

161: If a seignior had the betrothal-gift brought to the house of his (prospective) father-in-law (and) paid the marriage-price, and then a friend of his has so maligned him that his (prospective) father-in-law has said to the (prospective) husband, "You may not marry my daughter," he shall pay back double the full amount that was brought to him, but his friend may not marry his (intended) wife.

162: If, when a seignior acquired a wife, she bore him children and that woman has then gone to (her) fate, her father may not lay claim to her dowry, since her dowry belongs to her children.

163: If a seignior acquired a wife and that woman has gone to (her) fate without providing him with children, if his father-in-law has then returned to him the marriage-price which that seignior brought to the house of his father-in-law, her husband may not lay claim to the dowry of that woman, since her dowry belongs to her father's house.

164: If his father-in-law has not returned the marriage-price to him, he shall deduct the full amount of her marriage-price from her dowry and return (the rest of) her dowry to her father's house.

165: If a seignior, upon presenting a field, orchard, or house to his first-born, who is the favorite in his eye, wrote a sealed document for him, when the brothers divide after the father has gone to (his) fate, he shall keep the present which the father gave him, but otherwise they shall share equally in the goods of the paternal estate.

166: If a seignior, upon acquiring wives for the sons that he got, did not acquire a wife for his youngest son, when the brothers divide after the father has gone to (his) fate, to their youngest brother who did not acquire a wife, to him in addition to his share they shall assign money (enough)for the marriage-price from the goods of the paternal estate and thus enable him to acquire a wife.

167: If, when a seignior acquired a wife and she bore him children, that woman has gone to (her) fate (and) after her (death) he has then married another woman and she has borne children, when later the father has gone to (his) fate, the children shall not divide according to mothers; they shall take the dowries of their (respective) mothers and then divide equally the goods of the paternal estate.

168: If a seignior, having made up his mind to disinherit his son, has said to the judges, "I wish to disinherit my son," the judges shall investigate his record, and if the son did not incur wrong grave (enough) to be disinherited, the father may not disinherit his son.

169: If he has incurred wrong against his father grave (enough) to be disinherited, they shall let him off the first time; if he has incurred grave wrong a second time, the father may disinherit his son.

170: When a seignior's first wife bore him children and his female slave also bore him children, if the father during his lifetime has ever said "My children!" to the children whom the slave bore him, thus having counted them with the children of the first wife, after the father has gone to (his) fate, the children of the first wife and the children of the slave shall share equally in the goods of the paternal estate, with the first-born, the son of the first wife, receiving a preferential share.

171: However, if the father during his lifetime has never said "My children!" to the children whom the slave bore him, after the father has gone to (his) fate, the children of the slave may not share in the goods of the paternal estate along with the children of the first wife; freedom for the slave and her children shall be effected,   with the children of the first wife having no claim at all against the children of the slave for service; the first wife shall take her dowry and the marriage-gift which her husband, upon giving (it) to her, wrote down on a tablet for her, and living in the home of her husband, she shall have the usufruct (of it) as long as she lives, without ever selling (it), since her heritage belongs to her children.

172: If her husband did not give her a marriage-gift, they shall make good her dowry to her and she shall obtain from the goods of her husband's estate a portion corresponding to (that of) an individual heir; if her children keep plaguing her in order to make her leave the house, the judges shall investigate her record and place the blame on the children, so that woman need never leave her husband's house; if that woman has made up her mind to leave, she shall leave to her children the marriage-gift which her husband gave her (but) take the dowry from   her father's house in order that the man of her choice may marry her.

173: If that woman has borne children to her later husband in the place that she entered, and afterwards that woman has died, the earlier with the later children shall divide the dowry.

174: If she has not borne children to her later husband, only the children of her first husband shall receive her dowry.

175: If either a palace slave or a private citizen's slave married the daughter of a seignior and she has borne children, the owner of the slave may not lay claim to the children of the seignior's daughter for service.

176: Furthermore, if a palace slave or a private citizen's slave married the daughter of a seignior and when he married her she entered the house of the palace slave or the private citizen's slave with the dowry from her father's house and after they were joined together they set up a household and so acquired goods, but later either the palace slave or the private citizen's slave has gone to (his) fate, the seignior's daughter shall take her dowry, but they shall divide into two parts whatever her husband and she acquired after they were joined together and the owner of the slave shall take one-half, with the seignior's daughter taking one-half for her children.

176a: If the seignior's daughter has no dowry, they shall divide into two parts whatever her husband and she acquired after they were joined together and the owner of the slave shall take one-half, with the seignior's daughter taking one-half for her children.

177: If a widow, whose children are minors, has made up her mind to enter the house of another, she may not enter without the consent of the judges; when she wishes to enter the house of another, the judges shall investigate the condition of her former husband's estate and they shall entrust her former husband's estate to her later husband and that woman and they shall have them deposit a tablet (to the effect that) they will look after the estate and also rear the young (children), without ever selling the household goods, since the purchaser who purchases the household goods of a widow's children shall forfeit his money, with the goods reverting to their owner.

178: In the case of a nun, a hierodule, or a votary, whose father, upon presenting a dowry to her, wrote a tablet for her, if he did not write for her on the tablet which he wrote for her (permission) to give her heritage to whom she pleased and did not grant her full discretion, after the father has gone to (his) fate, her brothers shall take her field and orchard and they shall give her food, oil and clothing proportionate to the value of her share and thus make her comfortable; if her brothers have not given her food, oil and clothing proportionate to the value of her share and so have not made her comfortable, she may give her field and orchard to any tenant that she pleases and her tenant shall support her, since she shall have the usufruct of the field, orchard or whatever her father gave her as long as she lives, without selling (it or) willing (it) to another, since her patrimony belongs to her brothers.

179: In the case of a nun, a hierodule, or a votary, whose father, upon presenting a dowry to her, wrote a sealed document for her, if he wrote for her on the tablet which he wrote for her (permission) to give her heritage to whomever she pleased and has granted her full discretion, after her father has gone to (his) fate, she may give her heritage to whomever she pleases, with her brothers having no claim against her.

180: If a father did not present a dowry to his daughter, a hierodule in a convent or a votary, after the father has gone to (his) fate, she shall receive as her share in the goods of the paternal estate a portion like (that of) an individual heir, but she shall have only the usufruct of (it) as long as she lives, since her heritage belongs to her brothers.

181: If a father dedicated (his daughter) to deity as a hierodule, a sacred prostitute, or a devotee and did not present a dowry to her, after the father has gone to (his) fate, she shall receive as her share in the goods of the paternal estate her one-third patrimony, but she shall have only the usufruct of (it) as long as she lives, since her heritage belongs to her brothers.

182: If a father, since he did not present a dowry to his daughter, a hierodule of Marduk of Babylon, did not write a sealed document for her, after the father has gone to (his) fate, she shall share along with her brothers in the goods of the paternal estate to the extent of her one-third patrimony, but she shall not assume any feudal obligations, since a hierodule of Marduk may give her heritage to whomever she pleases.

183: If a father, upon presenting a dowry to his daughter, a lay priestess, when he gave her to a husband, wrote a sealed document for her, after the father has gone to (his) fate, she may not share in the goods of the paternal estate.

184: If a seignior did not present a dowry to his daughter, a lay priestess, since he did not give her to a husband, after the father has gone to (his) fate, her brothers shall present her with a dowry proportionate to the value of the father's estate and they shall give her to a husband.

185: If a seignior adopted a boy in his own name and has reared him, that foster child may never be reclaimed.

186: If a seignior, upon adopting a boy, seeks out his father and mother when he had taken him, that foster child may return to his father's house.

187: The (adopted) son of a chamberlain, a palace servant, or the (adopted) son of a votary, may never be reclaimed.

188: If a member of the artisan class[1] took a son as a foster child and has taught him his handicraft, he may never be reclaimed.

189: If he has not taught him his handicraft, that foster child may return to his father's house.

190: If a seignior has not counted among his sons the boy that he adopted and reared, that foster child may return to his father's house.

191: If a seignior, who adopted a boy and reared him, set up a family of his own, has later acquired children and so has made up (his) mind to cut off the foster child, that son shall not go off empty-handed; his foster father shall give him from his goods his one-third patrimony and then he shall go off, since he may not give him any of the field, orchard, or house.

---

[1] Lit. "the son of an artisan," where "son" is used in the technical sense of "belonging to the class of, species of," so common in the Semitic languages.

192: If the (adopted) son of a chamberlain or the (adopted) son of a votary has said to his foster father or his foster mother, "You are not my father," "You are not my mother," they shall cut out his tongue.

193: If the (adopted) son of a chamberlain or the (adopted) son of a votary found out his parentage and came to hate his foster father and his foster mother and so has gone off to his paternal home, they shall pluck out his eye.

194: When a seignior gave his son to a nurse and that son has died in the care of the nurse, if the nurse has then made a contract for another son without the knowledge of his father and mother, they shall prove it against her and they shall cut off her breast because she made a contract for another son without the knowledge of his father and mother.

195: If a son has struck his father, they shall cut off his hand.

Exod. 21:15

196: If a seignior has destroyed the eye of a member of the aristocracy,[1] they shall destroy his eye.

197: If he has broken a(nother) seignior's bone, they shall break his bone.

Exod. 21:23-25;
Lev. 24:19-20;
Deut. 19:21

198: If he has destroyed the eye of a commoner or broken the bone of a commoner, he shall pay one mina of silver.

199: If he has destroyed the eye of a seignior's slave or broken the bone of a seignior's slave, he shall pay one-half his value.

200: If a seignior has knocked out a tooth of a seignior of his own rank, they shall knock out his tooth.

201: If he has knocked out a commoner's tooth, he shall pay one-third mina of silver.

202: If a seignior has struck the cheek of a seignior who is superior to him, he shall be beaten sixty (times) with an oxtail whip in the assembly.

203: If a member of the aristocracy has struck the cheek of a(nother) member of the aristocracy who is of the same rank as himself, he shall pay one mina of silver.

204: If a commoner has struck the cheek of a(nother) commoner, he shall pay ten shekels of silver.

[1] Lit. "the son of a man," with "son" used in the technical sense already explained above and "man" clearly in the sense of "noble, aristocrat"; or it is possible that "son" here is to be taken in its regular sense to indicate a person younger than the assailant.

205: If a seignior's slave has struck the cheek of a member of the aristocracy, they shall cut off his ear.

206: If a seignior has struck a(nother) seignior in a brawl and has inflicted an injury on him, that seignior shall swear, "I did not strike him deliberately";[1]   and he shall also pay for the physician.

207: If he has died because of his blow, he shall swear (as before), and if it was a member of the aristocracy, he shall pay one-half mina of silver.

208: If it was a member of the commonalty, he shall pay one-third mina of silver.

Exod. 21:22-25

209: If a seignior struck a(nother) seignior's daughter and has caused her to have a miscarriage,[2]   he shall pay ten shekels of silver for her fetus.

210: If that woman has died, they shall put his daughter to death.

211: If by a blow he has caused a commoner's daughter to have a miscarriage, he shall pay five shekels of silver.

212: If that woman has died, he shall pay one-half mina of silver.

213: If he struck a seignior's female slave and has caused her to a have a miscarriage, he shall pay two shekels of silver.

214: If that female slave has died, he shall pay one-third mina of silver.

215: If a physician performed a major operation on a seignior with a bronze lancet and has saved the seignior's life, or he opened up the eye-socket of a seignior with a bronze lancet and has saved the seignior's eye, he shall receive ten shekels of silver.

216: If it was a member of the commonalty, he shall receive five shekels.

217: If it was a seignior's slave, the owner of the slave shall give two shekels of silver to the physician.

218: If a physician performed a major operation on a seignior with a bronze lancet and has caused the seignior's death, or he opened up the eye-socket of a seignior and has destroyed the seignior's eye, they shall cut off his hand.

219: If a physican performed a major operation on a commoner's slave with a bronze lancet and has caused (his) death, he shall make good slave for slave.

220: If he opened up his eye-socket with a bronze

---

[1] Lit. "while I was aware of (it)."
[2] Lit. "caused her to drop that of her womb (her fetus)."

lancet and has destroyed   his eye, he shall pay one-half his value in silver.

221: If a physician has set a seignior's broken bone, or has healed a sprained tendon, the patient[1]   shall give five shekels of silver to the physician.

222: If it was a member of the commonalty, he shall give three shekels of silver.

223: If it was a seignior's slave, the owner of the slave shall give two shekels of silver to the physician.

224: If a veterinary surgeon   performed a major operation on either an ox or an ass and has saved (its) life, the owner of the ox or ass shall give to the surgeon one-sixth (shekel) of silver as his fee.

225: If he performed a major operation on an ox or an ass and has caused (its) death, he shall give to the owner of the ox or ass one-fourth its value.

226: If a brander cut off the slave-mark of a slave not his own without the consent of the owner of the slave, they shall cut off the hand of that brander.

227: If a seignior deceived a brander so that he has cut off the slave-mark of a slave not his own, they shall put that seignior to death and immure him at his gate; the brander shall swear, "I did not cut (it) off knowingly," and then he shall go free.

228: If a builder constructed a house for a seignior and finished (it) for him, he shall give him two shekels of silver per *sar*[2] of house as his remuneration.

229: If a builder constructed a house for a seignior, but did not make his work strong, with the result that the house which he built collapsed and so has caused the death of the owner of the house, that builder shall be put to death.

230: If it has caused the death of a son of the owner of the house, they shall put the son of that builder to death.

231: If it has caused the death of a slave of the owner of the house, he shall give slave for slave to the owner of the house.

232: If it has destroyed goods, he shall make good whatever it destroyed; also, because he did not make the house strong which he built and it collapsed, he shall reconstruct the house which collapsed at his own expense.

233: If a builder constructed a house for a seignior and

---

[1] "owner of the injury."   [2] A measure equal to about 42 1/5 square yds.

has not done his work properly so that a wall has become unsafe, that builder shall strengthen that wall at his own expense.

234: If a boatman calked a boat of sixty *kur* for a seignior, he shall give him two shekels of silver as his remuneration.

235: If a boatman calked a boat for a seignior and did not do his work well with the result that that boat has sprung a leak in that very year, since it has developed a defect, the boatman shall dismantle that boat and strengthen (it) at his own expense   and give the strengthened boat back to the owner of the boat.

236: If a seignior let his boat for hire to a boatman and the boatman was so careless that he has sunk or wrecked the boat, the boatman shall make good the boat to the owner of the boat.

237: When a seignior hired a boatman and a boat and loaded it with grain, wool, oil, dates, or any kind of freight, if that boatman was so careless that he has sunk the boat and lost what was in it as well, the boatman shall make good the boat which he sank and whatever he lost that was in it.

238: If a boatman sank the boat of a seignior and has then refloated it, he shall give one-half its value in silver.

239: If a seignior hired a boatman, he shall give him six *kur* of grain per year.

240: If a rowboat rammed a sailboat and has sunk (it), the owner of the boat whose boat was sunk shall in the presence of god set forth the particulars regarding whatever was lost in his boat and the one in charge of the rowboat   which sank the sailboat shall make good to him his boat and his lost property.

241: If a seignior has distrained an ox as a pledge, he shall pay one-third mina of silver.

242, 243: If a seignior hired (it) for one year, he shall give to its owner four *kur* of grain as the hire of an ox in tandem, three *kur* of grain as that of a young lead-ox.

244: If a seignior hired an ox or an ass and a lion has killed it in the open, (the loss) shall be its owner's.

245: If a seignior hired an ox and has caused its death through carelessness or through beating, he shall make good ox for ox to the owner of the ox.

246: If a seignior hired an ox and has broken its foot or has cut its neck tendon, he shall make good ox for ox to the owner of the ox.

247: If a seignior hired an ox and has destroyed its eye, he shall give one-half its value in silver to the owner of the ox.

248: If a seignior hired an ox and has broken its horn, cut off its tail, or injured the flesh of its back, he shall give one-quarter its value in silver.

249: If a seignior hired an ox and god struck it and it has died, the seignior who hired the ox shall (so) affirm by god and then he shall go free.

250: If an ox, when it was walking along the street, gored a seignior to death, that case is not subject to claim.

Exod. 21:28-36

251: If a seignior's ox was a gorer and his city council made it known to him that it was a gorer, but he did not pad its horns (or) tie up his ox, and that ox gored to death a member of the aristocracy, he shall give one-half mina of silver.

252: If it was a seignior's slave, he shall give one-third mina of silver.

253: If a seignior hired a(nother) seignior to oversee his field, and lending him *feed-grain*, entrusting him with oxen, contracted with him to cultivate the field, if that seignior stole the seed or fodder and it has been found in his possession, they shall cut off his hand.

254: If he appropriated the *feed-grain* and thus has starved the oxen, he shall make good twofold the grain which he received.

255: If he has let the seignior's oxen out on hire or he stole the seed-grain and so has raised nothing in the field, they shall prove it against that seignior and at harvest-time he shall measure out sixty *kur* of grain per eighteen *iku*.

256: If he was not able to meet his obligation, they shall drag him through that field with the oxen.

257: If a seignior hired a *cultivator*, he shall give him eight *kur* of grain per year.

258: If a seignior hired a cattle-herder, he shall pay him six *kur* of grain per year.

259: If a seignior stole a plow from a field, he shall give five shekels of silver to the owner of the plow.

260: If he has stolen a *seeder* or a harrow, he shall give three shekels of silver.

261: If a seignior hired a shepherd to pasture cattle or sheep, he shall give him eight *kur* of grain per year.

262: If a seignior . . . and ox or a sheep to. . . .

263: If he has lost [the ox] or sheep which was committed to him, he shall make good ox for [ox], sheep for [sheep] to their owner.

264: If [a shepherd], to whom cattle or sheep were given to pasture, being in receipt of his wages in full, to his satisfaction, has then let the cattle decrease, has let the sheep decrease, thus lessening the birth rate, he shall give increase and profit in accordance with the terms of his contract.

265: If a shepherd, to whom cattle or sheep were given to pasture, became unfaithful and hence has altered the cattlemark or has sold (them), they shall prove it against him and he shall make good in cattle and sheep to their owner tenfold what he stole.

266: If a visitation of god has occurred in a sheepfold or a lion has made a kill, the shepherd shall prove himself innocent in the presence of god, but the owner of the sheepfold shall receive from him the animal stricken in the fold.

Exod. 22:10 ff.

267: If the shepherd was careless and has let lameness develop in the fold, the shepherd shall make good in cattle and sheep the loss through the lameness which he let develop in the fold and give (them) to their owner.

268: If a seignior hired an ox to thresh, twenty *qu* of grain shall be its hire.

269: If he hired an ass to thresh, ten *qu* of grain shall be its hire.

270: If he hired a goat to thresh, one *qu* of grain shall be its hire.

271: If a seignior hired oxen, a wagon and a driver for it, he shall give 180 *qu* of grain per day.

272: If a seignior hired simply a wagon by itself, he shall give forty *qu* of grain per day.

273: If a seignior hired a laborer, he shall give six *še* of silver per day from the beginning of the year till the fifth month; from the sixth month till the end of the year he shall give five *še* of silver per day.

274: If a seignior wishes to hire an artisan, he shall pay per day as the wage of a . . . five [*še*] of silver; as the wage of a *brickmaker* five *še* of silver; [as the wage of] a *linen-weaver* . . . [*še*] of silver; [as the wage] of a *seal-cutter* . . . [*še*] of silver; [as the wage of] a *jeweller* . . . [*še* of] silver; [as the wage of] a *smith* . . . [*še* of] silver; [as the wage of] a carpenter four *še* of silver; as the wage of a leatherworker ... *še* of silver; as the wage of a basketmaker ... *še* of silver; [as the wage of] a builder ... *še* of silver.

275: [If] a seignior hired a *long-boat*, its hire shall be three *še* of silver per day.

276: If a seignior hired a rowboat, he shall give two and one-half *še* of silver per day as its hire.

277: If a seignior hired a boat of sixty *ḳur*, he shall give one-sixth (shekel) of silver per day as its hire.

278: If a seignior purchased a male (or) female slave and when his month was not yet complete, epilepsy attacked him, he shall return (him) to his seller and the purchaser shall get back the money which he paid out.

279: If a seignior purchased a male (or) female slave and he has then received a claim (against him), his seller shall be responsible for the claim.

280: If a seignior has purchased in a foreign land the male (or) female slave of a(nother) seignior and when he has arrived home   the owner of the male or female slave has identified either his male or his female slave, if that male and female slave are natives of the land, their freedom shall be effected without any money (payment).

281: If they are natives of another land, the purchaser shall state in the presence of god what money he paid out and the owner of the male or female slave shall give to the merchant the money he paid out and thus redeem   his male or female slave.

282: If a male slave has said to his master, "You are not my master," his master shall prove him to be his slave and cut off his ear.

Documents from the Practice of Law

MESOPOTAMIAN LEGAL DOCUMENTS

ANET, 219-220

TRANSLATOR: THEOPHILE J. MEEK

NUZI AKKADIAN

(1) Sale-Adoption[1]

The tablet of adoption belonging to Kuzu, the son of Karmishe: he adopted Tehip-tilla, the son of Puhi-

---

[1] Sale-adoption was a legal device used in Nuzi whereby a landowner could circumvent the law prohibiting the sale of land outside the family by going through the form of adopting the purchaser. The Nuzi tablets come from the middle of the 2nd millennium B.C.

shenni. As his share [1] (of the estate) Kuzu gave Tehip-tilla 40 imers[2] of land in the district of Iphushshi. If the land should have a claimant, Kuzu shall clear (it) and give (it) back to Tehip-tilla. Tehip-tilla in turn gave 1 mina of silver to Kuzu as his honorarium. Whoever defaults shall pay 2 minas of silver (and) 2 minas of gold.

(The names of fourteen persons and the scribe as witnesses, each preceded by the witness-sign.)

(The names of two of the witnesses, one other person, and the scribe, each preceded by "The seal of.")

(2) Sale-Adoption

The tablet of adoption belonging to Nashwi, the son of Ar-shenni: he adopted Wullu, the son of Puhi-shenni. As long as Nashwi is alive, Wullu shall provide food and clothing; when Nashwi dies, Wullu shall become the heir. If Nashwi has a son of his own, he shall divide (the estate) equally with Wullu, but the son of Nashwi shall take the gods of Nashwi. However, if Nashwi does not have a son of his own, then Wullu shall take the gods of Nashwi.[3] Furthermore, he gave his daughter Nuhuya in marriage to Wullu, and if Wullu takes another wife he shall forfeit the lands and buildings of Nashwi. Whoever defaults shall make compensation with 1 mina of silver and 1 mina of gold.

Gen. 31:26 ff.

(The names of five persons and the scribe as witnesses, each preceded by the witness-sign.)

(The names of four of the witnesses and the scribe, each preceded by "The seal of.")

(3) Real Adoption

The tablet of adoption belonging to [Zike], the son of Akkuya: he gave his son Shennima in adoption to Shuriha-ilu, and Shuriha-ilu, with reference to Shennima, (from) all the lands . . . (and) his earnings of every sort gave to Shennima one (portion) of his property. If Shuriha-ilu should have a son of his own, as the principal (son) he shall take a double share; Shennima shall then be next in order (and) take his proper share. As long as Shuriha-ilu is alive, Shennima shall revere him. When Shuriha-ilu [dies], Shennima shall

---

[1] The word used here, *zittu*, means the double share of the first-born son.

[2] An imer was approximately 4½ acres.

[3] Possession of the household gods marked a person as the legitimate heir, which explains Laban's anxiety to recover his household gods from Jacob. It is to be noted too that Laban binds Jacob in verse 50 to marry no other wives besides his daughters, just as Wullu is bound in our text.

become the heir. Furthermore, Kelim-ninu has been given in marriage to Shennima. If Kelim-ninu bears (children), Shennima shall not take another wife; but if Kelim-ninu does not bear, Kelim-ninu shall acquire a woman of the land of Lullu as wife for Shennima, and Kelim-ninu may not send the offspring away. Any sons that may be born to Shennima from the womb of Kelim-ninu, to (these) sons shall be given [all] the lands (and) buildings of every sort. [However], if she does not bear a son, [then] the daughter of Kelim-ninu from the lands (and) buildings shall take one (portion) of the property. Furthermore, Shuriha-ilu shall not adopt another son in addition to Shennima. Whoever among them defaults shall compensate with 1 mina of silver (and) 1 mina of gold.

Furthermore, Yalampa is given as a handmaid to Kelim-ninu and Shatim-ninu has been made co-parent. As long as she is alive, she (i.e. Yalampa) shall revere her and Shatim-ninu shall not annul the [*agreement*].

If Kelim-ninu bears (children) and Shennima takes another wife, she may *take* her dowry and leave.

(The names of nine persons and the scribe as witnesses, each preceded by the witness-sign.)

The remaining sons of Zike may not lay claim to the lands (and) buildings belonging to the (above) one (portion) of the property.

The tablet was written after the proclamation.

(Sealed by eight persons, seven of whom were already named as witnesses.)

(4) Lawsuit

Tarmiya, the son of Huya, appeared with Shukriya and Kula-hupi, with (these) two brothers of his, the sons of Huya, in a lawsuit before the judges of Nuzi with reference to the female slave [Sululi-Ishtar], whereupon Tarmiya spoke thus before the judges, "My father, Huya, was sick and lay on a couch; then my father seized my hand and spoke thus to me, 'My other sons, being older, have acquired wives, but you have not acquired a wife; so I give you herewith Sululi-Ishtar as your wife.'" Then the judges demanded the witnesses of Tarmiya [and Tarmiya] had his witnesses appear [before the judges]: . . . , the son of Hurshaya, . . . , the son of Ikkiya, . . . , the son of Itrusha, (and) . . . , the son of Hamanna. [These] witnesses of [Tarmiya] were examined before the judges, whereupon the judges spoke to Shukriya and Kula-hupi, "Go and take the oath of the gods against the witnesses of Tarmiya." Shukriya and Kula-hupi shrank from the gods[1] so that Tarmiya prevailed in the lawsuit and the judges assigned the female slave, Sululi-Ishtar, to Tarmiya.

(The names of three persons, each preceded by "The seal of.")

The signature of Iliya.

(5) Hebrew Slave Document

Mar-Idiglat, a Hebrew from the land of Assyria, on his own initiative has entered (the house of) Tehip-tilla, the son of Puhi-shenni, as a slave.

(The names of eleven persons and the scribe as witnesses, each preceded by the witness-sign.)

(The names of two of the witnesses and the scribe, each preceded by "The seal of.")

(6) Hebrew Slave Document

Sin-balti, a Hebrew woman, on her own initiative has entered the house of Tehip-tilla as a slave. Now if Sin-balti defaults and goes into the house of another, Tehip-tilla shall pluck out the eyes of Sin-balti and sell her.

(The names of nine persons and the scribe as witnesses, each preceded by the witness-sign.)

(The names of two of the witnesses and the scribe, each preceded by "The seal of.")

[1] i.e. they refused to take the oath in fear of its consequences and thus showed themselves in the wrong.

ANET, 222-223

ARAMAIC PAPYRI FROM ELEPHANTINE

TRANSLATOR: H. L. GINSBERG

MIBTAHIAH'S FIRST MARRIAGE

Deed of 459 B.C., relating to reversion of property. Text: Sayce-Cowley, C; Cowley, 9.

On the 21st of Chisleu, that is the 1st of Mesore[1], year 6 of King Artaxerxes, Mahseiah b. Yedoniah, a Jew of Elephantine, of the detachment of Haumadata, said to Jezaniah b. Uriah of the said detachment as follows: There is the site of 1 house belonging to me, west of the house belonging to you, which I have given to your wife, my daughter Mibtahiah (*Mbṭhyh*), and in respect of which I have written her a deed. The measurements of the house in question are 8 cubits and a handbreadth (5) by 11, *by the measuring-rod*. Now do I, Mahseiah,

[1] Egyptian month-name.

say to you, Build and equip that site . . . and dwell thereon with your wife. But you may not sell that house or give it as a present to others; only your children by my daughter Mibtahiah shall have power over it after you two. If tomorrow or some other day you build upon this land, and then my daughter divorces you and leaves you, she shall have no power to take it or give it to others; only your children by (10) Mibtahiah shall have power over it, in return for the work which you shall have done. If, on the other hand, she recovers from you,[2] she [may] take half of the house, and [the] othe[r] half shall be at your disposal in return for the building which you will have done on that house. And again as to that half, your children by Mibtahiah shall have power over it after you. If tomorrow or another day I should institute suit or process against you and say I did not give you this land to build on and did not draw up this deed for you, I (15) shall give you a sum of 10 *karshin* by royal weight, at the rate of 2 R^3 to the ten, and no suit or process shall lie. This deed was written by 'Atharshuri b. Nabuzeribni in the fortress of Syene at the dictation of Mahseiah. Witnesses hereto (signatures).

[2] This must mean, "In the event of your divorcing her, in which case she does not forfeit all rights as when she divorces you." Perhaps there is a lacuna in the text.

[3] Probably stands for *rub'in* "quarters" (of a shekel). Does 2/4 × 10 (=1/5) indicate the proportion of alloy?

IN LIQUIDATION OF MIBTAHIAH'S SECOND MARRIAGE

See the Aramaic letter, "Settlement of Claim by Oath," Chap. XII.

CONTRACT OF MIBTAHIAH'S THIRD MARRIAGE

Text: Sayce-Cowley, G; Cowley, 15. Date: about 440 B.C.

On the 2[5]th of Tishri, that is the 6th day of the month Epiphi, [year . . . of] Kin[g Artaxerx]es, said Ashor b. [Seho],[1] builder to the king, to Mah[seiah, A]ramean of Syene, of the detachment of Varizata, as follows: I have [co]me to your house that you might give me your daughter Mipht⟨ah⟩iah in marriage. She is my wife and I am her husband from this day for ever. I have given you as the bride-price (5) of your daughter

[1] The name of Ashor's father (*sh'*) is preserved in another document. Both it and his own are Egyptian, but he eventually adopted the Hebrew one of Nathan.

Miphtahiah (a sum of) 5 shekels, royal weight. It has been received by you and your heart is content therewith.[1] (Lines 6-16, Miphtahiah's dowry.) (17) Should Ashor die tomorrow or an[othe]r day having no child, male or female, by his wife Mi[phtah]iah, Miphtahiah shall be entitled to the house, chattels and all worldly goods of Ashor. (20) Should Miphtahiah die tomorrow or ⟨another⟩ day having no child, male or female, by her husband Ashor, Ashor shall inherit her property and chattels. Should [Miph]tahiah, tomorrow [or] another [d]ay stand up in a congregation and say, I divorce my husband Ashor, the price of divorce shall be upon her head: she shall sit by the balance and weigh out to [As]hor a sum of 7 shekels 2 R.[2] But all that which she has brought in (25) with her she shall take out, shred and thread, and go whither she will, without suit or process. Should Ashor tomorrow or another day stand up in a congregation and say, I divorce my [wif]e Miphtahiah, [he shall] forfeit her bride-price, and all that she has brought in with her she shall take out, shred and thread, on one day at one stroke, and shall go whither she will, without suit or process. And [whoever] arises against Miphtahiah (30) to drive her away from the house, possessions, and chattels of Ashor shall give her the sum of 20 *karash*,[3] and the law of this deed shall [. . .] for her. And I shall have no right to say I have another wife besides Mipht⟨ah⟩iah or other children besides any Miphtahiah may bear to me. If I say I have chi[ldren] and wife other than Miphtahiah and her children, I shall give to Miphtahiah a su[m] of 20 *karash*, royal weight. (35) Neither shall I have the right to [wre]st my property and chattels from Miph[tah]iah. If I take *them* away from her (erasure), I shall give to Miphtahiah [a sum of] 20 *karash*, royal weight. [This deed] was written by Nathan b. *Ananiah* [at the dictation of Ashor]. Witnesses: (signatures).

---

[1] The bride-price was regularly added to the bride's dowry. In the following lines the value of each item of the dowry is given, and so is the total value; but the latter exceeds the value of the items by exactly the amount of the bride-price.

[2] This sum is exactly 1½ times the bride-price Ashor paid for her (line 5).

[3] A *karash* is 10 heavy shekels or 20 light ones.

VI. Egyptian Historical Texts

TRANSLATOR: JOHN A. WILSON

The Expulsion of the Hyksos

ANET, 233-234

It is an irony of history that our best contemporaneous source on the expulsion of the Hyksos from Egypt comes from the biographical record of a relatively modest citizen of Upper Egypt, the captain of a Nile vessel. In relating his participation in the campaigns of Ah-mose I (about 1570-1545 B.C.) and of Thutmose I (about 1525-1495), Ah-mose, son of the woman Eben, tells of the successive attacks on the Hyksos in Egypt and then of the follow-up campaigns into Asia.

The commander of a crew, Ah-mose, son of Eben, the triumphant, says:

I speak to you, all mankind, that I may let you know the favors which have come to me. I have been awarded gold seven times in the presence of the entire land, and male and female slaves in like manner, and I have been vested with very many fields.[1] The reputation of a valiant man is from what he has done, not being destroyed in this land forever.

He speaks thus:

I had my upbringing in the town of el-Kab, my father being a soldier of the King of Upper and Lower Egypt: Seqnen-Re, the triumphant,[2] his name being Bebe, (5) the son of (the woman) Ro-onet. Then I served as soldier in his place in the ship, "The Wild Bull," in the time of the Lord of the Two Lands: Neb-pehti-Re, the triumphant,[3] when I was (still) a boy, before I had taken a wife, (but) while I was (still) sleeping in a *net hammock*.[4]

But after I had set up a household, then I was taken on the ship, "Northern," because I was valiant. Thus I used to accompany the Sovereign—life, prosperity, health! —on foot, following his excursions in his chariot.[5] When the town of Avaris was besieged, then I showed valor on foot in the presence of his majesty. Thereupon I was appointed to the ship, "Appearing in Memphis."

Fig. 42

---

[1] In his tomb, Ah-mose gives a list of 9 male and 10 female slaves which were his booty. His grants of land from the king came to something like 70 acres.

[2] One of the pharaohs named Seqnen-Re in the 17th dynasty.

[3] Ah-mose I.

[4] Perhaps: "I was (still) sleeping with the phallic sheath attached"?

[5] Note the first use of the horse and chariot by the Egyptians. The Hyksos had introduced this war force into Egypt.

Then there was fighting on the water in *the canal Pa-Djedku* of Avaris. Thereupon I made a capture, (10) and I carried away a hand.[1] It was reported to the king's herald. Then the Gold of Valor was given to me. Thereupon there was fighting again in this place. Then I made a capture again there and brought away a hand. Then the Gold of Valor was given to me over again.

Then there was fighting in the Egypt which is south of this town.[2] Thereupon I carried off a man (as) living prisoner. I went down into the water—now he was taken captive on the side of the town[3] —and crossed over the water carrying him. Report was made to the king's herald. Thereupon I was awarded gold another time.

Then Avaris was despoiled. Then I carried off spoil from there: one man, three women, a total of four persons. Then his majesty gave them to me to be slaves.[4]

Josh. 19:6 Then (15) Sharuhen was besieged for three years.[5] Then his majesty despoiled it. Thereupon I carried off spoil from there: two women and a hand. Then the Gold of Valor was given to me, *and* my spoil was given to me to be slaves.

Now after his majesty had killed the Asiatics, then he sailed southward to Khenti-hen-nefer, to destroy the Nubian nomads. . . .

After this (Thut-mose I) went forth to Retenu,[6] to assuage his heart throughout the foreign countries. His majesty reached Naharin,[7] (37) and his majesty—life, prosperity, health!—found that enemy[8] while he was marshaling the battle array. Then his majesty made a great slaughter among them. There was no number to the living prisoners whom his majesty carried off by his victory. Now I was in the van of our army,[9] and his majesty saw how valiant I was. I carried off a chariot,

---

[1] It was an Egyptian army custom to cut off the hand of a dead enemy as a proof of killing.

[2] South of Avaris. This looks like a temporary retirement by the Egyptians.

[3] Beside the town, but across a body of water from the Egyptian army.

[4] In Ah-mose's "list of the male and female slaves of the spoil," most of the 19 names are good Egyptian. However, there appear a Pa-'Aam, "The Asiatic," a T'amutj, which is a feminine name similar to Amos, and an Ishtar-ummi, "Ishtar is My Mother."

[5] It lay in the extreme southwestern corner of the land of Canaan, in the territory of the tribe of Simeon. Perhaps it was modern Tell el-Fâr'ah.

[6] Syria-Palestine in general.

[7] "The Two Rivers," the area of the Euphrates bend.

[8] "That fallen one," a frequent designation of a major enemy.

[9] It has been pointed out that only in the stretch of patriotic enthusiasm of the first century of the 18th dynasty did the Egyptians speak of "our army," instead of ascribing the troops to the pharaoh.

its horse, and him who was in it as a living prisoner. They were presented to his majesty. Then I was awarded gold another time.[1] ...

[1] In the quarries of Maâsara is a record of the reopening of the quarries for stone to be used in certain temples. Part of the inscription runs: "The stone was dragged by the cattle which his [*victories*] throughout the lands of the Fenkhu had carried off." The accompanying scene shows Asiatics driving the cattle. Djahi and Fenkhu apply to the Phoenician coast running down into Palestine and including the hinterland—further north than southern Palestine.

Asiatic Campaign of Thut-mose III

THE BATTLE OF MEGIDDO

ANET, 234-238

Thut-mose III (about 1490-1436 B.C.) was the conquering pharaoh who set the Egyptian Empire on a foundation firm for almost a century. For twenty years he led campaigns into Asia almost every year. Some of these campaigns involved serious fighting, others were parades of strength. We have detailed information on his first campaign (perhaps 1468 B.C.), which attacked the focus of Asiatic resistance in the Canaanite city of Megiddo.

The "Annals" of Thut-mose III's military campaigns are carved on the walls of the Temple of Karnak, in recognition of the fact that the god Amon-Re had given victory.

Fig. 106

The Horus: Mighty Bull, Appearing in Thebes; ... (Thut-mose III).

His majesty commanded that [the victories which his father Amon had given to him] should be established [upon] a monument in the temple which his majesty had made for [his father Amon, in order to set down] (5) each individual campaign, together with the booty which [his majesty] carried [off from it, *and the dues of*] every [*foreign country*] which his father Re had given to him.

Year 22, 4th month of the second season, day 25.[1] [*His majesty passed the fortress of*] Sile;[2] on the first campaign of victory [*which his majesty made to extend*] the frontiers of Egypt, in valor, [in victory, in power, and in justification]. Now this was a [long] time in years ... (10) plunder, while every man *was* [*tributary*] before ... But it happened in later times that the garrison which was there was in the town of Sharuhen,[13] while from Iursa to the outer ends of the earth[3] had become rebellious against his majesty.

Josh. 19:6

[1] Tentatively, April 16, 1468 B.C., for the battle of Megiddo. The precise date will depend upon what the ancient Egyptians meant by a "new moon."
[2] Or Tjaru, the Egyptian frontier post, at or near modern Kantarah.
[3] From southern Palestine to northern Syria.

Year 23, 1st month of the third season, day 4, the day of the feast of the king's coronation—as far as the town of "That-Which-the-Ruler-Seized," [*of which the Syrian name is*] Gaza.[1]

[Year 23,] (15) 1st month of the third season, day 5—departure from this place, in valor, [in victory,] in power, and in justification, in order to overthrow that wretched enemy,[2] and to extend the frontiers of Egypt, according to the command of his father Amon-Re, the [*valiant*] and victorious, that he should capture.

Fig. 99

Year 23, 1st month of the third season, day 16[3] —as far as the town of Yehem. [His majesty] ordered a conference with his victorious army, speaking as follows: "That [wretched] enemy (20) of Kadesh has come and has entered into Megiddo. He is [there] at this moment. He has gathered to him the princes of [every] foreign country [which had been] loyal to Egypt, as well as (those) as far as Naharin and M[*itanni*], them of Hurru, them of Kode, their horses, their armies, [and their people], *for* he says—so it is reported—'I shall wait [here] (25) in Megiddo [to fight against his majesty].' Will ye tell me [what is in your hearts]?"[4]

They said in the presence of his majesty: "What is it like to go [on] this [road] which becomes (so) narrow? It is [reported] that the foe is there, waiting on [the outside, while they are] becoming (more) numerous. Will not horse (have to) go after [horse, and the army] (30) and the people similarly? Will the vanguard of us be fighting while the [rear guard] is waiting here in Aruna, unable to fight?[5] *Now* two (other) roads are here. One of the roads—behold, it is [*to the east of*] us, Judg. 5:19 so that *it* comes out at Taanach. The other—behold, it is to the (35) north side of Djefti,[6] and we will come out

---

[1] On Borchardt's reckoning, the Egyptians reached Gaza on April 25, 1468, having traveled at the respectable rate of 150 miles in 9 or 10 days. As this date was the anniversary of Thut-mose III's coronation, the year number changed from 22 to 23.

[2] The Prince of Kadesh was the leader of the coalition against Egypt.

[3] May 7, 1468 (Borchardt). After leaving the Egyptian-held city of Gaza, the army's rate was notably slower through territory which was actually or potentially rebellious. Perhaps 80 miles were covered in 11 or 12 days. Yehem (possibly Jahmai or similar) is tentatively located by Nelson at Yemma on the south side of the Carmel ridge.

[4] It is probable from the nature of this coalition and from Thut-mose's subsequent campaigns that this Kadesh was the city on the Orontes.

[5] If they went straight ahead on the narrow track debouching just south of Megiddo, they had to go in single file and would be particularly vulnerable.

[6] Two safer mountain tracks were offered as alternatives, one debouching at Taanach, 4 or 5 miles southeast of Megiddo, and one debouching at an unknown point north(west) of Megiddo.

to the north of Megiddo. Let our victorious lord proceed on the one of [them] which is [satisfactory to] his heart, (but) do not make us go on that difficult road!"

Then messages [were brought in *about that wretched enemy, and discussion was continued*] of [that] problem on which they had previously spoken. That which was said in the majesty of the Court—life, prosperity, health![1] —"I [swear], (40) as Re loves me, as my father Amon favors me, as my [nostrils] are rejuvenated with life and satisfaction, my majesty shall proceed upon this Aruna road! Let him of you who wishes go upon these roads of which you speak, and let him of you who wishes come in the following of my majesty! *'Behold,'* they will say, these (45) enemies whom Re abominates, 'has his majesty set out on another road because he has become afraid of us?'—so they will speak."

They said in the presence of his majesty: "May thy father Amon, Lord of the Thrones of the Two Lands, Presiding over Karnak, act [*according to thy desire*]! Behold, we are following thy majesty everywhere that [thy majesty] goes, for a servant will be after [his] lord."

[*Then* his majesty *laid a charge*] (50) upon the entire army: "[*Ye*] *shall* [*hold fast to the stride of your victorious lord on*] that road which becomes (so) na[r-row. Behold, his majesty has taken] an oath, saying: 'I will not let [my victorious army] go forth ahead of my majesty in [this place!'" *Now his majesty had laid it in his heart*] that he himself should go forth at the head of his army. [Every man] was made aware (55) of his order of march, horse following horse, while [his majesty] was at the head of his army.

Year 23, 1st month of the third season, day 19[2] —the awakening in [life] in the tent of life, prosperity, and health, at the town of Aruna. Proceeding northward by my majesty, carrying my father Amon-Re, Lord of the Thrones of the Two Lands, [that he might open the ways] before me,[3] while Har-akhti established [*the heart of my victorious army*] (60) and my father Amon strengthened the arm [of my majesty]. . . .

Num. 10:33; Deut. 1:33

Then [his] majesty issued forth[4] [at the head of] his [army], which was [prepared] in many ranks. [*He had*

---

[1] That is, the voice from the throne. The Court moved with the pharaoh.
[2] Three days after arrival in Yehem.   [3] The standard of Amon led the way.
[4] From the pass on to the Megiddo plain.

not met] a single [*enemy*. Their] southern wing was
in Taanach, [while their] nothern wing was on the
south side [of *the Qina Valley*.¹ Then] (65) his majesty
rallied them saying: "... ! They are fallen! While that
[wretched] enemy ... [*May*] ye [*give praise*] to (70)
[*him; may ye extol the might of*] his majesty, because
his arm is greater than (that of) [*any king. It has indeed protected the rear of*] his majesty's army in
Aruna!"

Now while the rear of his majesty's victorious army
was (still) at [the town] of Aruna, the vanguard had
come out into the [Qi]na Valley, and they filled the
mouth of this valley.

Then they said to his majesty—life, prosperity, health!
—(75) "Behold, his majesty has come forth with his
victorious army, and they have filled the valley. Let our
victorious lord listen to us this time, and let our lord
guard for us the rear of his army and his people. When
the rear of the army comes forth for us into the open,
then we shall fight against these foreigners, then we
shall not trouble our hearts [about] the rear of (80) our
army."

A halt was made by his majesty outside, [*seated*]
there and guarding the rear of his victorious army. Now
the [*leaders*] had just finished coming forth on this road
when the shadow turned.² His majesty reached the
south of Megiddo on the bank of the Qina brook, when
the seventh hour was in (its) course in the day.

Then a camp was pitched there for his majesty, and
a charge was laid upon the entire army, [saying]: "Prepare ye! Make your weapons ready, since one³ will
engage in combat with that wretched enemy in the
morning, because one is ... !"

Resting in the enclosure of life, prosperity, and
health.⁴ Providing for the officials. *Issuing rations* to the
retinue. Posting the sentries of the army. Saying to
them: "Be steadfast, be steadfast! Be vigilant, be vigilant!" Awakening in life in the tent of life, prosperity,
and health. They came to tell his majesty: "The desert
is well, and the garrisons of the south and north also!"

---

¹ The Qina is still represented by a brook flowing south of Megiddo.
When he said: "They are fallen!" he was anticipating the fall of the
Asiatics, because they had failed to guard the pass.
² It was noon, and the shadow clock should be turned around. The
Egyptian van thus reached the Megiddo plain seven hours before the rear
of the army emerged and Thut-mose could go into camp.   ³ Pharaoh.
⁴ The royal enclosure was doubtless an elaborate pavilion.

Year 23, 1st month of the third season, day 21, the day of the feast of the *true* new moon.[1] Appearance of the king at dawn. Now a charge was laid upon the entire army to *pass by* . . . (85) His majesty set forth in a chariot of fine gold, adorned with his accoutrements of combat, like Horus, the Mighty of Arm, a lord of action like Montu, the Theban, while his father Amon made strong his arms. The southern wing of his majesty's army was at a hill south of [the] Qina [*brook*], and the northern wing was to the northwest of Megiddo, while his majesty was in their center, Amon being the protection of his person (in) the melee and the strength of [*Seth pervading*] his members.

Thereupon his majesty prevailed over them at the head of his army. Then they saw his majesty prevailing over them, and they fled headlong [to] Megiddo with faces of fear. They abandoned their horses and their chariots of gold and silver, so that someone might draw them (up) into this town by *hoisting* on their garments. Now the people had shut this town against them, (but) they [let down] garments to *hoist* them up into this town. Now, if only his majesty's army had not given up their hearts to capturing the possessions of the enemy, they would [have captured] Megiddo at this time, while the wretched enemy of Kadesh and the wretched enemy of this town were being dragged (up) *hastily* to get them into their town, for the fear of his majesty entered [their bodies], their arms were weak, [*for*] his serpent-diadem had overpowered them.

Then their horses and their chariots of gold and silver were captured as an easy [prey. *Ranks*] of them were lying stretched out on their backs, like fish in the *bight of a net*, while his majesty's victorious army counted up their possessions. Now there was captured [that] wretched [enemy's] tent, which was worked [with *silver*], . . .

Then the entire army rejoiced and gave praise to Amon [because of the victory] which he had given to his son on [this day. They *lauded*] his majesty and extolled his victories. Then they presented the plunder which they had taken: hands,[2] living prisoners, horses, and chariots of gold and silver and of *painted work*. (90). . . .

---

[1] Borchardt's date for the battle is May 12, 1468.
[2] Cut off from the fallen foe as tokens of battle accomplishment.

[Then his majesty commanded] his army with the words: "Capture ye [effectively, my] victorious [army]! Behold, [*all foreign countries*] have been put [*in this town by* the command] of Re on this day, inasmuch as every prince of every [northern] country is shut up within it, for the capturing of Megiddo is the capturing of a thousand towns! Capture ye firmly, firmly! . . ."

[*Orders were issued to* the com]manders of the troops to pro[*vide for their divisions and to inform*] each [man] *of* his place. They measured [this] city, which was corralled with a moat and enclosed with fresh timbers of all their pleasant trees, while his majesty himself was in a fortress east of this town, [being] watchful . . . . [enclosed] with a girdle wall, . . . *by* its girdle wall. Its name was called "Men-kheper-Re-is-the-Corral-ler-of-the-Asiatics." People were appointed as sentries at the enclosure of his majesty, and they were told: "Be steadfast, be steadfast! Be vigilant, [be vigilant]!" . . . his majesty . . . . [Not one] of them [was permitted to go] outside from behind this wall, except to come out *at a knock* on the door of their fortress.[1]

Now everything which his majesty did to this town and to that wretched enemy and his wretched army is set down by the individual day, by the individual expedition, and by the individual [troop] commanders. . . . They [are] set down on a roll of leather in the temple of Amon today.

Now the princes of this foreign country came on their bellies to kiss the ground to the glory of his majesty and to beg breath for their nostrils, because his arm was (so) great, because the prowess of Amon was (so) great [over (95) every] foreign [country] . . . [all] the princes whom the prowess of his majesty carried off, bearing their tribute of silver, gold, lapis lazuli, and turquoise, and carrying grain, wine, and large and small cattle for the army of his majesty, with one gang of them bearing tribute southward. Then his majesty appointed princes anew for [*every town*]. . . .

[List of the booty which his majesty's army carried off from the town of] Megiddo: 340 living prisoners and 83 hands; 2,041 horses, 191 foals, 6 stallions, and . . . colts; 1 chariot worked with gold, with a *body* of gold, belonging to that enemy, [1] fine chariot worked with

Fig. 93

___
[1] The besieged Asiatics were permitted to appear only if Egyptians called them out?

gold belonging to the Prince of [*Megiddo*] . . . , and 892 chariots of his wretched army—total: 924; 1 fine bronze coat of mail belonging to that enemy, [1] fine bronze coat of mail belonging to the Prince of Meg[iddo, and] 200 [*leather*] coats of mail belonging to his wretched army; 502 bows; and 7 poles of *meru*-wood, worked with silver, of the tent of that enemy.

Now the army [of his majesty] carried off [*cattle*] . . . : 387 . . . , 1,929 cows, 2,000 goats, and 20,500 sheep.

List of what was carried off afterward by the king from the household goods of that enemy, who [was in] Yanoam, Nuges, and Herenkeru,[1] together with the property of those towns which had made themselves subject to him . . . : . . . ; 38 [*maryanu*] belonging to them,[2] 84 children of that enemy and of the princes who were with him, 5 *maryanu* belonging to them, 1,796 male and female slaves, as well as their children, and 103 pardoned persons, who had come out from that enemy because of hunger—total: 2,503—apart from bowls of costly stone and gold, various vessels, (100) . . . , a large *akunu*-jar in Syrian work, jars, bowls, *plates*, various drinking vessels, large kettles, [*x* +] 17 knives —making 1,784 *deben*;[3] gold in discs, found in the process of being worked, as well as abundant silver in discs —966 *deben* and 1 *kidet*;[4] a silver statue *in the form of* . . . , [*a statue*] . . . , with head of gold; 3 walking sticks with human heads; 6 carrying-chairs of that enemy, of ivory, ebony, and *carob*-wood, worked with gold, and the 6 footstools belonging to them; 6 large tables of ivory and *carob*-wood; 1 bed belonging to that enemy, of *carob*-wood, worked with gold and with every (kind of) costly stone, in the manner of a *kerker*,[5] completely worked in gold; a statue of that enemy which was there, of ebony worked with gold, its head of lapis [lazuli] . . . ; bronze vessels, and much clothing of that enemy.

Fig. 4

Now the fields were made into arable plots and assigned to inspectors of the palace—life, prosperity, health!—in order to reap their harvest. List of the harvest

---

[1] "Upper Retenu" properly stands for the mountain territory of north Palestine and southern Syria, and Yanoam seems to have been in the Lake Huleh area. The three towns would then be somewhere in that area.

[2] The *maryanu* were the warrior or officer class in Asia at this time.

[3] About 435 lb. troy of metal value (probably reckoned in silver) in the listed pieces.

[4] About 235 lb. troy. Uncertain whether of silver only, or of the combined value of gold and silver. [5] An unknown object of wood.

which his majesty carried off from the Megiddo acres: 207,300 [+x] sacks of wheat,[1] apart from what was cut as forage by his majesty's army, . . .

[1] Something like 450,000 bushels.

A Campaign of Seti I in Northern Palestine

ANET, 253-254 Internally and externally the Amarna Revolution had dealt a serious blow to Egyptian empire. Domestic reorganization was the first need. Then, when Seti I (about 1318-1301 B.C.) became pharaoh, he returned to campaigning in Asia. This stela from Palestinian soil gives a brief statement of his energy in meeting an attempted coalition of Asiatic princes.

Year 1, 3rd month of the third season, day 10.[1] Live the Horus: Mighty Bull, Appearing in Thebes, Making the Two Lands to Live; the Two Goddesses: Repeating Births, Mighty of Arm, Repelling the Nine Bows; the Horus of Gold: Repeating Appearances, Mighty of Bows in All Lands; the King of Upper and Lower Egypt, Lord of the Two Lands: Men-maat-Re [Ir]-en-Re; the Son of Re, Lord of Diadems: Seti Mer-ne-Ptah, beloved of Re-Har-akhti, the great god. The good god, potent with his arm, heroic and valiant like Montu, rich in captives, (5) knowing (how to) place his hand, alert wherever he is; speaking with his mouth, acting with his hands, valiant leader of his army, valiant warrior in the very heart of the fray, a Bastet[2] terrible in combat, penetrating into a mass of Asiatics and making them prostrate, crushing the princes of Retenu, reaching the (very) ends of (10) him who transgresses against *his* way. He causes to *retreat* the princes of Syria,[3] *all* the boastfulness *of whose* mouth was *(so) great.* Every foreign country of the ends of the earth, their princes say: "Where shall we go?" They spend the night *giving testimony* in his name, *saying: "Behold it, behold it!" in* their hearts. It is the strength of his father Amon that decreed to him valor and victory.

On this day[4] one came to speak to his majesty, as follows: (15) "The wretched foe who is in the town of Hamath[5] is gathering to himself many people, while he is seizing the town of Beth-Shan. *Then there will be*

[1] Around 1318 B.C., this date fell late in May.
[2] Bastet, an Egyptian cat-goddess, merged with Sekhmet, the lioness goddess of war. [3] *Kharu*, Syria-Palestine in general.
[4] The date at the beginning of the inscription.
[5] Not necessarily the Prince of Hamath. This may have been a prince from the north; note that Seti sends one army division north to Yanoam.

an alliance with them of Pahel. He does not permit the Prince of Rehob to go outside." [1]

Thereupon his majesty sent the first army of Amon, (named) "Mighty of Bows," to the town of Hamath, the first army of the (20) Re, (named) "Plentiful of Valor," to the town of Beth-Shan, and the first army of Seth, (named) "Strong of Bows," to the town of Yanoam. [2] When the space of a day had passed, they were overthrown to the glory of his majesty, the King of Upper and Lower Egypt: Men-maat-Re; the Son of Re: Seti Mer-ne-Ptah, given life.

[1] Ancient Beth-Shan is modern Tell el-Ḥuṣn, just northwest of modern Beisan. Hamath is almost certainly Tell el-Ḥammeh, about 10 mi. south of Beisan. Pahel or Pella is Khirbet Faḥil, about 7 mi. southeast of Beisan and across the Jordan. Rehob is probably Tell eṣ-Ṣârem, about 3 mi. south of Beisan. These cities all seem to have lain within a small range. It would seem that Hamath and Pahel were acting against Beth-Shan and Rehob.

[2] Seti I's dispositions were rapid and effective. One problem here is the reason for sending a unit against Yanoam, which was apparently considerably north of the center of disaffection. Yanoam may be modern Tell en-Nâ'ameh, north of Lake Huleh and thus nearly 50 mi. north of Beisan. Perhaps the real opposition to Egypt lay to the north, in the territory dominated by the Hittites. By throwing a road-block against reinforcements from the north, Seti I would be able to deal with a localized rebellion around Beth-Shan, without outside interference.

The Report of a Frontier Official

ANET, 259

In a group of letters which served as models for schoolboys, one communication presents the form in which an official on the eastern frontier of Egypt might report the passage of Asiatic tribes into the better pasturage of the Delta.

(51) The Scribe Inena communicating to his lord, the Scribe of the Treasury Qa-g[abu], . . . :—In life, prosperity, health! This is a letter [to] let [my lord] know: An[other communication to] my lord, to wit:

[I] have carried out every commission laid upon me, in good shape and strong as metal. I have not been lax.

Another communication to my [lord], to [wit: We] have finished letting the Bedouin tribes of Edom pass the Fortress [of] Mer-ne-Ptah Hotep-hir-Maat—life, prosperity, health!—which is (in) Tjeku, [1] (56) to the pools [2] of Per-Atum [3] [of] Mer-[ne]-Ptah Hotep-hir-Maat, which are (in) Tjeku, to keep them alive and to keep their cattle alive, through the great ka of Pharaoh —life, prosperity, health!—the good sun of every land,

Gen. 46:28; 47:1

Exod. 1:11

[1] The location is the eastern end of the Wadi Tumilat, the "land of Goshen." The Fortress of Mer-ne-Ptah will have been a frontier fortress. Tjeku—or probably Teku—could only with difficulty be Succoth and seems to be a broad designation for the region.   [2] The Semitic word birkeh is used.

[3] Per-Atum, "the House of Atum," is probably biblical Pithom.

in the year 8, 5 [intercalary] days, [the Birth of] Seth.[1]
I have had them brought in a copy of the *report* to the
[place where] my lord is, *as well as* the other names of
days when the Fortress of Mer-ne-Ptah Hotep-hir-Maat
—life, prosperity, health!—which is (in) [Tj]ek[u],
may be passed. . . .

[1] "The Birth of Seth" was the 3rd intercalary day at the end of the
year. Around 1215 B.C. this would be after the middle of June.

ANET, 260

A Syrian Interregnum

For an unknown number of years between the Nineteenth
and Twentieth Dynasties Egypt was in a chaotic state and for a
part of the time was under the rule of a Syrian. All that we know
of this episode comes from the following text.

The Great Papyrus Harris comes from Thebes and dates to the
end of the reign of Ramses III (about 1164 B.C.), forming a kind
of last will and testament for him. The troubles which he here
describes lay between the reign of the last king of the Nineteenth
Dynasty (about 1205 B.C.) and the beginning of the reign of
Ramses III's father, Set-nakht (about 1197 B.C.).

SAID King User-maat-Re Meri-Amon[1]—life, prosperity, health!—the great god,[2] to the officials and leaders
of the land, the infantry, the chariotry, the Sherden,[3]
the many bowmen, and all the souls of Egypt:

Hear ye, that I may make you aware of my bene-
factions which I accomplished while I was king of the
people. The land of Egypt had been cast aside, with
every man being his (*own standard of*) *right*. They
had no chief spokesman for many years previously up
to other times. The land of Egypt was officials and
mayors,[4] one slaying his fellow, both exalted and lowly.
Other *times* came afterwards in the empty years,[5] and
. . . ,[6] a Syrian (5) with them, made himself prince.
He set the entire land as tributary before him. One
joined his companion that their property might be plundered. They treated the gods like the people, and no
offerings were presented in the temples.

But when the gods reversed themselves to show mercy

[1] Ramses III (about 1195-1164 B.C.).
[2] The epithet normally means that the king is already dead.
[3] Egyptian captive or mercenary troops, from the Mediterranean area.
[4] That is, broken down under local rule only, without king or other
central government.
[5] Either years void of orderly rule, or years of emptiness, i.e. of economic
distress.
[6] The rule of an otherwise unknown Syrian ("Horite") is certain.

and to set the land right as was its normal state, they established their son, who had come forth from their body, to be Ruler—life, prosperity, health!—of every land, upon their great throne: User-kha-Re Setep-en-Re Meri-Amon—life, prosperity, health!—the Son of Re: Set-nakht Merer-Re Meri-Amon—life, prosperity, health! He was Khepri-Seth when he was enraged. He brought to order the entire land, which had been rebellious. He slew the disaffected of heart who had been in Egypt. He cleansed the great throne of Egypt.

The War Against the Peoples of the Sea

ANET, 262-263

In the latter half of the second millennium B.C. there were extensive movements in the eastern Mediterranean area. Masses of homeless peoples moved slowly across the sea and its coastlands, displacing or merging with the older populations. These migrations ended the Minoan civilization in Crete, contributed to the historical populations of Greece and Italy, wiped out the Hittite Empire, thrust the Philistines into Canaan, and washed up on the shores of Egypt. In Ramses III's eighth year (about 1188 B.C.) the pharaoh met and checked their attempt to push into the rich lands of the Nile. The victory was only a check, because the Egyptian Empire in Asia ended shortly after. The following accounts of this war come from Ramses III's temple of Medinet Habu at Thebes.

Fig. 7

Fig. 92

(1) Year 8 under the majesty of (Ramses III)....

(16) ... The foreign countries made a *conspiracy* in their islands. All at once the lands were removed and scattered in the fray. No land could stand before their arms, from Hatti, Kode, Carchemish, Arzawa, and Alashiya on,[1] being cut off *at* [*one time*]. A camp [was set up] in one place in Amor.[2] They desolated its people, and its land was like that which has never come into being. They were coming forward toward Egypt, while the flame was prepared before them. Their confederation was the Philistines, Tjeker, Shekelesh, Denye(n), and Weshesh,[3] lands united. They laid their hands upon the lands as far as the circuit of the earth, their hearts confident and trusting: "Our plans will succeed!"

Fig. 95

[1] Hatti was the Hittite Empire, Kode the coast of Cilicia and northern Syria, Carchemish the city on the Euphrates, Arzawa somewhere in or near Cilicia, and Alashiya probably Cyprus.

[2] Perhaps in the north Syrian plain or in Coele-Syria.

[3] Except for the Philistines (Peleset), these names are rendered close to the Egyptian writings. For the Tjeker, cf. the Wen-Amon story. The Shekelesh might be the Siculi, the Denyen (cuneiform Danuna) might be the Danaoi. The Weshesh cannot easily be related to any later people.

Now the heart of this god, the Lord of the Gods, was prepared and ready to ensnare them like birds. .... I organized my frontier in Djahi,[1] prepared before them:— princes, commanders of garrisons, (20) and *maryanu*. I have the river-mouths[2] prepared like a strong wall, with warships, galleys and coasters, *(fully) equipped*, for they were manned completely from bow to stern with valiant warriors carrying their weapons. The troops consisted of every picked man of Egypt. They were like lions roaring upon the mountain tops. The chariotry consisted of runners, of *picked men*, of every good and capable chariot-warrior. The horses were quivering in every part of their bodies, prepared to crush the foreign countries under their hoofs. I was the valiant Montu,[3] standing fast at their head, so that they might gaze upon the capturing of my hands. ....

Those who reached my frontier, their seed is not, their heart and their soul are finished forever and ever. Those who came forward together on the sea, the full flame was in front of them *at* the river-mouths, while a stockade of lances surrounded them on the shore.[4] They were dragged in, enclosed, and prostrated on the beach, killed, and made into heaps from tail to head. Their ships and their goods were as if fallen into the water.

I have made the lands turn back from (even) mentioning Egypt; for when they pronounce my name in their land, then (25) they are burned up. Since I sat upon the throne of Har-akhti and the Great-of-Magic[5] was fixed upon my head like Re, I have not let foreign countries behold the frontier of Egypt, to boast thereof to the Nine Bows.[6] I have taken away their land, their frontiers being added to mine. Their princes and their tribespeople are mine with praise, for I am on the ways of the plans of the All-Lord, my august, divine father, the Lord of the Gods.

---

[1] The Phoenician coast, running down into Palestine. From what little we know of Ramses III's sway, his defensive frontier was not north of Palestine. It is possible that the land battle against the Peoples of the Sea was in Asia, whereas the sea battle was on the coast of Egypt.

[2] Normally used for the mouths of the branches of the Nile in the Delta. Hence probably the line of defense in Egypt. Just possibly, the word might have been extended to harborages on the Asiatic coast.   [3] The god of war.

[4] One body had to be met on land (in Djahi?), whereas another body had to be met on sea (in the Delta?). The scenes show the boats of the Peoples of the Sea and also a movement by land in oxcarts, with women, children, and goods.

[5] The uraeus-serpent, symbol of kingship.   [6] Traditional enemies of Egypt.

The Megiddo Ivories

ANET, 263

A large collection of "Phoenician ivories" was found by excavation in a palace at Megiddo in Palestine. The carved designs were cosmopolitanly derived from various culture areas of the ancient Near East. The excavator tentatively dates the manufacture of the pieces between 1350 and 1150 B.C. Among the ivories are five bearing Egyptian hieroglyphs. A model pen case of an Egyptian envoy to foreign countries bears the name of Ramses III (about 1195-1164 B.C.), setting the *terminus ad quem* for the collection.

Figs. 29-31, 90

Ezra 2:65;
Neh. 7:67

Three plaques, which may have been used for inlay in furniture, bear the name of

the Singer of Ptah, South-of-His-Wall, Lord of the Life of the Two Lands, and Great Prince of Ashkelon, Kerker.

The Campaign of Sheshonk I

ANET, 263-264

Sheshonk I (about 945-924 B.C.) is the Shishak of the Old Testament. It is disappointing to find that the Egyptian texts do not enlarge our understanding of his campaign in Palestine in a sense which constitutes a real addition to the biblical account. To be sure, he has left us a listing of the Palestinian and Syrian towns which he claimed to have conquered, and this list may be reconstructed into a kind of itinerary. There is, however, no narrative account of the campaign by the pharaoh. The references in his inscriptions to "tribute of the land of Syria" or to his victories over the "Asiatics of distant foreign countries" are vague and generalized. How unhistorical his large claims were is clear from a statement to the pharaoh by the god Amon: "I have subjugated [for] thee the Asiatics of the armies of Mitanni." Mitanni as a nation had ceased to exist at least four centuries earlier.

I Kings 14:25-26;
II Chron. 12:2-9

Fig. 94

In addition to the list of towns, we do possess two documents attesting the name of Sheshonk on Asiatic soil. At Megiddo in Palestine was found a fragment of a monumental stela bearing the name of Sheshonk I and permitting the conclusion that the pharaoh had set up a triumphal monument there. At Byblos in Phoenicia another fragment, this time the chair of a seated statue, bears his name, although this monument may well be a princely gift, rather than a symbol of conquest.

Finally, the Walters Art Gallery in Baltimore has a basalt statuette of an Egyptian, the "Envoy of the Canaan and of Palestine, Pa-di-Eset, the son of Apy," which may date to the Twenty-second Dynasty. This piece does not involve conquest, but rather diplomatic relations.[1]

[1] G. Steindorff points out that the father's name may be Canaanite in origin.

VII. Assyrian and Babylonian
Historical Texts

TRANSLATOR: A. LEO OPPENHEIM

ASHURNASIRPAL II (883-859): EXPEDITION TO THE LEBANON

ANET, 275-276

From the annals inscribed on the large pavement slabs of the temple of Ninurta in Calah, the new royal residence built by Ashurnasirpal II.

Fig. 118

(iii 84—90)

At that time I seized the entire extent of the Lebanon mountain and reached the Great Sea of the Amurru country. I cleaned my weapons in the deep sea and performed sheep-offerings to (all) the gods. The tribute of the seacoast—from the inhabitants of Tyre, Sidon, Byblos, Mahallata, Maiza, Kaiza, Amurru, and (of) Arvad which is (an island) in the sea, (consisting of): gold, silver, tin, copper, copper containers, linen garments with multicolored trimmings, large and small monkeys, ebony, boxwood, ivory from walrus tusk— (thus ivory) a product of the sea,—(this) their tribute I received and they embraced my feet.

I ascended the mountains of the Amanus (*Ḫa-ma-ni*) and cut down (there) logs of cedars, stone-pines, cypresses (and) pines, and performed sheep-offerings to my gods. I (had) made a sculptured stela (commemorating) my heroic achievements and erected (it) there. The cedar beams from the Amanus mountain I *destined/sent* for/to the temple Esarra for (the construction of) a *iasmaku* -sanctuary as a building for festivals serving the temples of Sin and Shamash, the light(giving) gods.

SHALMANESER III (858-824): THE FIGHT AGAINST THE ARAMEAN COALITION

ANET, 277-281

First Year according to the so-called "Monolith Inscriptions."

(i.49—ii 13)

At that time, I paid homage to the greatness of (all) the great gods (and) extolled for posterity the heroic achievements of Ashur and Shamash by fashioning a (sculptured) stela with myself as king (depicted on it).

I wrote thereupon my heroic behavior, my deeds in combat and erected it beside the source of the Saluara river which is at the foot of the mountains of the Amanus. From the mountain Amanus I departed, crossed the Orontes river (*A-ra-an-tu*) and approached Alimush, the fortress town of Sapalulme from Hattina. To save his life, Sapalulme from Hattina [called for] Ahuni, man of Adini, Sangara from Carchemish, Haianu from Sam'al, Kate from Que, Pihirim from Hilukka, Bur-Anate from Iasbuq, Ada[. . . .] . . . Assyria. . . .

(ii)

[their/his army] I scattered, I stormed and conquered the town . . . I carried away as booty . . . , his horses, broken to the yoke. I slew with the sword. . . . During this battle I personally captured Bur-Anate from [Iasbuk]. I con[quered] the great cities (*maḫâzu*) of Hattina. . . . I overthrew the . . . of the Upper [Sea] of Amurru and of the Western Sea (so that they became) like ruin-hills (left by) the flood. I received tribute from the kings of the seashore. I marched straightaway, unopposed . . . throughout the wide seashore. I fashioned a stela with an image of myself as overlord in order to make my name/fame lasting forever and e[rected it] near the sea. I ascended the mountains of the Amanus, I cut there cedar and pine timber. I went to the mountain region Atalur, where the statue of the god Hirbe is set up and erected (there) a(nother) statue (of mine) beside his statue. I de[parted] from the sea; I conquered the towns Taia, Hazazu, Nulia (and) Butamu which (belong) to the country Hattina. I killed 2,900 of [their] battle-experienced soldiers; 14,600 I brought away as prisoners of war. I received the tribute of Arame, man of Gusi, (to wit): silver, gold, large [and small] cattle, wine, a couch of *whitish* gold.

Sixth Year according to the Monolith-Inscription.

(ii 78—102)

In the year of (the eponym) Daian-Ashur, in the month Aiaru, the 14th day, I departed from Nineveh. I crossed the Tigris and approached the towns of Giammu on the river Baliḫ. They became afraid of the terror emanating from my position as overlord, as well as of the splendor of my fierce weapons, and killed their master Giammu with their own weapons. I entered the towns Sahlala and Til-sha-Turahi and brought my gods/images into his palaces. I performed the *tašîltu* -festival in his (own) palaces. I opened (his) treasury, inspected what he had hidden; I carried away as booty his possessions, bringing (them) to my town Ashur. From Sahlala I departed and approached Kar-Shalmaneser. I crossed the Euphrates another time at its flood on rafts (made buoyant by means) of (inflated) goatskins. In Ina-Ashur-utir-asbat, which the people of Hattina call Pitru, on the other side of the Euphrates, on the river Sagur, I received tribute from the kings of the other side of the Euphrates—that is, of Sanagara from Carchemish, Kundashpi from Commagene, of Arame, man of Gusi, of Lalli from Melitene (*Melid*), of Haiani, son of Gabari, of Kalparuda from Hattina, (and) of Kalparuda of Gurgum—(consisting of): silver, gold, tin, copper (or bronze), copper containers. I departed from the banks of the Euphrates and approached Aleppo (*Ḫal-man*). They (i.e., the inhabitants of A.) were afraid to fight and seized my feet (in submission). I received silver and gold as their tribute and offered sacrifices before the Adad of Aleppo. I departed from Aleppo and approached the two towns of Irhuleni from Hamath (*Amat*). I captured the towns Adennu, Barga (and) Argana his royal residence. I removed from them his booty (as well as) his personal (lit.: of his palaces) possessions. I set his palaces afire. I departed from Argana and approached Karkara. I destroyed, tore down and burned down Karkara, his (text: my) royal residence. He brought along to help him 1,200 chariots, 1,200 cavalrymen, 20,000 foot soldiers

II Sam. 8:3 of Adad-'idri (i.e. Hadadezer) of Damascus (*Imērišu*), 700 chariots, 700 cavalrymen, 10,000 foot soldiers of Irhuleni from Hamath, 2,000 chariots, 10,000 foot sol-

I Kings 16:29 diers of Ahab, the Israelite (*A-ḫa-ab-bu* ^mat *Sir-'i-la-a-a*), 500 soldiers from Que, 1,000 soldiers from Musri, 10 chariots, 10,000 soldiers from Irqanata, 200 soldiers of Matinu-ba'lu from Arvad, 200 soldiers from Usanata, 30 chariots, 1[0?],000 soldiers of Adunu-ba'lu from Shian, 1,000 camel-(rider)s of Gindibu', from Arabia, [. . .],000 soldiers of Ba'sa, son of Ruhubi, from Ammon—(all together) these were twelve kings. They rose against me [for a] decisive battle. I fought with them with (the support of) the mighty forces of Ashur, which Ashur, my lord, has given to me, and the strong weapons which Nergal, my leader, has presented to me, (and) I did inflict a defeat upon them between the towns Karkara and Gilzau. I slew 14,000 of their soldiers with the sword, descending upon them like Adad when he makes a rainstorm pour down. I spread their corpses (everywhere), filling the entire plain with their widely scattered (fleeing) soldiers. During the battle I made their blood flow down the *ḫur-pa-lu* of the district. The plain was too small to let (all) their (text: his) souls descend[1] (into the nether world), the vast field gave out (when it came) to bury them. With their (text: sing.) corpses I spanned the Orontes before there was a bridge. Even during the battle I took from them their chariots, their horses broken to the yoke.

[1] This expression seems to indicate that the "souls" of the numerous dying soldiers were conceived as slipping down to the nether world through holes or cavities in the ground and that the massed corpses actually did cover the battlefield so completely as to make this descent difficult.

Eighteenth Year according to the fragment of an annalistic text

In the eighteenth year of my rule I crossed the Euphrates for the sixteenth time. Hazael of Damascus (*Imērišu*) put his trust upon his numerous army and called up his troops in great number, making the mountain Senir (Sa-ni-ru), a mountain, facing the Lebanon, to his fortress. I fought with him and inflicted a defeat upon him, killing with the sword 16,000 of his experienced soldiers. I took away from him 1,121 chariots, 470 riding horses as well as his camp. He disappeared to save his life (but) I followed him and besieged him in Damascus (*Di-maš-qi*), his royal residence. (There) I cut down his gardens (outside of the city, and departed). I marched as far as the mountains of Hauran (*šadê*ᵉ ᵐᵃᵗ*Ha-ú-ra-ni*), destroying, tearing down and burning innumerable towns, carrying booty away from them which was beyond counting. I (also) marched as far as the mountains of Ba'li-ra'si which is a promontory (lit.: at the side of the sea) and erected there a stela with my image as king. At that time I received the tribute of the inhabitants of Tyre, Sidon, and of Jehu, son of Omri (*Ia-ú-a mâr Hu-um-ri-i*).

Inscription from a marble bead

Booty (*kišitti*ᵗⁱ) of the temple of Sheru from the town of Mallaha, the royal residence of Hazael of Damascus (*Imērišu*) which Shalmaneser, son of Ashurnasirpal, has brought into the walls of Libbiali.[1]

II Kings 8:7-15;
Amos 1:4

[1] The name *Libbi-âli* denotes the central section of the town Ashur.

Epigraphs

From the rich iconographic documentation left by Shalmaneser III, five representations fall into the orbit of this book. They are provided with epigraphs which are given below in translation.

(a) From the Bronze Gates of Balawat

(Band III—Phoenicia, Tyre, Sidon, Gaza)

Fig. 98

I received the tribute (brought) on ships from the inhabitants of Tyre and Sidon.

(Band XIII—Syria)

I conquered Ashtamaku, the royal residence of Irhuleni of Hatti, together with 86 (other towns).

(b) From the Black Obelisk.

II

I Kings 19:16-17

Fig. 100

The tribute of Jehu (*Ia-ú-a*), son of Omri (*Ḫu-um-ri*); I received from him silver, gold, a golden *saplu*-bowl, a golden vase with pointed bottom, golden tumblers, golden buckets, tin, a staff for a king, (and) wooden *puruḫtu*.

ADAD-NIRARI III (810-783): EXPEDITION TO PALESTINE

ANET, 281   Stone Slab. From a broken stone slab found at Calah.

(1—14)

Property of Adad-nirari, great king, legitimate king, king of the world, king of Assyria—a king whom Ashur, the king of the Igigi (i.e. the dei superi) had chosen (already) when he was a youngster, entrusting him with the position of a prince without rival, (a king) whose shepherding they made as agreeable to the people of Assyria as (is the smell of) the Plant of Life, (a king) whose throne they established firmly; the holy high priest (and) tireless caretaker of the temple é.sár.ra, who keeps up the rites of the sanctuary, who acts (only) upon the trust-inspiring oracles (given) by Ashur, his lord; who has made submit to his feet the princes within the four rims of the earth; conquering from the Siluna mountain of the Rising Sun, the countries Saban, Ellipi, Harhar, Araziash, Mesu, the (country of the) Medians, Gizilbunda in its (full) extent, the countries Munna, Persia (*Parsua*), Allabria, Apdadana, Na'iri with all its regions, Andiu which lies far away in the *pitḫu* of the mountains with all its regions, as far as the Great Sea of the Rising Sun (and) from the banks of the Euphrates, the country of the Hittites, Amurru-country in its full extent, Tyre, Sidon, Israel (*mat*Hu-um-ri), Edom, Palestine (*Pa-la-as-tu*), as far as the shore of the Great Sea of the Setting Sun, I made them submit all to my feet, imposing upon them tribute.

TIGLATH-PILESER III (744-727): CAMPAIGNS AGAINST SYRIA AND PALESTINE

From a building inscription on clay preserved in various copies.

ANET, 282-284
Fig. 119

(56—63)

I installed Idi-bi'li as a Warden of Marches[2] on the border of Musur. In all the countries which . . . [I received] the tribute of Kushtashpi of Commagene[3] (*Kummuhu*), Urik of Qu'e, Sibitti-be'l of Byblos, . . . Enil of Hamath, Panammu of Sam'al, Tarhulara of Gumgum, Sulumal of Militene, . . . Uassurme of Tabal, Ushhitti of Tuna, Urballa of Tuhana, Tuhamme of Ishtunda, . . . [Ma]tan-be'l of Arvad, Sanipu of Bit-Ammon, Salamanu of Moab, . . . Mitinti of Ashkelon, Jehoahaz (*Ia-ú-ha-zi*) of Judah (*Ia-ú-da-a-a*), Kaush-malaku of Edom (*Ú-du-mu-a-a*), Muzr[i . . .], Hanno (*Ha-a-nu-ú-nu*) of Gaza (*Ha-za-at-a-a*) (consisting of) gold, silver, tin, iron, antimony,[1] linen garments with multicolored trimmings, garments of their native (industries) (being made of) dark purple wool . . . all kinds of costly objects be they products of the sea or of the continent, the (choice) products of their regions, the treasures of (their) kings, horses, mules (trained for) the yoke. . . .

[1] The term *abaru* (Sumerogram: A.BAR) denotes a rarely used metal, probably magnesite. For unknown reasons, it has mostly been used for small objects and tools (spoon, axe, etc.) prescribed for ritual purposes.

Year Unknown.

(150—157)

I received tribute from Kushtashpi of Commagene (*Kummuhu*), Rezon (*Ra-hi-a-nu*) of Damascus (*Ša-imērišu*), Menahem of Samaria (*Me-ni-hi-im-me* *al*Sa-me-ri-na-a-a*), Hiram (*Hi-ru-um-mu*) of Tyre, Sibitti-bi'li of Byblos, Urikki of Qu'e, Pisiris of Carchemish, I'nil of Hamath, Panammu of Sam'al, Tarhulara of Gurgum, Sulumal of Militene, Dadilu of Kaska, Uas-

II Kings 15:17

surme of Tabal, Ushhitti of Tuna, Urballa of Tuhana, Tuhamme of Ishtunda, Urimme of Hubishna (and) Zabibe, the queen of Arabia,[1] (to wit) gold, silver, tin, iron, elephant-hides, ivory, linen garments with multicolored trimmings, blue-dyed wool, purple-dyed[2] wool, ebony-wood, boxwood-wood, whatever was precious (enough for a) royal treasure; also lambs whose stretched hides were dyed purple, (and) wild birds whose spread-out wings were dyed blue,[3] (furthermore) horses, mules, large and small cattle, (male) camels, female camels with their foals.

Year Unknown. From a fragmentary annalistic text
. . . the town Hatarikka as far as the mountain Saua, [. . . the towns:] Byb[los], . . . Simirra, Arqa, Zimarra, . . . Uznu, [Siannu], Ri'-raba, Ri'-sisu, . . . the towns . . . of the Upper Sea, I brought under my rule. Six officers of mine I installed as governors over them. [. . . the town R]ashpuna which is (situated) at the coast of the Upper Sea, [the towns . . .]nite, Gal'za, Abilakka which are adjacent to Israel (*Bît Ḫu-um-ri-a*) [and the] wide (land of) [. . .]li, in its entire extent, I united with Assyria. Officers of mine I installed as governors upon them.

As to Hanno of Gaza (*Ḫa-a-nu-ú-nu* ᵃˡ*Ḫa-az-za-at-a-a*) who had fled before my army and run away to Egypt, [I conquered] the town of Gaza, . . . his personal property, his images . . . [and I placed (?)] (the images of) my [. . . gods] and my royal image in his own palace . . . and declared (them) to be (thenceforward) the gods of their country. I imposed upon th[em tribute]. [As for Menahem I ov]erwhelmed him [like a snowstorm] and he . . . fled like a bird, alone, [and bowed to my feet(?)]. I returned him to his place [and imposed tribute upon him, to wit:] gold, silver, linen garments with multicolored trimmings, . . . great . . . [I re]ceived from him. Israel (lit.: "Omri-Land" *Bît Ḫumria*) . . . all its inhabitants (and) their possessions I led to Assyria. They overthrew their king Pekah (*Pa-qa-ḫa*) and I placed Hoshea (*A-ú-si-'*) as king over them. I received from them 10 talents of gold, 1,000(?) talents of silver as their [tri]bute and brought them to Assyria.

II Kings 15:30

---

[1] The female rulers of Arab tribes attested in cuneiform documents from Tiglath-pileser III to Ashurbanipal, and perhaps Nabonidus.

[2] The terms used in this context are *takiltu* and *argamannu*; the first denoting a darker, the second a reddish shade of blue purple.

[3] This unique reference seems to mention stuffed and decorated animals.

SARGON II (721-705): THE FALL OF SAMARIA

ANET, 284-287

(a) Inscriptions of a General Nature

"Pavé des Portes," No. IV, lines 31-44.

(Property of Sargon, etc., king of Assyria, etc.) con- *Fig. 120*
queror of Samaria (*Sa-mir-i-na*) and of the entire (country of) Israel (*Bît-Ḫu-um-ri-a*) who despoiled Ashdod II Kings 18:9-10
(and) Shinuhti, who caught the Greeks who (live on
islands) in the sea, like fish, who exterminated Kasku,
all Tabali and Cilicia (*Ḫilakku*), who chased away
Midas (*Mi-ta-a*) king of Musku, who defeated Musur
(*Mu-ṣu-ri*) in Rapihu, who declared Hanno, king of
Gaza, as booty, who subdued the seven kings of the
country Ia', a district on Cyprus (*Ia-ad-na-na*), (who)
dwell (on an island) in the sea, at (a distance of) a
seven-day journey.

(b) From Annalistic Reports

So-called Annals and their parallels taken from the Display
Inscriptions. The Annals are quoted here according to A. G. Lie,
The Inscriptions of Sargon II, King of Assyria, Part 1. The
Annals (Paris, 1929).

First Year. (10—17)

At the begi[nning of my royal rule, I . . . the town of
the Sama]rians [I besieged, conquered] (2 lines destroyed) [for the god . . . who le]t me achieve (this)
my triumph. . . . I led away as prisoners [27,290 inhabitants of it (and) [equipped] from among [them
(soldiers to man)] 50 chariots for my royal corps. . . .
[The town I] re[built] better than (it was) before and
[settled] therein people from countries which [I] myself [had con]quered. I placed an officer of mine as
governor over them and imposed upon them tribute as
(is customary) for Assyrian citizens.

According to the Display Inscriptions. (23—26)

I besieged and conquered Samaria (*Sa-me-ri-na*), led
away as booty 27,290 inhabitants of it. I formed from
among them a contingent of 50 chariots and made remaining (inhabitants) assume their (social) positions.
I installed over them an officer of mine and imposed
upon them the tribute of the former king. Hanno, king
of Gaza and also Sib'e, the *turtan* of Egypt (*Mu-ṣu-ri*), II Kings 17:4 ff.
set out from Rapihu against me to deliver a decisive
battle. I defeated them; Sib'e ran away, afraid when
he (only) heard the noise of my (approaching) army,

and has not been seen again. Hanno, I captured personally. I received the tribute from Pir'u of Musuru, from Samsi, queen of Arabia (and) It'amar the Sabaean, gold in dust-form, horses (and) camels.

According to the Annals of the Room XIV.   (11—15)

Iamani from Ashdod, afraid of my armed force (lit.: weapons), left his wife and children and fled to the frontier of M[usru] which belongs to Meluhha (i.e., Ethiopia) and hid (lit.: stayed) there like a thief. I installed an officer of mine as governor over his entire large country and its prosperous inhabitants, (thus) aggrandizing (again) the territory belonging to Ashur, the king of the gods. The terror(-inspiring) glamor of Ashur, my lord, overpowered (however) the king of Meluhha and he threw him (i.e. Iamani) in fetters on hands and feet, and sent him to me, to Assyria. I conquered and sacked the towns Shinuhtu (and) Samaria, and all Israel (lit.: "Omri-Land" *Bît Ḫu-um-ri-ia*). I caught, like a fish, the Greek (Ionians) who live (on islands) amidst the Western Sea.

According to the Display Inscriptions.   (33—37)

Ia'ubidi from Hamath, a commoner[1] without claim to the throne, a cursed Hittite, schemed to become king of Hamath, induced the cities Arvad, Simirra, Damascus (*Di-maš-qa*[kl]) and Samaria to desert me, made them collaborate and fitted out an army. I called up the masses of the soldiers of Ashur and besieged him and his warriors in Qarqar, his favorite city. I conquered (it) and burnt (it). Himself I flayed; the rebels I killed in their cities and established (again) peace and harmony. A contingent of 200 chariots and 600 men on horseback I formed from among the inhabitants of Hamath and added them to my royal corps.   [1] *hubšu* denoting in Akkadian texts a special social class.

Seventh Year.   (120—125)

Upon a trust(-inspiring oracle given by) my lord Ashur, I crushed the tribes of Tamud, Ibadidi, Marsimanu, and Haiapa, the Arabs who live, far away, in the desert (and) who know neither overseers nor official(s) and who had not (yet) brought their tribute to any king. I deported their survivors and settled (them) in Samaria.

From Pir'u, the king of Musru, Samsi, the queen of

Arabia, It'amra, the Sabaean,—the(se) are the kings of the seashore and from the desert—I received as their presents, gold in the form of dust, precious stones, ivory, ebony-seeds,[1] all kinds of aromatic substances, horses (and) camels. [1] These are part of the Mesopotamian pharmacopoeia.

Eleventh Year. According to the Display Inscription
(90—112)

Azuri, king of Ashdod, had schemed not to deliver tribute any more and sent messages (full) of hostilities against Assyria, to the kings (living) in his neighborhood. On account of the(se) act(s) which he committed, I abolished his rule over the people of his country and made Ahimiti, his younger brother, king over them. But the(se) Hittites, always planning evil deeds, hated his reign and elevated to rule over them a Greek (*Ia-ma-ni*) who, without any claim to the throne, had no respect for authority—just as they themselves. In a sudden rage, I did not (wait to) assemble the full might of my army (or to) prepare the camp(ing equipment), but started out towards Ashdod (only) with those of my warriors who, even in friendly areas, never leave my side. But this Greek heard about the advance of my expedition, from afar, and he fled into the territory of Musru—which belongs (now) to Ethiopia —and his (hiding) place could not be detected. I besieged (and) conquered the cities Ashdod, Gath, Asdudimmu; I declared his images, his wife, his children, all the possessions and treasures of his palace as well as the inhabitants of his country as booty. I reorganized (the administration of) these cities (and) settled therein people from the [regions] of the East which I had conquered personally. I installed an officer of mine over them and declared them Assyrian citizens and they pulled (as such) the straps (of my yoke). The king of Ethiopia who [lives] in [a distant country], in an inapproachable region, the road [to which is . . .], whose fathers never—from remote days until now[17]—had sent messengers to inquire after the health of my royal forefathers, he did hear, even (that) far away, of the might of Ashur, Nebo (and) Marduk. The awe-inspiring glamor of my kingship blinded him and terror overcame him. He threw him (i.e. the Greek) in fetters, shackles and iron bands, and they brought him to Assyria, a long journey.

Isa. 20:1

(c) From Broken Prisms

According to the broken Prism A

[Aziru, king] of Ashdod (lacuna) on account of [this crime . . .] *from* . . . Ahimiti . . . his younger brother over [them . . .] I made (him) ruler . . . tribute . . . like (those of) the [former] kings, I imposed upon him. [But these] accursed [Hittites] conceived [the idea] of not delivering the tribute and [started] a rebellion against their ruler; they expelled him . . . (*Ia-ma-ni*) a Greek, comm[oner without claim to the throne] to be king over them, they made sit down [on the very throne] of his (former) master and [they . . .] their city of (or: for) the at[tack] (lacuna of 3 lines) . . . its neighborhood, a moat [they prepared] of a depth of 20 + x cubits . . . it (even) reached the underground water, in order to. . . . Then [to] the rulers of Palestine (*Pi-liš-te*), Judah (*Ia-ú-di*), Ed[om], Moab (and) those who live (on islands) and bring tribute [and] *tâmartu* -gifts to my lord Ashur—[he spread] countless evil lies to alienate (them) from me, and (also) sent bribes to Pir'u, king of Musru—a potentate, incapable to save them—and asked him to be an ally. But I, Sargon, the rightful ruler, devoted to the pronouncements (uttered by) Nebo and Marduk, (carefully) observing the orders of Ashur, led my army over the Tigris and the Euphrates, at the peak of the(ir) flood, the spring flood, as (if it be) dry ground. This Greek, however, their king who had put his trust in his own power and (therefore) did not bow to my (divinely ordained) rulership, heard about the approach of my expedition (while I was still) far away, and the splendor of my lord Ashur overwhelmed him and . . . he fled. . . .

Nimrud Inscription. (8)

(Property of Sargon, etc.) the subduer of the country Judah (*Ia-ú-du*) which is far away, the uprooter of Hamath, the ruler of which—Iau'bidi—he captured personally.[1]

---

[1] After his victory over Iau-bi'di at Qarqar, Sargon erected various stelae commemorating this event.

SENNACHERIB (704-681): THE SIEGE OF JERUSALEM

From the Prism of Sennacherib.   (ii 37—iii 49)   ANET, 287-288

In my third campaign I marched against Hatti. Luli, king of Sidon, whom the terror-inspiring glamor of my lordship had overwhelmed, fled far overseas and perished. The awe-inspiring splendor of the "Weapon" of Ashur, my lord, overwhelmed his strong cities (such as) Great Sidon, Little Sidon, Bit-Zitti, Zaribtu, Mahalliba, Ushu (i.e. the mainland settlement of Tyre), Akzib (and) Akko, (all) his fortress cities, walled (and well) provided with feed and water for his garrisons, and they bowed in submission to my feet. I installed Ethba'al (*Tuba'lu*) upon the throne to be their king and imposed upon him tribute (due) to me (as his) overlord (to be paid) annually without interruption.

As to all the kings of Amurru—Menahem (*Mi-in-ḫi-im-mu*) from Samsimuruna, Tuba'lu from Sidon, Abdili'ti from Arvad, Urumilki from Byblos, Mitinti from Ashdod, Buduili from Beth-Ammon, Kammusunadbi from Moab (and) Aiarammu from Edom, they brought sumptuous gifts (*igisû*) and—fourfold—their heavy *tâmartu* -presents to me and kissed my feet. Sidqia, however, king of Ashkelon, who did not bow to my yoke, I deported and sent to Assyria, his family-gods, himself, his wife, his children, his brothers, all the male descendants of his family. I set Sharruludari, son of Rukibtu, their former king, over the inhabitants of Ashkelon and imposed upon him the payment of tribute (and of) *katrû* -presents (due) to me (as) overlord—and he (now) pulls the straps (of my yoke)!

Fig. 102

In the continuation of my campaign I besieged Beth-Dagon, Joppa, Banai-Barqa, Azuru, cities belonging to Sidqia who did not bow to my feet quickly (enough); I conquered (them) and carried their spoils away. The officials, the patricians and the (common) people of Ekron[1]—who had thrown Padi, their king, into fetters (because he was) loyal to (his) solemn oath (sworn) by the god Ashur, and had handed him over to Hezekiah, the Jew (*Ha-za-qi-(i)a-ú* ^amel^*Ia-ú-da-ai*)— (and) he (Hezekiah) held him in prison, unlawfully, as if he (Padi) be an enemy—had become afraid and had called (for help) upon the kings of Egypt (*Muṣ(u)ri*) (and) the bowmen, the chariot(-corps) and the cavalry of the king of Ethiopia (*Meluḫḫa*), an army beyond

II Kings 18:21, 24

---
[1] Note the social stratification indicated in this passage.

counting—and they (actually) had come to their assistance. In the plain of Eltekeh (*Al-ta-qu-ú*), their battle lines were drawn up against me and they sharpened their weapons. Upon a trust(-inspiring) oracle (given) by Ashur, my lord, I fought with them and inflicted a defeat upon them. In the mêlée of the battle, I personally captured alive the Egyptian charioteers with the(ir) princes and (also) the charioteers of the king of Ethiopia. I besieged Eltekeh (and) Timnah (*Ta-am-na-a*), conquered (them) and carried their spoils away. I assaulted Ekron and killed the officials and patricians who had committed the crime and hung their bodies on poles surrounding the city. The (common) citizens who were guilty of minor crimes, I considered prisoners of war. The rest of them, those who were not accused of crimes and misbehavior, I released. I made Padi, their king, come from Jerusalem (*Ur-sa-li-im-mu*) and set him as their lord on the throne, imposing upon him the tribute (due) to me (as) overlord.

As to Hezekiah, the Jew, he did not submit to my yoke, I laid siege to 46 of his strong cities, walled forts and to the countless small villages in their vicinity, and conquered (them) by means of well-stamped (earth-)ramps, and battering-rams brought (thus) near (to the walls) (combined with) the attack by foot soldiers, (using) mines, breeches as well as sapper work. I drove out (of them) 200,150 people, young and old, male and female, horses, mules, donkeys, camels, big and small cattle beyond counting, and considered (them) booty. Himself I made a prisoner in Jerusalem, his royal residence, like a bird in a cage. I surrounded him with earthwork in order to molest those who were leaving his city's gate. His towns which I had plundered, I took away from his country and gave them (over) to Mitinti, king of Ashdod, Padi, king of Ekron, and Sillibel, king of Gaza. Thus I reduced his country, but I still increased the tribute and the *katrû* -presents (due) to me (as his) overlord which I imposed (later) upon him beyond the former tribute, to be delivered annually. Hezekiah himself, whom the terror-inspiring splendor of my lordship had overwhelmed and whose irregular and elite troops which he had brought into Jerusalem, his royal residence, in order to strengthen (it), had deserted him, did send me, later, to Nineveh, my lordly city, together with 30 talents of gold, 800 talents of

II Kings 18:15

silver, precious stones, antimony,[1] large cuts of red stone, couches (inlaid) with ivory, *nîmedu* -chairs (inlaid) with ivory, elephant-hides, ebony-wood, boxwood (and) all kinds of valuable treasures, his (own) daughters, concubines, male and female musicians. In order to deliver the tribute and to do obeisance as a slave he sent his (personal) messenger.

[1] This refers probably to stibnite, which might have been used as an eye paint (beside the cheaper and efficient substitute, burnt shells of almond and soot). Stibium is easily reduced and the metal is sporadically attested in Mesopotamia since the Neo-Sumerian period.

Epigraph from a relief showing the conquest of Lachish.   *Fig. 121*

Sennacherib, king of the world, king of Assyria, sat upon a *nîmedu* -throne and passed in review the booty (taken) from Lachish (*La-ki-su*).

II Kings 18:14
II Kings 19:8

ESARHADDON (680-669): THE SYRO-PALESTINIAN CAMPAIGN

ANET, 291

From the Prism B.

(v 54—vi 1)

I called up the kings of the country Hatti and (of the region) on the other side of the river· (Euphrates) (to wit): Ba'lu, king of Tyre, Manasseh (*Me-na-si-i*), king of Judah (*Ia-ú-di*), Qaushgabri, king of Edom, Musuri, king of Moab, Sil-Bel, king of Gaza, Metinti, king of Ashkelon, Ikausu, king of Ekron, Milkiashapa, king of Byblos, Matanba'al, king of Arvad, Abiba'al, king of Samsimuruna, Puduil, king of Beth-Ammon, Ahimilki, king of Ashdod—12 kings from the seacoast;

II Chron. 33:11

Ekishtura, king of Edi'il (Idalion), Pilagura (Pythagoras), king of Kitrusi (Chytros), Kisu, king of Sillu'ua (Soli), Ituandar, king of Pappa (Paphos), Erisu, king of Silli, Damasu, king of Kuri (Curium), Atmesu, king of Tamesi, Damusi, king of Qarti-hadasti (Carthage), Unasagusu, king of Lidir (Ledra), Bususu, king of Nuria,—10 kings from Cyprus (*Iadnana*) amidst the sea,

together 22 kings of Hatti, the seashore and the islands; all these I sent out and made them transport under terrible difficulties, to Nineveh, the town (where I exercise) my rulership, as building material for my palace: big logs, long beams (and) thin boards from cedar and pine trees, products of the Sirara and Lebanon

(*Lab-na-na*) mountains, which had grown for a long time into tall and strong timber, (also) from their quarries (lit.: place of creation) in the mountains, statues of protective deities (lit.: of Lamassû and Shêdu) made of a š n a n -stone, statues of (female) *abzaztu*, thresholds, slabs of limestone, of a š n a n -stone, of large- and small-grained breccia, of *alallu*-stone, (and) of g i . r i n . h i . l i . b a -stone.

ANET, 301   RECEIPT OF TRIBUTE FROM PALESTINE

The BrM text K 1295 is a receipt of tribute brought from Palestine.

Two minas of gold from the inhabitants of Bit-Ammon (*^{mat}Bit-Am-man-na-a-a*); one mina of gold from the inhabitants of Moab (*^{mat}Mu-'-ba-a-a*); ten minas of silver from the inhabitants of Judah (*^{mat}Ia-ú-da-a-a*); [. . . mi]nas of silver from the inhabitants of [Edom] (*^{mat}[U-du-ma]-a-a*). . . .

(reverse)

. . . the inhabitants of Byblos, the district officers of the king, my lord, have brought.

Historiographic Documents

ANET, 304-305   THE FALL OF NINEVEH

C. J. Gadd, *The Newly Discovered Babylonian Chronicle*, No. 21,901, in the British Museum (London, 1923), with transliteration and translation. Excerpt given is for the fourteenth year of Nabopolassar.

(reverse)

[Fourteenth year:] The king of Akkad cal[led up] his army and [Cyaxar]es, the king of the Manda-hordes (*Umman-manda*) marched towards the king of Akkad, [in] . . . they met each other. The king of Akkad . . . and [Cyaxar]es . . . [the . . .]s he ferried across and they marched (upstream) on the embankment of the Tigris and . . . [pitched camp] against Nineveh. . . . From the month Simanu till the month Abu, three ba[ttles were fought, then] they made a great attack against the city. In the month Abu, [the . . . th day, the city was seized and a great defeat] he inflicted [upon the] entire [population]. On that day, Sinsharishkun, king of Assy[ria fled to] . . . , many prisoners of the city, beyond counting, they carried away. The city [they turned] into ruin-hills and hea[ps (of debris). The king] and the army of Assyria escaped (however) before the king (of Akkad) and [the army] of the king of Akkad. . . . In the month Ululu, the 20th day, Cyaxares and his army returned to his country. Afterwards, the king of A[kkad] . . . marched as far as Nisibis. Booty and *ga-lu-tu* of . . . and (of) the country Rusapu they brought to the king of Akkad, to Nineveh. [In the month] . . . Ashuruballit . . . sat down in Harran upon the throne to become king of Assyria. Till the month . . . [the king of Akkad stayed] in Nineveh. . . . From the 20th day of the month [Tashritu] the king [of Akkad] . . . in the same month of Tashritu in the town. . . .

THE FALL OF JERUSALEM
(rev. 11-13)

Text from the seventh year of Nebuchadnezzar II. D. J. Wiseman, *Chronicles of Chaldaean Kings (626-556 B.C.) in the British Museum* (London, 1956). Tablet B.M. 21946 on plates V and XIV ff., also pp. 66 ff.

Seventh year: In the month Kislimu, the king of Akkad called up his army, marched against Syria (lit. Hattu-land), encamped against the city of Judah (URU Ia-a-hu-du) and seized the town on the second day of the month Adar. He captured the king. He appointed there a king of his own choice. He took much booty from it and sent (it) to Babylon.

Fig. 58

THE FALL OF BABYLON

ANET, 306-307

Eleventh year: The king (stayed) in Tema;[1] the crown prince, the officials and his army (were) in Akkad. The king did not come to Babylon for the (ceremonies of the) month Nisanu, Nebo did not come to Babylon, Bel did not go out (from Esagila in procession), the festival of the New Year was omitted, (but) the offerings for the gods of Babylon and Borsippa were given according to the complete (ritual).

(iii reverse)

. . . Tigris . . . [In the month of] Addaru the (image of the) Ishtar of Uruk . . . the . . . [the . . .]s of the Sea Country . . . [arm]y [made an] at[tack]. . . .

[Seventeenth year:] . . . Nebo [went] from Borsippa for the procession of [Bel . . .] [the king] entered the temple É.tùr.kalam.ma, in the t[emple] . . . (partly unintelligible)[2] [Be]l went out (in procession),

---

[1] Nabonidus' prolonged and apparently unmotivated stay in Tema has given rise to an extended literature.
[2] This incident seems to have occurred during the New Year's Festival.

they performed the festival of the New Year according to the complete (ritual). In the month of . . . [Lugal-Marada and the other gods] of the town Marad, Zababa and the (other) gods of Kish, the goddess Ninlil [and the other gods of] Hursagkalama entered Babylon. Till the end of the month Ululu (all) the gods of Akkad . . . those from above the IM and (those from) below the IM, entered Babylon. The gods from Borsippa, Kutha, . . . and Sippar (however) did not enter. In the month of Tashritu, when Cyrus attacked the army of Akkad in Opis on the Tigris, the inhabitants of Akkad revolted, but he (*Nabonidus*) massacred the confused inhabitants. The 14th day, Sippar was seized without battle. Nabonidus fled. The 16th day, Gobryas (*Ugbaru*), the governor of Gutium and the army of Cyrus entered Babylon without battle. Afterwards Nabonidus was arrested in Babylon when he returned (there). Till the end of the month, the shield(-carrying) Gutians were staying within Esagila (but) nobody carried arms in Esagila and its (pertinent) buildings, the correct time (for a ceremony) was not missed. In the month of Arahshamnu, the 3rd day, Cyrus entered Babylon, green twigs were spread in front of him— the state of "Peace" (*šulmu*) was imposed upon the city. Cyrus sent greetings to all Babylon. Gobryas, his governor, installed (sub-)governors in Babylon. From the month of Kislimu to the month of Addaru, the gods of Akkad which Nabonidus had made come down to Babylon . . . returned to their sacred cities. In the month of Arahshamnu, on the night of the 11th day, Gobryas died. In the month of [Arahshamnu, the . . .th day, the wi]fe of the king died. From the 27th day of Arahshamnu till the 3rd day of Nisanu a(n official) "weeping" was performed in Akkad, all the people (went around) with their hair disheveled. When, the 4th day, Cambyses, son of Cyrus, went to the temple é . NÍG.PA . k a l a m . m a . s u m . m̩a , the É . P A priest of Nebo who . . . the bull . . . they came (and) made the "weaving" by means of the *handles* and when [he le]d the image of Ne[bo . . . sp]ears and leather quivers, from. . . . Nebo returned to Esagila, sheep-offerings in front of Bel and the god Mâ[r]-b[íti].

(iv reverse)

(After lacuna, only the ends of 9 lines are preserved.)

NEBUCHADNEZZAR II (605-562)

(1) From administrative documents found in Babylon, some information concerning the fate of Jehoiachin, king of Judah, can now be gathered. These cuneiform tablets list deliveries of oil for the subsistence of individuals who are either prisoners of war or otherwise dependent upon the royal household. They are identified by name, profession, and/or nationality. The two tablets, so far published, also mention, beside Judeans, inhabitants of Ashkelon, Tyre, Byblos, Arvad, and, further, Egyptians, Medeans, Persians, Lydians, and Greeks.

II Kings 25:27-30

Jer. 52:31-34

(text Babylon 28122, obverse 29-33)

... t[o?] *Ia-'-ú-kin*, king ...
to the *qipūtu*-house of ...
... for Shalamiamu, the ...
... for 126 men from Tyre ...
... for Zabiria, the Ly[dian] ...

(text Babylon 28178, obverse ii 38-40)

10 (*sila* of oil) to ... [*Ia*]-'-*kin*, king of *Ia*[...]
2½ *sila* (oil) to [... so]ns of the king of Judah
(*Ia-a-ḫu-du*)
4 *sila* to 8 men from Judah (*amelIa-a-ḫu-da-a-a*) ...

(text Babylon 28186, reverse ii 13-18)

1½ *sila* (oil) for 3 carpenters from Arvad, ½ *sila* each
11½ *sila* for 8 ditto from Byblos, 1 sila each ...
3½ *sila* for 7 ditto, Greeks, ½ sila each
½ *sila* to *Nabû-êṭir* the carpenter
10 (*sila*) to *Ia-ku-ú-ki-nu*, the son of the king of *Ia-ku-du* (i.e. Judah)
2½ *sila* for the 5 sons of the king of Judah (*Ia-ku-du*)
through Qana'a [...]

(2) From a fragmentary historical text (BrM 78-10-15, 22, 37, and 38).   (13—22)

. . . [in] the 37th year, Nebuchadnezzar, king of Bab[ylon] mar[ched against] Egypt (*Mi-ṣir*) to deliver a battle. [*Ama*]*sis* (text: [. . .]-*a(?)-su*), of Egypt, [called up his a]rm[y] . . . [. . .]*ku* from the town *Puṭu-Iaman* . . . distant regions which (are situated on islands) amidst the sea . . . many . . . which/who (are) in Egypt . . . [car]rying weapons, horses and [chariot]s . . . he called up to assist him and . . . did [. . .] in front of him . . . he put his trust . . . (only the first signs at the beginning and the end of the following 7 or 8 lines are legible).

.ANET, 315-316 CYRUS (557-529)

Fig. 195 Inscription on a clay barrel.

(one line destroyed)

. . . [r]ims (of the world) . . . a weakling has been installed as the *enû*[1] of his country; [the correct images of the gods he removed from their thrones, imi]tations he ordered to place upon them. A replica of the temple Esagila he has . . . for Ur and the other sacred cities inappropriate rituals . . . daily he did blabber [incorrect prayers]. He (furthermore) interrupted in a fiendish way the regular offerings, he did . . . he established within the sacred cities. The worship of Marduk, the king of the gods, he [chang]ed into abomination, daily he used to do evil against his (i.e. Marduk's) city. . . . He [tormented] its [inhabitant]s with corvée-work (lit.: a yoke) without relief, he ruined them all.

Upon their complaints the lord of the gods became terribly angry and [he departed from] their region, (also) the (other) gods living among them left their mansions, wroth that he had brought (them) into Babylon (Š u . a n . n aᵏⁱ). (But) Marduk [who does care for] . . . on account of (the fact that) the sanctuaries of all their settlements were in ruins and the inhabitants of Sumer and Akkad had become like (living) dead, turned back (his countenance) [his] an[ger] [abated] and he had mercy (upon them). He scanned and looked (through) all the countries, searching for a righteous ruler willing to lead him (i.e. Marduk)-(in the annual procession). (Then) he pronounced the name of Cyrus (*Ku-ra-aš*), king of Anshan, declared him (lit.: pronounced [his] name) to be(come) the ruler of all the world. He made the Guti country and all the Manda-hordes bow in submission to his (i.e. Cyrus') feet. And he (Cyrus) did always endeavour to treat according to justice the black-headed whom he (Marduk) has made him conquer. Marduk, the great lord, a protector of his people/worshipers, beheld with pleasure his (i.e. Cyrus') good deeds and his upright mind (lit.: heart) (and therefore) ordered him to march against his city Babylon (K á . d i n g i r . r a). He

---

[1] The old Sumerian title appears here in a context which seems to indicate that the primitive concept concerning the intimate connection between the physical vitality of the ruler and the prosperity of the country, was still valid in the political speculations of the Babylonian clergy.

made him set out on the road to Babylon (DIN.TIR^{ki})
going at his side like a real friend. His widespread
troops—their number, like that of the water of a river,
could not be established—strolled along, their weapons
packed away. Without any battle, he made him enter
his town Babylon (Šu. a n . n a), sparing Babylon
(Ká. d i n g i r . r a^{ki}) any calamity. He delivered into
his (i.e. Cyrus') hands Nabonidus, the king who did not
worship him (i.e. Marduk). All the inhabitants of
Babylon (DIN.TIR^{ki}) as well as of the entire country of
Sumer and Akkad, princes and governors (included),
bowed to him (Cyrus) and kissed his feet, jubilant that
he (had received) the kingship, and with shining
faces. Happily they greeted him as a master through
whose help they had come (again) to life from death
(and) had all been spared damage and disaster, and
they worshiped his (very) name.

I am Cyrus, king of the world, great king, legitimate
king, king of Babylon, king of Sumer and Akkad,
king of the four rims (of the earth), son of Cambyses
(*Ka-am-bu-zi-ia*), great king, king of Anshan, grandson of Cyrus, great king, king of Anshan, descendant
of Teispes (*Ši-iš-pi-iš*), great king, king of Anshan, of
a family (which) always (exercised) kingship; whose
rule Bel and Nebo love, whom they want as king to
please their hearts.

When I entered Babylon (DIN.TIR^{ki}) as a friend and
(when) I established the seat of the government in the
palace of the ruler under jubilation and rejoicing,
Marduk, the great lord, [induced] the magnanimous
inhabitants of Babylon (DIN.TIR^{ki}) [to love me], and I
was daily endeavouring to worship him. My numerous
troops walked around in Babylon (DIN.TIR^{ki}) in peace,
I did not allow anybody to terrorize (any place) of
the [country of Sumer] and Akkad. I strove for peace
in Babylon (Ká. d i n g i r . r a^{ki}) and in all his (other)
sacred cities. As to the inhabitants of Babylon (DIN.TIR^{ki}),
[who] against the will of the gods [had/were . . . , I
abolished] the corvée (lit.: yoke) which was against
their (social) standing. I brought relief to their dilapi-
dated housing, putting (thus) an end to their (main)
complaints. Marduk, the great lord, was well pleased
with my deeds and sent friendly blessings to myself,
Cyrus, the king who worships him, to Cambyses, my
son, the offspring of [my] loins, as well as to all my

troops, and we all [praised] his great [godhead] joyously, standing before him in peace.

All the kings of the entire world from the Upper to the Lower Sea, those who are seated in throne rooms, (those who) live in other [types of buildings as well as] all the kings of the West land living in tents,[1] brought their heavy tributes and kissed my feet in Babylon (Š u . a n . n a). (As to the region) from . . . as far as Ashur and Susa, Agade, Eshnunna, the towns Zamban, Me-Turnu,[7] Der as well as the region of the Gutians, I returned to (these) sacred cities on the other side of the Tigris, the sanctuaries of which have been ruins for a long time, the images which (used) to live therein and established for them permanent sanctuaries. I (also) gathered all their (former) inhabitants and returned (to them) their habitations. Furthermore, I resettled upon the command of Marduk, the great lord, all the gods of Sumer and Akkad whom Nabonidus has brought into Babylon (Š u . a n . n a[ki]) to the anger of the lord of the gods, unharmed, in their (former) chapels, the places which make them happy.

May all the gods whom I have resettled in their sacred cities ask daily Bel and Nebo for a long life for me and may they recommend me (to him); to Marduk, my lord, they may say this: "Cyrus, the king who worships you, and Cambyses, his son, . . ." . . . all of them I settled in a peaceful place . . . ducks and doves, . . . I endeavoured to fortify/repair their dwelling places. . . .

(six lines destroyed)

[1] This phrase refers either to the way of life of a nomadic or a primitive society in contradistinction to that of an urban.

VIII. Palestinian Inscriptions

TRANSLATOR: W. F. ALBRIGHT

The Gezer Calendar

This little inscription was discovered at Gezer in 1908 by
R. A. S. Macalister; it is on a school exercise tablet of soft
limestone. For a number of years its date was uncertain, but
recent discoveries establish its relative archaism and point to the
second half of the tenth century or the very beginning of the
ninth as its probable time. The writer would date it in or about
the third quarter of the tenth century—about 925 B.C. in round
numbers. The language is good biblical Hebrew, in a very early
spelling; it is written in verse and seems to have been a kind
of mnemonic ditty for children.

His two months are (olive) harvest,   (tricolon, 2:2:2)
    His two months are planting (grain),
        His two months are late planting;
His month is hoeing up of flax,   (tricolon, 3:3:3)
    His month is harvest of barley,
        His month is harvest and *feasting*;
His two months are vine-tending,   (bicolon, 2:2)
    His month is summer fruit.

The Moabite Stone

This important inscription was discovered intact in 1868; it
was subsequently broken by the Arabs and in 1873 it was taken
to the Louvre.

The date of the Mesha Stone is roughly fixed by the reference
to Mesha, king of Moab, in II Kings 3:4, after 849 B.C. However, since the contents of the stela point to a date toward the
end of the king's reign, it seems probable that it should be placed
between 840 and 820, perhaps about 830 B.C. in round numbers.

I (am) Mesha, son of Chemosh-[. . .], king of Moab,
the Dibonite—my father (had) reigned over Moab
thirty years, and I reigned after my father,—(who)
made this high place for Chemosh in Qarhoh [. . .]
because he saved me from all the kings and caused me
to triumph over all my adversaries. As for Omri, (5)
king of Israel, he humbled Moab many years (lit.,
days), for Chemosh was angry at his land. And his son
followed him and he also said, "I will humble Moab."
In my time he spoke (thus), but I have triumphed
over him and over his house, while Israel hath perished
for ever! (Now) Omri had occupied the land of
Medeba, and (Israel) had dwelt there in his time and

half the time of his son (Ahab), forty years; but Chemosh dwelt there in my time.

And I built Baal-meon, making a reservoir in it, and I built (10) Qaryaten. Now the men of Gad had always dwelt in the land of Ataroth, and the king of Israel had built Ataroth for them; but I fought against the town and took it and slew all the people of the town as satiation (intoxication) for Chemosh and Moab. And I brought back from there Arel (or Oriel), its chieftain, dragging him before Chemosh in Kerioth, and I settled there men of Sharon and men of Maharith. And Chemosh said to me, "Go, take Nebo from Israel!" (15) So I went by night and fought against it from the break of dawn until noon, taking it and slaying all, seven thousand men, boys, women, girls and maid-servants, for I had devoted them to destruction for (the god) Ashtar-Chemosh. And I took from there the [...] of Yahweh, dragging them before Chemosh. And the king of Israel had built Jahaz, and he dwelt there while he was fighting against me, but Chemosh drove him out before me. And (20) I took from Moab two hundred men, all first class (warriors), and set them against Jahaz and took it in order to attach it to (the district of) Dibon.

It was I (who) built Qarhoh, the wall of *the forests* and the wall of the citadel; I also built its gates and I built its towers and I built the king's house, and I made both of its reservoirs for water inside the town. And there was no cistern inside the town at Qarhoh, so I said to all the people, "Let each of you make (25) a cistern for himself in his house!" And I cut *beams* for Qarhoh with Israelite captives. I built Aroer, and I made the highway in the Arnon (valley); I built Beth-bamoth, for it had been destroyed; I built Bezer— for it lay in ruins—with fifty men of Dibon, for all Dibon is (my) loyal dependency.

And I reigned [*in peace*] *over* the hundred towns which I had added to the land. And I built (30) [...] Medeba and Beth-diblathen and Beth-baal-meon, and I set there the [...] of the land. And as for Hauronen, there dwelt in it [.... And] Chemosh said to me, "Go down, fight against Hauronen. And I went down [and I fought against the town and I took it], and Chemosh dwelt there in my time. ...

The Ostraca of Samaria

This name is applied to a homogeneous group of 63 dockets on Israelite potsherds which were found by G. A. Reisner in 1910, while excavating a floor-level from the first phase of the second period of palace construction at Samaria. Owing to a mistake in stratigraphy, which was subsequently corrected by J. W. Crowfoot and his associates, this level was first attributed to Ahab; it is now reasonably certain that it should be assigned to the reign of Jeroboam II (about 786-746 B.C.). The four regnal years mentioned on the Ostraca extend from the ninth to the seventeenth (about 778-770 B.C.). These documents, though jejune in themselves, are of great significance for the script, spelling, personal names, topography, religion, administrative system, and clan distribution of the period.

Samaria Ostracon, No. 1

In the tenth year. To Shamaryau (Shemariah) from Beer-yam, a jar of old wine. Pega (son of) Elisha, 2; Uzza (son of) . . . , 1; Eliba, 1; Baala (son of) Elisha, 1; Jedaiah, 1.

Samaria Ostracon, No. 2

In the tenth year. To Gaddiyau from Azzo. Abibaal, 2; Ahaz, 2; Sheba, 1; Merib-baal, 1.

Samaria Ostracon, No. 18

In the tenth year. From Hazeroth to Gaddiyau. A jar of fine oil.

Samaria Ostracon, No. 30

In the fifteenth year. From Shemida to Hillez (son of) Gaddiyau. Gera (son of) Hanniab.

Samaria Ostracon, No. 55

In the tenth year. (From the) vineyard of Yehau-eli. A jar of fine oil.

An Order for Barley from Samaria

In 1932 several ostraca were found at Samaria, and were published the following year by E. L. Sukenik. One of them is outstanding because of its length and relative completeness. The script belongs to the eighth century, probably to its third quarter; it is characterized by extraordinarily long shafts of such letters as *l, m, n*, like other Israelite documents of this general period. The text is difficult, and the rendering below is tentative.

Baruch *(son of) Shallum* [. . .]

O Baruch . . . pay attention and [give (?) to . . . (son of)] Yimnah (Imnah) barley (to the amount of) two (or three?) *measures*.

The Siloam Inscription

Fig. 73

Accidentally discovered in 1880 in the rock wall of the lower entrance to the tunnel of Hezekiah south of the temple area in Jerusalem, the inscription is now in the Museum of the Ancient Orient at Istanbul. Its six lines occupy the lower half of a prepared surface, the upper part of which was found bare of inscription. It is, accordingly, almost certain that the first half of the original document is missing. Its contents and script point to the reign of Hezekiah (about 715-687 B.C.), a dating confirmed by II Kings 20:20 and especially II Chron. 32:30.

[. . . when] (the tunnel) was driven through. And this was the way in which it was cut through:—While [. . .] (were) still [. . .] axe(s), each man toward his fellow, and while there were still three cubits to be cut through, [there was heard] the voice of a man calling to his fellow, for there was *an overlap* in the rock on the right [and on the left]. And when the tunnel was driven through, the quarrymen hewed (the rock), each man toward his fellow, axe against axe; and the water flowed from the spring toward the reservoir for 1,200 cubits, and the height of the rock above the head(s) of the quarrymen was 100 cubits.

The Lachish Ostraca

These ostraca were discovered in the ruins of the latest Israelite occupation at Tell ed-Duweir in southern Palestine, which unquestionably represents biblical Lachish. The first 18 were found by the late J. L. Starkey in 1935; three more (making 21 in all) were added during a supplementary campaign in 1938. Most of the ostraca were letters, while others were lists of names, etc., but only a third of the documents are preserved well enough to be reasonably intelligible throughout. Nearly all of the ostraca come from the latest occupation level of the Israelite gate-tower, and they are generally placed immediately before the beginning of the Chaldean siege of Lachish, perhaps in the autumn of 589 (or 588) B.C. Since they form the only known corpus of documents in classical Hebrew prose, they have unusual philological significance, quite aside from the light which they shed on the time of Jeremiah.

Lachish Ostracon II

To my lord Yaosh: May Yahweh cause my lord to hear tidings of peace this very day, this very day! Who is thy servant (but) a dog that my lord hath remembered his servant? May Yahweh afflict those who re[port] an (evil) rumor about which thou art not informed!

II Sam. 9:8

Lachish Ostracon III

Thy servant Hoshaiah hath sent to inform my lord Yaosh: May Yahweh cause my lord to hear tidings of peace! And now thou hast sent a letter, but my lord did not enlighten thy servant concerning the letter which thou didst send to thy servant yesterday evening, though the heart of thy servant hath been sick since thou didst write to thy servant. And as for what my lord said, "Dost thou not understand?—call a scribe!", as Yahweh liveth no one hath ever undertaken to call a scribe for me; and as for any scribe who might have come to me, truly I did not call him nor would I give anything at all for him!

And it hath been reported to thy servant, saying, "The commander of the host, Coniah son of Elnathan, hath come down in order to go into Egypt; and unto Hodaviah son of Ahijah and his men hath he sent to obtain . . . from him."

And as for the letter of Tobiah, servant of the king, which came to Shallum son of Jaddua through the prophet, saying, "Beware!", thy servant hath sent it to my lord.

Lachish Ostracon IV

Fig. 80

May Yahweh cause my lord to hear this very day tidings of good! And now according to everything that my lord hath written, so hath thy servant done; I have written on the door according to all that my lord hath written to me. And with respect to what my lord hath written about the matter of *Beth-haraphid*, there is no one there.

And as for Semachiah, Shemaiah hath taken him and hath brought him up to the city. And as for thy servant, I am not sending *anyone* thither [today(?), but I will send] tomorrow morning.

And let (my lord) know that we are watching for the signals of Lachish, according to all the indications which my lord hath given, for we cannot see Azekah.

Lachish Ostracon V

May Yahweh cause my lord to hear [tidings of peace] and good [this very day, this very day!] Who is thy servant (but) a dog that thou hast sent to thy servant the [letters . . . Now] thy servant hath returned the letters to my lord. May Yahweh cause thee to see [. . .]. How can thy servant benefit or injure the king?

Lachish Ostracon VI

To my lord Yaosh: May Yahweh cause my lord to see this season in good health! Who is thy servant (but) a dog that my lord hath sent the [let]ter of the king and the letters of the prince[s, say]ing, "Pray, read them!" And behold the words of the pr[inces] are not good, (but) to weaken our hands [and to sla]cken the hands of the m[en] *who are informed about them* [. . . And now] my lord, wilt thou not write to them, saying, "Why do ye thus [*even*] in Jerusalem? Behold unto the king and unto [*his house*] are ye doing this thing!" [And,] as Yahweh thy God liveth, truly since thy servant read the letters there hath been no [*peace*] for [thy ser]vant. . . .

Jer. 38:4

Lachish Ostracon VIII

May Yahweh cause my lord to hear tidings of good this very day! [. . .]. *The Lord hath humbled me* before thee. *Nedabiah* hath fled to the mountains [. . .]. Truly I lie not—let my lord *send* thither!

Lachish Ostracon IX

May Yahweh cause my lord to hear [tidings] of peace! [. . .] let him send [. . .] *fifteen* [. . .]. Return word to thy servant through *Shelemiah* (telling us) what we shall do tomorrow!

IX. Canaanite and Aramaic Inscriptions

TRANSLATOR: FRANZ ROSENTHAL

Building Inscriptions

YEHIMILK OF BYBLOS

ANET, 499

This inscription records the dedication of a new building, possibly a temple, and is now quite generally dated in the tenth century. It was found in Byblos in 1929.

A house built by Yehimilk, king of Byblos, who also has restored all the ruins of the houses here.

May Ba'lshamem and the Lord of Byblos[1] and the Assembly of the Holy Gods of Byblos prolong the days and years of Yehimilk in Byblos, for (he is) a righteous king and an upright king before the Holy Gods of Byblos!

[1] A correction to "Lady of Byblos," a frequently mentioned deity, has been suggested.

AZITAWADDA OF ADANA

ANET, 499-500

This unusually long inscription comes from a locality called Karatepe situated about thirty-eight miles southwest of Mar'ash beside the River Jeyhan. Three versions of the Phoenician text, together with some Hittite versions, were discovered in 1946-47. They contain an autobiographical account which king Azitawadda composed on the occasion of the dedication of a citadel and city founded by him. The exact date of the inscriptions is still uncertain and depends on a further study of the archaeological and historical evidence. The text seems to antedate events described in the inscription of Kilamuwa (see no. 3), but at present a much later, eighth-century date cannot be ruled out.

One version of the inscription is written in four columns on four sides of a statue. Another version starts on a gate lion and is continued on two orthostats. The third version consists of three columns distributed over four orthostats and continued on the bases of the fourth and adjacent orthostats to a gate lion.

I am Azitawadda, the blessed of Ba'l,[1] the servant of Ba'l, whom Awrikku[2] made powerful, king of the Danunites.

Ba'l made me a father and a mother to the Danunites. I have restored the Danunites. I have expanded the country of the Plain of Adana from the rising of the sun to its setting. In my days, the Danunites had everything good and plenty to eat and well-being. I have

[1] Or perhaps: "chief official (habarakku) of Ba'l."
[2] Awrikku most probably was the father of Azitawadda.

filled the storehouses of Pa'r. I have added horse to horse, shield to shield, and army to army, by virtue of Ba'l and the Gods (*El*). I shattered the wicked. I have removed all the evil that was in the country. I have set up my lordly houses in good shape and I have acted kindly toward the roots of my sovereignty.[1]

I have been sitting upon the throne of my father. I have made peace with every king. Yea, every king considered me his father because of my righteousness and my wisdom and the kindness of my heart.

I have built strongholds in all the outposts at the borders in places where there were evil men, gang-leaders, none of whom had been subservient to the House of Mupsh. I, Azitawadda, placed them underneath my feet. I have built strongholds in those places, so that the Danunites might dwell in peace of mind.

I have subdued powerful countries in the west which the kings who were before me had not been able to subdue. I, Azitawadda, subdued them. I have brought them (their inhabitants) down and established them at the eastern end of my borders, and I have established Danunites there (in the west). In my days, there was, within all the borders of the Plain of Adana, from the rising of the sun to its setting, even in places which had formerly been feared, where a man was afraid to walk on the road but where in my days a woman was able *to stroll, peaceful activity*,[2] by virtue of Ba'l and the Gods (*El*). And in all my days, the Danunites and the entire Plain of Adana had plenty to eat and well-being and a good situation and peace of mind.

I have built this city. I have given it the name of Azitawaddiya, for Ba'l and Reshef-*Ṣprm* commissioned me to build it. I have built it, by virtue of Ba'l and by virtue of Reshef-*Ṣprm*, with plenty to eat and well-being and in a good situation and in peace of mind to be a protection for the Plain of Adana and the House of Mupsh, for in my days, the country of the Plain of Adana had plenty to eat and well-being, and the Danunites *never* had *any night* in my days.

Having built this city and having given it the name of Azitawaddiya, I have established Ba'l-*Krntryš* in it. A sacrific(ial order) was established for all the molten images: for the yearly sacrifice an ox, at the [time of

---

[1] The "roots" may be the residential and capital cities of the realm, or the royal offspring.　　[2] Literally: *"work* (Akk. *dullu*) *with spindles."*

pl]owing a sheep, and at the time of harvesting a sheep.

May Ba'l-*Krntryš* bless Azitawadda with life, peace, and mighty power over every king, so that Ba'l-*Krntryš* and all the gods of the city may give Azitawadda length of days, a great number of years, good authority, and mighty power over every king! And may this city possess plenty to eat and wine (to drink), and may this people that dwells in it possess oxen and small cattle and plenty to eat and wine (to drink)! May they have many children, may they be strong numerically, may they serve Azitawadda and the House of Mupsh in large numbers, by virtue of Ba'l and the Gods (*El*)!

If there be a king among kings and a prince among princes or a man who is (just) called a man who shall wipe out the name of Azitawadda from this gate and put down his own name, even if he has good intentions toward this city but removes this gate which was made by Azitawadda and makes for the (new) gate a (new) *frame* and puts his name upon it, whether he removes this gate with good intentions or out of hatred and evil, let Ba'lshamem and El-the-Creator-of-the-Earth and the Eternal-Sun and the whole Group of the Children of the Gods (*El*) wipe out that ruler and that king and that man who is (just) called a man! However, the name of Azitawadda shall endure forever like the name of sun and moon!

KILAMUWA OF Y'DY-SAM'AL

ANET, 500-501

This autobiographical account, composed in connection with the dedication of a palace, was discovered in 1902 in modern Zinjirli in northwest Syria. It dates from the second half of the ninth century B.C. The text consists of two parts. In the first part, king Kilamuwa boasts of his success in foreign policy, and in the second part, he praises his domestic accomplishments. He states that he improved the position of the *mškbm*, possibly an oppressed sedentary element of the population, on whose undisturbed relations with another group, the *b'rrm*, possibly referring to "wild" Bedouins, peace in his realm depended.

Y'dy, whose vocalization is uncertain, might be the capital city of the realm, to be vocalized Yu'addiya or the like (cf. Azitawadda-Azitawaddiya), which later on came to be known as Sam'al. The latter, however, might have been the name of a larger region or country.

I am Kilamuwa, the son of Hayya. Gabbar became king over *Y'dy* but he was ineffective. There was *Bmh* but he was ineffective. There was my father Hayya but he was ineffective. There was my brother Sha'il but he was ineffective. But I, Kilamuwa, the son of *Tm*,[1] what I achieved, the former (kings) did not achieve.

My father's house was in the midst of mighty kings. Everybody stretched forth his hand to eat it. But I was in the hands of the kings like a fire that eats the beard, like a fire that eats the hand. The king of the Danunites (tried to) overpower me, but I hired against him the king of Assyria, (who) gave a maid for a lamb, a man for a garment.[2]

I, Kilamuwa, the son of Hayya, sat upon the throne of my father. Before the former kings, the *mškbm* went (cowed) like dogs. I, however, to some I was a father. To some I was a mother. To some I was a brother. Him who had never seen the face of a sheep, I made the possessor of a flock. Him who had never seen the face of an ox, I made the possessor of a herd of cattle and a possessor of silver and a possessor of gold. He who had not (even) seen linen since his youth, in my days he was covered with byssus. I took the *mškbm* by the hand. They were disposed (toward me) as an orphan is to his mother.

If one of my children who shall sit in my place should damage this inscription, may the *mškbm* not respect the *b'rrm*, and may the *b'rrm* not respect the *mškbm*!

He who smashes this inscription, may his head be smashed by Ba'l-Samad who belongs to Gabbar, and may his head be smashed by 'Ba'l-Hamman who belongs to *Bmh*, and by Rakabel, the Lord of the dynasty!

---

[1] Many suggestions have been made to explain these two letters but the one considering them the name of Kilamuwa's mother—to be corrected to Tammat—remains the most plausible one for the time being.

[2] Kilamuwa apparently used a proverb in which a buyer boasts of a good bargain. He not only hired the mighty king of Assyria, but was able to do so cheaply.

ANET, 501

BARRAKAB OF Y'DY-SAM'AL

Fig. 127

This inscription of a remote successor of the afore-mentioned Kilamuwa was found in Zinjirli in 1891. It was set up about 730 B.C.

I am Barrakab, the son of Panamu, king of Sam'al, servant of Tiglath-pileser, the lord of the (four) quarters of the earth.

Because of the righteousness of my father and my own righteousness, I was seated by my Lord Rakabel and my Lord Tiglath-pileser upon the throne of my father. The house of my father has profited more than anybody else, and I have been running at the wheel of my Lord, the king of Assyria, in the midst of mighty kings, possessors of silver and possessors of gold. I took over the house of my father and made it more prosperous than the house of one of the mighty kings. My brethren, the kings, *are envious* because of all the prosperity of my house.

My fathers, the kings of Sam'al, had no good house. They had the house of Kilamu, which was their winter house and also their summer house. But I have built this house.

Cultic Inscriptions

BEN-HADAD OF DAMASCUS

ANET, 501

The stela with this inscription was discovered, apparently in 1939, in an ancient cemetery about four miles north of Aleppo, probably not *in situ*. It may, however, have originally been set up somewhere in the neighborhood of Aleppo. It dates from about 860 B.C.

Fig. 139

A stela set up by Barhadad, the son of T[abrimmon, the son of Hezion], king of Aram, for his Lord Melqart, which he vowed to him and he (then) heard his voice.

KILAMUWA OF *Y'DY*-SAM'AL

ANET, 501

A gold sheath found in Zinjirli.

A *smr* (*sheath, scepter?*) fashioned by Kilamuwa, the son of Hayya, for Rakabel.

May Rakabel give him a long life!

ZAKIR OF HAMAT AND LU'ATH

ANET, 501-502

This historical inscription, dating from the early years of the eighth century B.C., was composed in connection with the dedication of a statue of Ilu-Wer, an avatar of Hadad. It was found in 1904 in a place about twenty-five miles southeast of Aleppo which in modern times is called Afis and which appears to have been mentioned in this inscription as Apish.

A stela set up by Zakir, king of Hamat and Lu'ath, for Ilu-Wer, [*his god*].

I am Zakir, king of Hamat and Lu'ath. A humble man I am. Be'elshamayn [*helped me*] and stood by me. Be'elshamayn made me king over Hatarikka (Hadrach).

Barhadad, the son of Hazael, king of Aram, united [seven of] a group of ten kings against me: Barhadad and his army; Bargush and his army; the king of Cilicia and his army; the king of 'Umq and his army; the king of Gurgum and his army; the king of Sam'al and his army; the king of Milidh and his army. [All these kings whom Barhadad united against me] were seven kings and their armies. All these kings laid siege to Hatarikka. They made a wall higher than the wall of Hatarikka. They made a moat deeper than its moat. But I lifted up my hand to Be'elshamayn, and Be'elshamayn heard me. Be'elshamayn [spoke] to me through seers and through diviners. Be'elshamayn [said to me]: Do not fear, for I made you king, and I shall stand by you and deliver you from all [these kings who] set up a siege against you. [Be'elshamayn] said to me: [I shall destroy] all these kings who set up [a siege against you and made this moat] and this wall which . . . .

[. . .] charioteer and horseman [. . .] its king in its midst [. . .]. I [enlarged] Hatarikka and added [to it] the entire district of [. . .] and I made him ki[ng . . .] all these strongholds everywhere within the bor[ders].

I built houses for the gods everywhere in my country. I built [. . .] and Apish [. . .] and the house of [. . .].

I set up this stela before Ilu-Wer, and I wrote upon it my achievements [. . .]. Whoever shall remove (this record of) the achievements of Zakir, king of Hamat and Lu'ath, from this stela and whoever shall remove this stela from before Ilu-Wer and banish it from its [place] or whoever shall stretch forth his hand [to . . .], [may] Be'elshamayn and I[lu-Wer and . . .] and Shamash and Sahr [and . . .] and the Gods of Heaven [and the Gods] of Earth and Be'el-'[. . . deprive him of h]ead and [. . . and] his root and [. . . , and may] the name of Zakir and the name of [his house endure forever]!

ANET, 502

YEHAWMILK OF BYBLOS

Fig. 130

This ex-voto has been known since 1869, but a fragment completing most of its lower right-hand corner was found only sixty years later. It appears to date from the fifth or fourth century. The identity of the second of the three main objects which

Yehawmilk here dedicates to his goddess has not yet been fully cleared up. Instead of an *engraved object*, it might have been a *door*.

I am Yehawmilk, king of Byblos, the son of *Yehar-ba'l*, the grandson of Urimilk, king of Byblos, whom the mistress, the Lady of Byblos, made king over Byblos.

I have been calling my mistress, the Lady of Byblos, [and she heard my voice]. Therefore, I have made for my mistress, the Lady of Byblos, this altar of bronze which is in this [*courtyard*], and this *engraved object* of gold which is in front of this *inscription* of mine, with the *bird* (?) of gold that is set in a (*semiprecious*) stone, which is upon this *engraved object* of gold, and this portico with its columns and the [*capitals*] which are upon them, and its roof: I, Yehawmilk, king of Byblos, have made (these things) for my mistress, the Lady of Byblos, as I called my mistress, the Lady of Byblos, and she heard my voice and treated me kindly.

May the Lady of Byblos bless and preserve Yehaw-milk, king of Byblos, and prolong his days and years in Byblos, for he is a righteous king. And may [the mistress,] the Lady of Byblos, give [him] favor in the eyes of the gods and in the eyes of the people of this country and (that he be) pleased with the people of this country.

[Whoever you are,] ruler and (ordinary) man, who might [*continue*] to do work on this altar and this *engraved work* of gold and this portico, my name, Yehawmilk, king of Byblos, [you should put with] yours upon that work, and if you do not put my name with yours, or if you [*remove*] this [*work and transfer this work from its foundation*] *upon this* place *and* [. . . , may] the mistress, the Lady of Byblos, [*destroy*] that man and his seed before all the Gods of Byblos.

THE MARSEILLES TARIFF

ANET, 502-503

The two blocks of stone containing this inscription were found in Marseilles in 1845. The stone used for them is known to occur in the region of Carthage. Thus, it is possible that the document originally belonged to a temple in Carthage. However, the possibility that a similar kind of stone might also have been quarried in the neighborhood of Marseilles apparently has not yet been sufficiently explored. The date of the inscription is uncertain; it may date from the third century or the early part of the second century B.C. The text is carefully engraved. It is provided with a title, and each paragraph begins with a new line.

TEMPLE OF BA'L-[*ZAPHON*]

Tariff of payments set up [by the men in
charge of] the payments in the time of [the
lords Hilles]ba'l, the suffete, the son of Bod-
tanit, the son of Bod[eshmun, and Hillesba'l,]
the suffete, the son of Bodeshmun, the son of
Hillesba'l, and their colleagues.

For an ox, as a whole offering or a *substitute offering*
or a complete whole offering, the priests shall have ten
—10—silver (pieces) for each. In the case of a whole
offering, they shall have, over and above this payment,
meat [weighing *three hundred—300*]. In the case of a
substitute offering, they shall have *neck* and *shoulder
joints (chuck)*, while the person offering the sacrifice
shall have the skin, *ribs*, feet, and the rest of the meat.

For a calf whose horns are *still lacking somewhat and
. . .* , or for a stag, as a whole offering or a *substitute
offering* or a complete whole offering, the priests shall
have five—5—silver [pieces for each. In the case of a
whole offering, they shall have, over and] above this
payment, meat weighing one hundred and fifty—150.
In the case of a *substitute offering*, they shall have *neck*
and *shoulder joints*, while [the person offering the
sacrifice] shall have the skin, *ribs*, feet, [and the rest
of the meat].

For a ram or a goat, as a whole offering or a *substitute offering* or a complete whole offering, the priests
shall have one—1—shekel of silver and 2 *zr*[1] for each.
In the case of a *substitute offering*, they shall have,
[over and above this payment, *neck*] and *shoulder
joints*, while the person offering the sacrifice shall
have the skin, *ribs*, feet, and the rest of the meat.

For a lamb or for a kid or for a *young* stag, as a
whole offering or a *substitute offering* or a complete
whole offering, the priests shall have three quarters of
silver and [2] *zr* [for each. In the case of a *substitute
offering*, they shall have, over and] above this payment,
neck and *shoulder joints*, while the person offering
[the sacrifice] shall have the skin, *ribs*, feet, and the
rest of the meat.

For an *'gnn* bird or a *ṣṣ* (bird), as a complete whole
offering or a *ṧṣf offering* or a *ḥzt offering*, the priests

---

[1] *zr* is the name of a small coin or, possibly, the abbreviation for such a
coin, as *'a* below is an abbreviation of the name of another unit smaller
than *zr*.

shall have three quarters of silver and 2 *zr* for each. [The person offering the sacrifice] shall have the meat.

[For] any (other) bird or a holy *oblation* or a hunt offering or an oil offering, the priests shall have 10 *'a* of silver for each [. . .].

For any *substitute offering* which they shall have to carry to the God, the priests shall have *neck* and *shoulder joints*, and for a *substitute offering* [. . .].

Upon a *cake*² and upon milk and upon fat and upon any sacrifice which someone is to offer as a meal-offering, [the priests shall have . . .].

For any sacrifice which shall be offered by persons poor³ in cattle or poor in fowl, the priests shall have nothing [whatever].

Any *citizen* and any scion (*of a noble clan*) and any participant in a banquet for the God and anybody who shall offer a sacrifice [. . .], those men shall make payment per sacrifice as specified in a written document [which was set up under . . .].

Any payment which is not specified in this tablet shall be made according to the written document which [was also set up . . . under Hillesba'l, the son of Bodtan]it and Hillesba'l, the son of Bodeshmun, and their colleagues.

Any priest who shall accept a payment contrary to what is specified in this tablet shall be fined [. . .].

Any person offering a sacrifice who shall not give the [*money for*] the payment [which is specified in this tablet . . .].

² *bll* may mean "fodder" as in Hebrew. It is certainly possible that fodder was offered for the animals of the temple.
³ Or rather: "without."

THE CARTHAGE TARIFF

ANET, 503

A number of fragments very similar in contents to the preceding Marseilles Tariff have also been found in Carthage itself over a number of years beginning with 1858. Three of those fragments, though not parts of the same monument, were recognized by J.-B. Chabot as belonging to identical texts, and Chabot's reconstruction has been followed in this translation. The date of the Carthage Tariff is about the same as that of the Marseilles Tariff.

> Tariff of payments set up by [the
> men in charge of the payments . . .].

[For an ox, as whole offerings or *substitute offerings*],

the priests [shall have] the skins, and the person offering the sacrifice the *fat parts* [...].

For a stag, [as whole offerings or *substitute offerings*], the priests [shall have] the skins, and the person offering the sacrifice the *fat parts* [...].

For a ram or a goat, as whole offerings or as *substitute offerings*, the priests shall have the skins of the goats, and the person offering the sacrifice shall have the *ribs* [...].

For a lamb or for a kid or for a *young* stag, as whole offerings or *substitute offerings*, the priests shall have the skins [...].

For any sacrifice which shall be offered by persons poor in cattle, the priest shall have nothing whatever.

For an *'gnn* bird or for a *ṣṣ* (bird), 2 *zr* of silver for each.

[For any *substitute offering* wh]ich he shall have to carry to the God, the priest shall have *necks* and *shoulder joints* [...].

[Upon any] holy [*oblation*] and upon a hunt offering and upon an oil offering [...].

Upon a *cake* (*fodder*) and upon milk (fat) and upon a sacrifice as a meal-offering and upon [...].

Any payment which is not specified in this tablet shall be made [according to the written document ...].

Any priest who shall take [...].

Any person offering a sacrifice who [...].

Any person who shall trade [... , and who] shall shatter this tablet [...].

Pds, the son of Eshmunhilles [...].

X. Rituals and Hymns

Egyptian Execration Texts

TRANSLATOR: JOHN A. WILSON

THE EXECRATION OF ASIATIC PRINCES

ANET, 328-329

In the Middle Kingdom period the Egyptians practiced the magical cursing of their actual or potential enemies. In the Berlin Museum are fragments of pottery bowls which had been inscribed with the names of such foes and then smashed. In the Cairo and Brussels Museums inscribed figurines carry the same kind of curse. As they smashed such pottery, so they thought to break the power of their enemies. The exorcised elements were Nubians, Asiatics, Libyans, hostile Egyptians, and evil forces. The translation below, from the Berlin material, gives some Asiatics, some Egyptians, and the forces.

Fig. 153
Jer. 19:10-11

Asiatics

(e 1) The Ruler of Iy-'anaq,[1] *Erum*, and all the *retainers*[2] who are with him; the Ruler of Iy-'anaq, Abi-*yamimu*, and all the *retainers* who are with him; the Ruler of Iy-'anaq, 'Akirum, and all the *retainers* who are with him;

(4) the Ruler of Shutu,[3] Ayyabum,[4] and all the *retainers* who are with him; the Ruler of Shutu, Kushar, and all the *retainers* who are with him; the Ruler of Shutu, Zabulanu,[5] and all the *retainers* who are with him; . . .

Num. 24:17

(23) the Ruler of Asqanu,[6] *Khalu-kim*, and all the *retainers* who are with him; . . .

(27) the Ruler of Jerusalem, Yaqar-'Ammu, and all the *retainers* who are with him; the Ruler of Jerusalem, Setj-'Anu, and all the *retainers* who are with him; . . .[7]

(31) all the rulers of *Iysipi* and all the *retainers* who are with them;

(f 1) all the Asiatics—of Byblos, of Ullaza, of Iy-'anaq, of Shutu, of *Iymu'aru*, of *Qehermu*, of *Rehob*,[8] of

---

[1] Many of the geographic names are unknown, and identifications for most of the others must be tentative. The present name has been related to the *'Anaqim* "giants" who were in the land of Canaan at the time of the Conquest.

Deut. 2:10

[2] Taken as the Egyptian word for "trusted men." Perhaps the same word as the *hanik* of Gen. 14:14.

[3] Probably Moab.

[4] Job; cuneiform Ayyab.   [5] Similarly cuneiform, for Zebulon.

[6] Ashkelon; cuneiform Ashqaluna.

[7] The figurines in Brussels and Cairo have further identifiable names.

[8] Probably any one of several Rehobs.

Yarimuta, of *Inhia*, of *Aqhi*, of 'Arqata, [2] of Yari-muta, of *Isinu*, [3] of Asqanu, of *Demitiu*, of *Mut-ilu*, of Jerusalem of *'Akhmut*, of *Iahenu*, and of *Iysipi*;

(g 1) their strong men, their swift runners, their allies, their associates, and the Mentu [4] in Asia;

(h 1) who may rebel, who may plot, who may fight, who may talk of fighting, or who may talk of rebelling —in this entire land.

Egyptians

(m 1) All men, all people, all folk, all males, all *eunuchs*, all women, and all officials,

(n 1) who may rebel, who may plot, who may fight, who may talk of fighting, or who may talk of rebelling, and every rebel who talks of rebelling—in this entire land.

Josh. 1:18

(o 1) Ameni shall die, the tutor of Sit-Bastet, the *chancellor* of Sit-Hat-Hor, (daughter of) Nefru. [5]

Sen-Usert the younger, called Ketu, shall die, the tutor of Sit-Ipi, (daughter of) Sit-Hat-Hor, and tutor of Sit-Ipi, (daughter of) Sit-Ameni, the *chancellor* of Ii-menet, (daughter of) Sit-Hat-Hor. . . .

(8) Ameni, born to Hetep and son of Sen-Usert, shall die.

Baneful Forces

(p 1) Every evil word, every evil speech, every evil slander, every evil thought, every evil plot, every evil fight, every evil quarrel, every evil plan, every evil thing, all evil dreams, and all evil slumber.

[2] Or 'Iraqtum, another name for the same, in Phoenicia.
[3] This has been compared to (Beth)-Shan.
[4] The "Mentu in Setet" is an old designation for Egypt's immediate neighbors to the northeast.
[5] There are two significant factors about these specifically named Egyptians. First, the names are names characteristic of the 12th dynasty royal family. Second, several of them are functionaries of women who seem to be princesses or queens. One thinks of a harem conspiracy as the setting for such curses.

Egyptian Hymns

TRANSLATOR: JOHN A. WILSON

ANET, 369-371

THE HYMN TO THE ATON

The Pharaoh Amen-hotep IV broke with the established religion of Egypt and instituted the worship of the Aton, the sun disc as the source of life. "The Amarna Revolution" attempted a distinct break with Egypt's traditional and static ways of life in religion, politics, art, and literature. Pharaoh changed his name to Akh-en-Aton (perhaps "He Who Is Serviceable to the Aton") and moved his capital from Thebes to Tell el-Amarna. Pharaoh's own attitude to the god is expressed in the famous hymn which follows. Beyond doubt, the hymn shows the universality and beneficence of the creating and re-creating sun disc. A similarity of spirit and wording to the 104th Psalm has often been noted, and a direct relation between the two has been argued.[1] Because Akh-en-Aton was devoted to this god alone, the Amarna religion has been called monotheistic. This is a debatable question, and a reserved attitude would note that only Akh-en-Aton and his family worshiped the Aton, Akh-en-Aton's courtiers worshiped Akh-en-Aton himself, and the great majority of Egyptians was ignorant of or hostile to the new faith.

Figs. 108, 110

[1] As in Breasted.

Praise of Re Har-akhti, Rejoicing on the Horizon, in His Name as Shu Who Is in the Aton-disc,[2] living forever and ever; the living great Aton who is in jubilee, lord of all that the Aton encircles, lord of heaven, lord of earth, lord of the House of Aton in Akhet-Aton;[3] (and praise of) the King of Upper and Lower Egypt, who lives on truth, the Lord of the Two Lands: Nefer-kheperu-Re Wa-en-Re; the Son of Re, who lives on truth, the Lord of Diadems: Akh-en-Aton, long in his lifetime; (and praise of) the Chief Wife of the King, his beloved, the Lady of the Two Lands: Nefer-neferu-Aton Nefert-iti, living, healthy, and youthful forever and ever; (by) the Fan-Bearer on the Right Hand of the King ... Eye. He says:

Thou appearest beautifully on the horizon of heaven,
Thou living Aton, the beginning of life!
When thou art risen on the eastern horizon,
Thou hast filled every land with thy beauty.
Thou art gracious, great, glistening, and high over
 every land;
Thy rays encompass the lands to the limit of all that
 thou hast made:
As thou art Re, thou reachest to the end of them;[4]
(Thou) subduest them (for) thy beloved son.[5]
Though thou art far away, thy rays are on earth;
Though thou art in *their* faces, *no one knows thy*
 going.

When thou settest in the western horizon,
The land is in darkness, in the manner of death.

---

[2] The Aton had a dogmatic name written within a royal cartouche and including the three old solar deities, Re, Har-of-the-Horizon, and Shu.
[3] Akhet-Aton was the name of the capital at Tell el-Amarna.
[4] Pun: *Ra* "Re," and *er-ra* "to the end."   [5] Akh-en-Aton.

They sleep in a room, with heads wrapped up,
Nor sees one eye the other.
All their goods which are under their heads might
   be stolen,
(But) they would not perceive (it).
Every lion is come forth from his den;
All creeping things, they sting.
Darkness *is a shroud*, and the earth is in stillness,
Ps. 104:20-21 For he who made them rests in his horizon.

At daybreak, when thou arisest on the horizon,
When thou shinest as the Aton by day,
Thou drivest away the darkness and givest thy rays.
The Two Lands are in festivity *every day*,
Awake and standing upon (their) feet,
For thou hast raised them up.
Washing their bodies, taking (their) clothing,   (5)
Their arms are (raised) in praise at thy appearance.
Ps. 104:22-23 All the world, they do their work.

All beasts are content with their pasturage;
Trees and plants are flourishing.
The birds which fly from their nests,
Their wings are (stretched out) in praise to thy *ka*.
All beasts spring upon (their) feet.
Whatever flies and alights,
Ps. 104:11-14 They live when thou hast risen (for) them.
The ships are sailing north and south as well,
For every way is open at thy appearance.
The fish in the river dart before thy face;
Ps. 104:25-26 Thy rays are in the midst of the great green sea.

Creator of seed in women,
Thou who makest fluid into man,
Who maintainest the son in the womb of his mother,
Who soothest him with that which stills his weeping,
Thou nurse (even) in the womb,
Who givest breath to sustain all that he has made!
When he descends from the womb to *breathe*
On the day when he is born,
Thou openest his mouth completely,
Thou suppliest his necessities.
When the chick in the egg speaks within the shell,
Thou givest him breath within it to maintain him.
When thou hast made him his fulfillment within the
   egg, to break it,

He comes forth from the egg to speak at his completed
   (time);
He walks upon his legs when he comes forth from it.

How manifold it is, what thou hast made!   Ps. 40:5
They are hidden from the face (of man).
O sole god, like whom there is no other!
Thou didst create the world according to thy desire,
Whilst thou wert alone: Ps. 104:24
All men, cattle, and wild beasts,
Whatever is on earth, going upon (its) feet,
And what is on high, flying with its wings.

The countries of Syria and Nubia, the *land* of Egypt,
Thou settest every man in his place,
Thou suppliest their necessities:
Everyone has his food, and his time of life is   Ps. 90:10
   reckoned.   Ps. 104:27
Their tongues are separate in speech,
And their natures as well;
Their skins are distinguished,
As thou distinguishest the foreign peoples.
Thou makest a Nile in the underworld,
Thou bringest it forth as thou desirest
To maintain the people (of Egypt)[1]
According as thou madest them for thyself,
The lord of all of them, wearying (himself) with
   them,
The lord of every land, rising for them,
The Aton of the day, great of majesty.

All distant foreign countries, thou makest their life
   (also),
For thou hast set a Nile in heaven,
That it may descend for them and make waves upon
   the mountains,   (10)   Ps. 104:6, 10
Like the great green sea,
To water their fields in their towns.[2]
How effective they are, thy plans, O lord of eternity!
The Nile in heaven, it is for the foreign peoples
And for the beasts of every desert that go upon
   (their) feet;

---

[1] The Egyptians believed that their Nile came from the waters under
the earth, called by them Nun.
[2] The rain of foreign countries is like the Nile of rainless Egypt.

(While the true) Nile comes from the underworld
for Egypt.

Thy rays suckle every meadow.
When thou risest, they live, they grow for thee.
Ps. 104:19 Thou makest the seasons in order to rear all that
thou hast made,
The winter to cool them,
And the heat that *they* may taste thee.
Thou hast made the distant sky in order to rise therein,
In order to see all that thou dost make.
Whilst thou wert alone,
Rising in thy form as the living Aton,
Appearing, shining, *withdrawing or approaching*,
Thou madest millions of forms of thyself alone.
Cities, towns, fields, road, and river—
Every eye beholds thee over against them,
For thou art the Aton of the day over *the earth*. . . .

Thou art in my heart,
And there is no other that knows thee
Save thy son Nefer-kheperu-Re Wa-en-Re,[1]
For thou hast made him well-versed in thy plans and
in thy strength.[2]

The world came into being by thy hand,
According as thou hast made them.
Ps. 104:30 When thou hast risen they live,
Ps. 104:29 When thou settest they die.
Thou art lifetime thy own self,
For one lives (only) through thee.
Eyes are (fixed) on beauty until thou settest.
All work is laid aside when thou settest in the west.
(But) when (thou) risest (again),
[*Everything is*] made to flourish for the king, . . .
Since thou didst found the earth
And raise them up for thy son,
Who came forth from thy body:
the King of Upper and Lower Egypt, . . . Akh-en-
Aton, . . . and the Chief Wife of the King . . . Nefert-iti,
living and youthful forever and ever.

---

[1] Even though the hymn was recited by the official Eye, he states that
Akh-en-Aton alone knows the Aton.
[2] Pharaoh was the official intermediary between the Egyptians and their
gods. The Amarna religion did not change this dogma.

HYMN OF VICTORY OF MER-NE-PTAH ("ISRAEL STELA")

The date of this commemorative hymn (or series of hymns) relates it to Mer-ne-Ptah's victory over the Libyans in the spring of his fifth year (about 1230 B.C.). However, the text is not historical in the same sense as two other records of that victory, but is rather a poetic eulogy of a universally victorious pharaoh. Thus it was not out of place to introduce his real or figurative triumph over Asiatic peoples in the last poem of the hymn. In that context we meet the only instance of the name "Israel" in ancient Egyptian writing.

ANET, 376, 378

. . . .

The princes are prostrate, saying: "Mercy!"[1]
Not one raises his head among the Nine Bows.
Desolation is for Tehenu; Hatti is pacified;
Plundered is the Canaan with every evil;
Carried off is Ashkelon; seized upon is Gezer;
Yanoam is made as that which does not exist;[2]
Israel is laid waste, his seed is not;[3]
Hurru is become a widow for Egypt![4]
All lands together, they are pacified;
Everyone who was restless, he has been bound
by the King of Upper and Lower Egypt: Ba-en-Re Meri-
Amon; the Son of Re: Mer-ne-Ptah Hotep-hir-Maat,
given life like Re every day.

Fig. 96
Jer. 49:10
Lam. 1:1

[1] Or "Peace!" The Canaanite word *shalam* is used here.
[2] Hatti was the land of the Hittites. Yanoam was an important town of northern Palestine.
[3] Much has been made of the fact that the word Israel is the only one of the names in this context which is written with the determinative of people rather than land. Thus we should seem to have the Children of Israel in or near Palestine, but not yet as a settled people. This would have important bearing on the date of the Conquest. This is a valid argument. Determinatives should have meaning, and a contrast between determinatives in the same context should be significant. This stela does give the country determinatives to settled peoples like the Rebu, Temeh, Hatti, Ashkelon, etc., and the determinative of people to unlocated groups like the Madjoi, Nau, and Tekten. The argument is good, but not conclusive, because of the notorious carelessness of Late-Egyptian scribes and several blunders of writing in this stela.
The statement that the "seed," i.e. offspring, of Israel had been wiped out is a conventional boast of power at this period.
[4] The land of the biblical Horites, or Greater Palestine.

An Akkadian Hymn

TRANSLATOR: FERRIS J. STEPHENS

HYMN TO ISHTAR

ANET, 383

After extolling the charms and virtues of the goddess, the hymn concludes by enumerating the blessings which she has bestowed upon the king, Ammiditana. While these are represented as accomplished facts, the statements should be taken as indications of the hope of the king for their eventual realization. The text publication does not indicate the provenience of the tablet. It was written in the latter part of the First Dynasty of Babylon, approximately 1600 B.C. Text: *RA*, XXII, 170-1; translation: *RA*, XXII, 174-7; metrical transcription: *ZA*, XXXVIII, 19-22.

Praise the goddess, the most awesome of the goddesses.
Let one revere the mistress of the peoples, the greatest
  of the Igigi.[1]
Praise Ishtar, the most awesome of the goddesses.
Let one revere the queen of women, the greatest of the
  Igigi.

Song of Sol. 4:1-3   She is clothed with pleasure and love.
She is laden with vitality, charm, and voluptuousness.
Ishtar is clothed with pleasure and love.
She is laden with vitality, charm, and voluptuousness.

In lips she is sweet; life is in her mouth.
At her appearance rejoicing becomes full.   (10)
She is glorious; veils are thrown over her head.
Her figure is beautiful; her eyes are brilliant.

The goddess—with her there is counsel.
The fate of everything she holds in her hand.
At her glance there is created joy,
Power, magnificence, the protecting deity and guardian
  spirit.

She dwells in, she pays heed to compassion and friendli-
  ness.
Besides, agreeableness she truly possesses.
Be it slave, unattached girl, or mother, she preserves
  (her).
One calls on her; among women one names
  her name.   (20)

Who—to her greatness who can be equal?
Strong, exalted, splendid are her decrees.
Ishtar—to her greatness who can be equal?
Strong, exalted, splendid are her decrees.

She is sought after among the gods; extraordinary is
  her station.
Respected is her word; it is *supreme* over them.

---

[1] A collective name for the great gods of heaven.

Ishtar among the gods, extraordinary is her station.
Respected is her word; it is *supreme* over them.

She is their queen; they continually cause her commands
    to be executed.
All of them bow down before her.   (30)
They receive her light before her.
Women and men indeed revere her.

In their assembly her word is powerful; it is dominating.
Before Anum their king she fully supports them.
She rests in intelligence, cleverness, (and) wisdom.
They take counsel together, she and her lord.

Indeed they occupy the throne room together.
In the divine chamber, the dwelling of joy,
Before them the gods take their places.
To their utterances their attention is turned.

The king their favorite, beloved of their hearts,
Magnificently offers to them his pure sacrifices.
Ammiditana, as the pure offering of his hands,
Brings before them fat oxen and gazelles.

From Anum, her consort, she has been pleased to ask
    for him
An enduring, a long life.
Many years of living, to Ammiditana
She has granted, Ishtar has decided to give.

By her orders she has subjected to him
The four world regions at his feet;
And the total of all peoples
She has decided to attach them to his yoke.

XI. Wisdom, Prophecy, and Songs

Egyptian Instructions

TRANSLATOR: JOHN A. WILSON

THE INSTRUCTION OF THE VIZIER PTAH-HOTEP

ANET, 412-414   The Egyptians delighted in compilations of wise sayings, which were directive for a successful life. To them, this was "wisdom." One of the earliest of these compilations purports to come from Ptah-hotep, the vizier of King Izezi of the Fifth Dynasty (about 2450 B.C.). The old councilor is supposed to be instructing his son and designated successor on the actions and attitudes which make a successful official of the state. Excerpts from the document follow.

.... Then he said to his son:

Let not thy heart be puffed-up because of thy knowledge; be not confident because thou art a wise man. Take counsel with the ignorant as well as the wise. The (full) limits of skill cannot be attained, and there is no skilled man equipped to his (full) advantage. [1] Prov. 2:4 Good speech is more hidden than the emerald, but it may be found with maidservants at the grindstones. ...

IF THOU ART A LEADER (85) commanding the affairs of the multitude, seek out for thyself every beneficial deed, until it may be that thy (own) affairs are without wrong. Justice is great, and its appropriateness is lasting; it has not been disturbed since the time of him who made it, (whereas) there is punishment for him who passes over its laws. It is the (right) path before him who knows nothing. Wrongdoing has never brought its undertaking into port. (It may be that) it is fraud that gains riches, (95) (but) the strength of justice is that it lasts, and a man may say: "It is the property of my father."...

Prov. 23:1-3   IF THOU ART ONE OF THOSE SITTING (120) at the table of one greater than thyself, take what he may give, when it is set before thy nose. Thou shouldst gaze at what is before thee. Do not pierce him with many stares, (for such) an aggression against him is an abomination to the *ka*. [2] Let thy face be cast down until he addresses thee, and thou shouldst speak (only) when he addresses thee. (130) Laugh after he laughs, and it will be very pleasing to his heart and what thou mayest

[1] *Ma'at* "justice" or "truth," was an inheritable value.
[2] The *ka* was the protecting and guiding vital force of a man, and thus his social mentor.

do will be pleasing to the heart. No one can know what is in the heart.

As for the great man when he is at meals, his purposes conform to the dictates of his *ka*. He will give to the one whom he favors. (140) The great man gives to *the man whom he can reach*, (but) it is the *ka* that lengthens out his arms. The eating of bread is under the planning of god[1] —it is (only) a fool who would *complain of* it.

IF THOU ART A MAN OF INTIMACY, whom one great man sends to another, be thoroughly reliable when he sends thee. Carry out the errand for him as he has spoken. (150) Do not be reserved about what is said to thee, and beware of (any) act of forgetfulness. Grasp hold of truth, and do not exceed it. (*Mere*) *gratification is by no means to be repeated*. Struggle against making words worse, (thus) *making* one great man *hostile* to another *through vulgar speech*. (160) A great man, a little man—it is the *ka*'s abomination.[2] ...

Prov. 25:13

(175) IF THOU ART A POOR FELLOW, FOLLOWING A MAN OF DISTINCTION, one of good standing with the god, know thou not his former insignificance. Thou shouldst not be puffed-up against him because of what thou didst know of him formerly. Show regard for him in conformance with what has accrued to him—property does not come of itself. It is their law for him who wishes them. *As for him who oversteps, he is feared.* It is god who makes (a man's) quality, (185) and he defends him (even) while he is asleep....

If thou art one to whom petition is made, (265) be calm as thou listenest to the petitioner's speech. Do not rebuff him before he has swept out his body or before he has said that for which he came. A petitioner likes attention to his words better than the fulfilling of that for which he came. He is rejoicing thereat more than any (other) petitioner, (even) before that which has been heard has come to pass. As for him who plays the rebuffer of a petitioner, men say: "Now why is he doing it?" (275) It is not (*necessary*) that everything about which he has petitioned *should* come to pass, (but) a good hearing is a soothing of the heart.

IF THOU DESIREST to make friendship last in a home to which thou hast access as master, as a brother,

---

1 "God" in these wisdom texts sometimes means the king, sometimes the supreme or creator god, and sometimes the force which demands proper behavior—a force not clearly defined, but perhaps the local god.

2 Do not draw invidious distinctions?

or as a friend, into any place where thou mightest enter, beware of approaching the women. It does not go well with the place where that is done. *The face has no alertness by splitting it.*[1] A thousand men *may be distracted from* their (own) advantage. (285) One is made a fool by limbs of fayence, as she stands (there), become (all) carnelian. A mere trifle, the likeness of a dream—and one attains death through knowing her. . . . Do not do it—it is really an abomination—(295) and thou shalt be free from sickness of heart every day. As for him who escapes from gluttony for it, all affairs will prosper with him. . . .

Prov. 6:29
Prov. 6:24
Prov. 7:5

Prov. 7:27

Do not be covetous at a division. Do not be greedy, unless (it be) for thy (own) portion. Do not be covetous against thy (own) kindred. Greater is the respect for the mild than (for) the strong. (320) He is a mean person who *exposes* his kinsfolk; he is empty of *the fruits of conversation.*[2] It is (only) a little of that for which one is covetous that turns a calm man into a contentious man.

Prov. 15:27

If thou art a man of standing, thou shouldst found thy household and love thy wife at home as is fitting. Fill her belly; clothe her back. Ointment is the prescription for her body. Make her heart glad as long as thou livest. (330) She is a profitable field for her lord.[3] Thou shouldst not contend with her at law, and keep her far from gaining control. . . . Her eye is her stormwind. Let her heart be soothed through what may accrue to thee; it means keeping her long in thy house. . . .

Prov. 31:10-12, 31

Prov. 12:4

If thou art (now) important after thy (former) unimportance, so that thou mayest do things after a neediness (430) formerly in the town which thou knowest, in contrast to what was thy lot before, do not be miserly with thy wealth, which has accrued to thee as the gift of god. Thou art not behind[4] some other equal of thine to whom the same has happened. . . .

Eccles. 6:2

If a son accepts what his father says, (565) no project of his miscarries. He whom thou instructest as thy obedient son, who will stand well in the heart of the official, his speech is guided with respect to what has been said to him, one regarded as obedient. . . . (But)

---

[1] Perhaps: He who has a wandering eye for the women cannot be keen.
[2] "A mean person is he who goes out (from?) under his kinsfolk.
[3] The desire for children—particularly male children—was perennial in the orient.   [4] Not behind or ahead of, but the same as?

the *induction*[1] of him who does not hearken miscarries. The wise man rises early in the morning to establish himself, (but) the fool rises early in the morning (only) to *agitate* himself....

[1] Induction into the official service?

THE INSTRUCTION OF AMEN-EM-OPET

ANET, 421-424

A general parallelism of thought or structure between Egyptian and Hebrew literature is common. It is, however, more difficult to establish a case of direct literary relation. For this reason, special attention is directed to the Instruction of Amen-em-Opet, son of Ka-nakht, and its very close relation to the Book of Proverbs, particularly Prov. 22:17-24:22. Amen-em-Opet differs from earlier Egyptian books of wisdom in its humbler, more resigned, and less materialistic outlook.[1]

The hieratic text is found in British Museum Papyrus 10474 and (a portion only) on a writing tablet in Turin. The papyrus is said to have come from Thebes. The date of the papyrus manuscript is debated. It is certainly subsequent to the Egyptian Empire. A date anywhere between the 10th and 6th centuries B.C. is possible, with some weight of evidence for the 7th-6th centuries. Some introductory lines have been omitted here.

HE SAYS: FIRST CHAPTER:

Give thy ears, hear what is said,
Give thy heart to understand them.   (10)
To put them in thy heart is worth while,
(But) it is damaging to him who neglects them.
Let them rest in the casket of thy belly,
That they may be a *key* in thy heart.
At a time when there is a whirlwind of words,   (15)
They shall be a mooring-stake *for* thy tongue.
If thou spendest thy time while this is in thy heart,
Thou wilt find it a success;
Thou wilt find my words a treasury of life,   (iv 1)
And thy body will prosper upon earth.

Prov. 22:17-18a

Prov. 22:18-19

SECOND CHAPTER:

Guard thyself against robbing the oppressed
And against overbearing the disabled.   (5)
Stretch not forth thy hand against the approach of
　an old man,
Nor *steal away* the speech of the *aged*.
Let not thyself be sent on a dangerous errand,
Nor love him who carries it out.
Do not cry out against him whom thou hast
　attacked,   (10)
Nor return him answer on thy own behalf.

Prov. 22:22

He who does evil, the (very) river-bank abandons
   him,
And his *floodwaters* carry him off.
The north wind comes down that it may end his
   hour;
It is joined to the tempest; (15)
The thunder is loud, and the crocodiles are wicked.
Thou heated man,[1] how art thou (now)?
He is crying out, and his voice (reaches) to heaven.
O moon,[2] establish his crime (against him)!
So steer that we may bring the wicked man
   across, (v 1)
For we shall not act like him—
Lift him up, give him thy hand;
Leave him (in) the arms of the god;

Prov. 25:21-22 Fill his belly with bread of thine, (5)
So that he may be sated and may *be ashamed*.
Another good deed in the heart of the god
Is to pause before speaking. . . .

FOURTH CHAPTER:

Ps. 1; Jer. 17:5-8 As for the heated man of a temple, (vi 1)
He is like a tree growing in the open.
In the completion of a moment (comes) its loss of
   foliage,
And its end is reached in the shipyards;
(Or) it is floated far from its place, (5)
And the flame is its burial shroud.
(But) the truly silent man holds himself apart.
He is like a tree growing in a *garden*.
It flourishes and doubles its yield;
It (stands) before its lord. (10)
Its fruit is sweet; its shade is pleasant;
And its end is reached in the garden. . . .

SIXTH CHAPTER:

Do not carry off the landmark at the boundaries of
   the arable land,
Nor disturb the position of the measuring-cord;
Be not greedy after a cubit of land,
Nor encroach upon the boundaries of

Prov. 22:28; 23:10 a widow. . . . (vii 15)
Guard against encroaching upon the boundaries of
   the fields,

---

[1] The "hot" man is the passionate or impulsive man, in contrast to the
"silent" or humbly pious man.   [2] Thoth was the barrister of the gods.

Lest a terror carry thee off.   (viii 10)
One satisfies god with the will of the Lord,
Who determines the boundaries of the arable land. ...   Prov. 23:11
Plow in the fields, that thou mayest find thy
   needs,   (17)
That thou mayest receive bread of thy own threshing
   floor.
Better is a measure that the god gives thee
Than five thousand (taken) illegally.
They do not spend a day (in) the granary or
   barn;   (ix 1)
They make no provisions for the beer-jar.
The completion of a moment is their lifetime in the
   storehouse;
At daybreak they are sunk (from sight).
Better is poverty in the hand of the god   (5)
Than riches in a storehouse;
Better is bread, when the heart is happy,   Prov. 15:16-17
Than riches with sorrow.

SEVENTH CHAPTER:
Cast not thy heart in pursuit of riches,   (10)
(For) there is no ignoring Fate and Fortune.[1]
Place not thy heart upon externals,
(For) every man belongs to his (appointed) hour.
Do not strain to seek an excess,
When thy needs are safe for thee.   (15)
If riches are brought to thee by robbery,
They will not spend the night with thee;
At daybreak they are not in thy house:
Their places may be seen, but they are not.
The ground has opened its mouth . . . that it might
   swallow them up,
And might sink them into the underworld.   (x 1)
(Or) they have made themselves a great breach of
   their (own) size
And are sunken down in the storehouse.
(Or) they have made themselves wings like geese
And are flown away to the heavens.   (5)   Prov. 23:4-5
Rejoice not thyself (over) riches (gained) by robbery,
Nor mourn because of poverty.
If an archer *in the van* advances (too far),
Then his *squad* abandons him.
The ship of the covetous is left (in) the mud,   (10)

---

[1] The god *Shay* and the goddess *Renenut* were two deified concepts,
whose governing role was particularly strong at this time.

While the boat of the silent man (has) a fair breeze.
Thou shouldst make prayer to the Aton when he
    rises,
Saying: "Give me prosperity and health."
He will give thee thy needs for this life,
And thou wilt be safe from terror. ...

NINTH CHAPTER:

Prov. 22:24   Do not associate to thyself the heated man,
Nor visit him for conversation.
Preserve thy tongue from answering thy
    superior,   (xi 15)
And guard thyself against reviling him.
Do not make him cast his speech to lasso thee,
Nor make (too) free with thy answer.
Thou shouldst discuss an answer (*only*) *with* a man
    of thy (own) size,
And guard thyself against plunging headlong into it.
Swifter is speech when the heart is hurt   (xii 1)
Than wind *of the head-waters*. ...

Prov. 22:25   Do not leap to hold to such a one,
Lest a terror carry thee off.

TENTH CHAPTER: (xiii 10)
Do not greet thy heated (opponent) in thy violence,
Nor hurt thy own heart (thereby).
Do not say to him: "Hail to thee!" falsely,
When a terror is in thy belly.

Prov. 12:22   Do not talk with a man falsely—   (15)
The abomination of the god.
Do not cut off thy heart from thy tongue,
That all thy affairs may be successful.
Be sincere   in the presence of the common people,
For one is safe in the hand of the god.   (xiv 1)
God hates him who falsifies words;
His great abomination is the contentious of belly.

ELEVENTH CHAPTER:
Be not greedy for the property of a poor man,   (5)
Nor hunger for his bread.
As for the property of a poor man, it (is) a blocking
    to the throat,
It makes a *vomiting* to the gullet.
If he has *obtained* it by false oaths,

Prov. 23:6-7   His heart is perverted by his belly. ...   (xiv 10)
The mouthful of bread (too) great thou
    swallowest and vomitest up,   (xiv 17)
Prov. 23:8   And art emptied of thy good. ...

THIRTEENTH CHAPTER:
Do not confuse a man with a pen upon
    papyrus—   (xv 20)
The abomination of the god.
Do not bear witness with false words,   (xvi 1)   Prov. 14:15
Nor *support* another person (*thus*) with thy tongue.
Do not take an accounting of him who has nothing,
Nor falsify thy pen.
If thou findest a large debt against a poor man,   (5)   Prov. 22:26-27
Make it into three parts,
Forgive two, and let one stand.
Thou wilt find it like the ways of life;
Thou wilt lie down and sleep (soundly); in the
    morning
Thou wilt find it (again) like good news.   (10)
Better is praise as one who loves men
Than riches in a storehouse;
Better is bread, when the heart is happy,   Prov. 16:8
Than riches with sorrow. ...

SIXTEENTH CHAPTER:
Do not *lean on* the scales nor falsify the weights,
                                      Prov. 20:23
Nor damage the fractions of the measure.
Do not wish for a (common) country
    measure,   (xvii 20)
And neglect those of the treasury.
The ape[1] sits beside the balance,
And his heart is the plummet.   (xviii 1)
Which god is as great as Thoth,
He that discovered these things, to make them?
Make not for thyself weights which are deficient;
They *abound in grief* through the will of god. ...   Prov. 16:11

EIGHTEENTH CHAPTER: (xix 10)
Do not spend the night fearful of the morrow.
At daybreak what is the morrow like?   Prov. 27:1
Man knows not what the morrow is like.
God is (always) in his success,
Whereas man is in his failure;   (15)
One thing are the words which men say,   Prov. 19:21
Another is that which the god does.
Say not: "I have no wrongdoing,"   Prov. 20:9
Nor (yet) strain to seek quarreling.
As for wrongdoing, it belongs to the god;   (20)
It is sealed with his finger.
There is no success in the hand of the god,

[1] The animal sacred to Thoth, god of just measure.

But there is no failure before him.
If he [1] pushes himself to seek success,   (xx 1)
In the completion of a moment he damages it.
Be steadfast in thy heart, make firm thy breast.
Steer not with thy tongue (alone).
If the tongue of a man (be) the rudder of a boat,   (5)
The All-Lord is its pilot. ...

TWENTIETH CHAPTER:
Do not confuse a man in the law court,
Nor *divert* the righteous man.
Give not thy attention (only) to him clothed in
    white,   (xxi 1)
Nor give consideration to him that is unkempt.
Do not accept the bribe of a powerful man,
Nor oppress for him the disabled.
As for justice, the great reward of god,   (5)
He gives it to whom he will....
Do not falsify the *income* on the records,
Nor damage the plans of god.
Do not discover for thy own self the will of god, (15)
Without (reference to) Fate and Fortune. ...

TWENTY-FIRST CHAPTER:

Prov. 20:22   Do not say: "I have found a strong superior, (xxii 1)
For a man in thy city has injured me."
Do not say: "I have found a *patron*,
For one who hates me has injured me."
For surely thou knowest not the plans of god,   (5)
Lest thou *be ashamed* on the morrow.

Prov. 20:22; 27:1   Sit thou down at the hands of the god,
And thy silence will cast them down. ...
Empty not thy belly to everybody,
Nor damage (thus) the regard for thee.

Prov. 20:19; 23:9   Spread not thy words to the common people,
Nor associate to thyself one (too) outgoing of heart.

Prov. 12:23   Better is a man whose talk (remains) in his belly (15)
Than he who speaks it out injuriously.
One does not run to reach success,
One does not *throw* to his (own) damage. ...

TWENTY-THIRD CHAPTER:
Do not eat bread before a noble,
Nor lay on thy mouth at first.
If thou art satisfied with false chewings,   (xxiii 15)
They are a pastime for thy spittle.

Prov. 23:1-3   Look at the cup which is before thee,   [1] A man.

And let it serve thy needs.
As a noble is great in his office,
He is as a well abounds (in) the drawing (of
water). ...

TWENTY-FIFTH CHAPTER:
Do not laugh at a blind man nor tease a dwarf   Prov. 17:5
Nor injure the affairs of the lame.   (xxiv 10)
Do not tease a man who is in the hand of the god, [1]
Nor be fierce of face against him if he errs.
For man is clay and straw,   Ps. 103:14
And the god is his builder.
He is tearing down and building up every day.   (15)
He makes a thousand poor men as he wishes,
(Or) he makes a thousand men *as overseers*,
When he is in his hour of life.
How joyful is he who reaches the West,
When he is safe in the hand of the god. [2] ...

TWENTY-EIGHTH CHAPTER:
Do not *recognize* a widow if thou catchest her in the
     fields, [3]
Nor fail to be *indulgent* to her reply.   (xxvi 10)
Do not neglect a stranger (with) thy oil-jar,
That it be doubled before thy brethren.
God desires respect for the poor   Prov. 22:22-23
More than the honoring of the exalted. ...

THIRTIETH CHAPTER:
See thou these thirty chapters:
They entertain; they instruct;
They are the foremost of all books;
They make the ignorant to know.   (xxvii 10)
If they are read out before the ignorant,
Then he will be cleansed by them.
Fill thyself with them; put them in thy heart,
And be a man who can interpret them,
Who will interpret them as a teacher.   (15)
As for the scribe who is experienced in his office,   Prov. 22:29
He will find himself worthy (to be) a courtier.

     (colophon:)   It has come to its end
In the writing of Senu, son of the God's Father
     Pa-miu.[4]   (xxviii 1)

---

[1] The insane.
[2] Death releases a man from the helplessness of this world.
[3] Literally: "Do not find a widow." The reference is to the poor glean-
ing in the fields.
[4] Senu was the scribe who made this copy.

Proverbs from Mesopotamia

TRANSLATOR: ROBERT H. PFEIFFER

ANET, 425

A. K 4347

(20) Deal not badly with a matter, then [no sor]row [will fa]ll into your heart. (21) Do [no] evil, then you will [not] clutch a lasting [sorr]ow. (27) Without copulation she conceived, without eating she became plump![1] (28) Copulation causes the breast to give suck.[2] (29) When I labor they take away (my reward): when I increase my efforts, who will give me anything? (34) The strong man is fed through the price of his hire, the weak man through the price (or: the wages) of his child. (37) He is fortunate in everything, since he wears a (fine) garment. (38) Do you strike the face of a walking ox with a strap? (39) My knees keep walking, my feet are tireless, yet

Eccles. 9:11

a man devoid of understanding pursues me with sorrow. (40) Am I (not) a thoroughbred steed? Yet I am harnessed with a mule and must draw a wagon loaded with reeds. (44) I dwell in a house of asphalt

Eccles. 1:9-10

and bricks, yet some clay ... pours over me.[3] (50) The life of the day before yesterday is that of any day. (53) You are placed into a river and your water becomes at once stinking; you are placed in an orchard and your date-fruit becomes bitter.[4] (55) If the shoot is not right it will not produce the stalk, nor create seed. (56) Will ripe grain grow? How do we know? Will dried grain grow? How do we know? (57) Very soon he will be dead; (so he says), "Let me eat up

Isa. 22:13

(all I have)!" Soon he will be well; (so he says), "Let me economize!" (60) From before the gate of the city whose armament is not powerful the enemy cannot be repulsed. (64) You go and take the field of the enemy; the enemy comes and takes your field.

[1] To indicate something impossible; cf. Amos 6:12a. The Sumerian original reads: "Without his cohabiting with you, can you be pregnant? Without his feeding you, can you be fat?" [2] i.e. cause and effect.

[3] The Sumerian seems to mean: "In the house the asphalt was removed from the brick; ... last year the roof drain was dripping on me."

[4] Said of a man afflicted with persistent bad luck, or of one bringing misfortune to others through the evil eye.

The following Sumerian proverbs appear on tablets dating to the Early Old Babylonian period which have been found at Nippur and Ur. The translations here provided are by Edmund I. Gordon, Research Associate, Babylonian Section, University Museum, University of Pennsylvania.

(1) A perverse child—his mother should never have given birth to him; his (personal) god should never have fashioned him! (2) The fox had a stick with him: "Whom shall I hit?" He carried a legal document with him: "What can I challenge?" (3) Upon my escaping from the wild-ox, the wild-cow confronted me! (4) As long as he is alive, he is his friend; on the day of (his) death, he is his greatest adversary! (5) He could not bring about an agreement; the women were all talking to one another! (6) Into an open mouth, a fly will enter! (7) Like a barren cow, you are looking for a calf of yours which does not exist! (8) The horse, after he had thrown off his rider, said: "If my burden is always to be this, I shall become weak!" (9) The dog understands "Take it!" He does not understand "Put it down!"

Aramaic Proverbs and Precepts

TRANSLATOR: H. L. GINSBERG

THE WORDS OF AHIQAR

ANET, 427-430

The text is preserved as the more recent writing on eleven sheets of palimpsest papyrus of the late fifth century B.C. recovered by German excavators from the debris of Elephantine, Upper Egypt, in the years 1906-7. The first four papyri, with a total of five columns, contain the story of Ahiqar, which is in the first person; the remaining seven, with a total of nine columns, contain Ahiqar's sayings. The composition of the work may antedate the preserved copy by as much as a century.

Prior to the recovery of the old Aramaic text, several post-Christian recensions of the book of Ahiqar were known, the Syriac one being the oldest. The man Ahiqar is mentioned in the book of Tobit (1:22; 14:10; etc.).

. . .

(vi 79-94) [Wh]at is stronger than a braying ass? The l[o]ad. The son who is trained and taught and on [whose] feet the fetter is put [*shall prosper*]. Withhold not thy son from the rod, else thou wilt not be able to save [him from *wickedness*]. If I smite thee, my son, thou wilt not die, but if I leave thee to thine own heart [thou wilt not live]. A blow for a bondman, *a reb[uke]* for a bondwoman, and for all thy slaves dis[cipline. One who] buys a run[away] slave [or] a thievish handmaid *squanders his fortune* and disgraces] the name of his father and his offspring with the reputation of his wantonness.—The scorpion [finds] bread but is not p[*leased, and something b]ad* and is more pleased than if one fe[eds it . . .] The lion will *lie in wait* for the stag in the concealment of the . . . and he [. . .] and will shed its blood and eat its flesh. Even so is the meeting of [*me*]*n.—.* . . a lion. . . . An ass which leaves [*its load*] and *does not carry it* shall take a *load* from its companion and take the b[urde]n which is not its [own with its own] and shall be made to bear a camel's load.—The ass *bend*[*s down*] to the she-ass [from lo]ve of her, and the birds [. . .]. Two things [which] are meet, and the third pleasing to Shamash: one who dr[inks] wine and gives it to drink, one who guards wisdom, and one who hears a word and does not tell.—Behold that is dear [to] Shamash. But he who drinks wine and does not [give it to drink], and one whose wisdom goes astray, [and . . .] is seen.—

[. . . Wisdom . . .].

(vii 95-110) To gods also she is dear. F[or all time] the kingdom is [hers]. In he[av]en is she established, for the lord of holy ones has exalted [her.—My s]on, ch[at]ter not overmuch so that thou speak out [every w]ord [that] comes to thy mind; for men's (eyes) and ears are everywhere (trained) u[pon] thy mouth.

Prov. 4:23

Beware lest it be [thy] *undoing.* More than all watchfulness watch thy mouth, and [over] what [*thou*] h[*earest*] harden thy heart. For a word is a bird: once released no man *can re*[*capture it*]. First *co*[*un*]*t the secrets of* thy mouth; then bring out thy [words] by *number.* For the *instruction* of a mouth is stronger

Prov. 4:22; 16:24

than the *instruction* of war. Treat not lightly the word of a king: let it be healing for thy [flesh]. Soft is the utterance of a king; (yet) it is sharper and stronger than a [two]-edged knife. Look before thee: a hard look [on the f]ace of a k[ing] (means) "Delay not!" His wrath is swift as lightning: do thou take heed unto

Eccles. 8:2-3

thyself that he disp[lay i]t not against thine ut[tera]nces and thou perish [be]fore thy time. [The wr]ath of a king, if thou be commanded, is a burning fire. Obey [it] at once. Let it not be kindled against thee and cover (read: *burn*) thy hands. [Cov]er up the word of a king with the veil of the heart.—Why should wood strive

Eccles. 6:10

with fire, flesh with a knife, a man with [*a king*]? I have tasted even the bitter medlar, and [*I have eaten*] endives; but there is naught which is more [bi]tter than poverty. Soft is the tongue of *a k*[*ing*], but it

Prov. 25:15

breaks a dragon's ribs; like a plague, which is not

seen.—Let not thy heart rejoice over the multitude of children [nor grieve] over their fewness. A king is like *the Merciful*; his voice also is loud: who is there that can stand before him, except one with whom is God? Beautiful is a king to behold, and noble is his majesty to them that walk the earth *as [free]men*. A good vessel cove[rs] a word in its heart, and a broken one lets it out. The lion approached to [greet the ass]: "Peace be unto thee." The ass answered and said to the lion: . . .

(viii 111-125) I have lifted sand, and I have carried salt; but there is naught which is heavier than [*rage*]. I have lifted bruised straw, and I have taken up bran; but there is naught which is lighter than a sojourner. [1] War troubles calm waters between good *friends*. If a man be small and grow great, his words *soar* above him. For the opening of his mouth is an *utte[ra]nce* of gods, and if he be beloved of gods they will put something good in his mouth to say. Many are [the st]ar[s] of heaven wh]ose names no man knows. By the same token, no man knows mankind. There is [n]o lion in the sea, therefore they call a flood a *lb'*. The leopard met the goat when she was cold. The leopard answered and said to the goat, "Come, I will cover thee with my hide." The goat [answered] and said to the leopard, "What need have I for it, *my lord?* Take not my skin from me." For he does not greet the gazelle [2] except to suck its blood.—The bear went to the lam[bs. "Give me one of you and I] will be content." The lam[bs] answered and said to him, "Take whichever thou wilt of us. We are [thy] la[mbs]." Truly, 'tis not in the power of m[e]n to li[ft u]p their feet or to put them down with[out the gods]. Truly, 'tis not in thy power to li[ft u]p thy foot [o]r to put it down.—If a good thing come forth from the mouths of m[en, it is well for them], and if an evil thing come [forth] from their mouths, the gods will do evil unto them.—If God's eyes are on men, a man may chop wood in the dark without seeing, like a thief, who demolishes a house and . . . (ix 123-141) [Bend not] thy [b]ow and shoot not thine arrow at a righteous man, lest God come to his help and turn it back upon thee. [If] thou [be hungry], my son, *take every trouble* and do every labor, then wilt thou eat and be satisfied and give

Prov. 27:3;
Job. 6:2-3

Prov. 16:1

Isa. 40:26; Ps. 147:4

---

[1] i.e. there is nothing less respected.
[2] The goat seems to have become a gazelle through inadvertence.

to thy children. [If thou be]nd thy bow and shoot thine arrow at a righteous man, from thee is the arrow but from God the *guidance*. [If] thou [be needy], my son, borrow corn and wheat that thou mayest eat and be sated and give to thy children with thee. Take not a heavy loan, from an evil man. More[over, if] thou take a loan, give no rest to thyself until [thou repay the l]oan. [A loa]n is sweet as [. . .], but its repayment is grief. My [son, hearken not] with thine ears to [a lying man]. For a man's charm is his truthfulness; his repulsiveness, the lies of his lips. [At fi]rst a throne [is set up] for the liar, but in the e[nd they fi]nd out his lies and spit in his face. A liar's neck is cut [i.e. he speaks very softly?] like a . . . virgin that [is hidden] from sight, like a man who causes misfortune which does not proceed from God.—[Despise not] that which is in thy lot, nor covet a wealth which is denied thee. [Multiply not] riches and make not great thy heart. [Whosoever] *takes no pride* in the names of his father and mother,

Prov. 20:20 may the s[un] not shine [upon him]; for he is a wicked man. [From myself] has my misfortune proceeded: with whom shall I be justified?—The son of my body has spied out my house: [wh]at can I say to strangers? [*My son* has] been a false witness against me: who, then, has justified me?—From my house has gone forth wrath: with whom shall I strive? Reveal

Prov. 25:9-10 not thy [*secrets*] before thy [fri]ends, lest thy name become despised of them. (x 142-158) With him who is more exalted than thou, *quarrel not*. With him who is . . . and stronger than thou, [*contend not; for he will take*] of thy portion and [*add it to*] his. Behold even so is a small man (who strives) with [a great one]. Remove not wisdom from thee [. . .]. Gaze not overmuch [les]t thy vi[sion] be dimmed. Be not (too) sweet, lest they [swallow] thee: be not (too) bitter [*lest they spit thee out*]. If thou wouldst be [exalted], my son, [humble thyself before God], who humbles an [exalted] man and [exalts a lowly man]. What me[n's] l[i]ps curse, God does n[ot] curse. (lines 152-5 badly damaged and omitted here) God shall twist the twister's mouth and tear out [his] tongue. Let not good [ey]es be darkened, nor [good] ears [be stopped, and let a good mouth love] the truth and speak it. (xi 159-172) A man of [beco]ming conduct whose heart is good is like a mighty c[it]y which is si[*tuated*] upon a m[ountain]. There is [*none that can bring him down.*

Except] a man *dwell* with God, how can he be guarded by his own refuge? ..., but he with whom God is, who ca[n cas]t him down? (line 162 difficult and omitted here) A man [knows not] what is in his fellow's heart. So when a good man [se]es a wi[cked] man [let him beware of him]. Let him [not] join with him on a journey or be a *neighbor* to him—a good man [wi]th a ba[d] m[an]. The [bram]ble sent to [the] pomegranate tree [saying], "The bramble to the pomegranate: Wherefore the mul(titude) of (thy) thorns [to him that to]uches thy [fru]it?" ... The [pomegranate tree] answered and said to the bramble, "Thou art al[l] thorns to him that touches thee." All that come in contact with a righteous man are on his side. [*A city*] of wicked men shall on a gusty day be pulled apart, and in ... its gates be brought low; for the spoil [of the righteous are they].—Mine eyes which I lifted up unto thee and my heart which I gave thee in wisdom [hast thou scorned, and thou ha]st brought my name into disg[race]. If the wicked man seize the corner of thy garment, leave it in his hand. Then approach Shamash: he will [t]ake his and give it to thee.

(xii 173-190) (Ends of all lines and beginnings of some missing. Only the point of line 188 is entirely clear: "Hunger makes bitterness sweet, and thirst [sourness]."̇ In column xiii 191-207, only of a few sayings is enough preserved for making out the point.)

Prov. 27:7

... If thy master entrust to thee water to keep [*and thou do it faithfully, he may*] leave gold with thee. .... [A man] one [day said] to the wild ass, "[Let me ride] upon thee, and I will maintain thee [...." Said the wild ass, "Keep] thy maintenance and thy fodder, and let me not see thy riding."—Let not the rich man say, "In my riches I am glorious."

Jer. 9:23

(Column xiv 208-223 has only shreds preserved; the point of the first one can be guessed: "[*Do not sh*]*ow* an Arab the sea nor a Sidonian the de[*sert*]; for their work is *different*.")

Akkadian Observations on Life

TRANSLATOR: ROBERT H. PFEIFFER

A PESSIMISTIC DIALOGUE BETWEEN MASTER AND SERVANT

ANET, 437-438

(I) ["Servant,] obey me." Yes, my lord, yes. ["Bring me at once the] chariot, hitch it up. I will ride to the palace." [Ride, my lord, ride! All your wishes] will be realized for you. The king] will be gracious to you. (5) ["No, servant,] I shall not ride [to] the palace." [Do not ride], my lord, do not ride. [To a place . . .] he will send you. [*In a land which*] you know [not] he will let you be captured. [Day and] night he will let you see trouble.

(II) (10) "Servant, obey me." Yes, my lord, yes. ["Bring me at] once water for my hands, and give it to me: I wish to dine." [Dine,] my lord, dine. To dine regularly is the opening of the heart (i.e. brings joy). [To a dinner] eaten in happiness and with washed hands (the sun-god) Shamash comes. "No, [servant,] I shall not dine." (15) Do not dine, my lord, do not dine. To be hungry and eat, to be thirsty and drink, comes upon (every) man.

(III) "Servant, obey me." Yes, my lord, yes. "Bring me at once the chariot, hitch it up. I will ride to the wilderness." Ride, my lord, ride. The fugitive's stomach is full. (20) The hunting dog will break a bone; the fugitive *ḫaḫur* bird will build its nest; the wild ass running to and fro will . . . . "No, servant, to the wilderness I will not ride." Do not ride, my lord, do not ride. (25) The fugitive's mind is variable. The hunting dog's teeth will break; the house of the fugitive *ḫaḫur* bird is in [*a hole*] of the wall; and the abode of the wild ass running to and fro is the desert.

(IV) "Servant, [obey me." Yes, my lord, yes.] (20-31) (fragments). . . . the silence of the evil one make complete. ["My enemy] I shall capture and *quickly* shackle. I shall lie in wait for my adversary." (35) Lie (in wait), my lord, lie (in wait). . . . A house you will not build. He who proceeds [rashly] destroys his father's house.

(V) . . . "I will not build a house." You will not build it.

(VI) ["Servant, obey me." Yes, my lord, yes.] "At the

[word of my adversary I shall remain silent."] (40)
Remain silent, my lord, remain [silent. Silence is better
than speech.] "No, servant, at the [word of my adversary
I shall not remain silent."] Do not remain silent, my
lord, [do not remain silent.] If you do not speak
with your mouth . . . . Your adversary will be angry
with you . . . .

(VII) (45) "Servant, obey me." Yes, my lord, yes. "I
intend to start a rebellion." Do (it), my lord, [do (it)].
If you do not start a rebellion what becomes of your
clay?[1] Who will give you (something) to fill your
stomach? "No, servant, I shall not do something violent." (50) [Do (it) not, my lord, do (it) not.] The
man doing something violent is killed or [ill-treated],
or he is maimed, or captured and cast into prison.

Prov. 24:21-22

(VIII) "Servant, obey me." Yes, my lord, yes. (55)
"A woman will I love." Yes, love, my lord, love. The
man who loves a woman forgets pain and trouble.
"No, servant, a woman I shall not love." [Do not love,]
my lord, do not [love]. Woman is a well, (60) woman
is an iron dagger—a sharp one!—which cuts a man's
neck.

(IX) "Servant, obey me." Yes, my lord, yes. "Bring
me at once water for my hands, and give it to me:
I will offer a sacrifice to my god." Offer, my lord,
offer. A man offering sacrifice to his god is happy,
loan upon loan he makes. "No, servant, a sacrifice to
my god will I not offer." Do not offer (it), my lord,
do not offer (it). You may teach a god to trot after
you like a dog when he requires of you, (saying),
"(Celebrate) my ritual" or "do not inquire (by re-
questing an oracle)" or anything else.

(X) ["Servant,] obey me." Yes, my lord, yes. (70)
"I shall give food to our country." Give it, my lord, give
it! [The man who] gives food [to his country]—his
barley (remains) his own but his receipts from interest
(payments) become immense. ["No, servant,] food to
my country I shall not give." [Do not give, my lord,]
do not give. Giving is like lov[ing]. . . . giving birth
to a son. (75) . . . they will curse you. [They will eat]
your barley and destroy you.

(XI) "Servant, obey me." Yes, my lord, yes. "I will
do something helpful for my country." Do (it), my
lord, do (it). The man who does something helpful
for his country,—his helpful deed is placed in the

---

[1] "Your clay" means of course "your body" (cf. Gen. 2:7).

bowl of Marduk.[1] (80) "No, servant, I will not do
something helpful for my country." Do it not, my lord,
do it not. Climb the mounds of ancient ruins and walk
about: look at the skulls of late and early (men); who
(among them) is an evildoer, who a public benefactor?

(XII) "Servant, obey me." Yes, my lord, yes. "Now,
what is good? (85) To break my neck, your neck,
throw (both) into the river—(that) is good." Who is
tall enough to ascend to heaven? Who is broad enough
to embrace the earth? "No, servant, I shall kill you and
send you ahead of me." (Then) would my lord (wish
to) live even three days after me? (Colophon) Written
according to the original and collated.

[1] The tablets listing men's deeds were stored in Marduk's bowl.

Egyptian Prophecy

TRANSLATOR: JOHN A. WILSON

ANET, 444-446 THE PROPHECY OF NEFER-ROHU

The Middle Kingdom delivered Egypt from the civil war and
anarchy which had followed the Old Kingdom. These troubles
and their ultimate resolution produced a sense of messianic
salvation, a feeling which the early pharaohs of the Middle
Kingdom probably fostered in their own interests. The following
text was apparently composed at that time of happy deliverance,
although the earliest extant copies happen to date from the
Eighteenth Dynasty, about five centuries later. The text purports to relate how King Snefru of the Fourth Dynasty sought
entertainment and how a prophet foretold the downfall of the
Old Kingdom and the reestablishment of order by Amen-em-
het I, the first king of the Twelfth Dynasty.

Now IT HAPPENED THAT the majesty of the King of
Upper and Lower Egypt: Snefru, the triumphant, was
the beneficent king in this entire land. On one of these
days it happened that the official council of the Residence City entered into the Great House—life, [pros-
perity], health!—to offer greeting. Then they went
out, that they might offer greetings (elsewhere), according to their daily procedure. Then his majesty—life,
prosperity, health!—said to the seal-bearer who was at
his side: "Go and bring me (back) the official council
of the Residence City, which has gone forth hence to
offer greetings on this [day]." (Thereupon they) were
ushered in to him (5) immediately. Then they were

on their bellies in the presence of his majesty a second time.

Then his majesty—life, prosperity, health!—said to them: "(My) people, behold, I have caused you to be called to have you seek out for me a son of yours who is wise, or a brother of yours who is competent, or a friend of yours who has performed a good deed, one who may say to me a few fine words or choice speeches, at the hearing of which my [majesty] may be entertained."

Then they put (themselves) upon their bellies in the presence of his majesty—life, prosperity, health!—once more. THEN THEY SAID BEFORE his majesty—life, prosperity, health!: "A great lector-priest of Bastet,[2] O sovereign, our lord, (10) whose name is Nefer-rohu—he is a commoner valiant [with] his arm, a scribe competent with his fingers; he is a man of rank, who has more property than any peer of his. Would that he [*might be permitted*] to see his majesty!" Then his majesty—life, prosperity, health!—said: "Go and [bring] him to me!"

Then he was ushered in to him immediately. Then he was on his belly in the presence of his majesty—life, prosperity, health! Then his majesty—life, prosperity, health!—said: "Come, pray, Nefer-rohu, my friend, that thou mayest say to me a few fine words or choice speeches, at the hearing of which my majesty may be entertained!" Then the lector-priest Nefer-rohu said: "Of what has (already) happened or of what is going to happen, O Sovereign—life, prosperity, health! —[my] lord?" (15) Then his majesty—life, prosperity, health!—said: "Rather of what is going to happen. If it has taken place *by* today, *pass it* [*by*]."[3] Then he stretched forth his hand for the box of writing equipment; then he drew forth a scroll of papyrus and a palette; thereupon he put (it) into writing.[4]

What the lector-[priest] Nefer-rohu said, that wise man of the east, he who belonged to Bastet at her appearances, that child of the Heliopolitan nome,[5] AS HE BROODED over what (was to) happen in the land, as he

---

[2] The lector-priest (literally, "he who carries the ritual") was initiated into the sacred writings and thus was priest, seer, and magician. Bastet was the cat-goddess of Bubastis in the eastern half of the Delta.

[3] This must be the general sense, although the wording is obscure. An Egyptian interest in the future, rather than the past, was not normal, but a prophecy which promised that the future would restore the past would be acceptable.

[4] The pharaoh himself wrote down the prophecy. The Egyptian texts treat Snefru as a friendly and approachable ruler.

[5] Although now serving in Bubastis, he was born in the Heliopolitan nome.

called to mind the state of the east, when the Asiatics would move about with their strong arms, would disturb the hearts [of] those who are at the harvest, and would take away the spans of cattle at the plowing. (20) He said:

Reconstruct, O my heart, (*how*) thou bewailest this land in which thou didst begin! To be silent is *repression.* Behold, there is something about which men speak as *terrifying,* for, behold, the great man is a thing passed away (in the land) where thou didst begin. BE NOT LAX; BEHOLD, IT is before thy face! Mayest thou rise up against what is before thee, for, behold, although great men are concerned with the land, what has been done is as what is not done. *Re must begin the foundation (of the earth over again).* The land is completely perished, (so that) no remainder exists, (so that) not (even) the black of the nail survives from what was fated. [1]

Isa. 24:3

THIS LAND IS (SO) DAMAGED (that) there is no one who is concerned with it, no one who speaks, no eye that weeps. How is this land? The sun disc is covered over. (25) It will not shine (so that) people may see. No one can live when clouds cover over (the sun). Then everybody is deaf for lack of it.

Amos 8:9

I shall speak of what is before my face; I cannot foretell what has not (yet) come.

THE RIVERS of Egypt are empty, (so that) the water is crossed on foot. Men seek for water for the ships to sail on it. Its course is [become] a sandbank. The sandbank *is against* the flood; the place of water *is against* the [flood]—(*both*) the place of water *and* the sandbank.[2] The south wind will oppose the north wind; the skies are no (longer) in a single wind.[3] A foreign bird will be born in the marshes of the Northland. It has made a nest beside (30) men. and people have let it approach through want of it.[4] DAMAGED INDEED ARE THOSE good things, those fish-ponds, (where there were) those who clean fish, overflowing with fish and fowl. Everything good is disappeared, and the land is

Isa. 19:5
Ezek. 30:12

Isa. 19:8

---

[1] Not so much of the "Black Land" of Egypt survives as might be under a fingernail.

[2] Perhaps mistranslated, but attempting to hold the idea that neither the banks nor the bed of the stream would receive the life-giving inundation.

[3] The pleasant north wind is the normal wind of Egypt.

[4] A strange passage, which either emphasizes the unnaturalness of nature in the distressed times or else is an oblique reference to Asiatics infiltrating into the Delta.

prostrate because of woes from that *food*,[1] the Asiatics
who are throughout the land.

Foes have arisen in the east, and Asiatics have come
down into Egypt. . . . No protector will listen. . . . Men
will enter into the *fortresses*. Sleep will *be banished*
from my eyes, (35) as I spend the night wakeful. THE
WILD BEASTS OF THE DESERT WILL drink at the rivers of
Egypt and be at their ease on their banks for lack of
some one to scare them away.

Isa. 19:18

Zeph. 2:15

This land is helter-skelter, and no one knows the
result which will come about, which is hidden from
speech, sight, or hearing. The face is deaf, for silence
confronts. I show thee the land topsy-turvy. That
which never happened has happened. Men will take up
weapons of warfare, (so that) the land lives in (40)
confusion. MEN WILL MAKE ARROWS of metal,[2] beg for
the bread of blood, and laugh with the laughter of
sickness.[3] There is no one who weeps because of death;
there is no one who spends the night fasting because
of death; (but) a man's heart pursues himself (alone).
(Dishevelled) mourning is no (longer) carried out today, (for) the heart is completely *separated from* it. A
man sits *in his corner*, (*turning*) his back while one
man kills another. I show thee the son as a foe, the
brother as an enemy, and a man (45) killing his (own)
father.

Isa. 19:2

EVERY MOUTH IS FULL OF "LOVE ME!", AND everything
GOOD has disappeared. The land is perished, (*as though*)
laws *were* destined *for it*: the damaging of what had
been done, the emptiness of what had been found,[4]
and the doing of what had not been done. Men take
a man's property away from him, and it is given to him
who is from outside. I show thee the possessor in need
and the outsider satisfied. He who never filled for himself (*now*) *empties*.[5] Men will [*treat*] (fellow) citizens
as hateful, in order to silence the mouth that speaks.
If a statement is answered, an arm goes out with a
stick, and men speak with: "Kill him!" THE UTTERANCE

---

[1] The Asiatics are a bitter diet for the Egyptians?

[2] Note that metal arrow-points were first used in Egypt in the 11th
dynasty (about 2100 B.C.).   [3] Hysteria.

[4] A pious obligation resting upon the Egyptians was to restore the
inscriptions of the ancestors which were "found empty," i.e. damaged or
containing lacunae. Under the present unsettled conditions what was found
empty was left empty.

[5] Perhaps: he who never had to insist on full measure for himself now
scrapes the bottom.

OF SPEECH IN THE HEART is like a fire. (50) Men cannot suffer what issues from *a man's* mouth.

The land is diminished, (but) its administrators are many; bare, (but) its taxes are great; little in grain, (but) the measure is large, and it is measured to overflowing. [1]

Re separates himself (from) mankind. If he shines forth, it is (but) an hour. No one knows when midday falls, for his shadow cannot be distinguished.[2] There is no one bright of face when seeing [him]; the eyes are not moist with water, when he is in the sky like the moon. His prescribed time does not fail. His rays are indeed in (men's) faces in his former way.

Isa. 24:1   I SHOW THEE THE LAND TOPSY-TURVY. The weak of arm is (now) the possessor of an arm. Men (55) salute (respectfully) him who (formerly) saluted. I show thee the undermost on top, turned about *in proportion to* the turning about *of my belly*. Men live in the necropolis. The poor man will make wealth. ... It is the paupers who eat the offering-bread, while the servants *jubilate*. The Heliopolitan nome, the birthplace of every god, will no (*longer*) *be on earth.*

(THEN) IT IS THAT a king WILL COME, BELONGING TO THE SOUTH, Ameni, the triumphant, his name. He is the son of a woman of the land of Nubia; he is one born in Upper Egypt. [3] He will take the [White] Crown; he will wear the Red Crown; (60) he will unite the Two Mighty Ones; [4] he will satisfy the Two Lords [5] with what they desire. The encircler-of-the-fields (will be) in his grasp, the oar ... [6]

REJOICE, ye people of his time! The son of a man will make his name forever and ever. They who incline toward evil and who plot rebellion have subdued their speech for fear of him. The Asiatics will fall to his sword, and the Libyans will fall to his flame. The rebels belong to his wrath, and the treacherous of heart to (65) the awe of him. The uraeus-serpent which is on his brow stills for him the treacherous of heart.

---

[1] A land smaller and poorer has more bureaucrats and higher and more exacting taxes.

[2] The sun's shadow on the shadow-clock determined the hour of noon.

[3] Ameni was an abbreviated name for Amen-em-het (I).

[4] The two tutelary goddesses of Upper and Lower Egypt, who united as the Double Crown.   [5] Horus and Seth.

[6] As one act of the coronation ceremonies, the pharaoh, grasping an oar and some other object, dedicated a field by running around it four times.

THERE WILL BE BUILT the Wall of the Ruler—life, prosperity, health![1]—and the Asiatics will not be permitted to come down into Egypt that they might beg for water in the customary manner, in order to let their beasts drink. And justice will come into its place, while wrongdoing is *driven* out.[2] Rejoice, he who may behold (this) (70) and who may be in the service of the king!

The learned man will pour out water for me,[3] when he sees what I have spoken come to pass.

IT HAS COME (TO ITS END) in [success], by the *Scribe* . . .

[1] A series of fortresses along the eastern frontier, as in *Si-nuhe*.
[2] The coronation of each pharaoh reinstituted the old order of *ma'at* "justice," and expelled "deceit."   [3] As a libation at the tomb.

Egyptian Songs and Poems

TRANSLATOR: JOHN A. WILSON

LOVE SONGS

ANET, 467-469

The later Egyptian Empire (1300-1100 B.C.) has provided us with several collections of love songs. They were apparently intended to be sung to the accompaniment of some musical instrument. They express an enjoyment of nature and the out-of-doors. As in the Song of Songs, the lovers are called "my brother" and "my sister."

a

The voice of the swallow speaks and says:
"The land has brightened—What is thy road?"[1]
Thou shalt not, O bird, *disturb* me!
I have found my brother in his bed,
And my heart is still more glad,
(*When he*) said to me:
"I shall not go afar off.
My hand is in thy hand,
I shall stroll about,
And I shall be with thee in every pleasant place."
He makes me the foremost of maidens.
He injures not my heart.
THE END.

Song of Sol. 2:12-13

[1] Where are you walking in the early morning?

b

SEVENTH STANZA.[1]
Seven (days) to yesterday I have not seen the sister,
  And a sickness has invaded me.
My body has become heavy,
  Forgetful of my own self.[2]

Song of Sol. 2:5; 5:8

[1] Here the word "seven" is employed in place of a pun.
[2] Often in the sense of losing consciousness.

If the chief of physicians come to me,
My heart is not content (with) their remedies;
The lector priests,[2] no way (out) is in them:—
My sickness will not be probed.
To say to me: "Here she is!" is what will revive me;
Her name is what will lift me up;
The going in and out of her messengers
Is what will revive my heart.
More beneficial to me is the sister than any remedies;
She is more to me than the collected writings.
My health is her coming in from outside:
When (I) see her, then (I) am well.
If she opens her eye, my body is young (again);
If she speaks, then I am strong (again);
When I embrace her, she drives evil away from me—
But she has gone forth from me for seven days!

[2] Who read magic spells for the cure of disease.

c

Song of Sol. 1:9

Would that thou wouldst come (to the sister speedily),
Like a horse of the king,
Picked from a thousand of all steeds,
The foremost of the stables!
It is distinguished in its food,
And its master knows its paces.
If it hears the sound of the whip,
It knows no delay,
And there is no foremost of the chasseurs[1]
Who can stay before it (to hold it).
How well the sister's heart knows
That he is not far from the sister!   THE END.

[1] *Teher*, a foreign word (perhaps Hittite) for a chariot-warrior.

ANET, 470-471   IN PRAISE OF THE CITY RAMSES

The pharaohs of the Nineteenth Dynasty established their residence city, the biblical Ramses or Raamses, in the northeastern Delta. The glories of this new capital were celebrated in poetical compositions like the following.

The Scribe Pai-Bes communicating to his lord, the Scribe Amen-em-Opet: In life, prosperity, health! It is a letter to let [my] lord know. Another communication to my lord, to wit:

I have reached Per-Ramses,   and have found (ii 1) it in [very, very] good condition, a beautiful district, without its like, after the pattern of Thebes. It was [Re] himself [who founded it.]

The Residence is pleasant in life; its field is full of everything good; it is (full) of supplies and food every day, its *ponds* with fish, and its lakes with birds. Its meadows are verdant with grass; its banks bear dates; its melons are abundant on the sands. . . . Its granaries are (so) full of barley and emmer (that) they come near to the sky. Onions and leeks (5) are *for food*, and lettuce of the *garden*, pomegranates, apples, and olives, figs of the orchard, sweet wine of *Ka*-of-Egypt,[1] surpassing honey, red *wedj*-fish of the canal of the Residence City, *which* live on lotus-flowers, *bedin*-fish of the *Hari*-waters, . . .

Num. 11:5

The Shi-Hor[2] has salt, and *the Her canal* has natron. Its ships go out and come (back) to mooring, (so that) supplies (10) and food are in it every day. One rejoices to dwell within it, and there is none who says: "Would that!" to it.[3] The small in it are like the great.

Josh. 13:3

Come, let us celebrate for it its feasts of the sky, as well as its feasts at the beginning of the seasons.[4]

The reed-thicket[5] comes to it with papyrus; the Shi-Hor with rushes. . . . (iii 1) . . . The young men of "Great of Victories" are dressed up every day, with sweet oil upon their heads and newly dressed hair. They stand beside their doors, their hands bowed down with flowers, with greenery of the House of Hat-Hor and flax of *the Her canal*, on the day when User-maat-Re Setep-en-Re —life, prosperity, health!—Montu-in-the-Two-Lands enters in, on the morning of the Feast of Khoiakh. (5) Every man is like his fellow in uttering their petitions.

The ale of "Great of Victories" is sweet; . . . beer of Kode[6] from the harbor, and wine of the vineyards. The ointment of the *Segbeyen* waters is sweet, and the garlands of the *garden*. The singers of "Great of Victories" are sweet, being instructed in Memphis.

(So) dwell content of heart and free, without stirring from it, O User-maat-Re Setep-en-Re—life, prosperity, health!—Montu-in-the-Two-Lands, Ramses Meri-Amon —life, prosperity, health!—thou god! THE END.

---

[1] A well-known vineyard of the Delta.

[2] The biblical "the Shihor (which is before Egypt)," or "the Waters of Horus." Presumably the Tanite branch of the Nile, with its salt-flats.

[3] No one feels a lack in the city Ramses.

[4] The "feasts of the sky" were those astronomically set, such as those of the phases of the moon. The seasonal feasts included the Coronation Feast, the Rising of the Dog-Star, the Feast of Opet, etc.

[5] The word used appears also in Hebrew in "the Sea of Reeds" (conventionally translated "Red Sea").

[6] Kode or Qedi was the north Phoenician coast, carrying into Cilicia.

XII. Letters

Akkadian Letters

TRANSLATOR: W. F. ALBRIGHT[*]

THE MARI LETTERS

In 1935-38 André Parrot excavated the palace of king Zimri-Lim (about 1730-1700 B.C.) at Tell el-Hariri, ancient Mari on the Middle Euphrates. Among nearly 20,000 cuneiform tablets found in this palace were some 5,000 letters, mostly written by native Amorites (Northwestern Semites) in a Babylonian full of West-Semitic words and grammatical usages. Personal names, language and customs reflect the culture of the Patriarchal Age in Genesis.

a

Published and translated by G. Dossin in *RA*, xxxv (1938), pp. 178 f.

To my lord say: Thus Bannum, thy servant. Yesterday, (5) I departed from Mari, and spent the night at Zuruban. All the Benjaminites raised fire-signals.[1] (10) From Samanum to Ilum-Muluk, from Ilum-Muluk to Mishlan, all the cities of the Benjaminites (15) of the Terqa district raised fire signals in response, and so far I have not ascertained the meaning of those signals. Now, I shall (20) determine the meaning, and I shall write to my lord whether it is thus or not. Let the guard of the city of Mari be strengthened, (25) and let my lord not go outside the gate.

Jer. 6:1

b

Published by C. F. Jean in *Archives royales de Mari*, ii, No. 22. For his preliminary translation see *RA*, xxix, pp. 64 f.; the following is fully revised.

To my lord say: Thus Ibal-pi-Il, thy servant. (5) Hammurabi spoke to me as follows: "A heavily armed force had gone out to raid the enemy column, but there was no suitable base to be found, so that force has returned empty-handed and the column of the enemy is proceeding in good order without panic. Now let a light armed force go to raid the enemy column and capture informers."

Thus Hammurabi spoke to me. I am sending Sakirum with three hundred troops to Shabazum, (20) and

---

* In collaboration with George E. Mendenhall.
[1] With their aid the ancients were able to communicate with great rapidity over considerable distances.

the troops which I have sent are one hundred fifty [Hanu], fifty Suhu, and one hundred troops from the bank of the Euphrates River; and there are three hundred troops of Babylon. In the van of the troops of my lord there goes Ilu-nasir, the seer,[1] the subject of my lord, (25) and one Babylonian seer goes with the troops of Babylon. These six hundred troops are based in Shabazum, and the seer assembles the omens. When the appearance of their (30) omens is favorable, one hundred fifty go out and one hundred fifty come in. May my lord know this. The troops of my lord are well.

Num. 22-24

c

Published by C. F. Jean in *Archives royales de Mari*, II, No. 37, and translated in *Revue des études sémitiques*, 1944, pp. 10 f.; the following is fully revised.

To my lord say: Thus Ibal-Il, thy servant. The tablet of Ibal-Adad from Aslakka (5) reached me and I went to Aslakka to "kill an ass"[2] between the Hanu and Idamaras. A "puppy and lettuce" they brought, but I obeyed my lord and (10) I did not give the "puppy and lettuce." I caused the foal of an ass to be slaughtered. I established peace between the Hanu and Idamaras. (15) In Hurra, in all of Idamaras, the Hanu are victorious, as a victor who has no enemy.[3] May my lord be pleased. This tablet of mine (20) I will have delivered to my lord in Rataspatum. I will reach my lord by the third day after this tablet of mine. (25) The camp and the Banu-Sim'al[8] are well.

Zech. 9:9

d

Published by C. F. Jean in *Archives royales de Mari*, II, No. 131, and translated in *Revue des études sémitiques*, 1944, pp. 26 f.; the following is fully revised.

To my lord say: Thus Mashum, thy servant. (5) Sintiri wrote to me for help, and I reached him with troops at Shubat-Shamash. The next day word of the enemy (10) came as follows: "Yapah-Adad has made ready the settlement Zallul on this side on the bank of the Euphrates River, and with two thousand troops

---

[1] Cuneiform *barum*. In later times Balaam was just such a *baru*.

[2] This expression is always in Amorite, transcribed in cuneiform *hayaram qatalum* (Heb. *qatol 'air*); it means simply "make a treaty," which was solemnized by the sacrifice of a young ass, much as the later Saracens of St. Nilus' time sacrificed a camel.

[3] The cuneiform text must be read *šabi'um gerem ul išu*, obviously referring to the bloodless victory of the Hanu (the most important tribe of Mari) over their former foes in the southeastern marches.

of the Hapiru of the land (15), is dwelling in that city." This word came to me, and from Shubat-Shamash, with troops of my command and with troops of the command of (20) Sintiri, I hurried, and made ready the town of Himush over against the town of Zallul. Between the two (25) cities (there is a distance of) thirty "fields." When I had made ready the city of Himush over against him, and he saw that the land was hastening to (my) aid, (30) he raised a fire signal, and all the cities of the land of Ursum on the other side acknowledged it. The *security* forces which are stationed within the brick-*enclosure* are numerous, and, lest they (35) wipe out the troops, I did not draw near the city. This tablet of mine I send to my lord from the bank of the Euphrates River. The troops and *cattle* are well.

Jer. 6:1

ANET, 483-490

THE AMARNA LETTERS

In 1887 an Egyptian peasant woman discovered a collection of cuneiform tablets at Tell el-Amarna in Middle Egypt, the site of Akh-en-Aton's capital in the early fourteenth century B.C. These tablets were sold to European museums and private dealers; some of them escaped attention for nearly thirty years. Subsequently excavation disclosed enough additional tablets to bring the total collection up to about 377 numbers. Almost all of them are letters belonging to the royal archives of Amenhotep III and his son Akh-en-Aton. Nearly 300 letters were written by Canaanite (or rarely Egyptian) scribes in Palestine, Phoenicia, and southern Syria, about half of them in Palestine proper. These letters are written in a conventional vulgar Akkadian, full of canaanitisms in grammar and vocabulary. Occasionally we find a letter written mostly in Canaanite with scattered Akkadian formulas and ideograms. They date from the last years of Amen-hotep III and the reign of his successor; a very few may date from the ephemeral reign of Akh-en-Aton's son-in-law and successor, Smenkhkere.

Fig. 107

The translations offered below represent the combined work of W. F. Albright and George E. Mendenhall, with a few corrections by W. L. Moran, S. J.—ED.

EA, No. 234 [1]

To the king, my lord, the Sun-god from heaven: Thus Zatatna, prince of Accho, thy servant, the servant of the king, and (5) the dirt (under) his two feet, the ground which he treads. At the two feet of the king, my lord, the Sun-god from heaven, seven times,

[1] This letter comes from the time of Akh-en-Aton. Shuta (pronounce *Suta*) was an Egyptian officer, probably the great-grandfather of Ramses II; Biryawaza (whose name was formerly read erroneously *Namyawaza*) was prince of Damascus under Egyptian suzerainty. All personal names (except Shuta) are Indo-Aryan.

seven times I fall, both prone and supine. (10) Let the king, my lord, hear the word of his servant! [Zir]dam-yashda has withdrawn from Biryawaza. [He was] with Shuta, the s[ervant] of the (15) king in the city of [....] He did not say anything to him. The army of the king, my lord, has departed. He was with it in Megiddo. (20) I said nothing to him, but he deserted to me, and now Shuta has written to me: "Give (25) Zirdamyashda to Biryawaza!" But I did not consent to give him up. Behold, Accho is (as Egyptian) as Magdal (30) in Egypt, but the king, my lord, has not heard that [Shut]a has turned against me. Now let the king, my lord, send (35) his commissioner and fetch him.

Exod. 14:2

EA, No. 244[1]

To the king, my lord, and my Sun-god, say: Thus Biridiya, the faithful servant of the (5) king. At the two feet of the king, my lord, and my Sun-god, seven and seven times I fall. Let the king know that (10) ever since the archers returned (to Egypt?), Lab'ayu has carried on hostilities against me, and we are not able to pluck the wool, and we are not able to go outside the gate in the presence of Lab'ayu, since he learned that thou hast not given (20) archers; and now his face is set to take Megiddo, (25) but let the king protect his city, lest Lab'ayu seize it. (30) Verily, the city is destroyed by death from pestilence and *disease*. Let the king give (35) one hundred garrison troops to guard the city lest Lab'ayu seize it. Verily, there is no other purpose in (41) Lab'ayu. He seeks to destroy Megiddo.

EA, No. 245[2]

Further, I said to my brethren, "If the gods of the king, our lord, grant (5) that we capture Lab'ayu, then we will bring him alive to the king, our lord"; but my mare was felled by an arrow, and I alighted (10) afterwards and rode with Yashdata, but before my arrival, they had slain him. (15) Verily, Yashdata is thy servant, and he entered the battle with me. And

[1] Biridiya was prince of Megiddo at the end of the reign of Amen-hotep III and the beginning of the reign of Akh-en-Aton; his name is Indo-Aryan like most other princely names of northern Palestine at that time. Lab'ayu (whose name meant approximately "lion-like" in Canaanite) was prince of Shechem in the central hill-country and was constantly raiding the territory and caravans of his neighbors on all sides.

[2] This is the latter part (all that is preserved) of a continued letter from Biridiya of Megiddo. Zurata, whom Biridiya accuses of treachery, was prince of Acre (biblical Accho).

verily, [...] (20) the life of the king, m[y lord] [and] [...] all in [...] of the king, [my] lord, [...], and Zurata (25) removed Lab'ayu from Megiddo, saying to me: "I will send him by ship (30) to the king," and Zurata took him and sent him home from Hannathon, for Zurata had received his ransom money (35) in his hand.

Further, what have I done to the king, my lord, that he should despise me and honor (40) my younger brothers? Zurata has sent Lab'ayu, and Zurata has sent Ba'lu-mihir to their homes, and let the king, my lord, be informed!

RA, xix, p. 97 [1]

To the king, my lord, and my Sun-god say: Thus Biridiya, the true servant of the king. (5) At the feet of the king, my lord, and my Sun-god, seven times and seven times I fall. Let the king be informed concerning his servant and concerning his city. (10) Behold, I am working in the town of Shunama, and I bring men of the corvée, (15) but behold, the governors who are with me do not as I (do): they do not (20) work in the town of Shunama, and they do not bring men for the corvée, but I alone (25) bring men for the corvée from the town of Yapu. They come from Shu[nama], and likewise from the town of Nuribda. (30) So let the king be informed concerning his city!

Gen. 49:15

EA, No. 250 [2]

˹To˺ the king, my lord, say: Thus Ba'lu-UR.SAG, thy servant. At the feet of the king, my lord, seven times, seven times, I fall. Let the king, my lord, know that (5) the two sons of a rebel against the king my lord, the two sons of Lab'ayu, have determined to destroy the land of the king, my lord, after their father's death. And let the king, my lord, know that (10) many days the two sons of Lab'ayu have *accused* me (saying): "Why hast thou given the town of Giti-padalla into the hand of the king, thy lord—the city which Lab'ayu, our

---

[1] This letter from the prince of Megiddo is very instructive because of the light it throws on forced labor for the king in the Plain of Esdraelon, several of whose towns and villages are mentioned. The word for "corvée" is the Hebrew *mas*, which is employed a little later of the tribe of Issachar in this very region.

[2] The prince from whom this letter comes was in control of a district in the northern coastal plain of Palestine, south of Carmel. Here Lab'ayu's sons are described as continuing their father's activities. Biryawaza, whose help is wanted to subdue the recalcitrants, was prince of Damascus. Milkilu was prince of Gezer, whose territory adjoined the territory of Ba'lu-UR.SAG ("Baal is a warrior") on the south.

father, captured?" (15) So thus the two sons of Lab'ayu
spoke to me: "Declare war against the people of the
land of Qena, because they slew our father; and if you
do not declare war, then we are hostile to you."

But I answered them: (20) "May the god of the king,
my lord, preserve me from making war against the
people of the land of Qena, the servants of the king,
my lord!" Now may it be agreeable to the king, my
lord, to send one of his officers to Biryawaza (25) and
let him say to him: "Wilt thou march against the two
sons of Lab'ayu, or art thou a rebel against the king?"
And after him, let the king, my lord, send to me [...]
the deed (30) ⌐of the king,⌐ thy ⌐lord⌐, against the
two sons of Lab'ayu [...] Milkilu *has gone in to
them*[? ...] (35) ... ⌐land of the king, my lord, with
them after Milkilu and Lab'ayu died.⌐ (40) And thus
the two sons of Lab'ayu spoke: "Be hostile to the king,
thy lord, like our father, when he attacked Shunama
and Burquna and Harabu, and (45) destroyed them/
smote them. And he took Giti-rimuni, and he betrayed
the helpers of the king, thy lord."

But I answered them: "The god of the king, my lord,
preserve me from making (50) war against the king,
my lord. The king, my lord, I serve, and my brothers
who hearken to me." But the courier of Milkilu does
not move from the two sons of Lab'ayu (55) a (*single*)
day. Behold, Milkilu seeks to destroy the land of the
king, my lord. But there is no other intention with me—
I serve the king, my lord, and the word which the
king, my lord, speaks do I hear.

EA, No. 252 [1]

To the king, my lord, say: Thus Lab'ayu, thy servant.
At the feet of my lord I fall. (5) As for what thou
hast written, "Are the people strong who have captured
the town? How can the men be arrested?" (I reply)
"By fighting was the town captured, (10) in spite of
the fact that I had taken an oath of conciliation and that,
when I took the oath, an (Egyptian) officer took the
oath with me! The city as well as my god are captured.
I am slandered/blamed (15) before the king, my
lord."

[1] This letter is written in almost pure Canaanite and was not understood until very recently. Lab'ayu virtuously protests that he was only
repelling aggressors who had attacked his native town (not Shechem,
which was his capital) in spite of a previous treaty sworn in the presence
of an Egyptian official.

Further, when (even) ants are smitten, they do not accept it (passively), but they bite the hand of the man who smites them. (20) How could I hesitate this day when two of my towns are taken?

Further, even if thou shouldst say: "(25) Fall beneath them, and let them smite thee," I should still repel my foe, the men who seized the town and (30) my god, the despoilers of my father, (yea) I would repel them.

EA, No. 254[1]

To the king, my lord and my Sun-god: Thus Lab'ayu, thy servant, and the dirt on which thou dost tread. At the feet of the king, my lord, (5) and my Sun-god, seven times and seven times I fall.

I have heard the words which the king wrote to me, and who am I that the king should lose his land (10) because of me? Behold, I am a faithful servant of the king, and I have not rebelled and I have not sinned, and I do not withhold my tribute, and I do not refuse (15) the requests of my commissioner. Now they wickedly slander me, but let the king, my lord, not impute rebellion to me!

Further, (20) my crime is namely that I entered Gezer and said publicly: (25) "Shall the king take my property, and not likewise the property of Milkilu?" I know the deeds which Milkilu has done against me.

(30) Further, the king wrote concerning my son. I did not know that my son associates with the 'Apiru (36), and I have verily delivered him into the hand of Addaya.

Further, if the king should write for my wife, (40) how could I withhold her? If the king should write to me, "Plunge a bronze dagger into thy heart and (45) die!", how could I refuse to carry out the command of the king?

EA, No. 256[2]

To Yanhamu, my lord say: Thus Mut-ba'lu, thy servant. At the two feet of my lord I fall. How is it said (5)

---

[1] In this letter Lab'ayu protests his innocence of all charges against him and assures the king (Amen-hotep III) that he is more loyal than the neighbors who complain against him.

[2] Mut-ba'lu (literally "Man of Baal") was prince of Pella in the northern Jordan Valley, opposite Beth-Shan; Ayab (Ayyab, Hebrew Job) was prince of Ashtartu (biblical Ashtaroth) in Bashan. The land of Garu lay in southern Golan between Pella and Ashtartu. Yanhamu, to whom the letter is addressed, was a high Egyptian official of Canaanite (possibly of Hebrew) origin, who seems to have been the Egyptian governor of Palestine at the beginning of the reign of Akh-en-Aton.

before thee, "Mut-ba'lu has fled, Ayab has hidden himself?" How can the prince of Pella flee from the face of the commissioner (10) of the king, his lord? As the king my lord lives, as the king my lord lives, Ayab is not in Pella. Behold, he has not been (here) for two months(?). (15) Indeed, ask Ben-ilima, ask Taduwa, ask Yashuya. Again, *at the instance of* (20) the house of Shulum-Marduk, the city of Ashtartu came to (my) help, when all the cities of the land of Garu were hostile, (namely) Udumu, Aduru, (25) Araru, Meshqu, Magdalu, Eni-anabu and Zarqu, and when Hayanu and Yabilima were captured.

Further, behold—after (30) thy writing a tablet to me, I wrote to him. Before thou dost arrive with thy caravan, behold, he will have reached Pella, and he will hear (thy) words.

EA, No. 270[1]

To the king, my lord, my pantheon, my Sun-god, say: Thus Milkilu, thy servant, (5) the dirt (under) thy feet. At the feet of the king, my lord, my pantheon, my Sun-god, seven times, seven times I fall. Let the king, my lord, know (10) the deed which Yanhamu did to me after I left the presence of the king, my lord. Now he seeks (15) two thousand (shekels) of silver from my hand, saying to me: "Give me thy wife and (20) thy children, or I will smite!" Let the king know this deed, and let my lord send to me (26) chariots, and let him take me to himself lest I perish!

EA, No. 271[2]

To the king, my lord, my pantheon, my Sun-god, say: Thus Milkilu, thy servant, (5) the dirt (under) thy feet. At the feet of the king, my lord, my pantheon, my Sun-god, seven times, seven times, I fall. Let the king know (10) that powerful is the hostility against me and against Shuwardata. Let the king, my lord, protect his land (15) from the hand of the 'Apiru. If not, (then) let the king, my lord, send chariots (20) to fetch us, lest our servants smite us.

[1] Milkilu (Heb. Malchiel) was prince of Gezer. For Yanhamu see the previous letter.

[2] For Milkilu see the previous letter. Shuwardata (with an Indo-Aryan name) was prince of the Hebron region in the southern hill-country, and frequently appears in association with Milkilu. The 'Apiru (formerly called Habiru) were a strong semi-nomadic people, or rather class of population in Syria and Palestine. While there is much reason to identify them with the Hebrews of the Patriarchal Age, the combination still remains uncertain and cannot be made the basis for any historical inferences.

Further, let the king, my lord, ask (25) Yanhamu, his servant, concerning that which is done in his land.

RA, xxxi, pp. 125-136[1]

To Milkilu, prince of Gezer. Thus the king. Now I have sent thee this tablet to say to thee: Behold, (5) I am sending to thee Hanya, the commissioner of the archers, together with goods, in order to procure fine concubines (i.e.) *weaving women*: silver, gold, (linen) garments, (10) *turquoise*, all (sorts of) precious stones, chairs of *ebony*, as well as every good thing, totalling 160 deben. Total: 40 concubines: the price of each concubine is 40 (shekels) of silver. (15) So send very fine concubines in whom there is no blemish. (19) And let the king, thy lord, say to thee, "This is good. To thee life has been *decreed*." And mayest thou know that (25) the king is well, like the Sun-god. His troops, his chariots, his horses are very well. Behold, the god Amon has placed the upper land, (30) the lower land, the rising of the sun, and the setting of the sun under the two feet of the king.

EA, No. 280 [2]

To the king, my lord, my pantheon, my Sun-god, say: Thus Shuwardata, (5) thy servant, the dirt (under) thy feet! At the feet of the king, my lord, my pantheon, my Sun-god, seven times, seven times, I fall! (9) The king, my lord, sent me to make war against Keilah. I have made war (and) I was successful; my town has been restored (15) to me. Why did 'Abdu-Heba write to the people of Keilah (saying): "Take (my) silver and (20) follow me!" And let the king, my lord, know that 'Abdu-Heba had taken the town from my hand.

Further, (25) let the king, my lord, investigate; if I have taken a man or a single ox or an ass from him, then he is in the right! (30)

Further, Lab'ayu is dead, who seized our towns; but behold, 'Abdu-Heba is another Lab'ayu, and (35) he (also) seizes our towns! So let the king take thought

[1] This letter from pharaoh to Milkilu of Gezer throws an interesting light on the rôle of the Canaanite princes in organizing royal commerce in Asia; Egyptian products and manufactured articles are to be exchanged for the best quality of slave-girls.

[2] Shuwardata, prince of the Hebron district, here protests to pharaoh (Akh-en-Aton) that 'Abdu-Heba, prince of Jerusalem, is just as aggressive as the unlamented Lab'ayu (see the previous letters).

for his servant because of this deed! And I will not do anything until the king sends back a message to his servant.

RA, xix, p. 106[1]

To the king, my lord, my Sun-god, my pantheon say: Thus Shuwardata, thy servant, servant of the king (5) and the dirt (under) his two feet, the ground (on) which thou dost tread! At the feet of the king, my lord, the Sun-god from heaven, seven times, seven times I fall, both (10) prone and supine.

Let the king, my lord, learn that the chief of the Apiru has risen (in arms) against the lands which the god of the king, my lord, gave me; (16) but I have smitten him. Also let the king, my lord, know that all my brethren have abandoned me, and (20) it is I and 'Abdu-Heba (who) fight against the chief of the 'Apiru. And Zurata, prince of Accho, and Indaruta, prince of Achshaph, it was they (who) hastened (25) with fifty chariots—for I had been robbed (by the 'Apiru)—to my help; but behold, they are fighting against me, so let it be agreeable to the king, my lord, and (30) let him send Yanhamu, and let us make war in earnest, and let the lands of the king, my lord, be restored to their (former) limits!

EA, No. 286[2]

To the king, my lord, say: Thus 'Abdu-Heba, thy servant. At the two feet of my lord, the king, seven times and seven times I fall. (5) What have I done to the king, my lord? They blame me before the king, my lord (saying): " 'Abdu-Heba has rebelled against the king, his lord." Behold, as for me, (it was) not my father (10) and not my mother (who) set me in this

---

[1] This letter, from the beginning of Akh-en-Aton's reign, is an extraordinarily illuminating illustration of the situation in Palestine at that time. Just who this redoubtable 'Apiru chieftain was we do not learn, since the proud feudal princes disdained even to mention names of the semi-nomadic 'Apiru. However, he was sufficiently dangerous to unite the arch-foes, 'Abdu-Heba and Shuwardata, and to induce them to offer fifty chariots (a very considerable offer for Palestinian chieftains) to the princes of Accho and Achshaph in the Plain of Acre, far to the north. One suspects that Milkilu of Gezer and Lab'ayu of Shechem, who are not mentioned at all, were—either or both—involved with the 'Apiru.

[2] This letter is characteristic of the continuous requests of 'Abdu-Heba, prince of Jerusalem, for Egyptian assistance in his chronic struggle with the 'Apiru. However, it seems certain from other letters that he was inclined to lump his enemies among the "governors" (i.e. the native princes) with the 'Apiru. It is uncertain whether the Ilimilku (Elimelech) of lines 35 ff. was an 'Apiru chieftain, was one of the sons of Lab'ayu, or was even Milkilu of Gezer (whose name might have been transposed accidentally by the scribe).

place; the arm of the mighty king brought me into the house of my father! Why should I commit (15) transgression against the king, my lord? As long as the king, my lord, lives, I will say to the commissioner of the king, my lord, "Why do ye favor the 'Apiru and oppose the governors?"—And thus (21) I am blamed in the presence of the king, my lord. Because it is said, "Lost are the lands of the king, my lord," thus am I blamed to the king, my lord! (25) But let the king, my lord, know that (when) the king had established a garrison, Yanhamu took ⌜it all⌝ away, [and . . .] ⌜the troops⌝ (30) [of archers(?) . . .] the land of Egypt [. . .] O king, my lord, there are no garrison troops (here)! [So] let the king take care of his land! (35) Let the king take care of his land! [The land]s of the king have all rebelled; Ilimilku is causing the loss of all the king's land. So let the king take care of his land! I keep saying, "Let me enter (40) into the presence of the king, my lord, and let me see the two eyes of the king, my lord." But the hostility against me is strong, so I cannot enter into the presence of the king, my lord. So may it please the king (45) to send me garrison troops in order that I may enter and see the two eyes of the king, my lord. As truly as the king, my lord, lives, when the commis[sioners] go forth I will say, "Lost are the lands of the king! (50) Do you not hearken unto me? All the governors are lost; the king, my lord, does not have a (single) governor (left)!" Let the king turn his attention to the archers, and let the king, my lord, send out (55) troops of archers, (for) the king has no lands (left)! The 'Apiru plunder all the lands of the king. If there are archers (here) in this year, the lands of the king, my lord, will remain (intact); but if there are no archers (here) (60) the lands of the king, my lord, will be lost!

To the scribe of the king, my lord: Thus 'Abdu-Heba, thy servant. Present eloquent words to the king, my lord.—All the lands of the king, my lord, are lost!

EA, No. 287[1]

[To the kin]g, my lord, [say:] [Thus] 'Abdu-Heba, thy servant. [At the feet] of my lord seven t[imes and seven times I fall.] [Let my king] [know (?) this]

---

[1] In this letter the prince of Jerusalem complains about a number of events which recur in other letters. In the first place he excoriates Milkilu of Gezer and Tagu of the northern Coastal Plain of Palestine for their

matter! [Milkili and Tagu (?)] (5) have caused [their troops (?)] to enter [the town of Rubutu (?)] [Behold] the deed which [Milkilu (?)] has done; [bows] (and) copper arrows [... he has given (?) ...] word [... (10) ...] into the town of [Rubutu (?)] they brought in. Let my king know that all the lands are at peace (but that) there is war against me. So let my king take care of his land!

Behold the land of Gezer, the land of Ashkelon, (15) and ⌜Lachish,⌝ they have given them grain, oil, and all their requirements; and let the king (thus) take care of his archers! Let him send archers against the men who transgress against the king, my lord. (20) If there are archers (here) in this year, then the lands and the governor⟨s⟩ will (still) belong to the king, my lord; [but] if there are no archers, the lands and the governors will (no longer) belong to the king! (25) Behold this land of Jerusalem: (It was) not my father (and) not my mother (who) gave (it) to me, (but) the arm of the mighty king (which) gave (it) to me.

Behold, this deed is the deed of Milkilu (30) and the deed of the sons of Lab'ayu who have given the land of the king to the 'Apiru. Behold, O king, my lord, I am right!

With reference to the Nubians, let my king ask the commissioners whether my house is (not) very strong! (35) Yet they attempted a very great crime; they took their implements and breached ... of the roof. [If] they send into the land [of Jerusalem] ⌜troops⌝, let them come up with [an (Egyptian) officer (40) for] (regular) service. Let [my king] take heed for them —for [all] the lands are impoverished by them— [and] let my king requisition for them much grain, much oil, (and) much clothing, (45) until Pawure, the royal commissioner, comes up to the land of Jerusalem.

Addaya has left, together with the garrison (and)

aggression against Rubutu, which lay somewhere in the region southwest of Megiddo and Taanach. In the second place he urges the king to instruct his officers to supply the Egyptian archers from the towns of the Philistine Plain and Sharon (in order to avert heavy drain on the scanty supplies of Jerusalem). He goes on to complain that the Nubian (biblical Cushite) slave-troops (or mercenaries) of Egypt, stationed as garrison in Jerusalem, had burglarized the residence of 'Abdu-Heba himself, nearly killing the prince in his own house. He finally complains that his last caravan containing tribute and captives for the king was attacked and robbed near Ajalon, presumably by the men of Milkilu of Gezer and the sons of Lab'ayu.

the (Egyptian) officer which my king had given (me).
Let the king know! Addaya spoke to me, (saying,)
(50) [Loo]k, let me go, (but) do not thou leave it
(the city)! So send me a garrison this [year], and send
me a commissioner likewise, O my king. I have sent
[gifts (?)] to the king, my lord: [. . .] captives, five
thousand [silver (shekels)] (55) and eight porters for
the caravans of the king, *my lord*; (but) they were
captured in the plain of Ajalon. Let the king, my lord,
know that I cannot send a caravan to the king, my
lord. For thy information!

(60) Behold, the king has set his name in the land of
Jerusalem for ever; so he cannot abandon the lands of

II Kings 21:4, 7   Jerusalem!

To the scribe of the king, my lord, (65) say: Thus
'Abdu-Heba, thy servant. At thy two feet I fall—thy
servant am I! Present eloquent words to the king, my
lord. I am (only) a petty officer of the king; (70) I am
more insignificant (?) than thou!

But the men of the land of Nubia have committed
an evil deed against ⟨me⟩; I was almost killed by the
men of the land of Nubia (75) in my own house. Let
the king [call] them to (account). Seven times and

Gen. 4:24   seven times let the [king,] my lord, [avenge (?)] me!

EA, No. 288[1]

To the king, my lord, my Sun-god, say: Thus 'Abdu-
Heba, thy servant. At the two feet of the king, my
lord, seven times and seven times I fall. (5) Behold the
king my lord, has set his name at the rising of the sun,
and at the setting of the sun! (It is) vile what they
have done against me. Behold, I am not a governor
(10) (nor even a) petty officer of the king, my lord;
behold, I am a shepherd of the king, and a bearer of
the royal tribute am I. It was not my father (and) not
my mother, (but) the arm of the mighty king (15)
(which) placed me in the house of my father. [. . .]
came to me [. . .] I delivered ten slaves [into his] hand.
Shuta, the royal commissioner, came (20) to me.
Twenty-one maidens (and) eighty captives I delivered
into the hand of Shuta as a gift for the king, my lord.
Let my king take thought for his land! The land of the

---

[1] This letter continues the complaints of the previous letter, and incidentally paints a vivid picture of the anarchic condition of the country
early in the reign of Akh-en-Aton. The references to "the very gate of
Sile (Zilu)" mean that the outrages against the *pax Aegyptiaca* extend to
the frontiers of Egypt itself, near modern Qantarah.

king is lost; in its entirety (25) it is taken from me; there is war against me, as far as the lands of Seir (and) as far as Gath-carmel! All the governors are at peace, but there is war against me. I have become like an 'Apiru (30) and do not see the two eyes of the king, my lord, for there is war against me. I have become like a ship in the midst of the sea! The arm of the mighty king (35) conquers the land of Naharaim and the land of Cush, but now the 'Apiru capture the cities of the king. There is not a single governor (remaining) (40) to the king, my lord—all have perished! Behold, *Turbazu* has been slain in the (very) gate of Sile, (yet) the king holds his peace. Behold Zimreda, the townsmen of Lachish have smitten him, slaves who had become 'Apiru. (45) Yaptih-Hadad has been slain [in] the (very) gate of Sile, (yet) the king holds his peace. [Wherefore] does not [the king] call them to account? [So] let the king take care of his land; [and l]et the king decide, and let the king send (50) archers to his land! [But] if there are no archers (here) this year, all the lands of the king, my lord, will be lost. They shall not say to the king, my lord, (55) that the land of the king, my lord, has been lost, and (that) all of the governors have perished! If there are no archers (here) this year, let the king send a commissioner, and let him take me (60) to himself (!) together with ⟨my⟩ brothers, and we shall die near the king, our lord!

[To] the scribe of the king, my lord: [Thus] 'Abdu-Heba, ⟨thy⟩ servant. At [thy (?)] two feet I fall. Present eloquent words (65) [. . .] to the king, [my lord! Thy] servant [and] thy son am I.

EA, No. 289[1]

To the king, my lord, [say]: Thus 'Abdu-Heba, thy servant. At the two feet of my lord, the king, seven times and seven times I [fall.] (5) Behold, Milkilu does not break (his alliance) with the sons of Lab'ayu and with the sons of Arzayu in order to covet the land of the king for themselves. As for a governor who does (such a) deed (as) this, (10) why does not my king call him to account? Behold Milkilu and Tagu! The deed which they have done is this, that they(!) have taken it, the town of Rubutu. And now as for Jerusalem—(15) Behold this land belongs to the king, or

---

[1] Addaya was the Egyptian resident governor of Palestine, with his seat at Gaza.

why like the town of Gaza is it loyal to the king? Behold the land of the town of Gath-carmel, it belongs to Tagu, and the men of Gath (20) have a garrison in Beth-Shan. Or shall we do like Lab'ayu, who gave the land of Shechem to the 'Apiru? (25) Milkilu has written to Tagu and the sons of ⟨Lab'ayu⟩, (saying) "Ye are (members of) my house. Yield all of their demands to the men of Keilah, and let us break our alliance ⟨with⟩ Jerusalem!" (30) The garrison which thou didst send through Haya, son of Miyare, Addaya has taken (and) has put into his residence in Gaza, [and] twenty men to Egypt (35) he has sent. Let my king know (that) there is no royal garrison with me. So now, as my king lives, truly the commissioner, Puwure, has taken leave of me (40) and is in Gaza; and let my king look out for him! And let the king send fifty men as a garrison to guard the land! The entire land of the king has revolted. (45) Send me Yanhamu and let him take care of the land of the king!

To the scribe of the king, [my lord]: Thus 'Abdu-Heba, [thy] servant. Present eloquent words (50) to the king. I am much more insignificant than thou; I am thy servant.

EA, No. 290 [1]

[To] the king, my lord, say: Thus ['Abdu]-Heba, thy servant. At the two feet of the [king,] my lord, seven times and seven times I fall. (5) Behold the deed which Milkilu and Shuwardata did to the land of the king, my lord! They rushed troops of Gezer, troops of Gath (10) and troops of Keilah; they took the land of Rubutu; the land of the king went over to the 'Apiru people. But now even (15) a town of the land of Jerusalem, Bit-*Lahmi* by name, a town belonging to the king, has gone over to the side of the people of Keilah. Let my king hearken to 'Abdu-Heba, thy servant, (20) and let him send archers to recover the royal land for the king! But if there are no archers, the land of the king will pass over to the 'Apiru people. (25) This was done at the command of Milkilu [and at] the command of Shuwardata (?) ... So let my king (30) take care of [his] land!

---

[1] In lines 15 ff. there is an almost certain reference to the town of Bethlehem, which thus appears for the first time in history. Keilah may have been the home of Shuwardata, prince of the Hebron district.

EA, No. 292[1]

To the king, my lord, my pantheon, my Sun-god say: Thus Ba'lu-shipti, thy servant, the dirt (under) thy two feet. (5) At the feet of the king, my lord, my pantheon, my Sun-god, seven times, seven times I fall. I have looked this way, and I have looked that way, (10) but it was not bright. I looked toward the king, my lord, and it was bright. A brick may move from beneath its companions, (15) but I will not move from beneath the two feet of the king, my lord. I have heard the words, which the king, my lord, wrote to his servant: (20) "Guard thy commissioner, and guard the cities of the king, thy lord." Behold, I guard, and behold, I hearken day (25) and night to the words of the king, my lord. But let the king, my lord, *learn* concerning his servant, (that) there is hostility against me from the mountains, so I have built (30) a house— Manhatu is its name—in order to make ready before the archers of the king, my lord; but Maya took it from my hands, and installed (35) his commissioner within it. So command Reanap, my commissioner, to restore the city to my hands, that I may make ready for (40) the archers of the king, my lord.

Further, behold the deed of Peya, the son of Gulate, against Gezer, the maidservant of the king, my lord, how many days he plundered it, so that it has become an empty cauldron because of him. From the mountains (50) people are ransomed for thirty (shekels) of silver, but from Peya for one hundred (shekels) of silver; so know these words of thy servant!

Exod. 21:32

EA, No. 297[2]

To the king, my lord, my pantheon, my Sun-god, say: Thus Yapahu, thy servant, the dirt (under) thy two feet. (5) At the feet of the king, my lord, my pantheon, my Sun-god, seven times, seven times, I fall. Everything which the king, my lord, said to me (10) I have heard most attentively.

---

[1] Ba'lu-shipti was prince of Gezer in the period following the death of Milkilu, and this letter comes from the middle of the reign of Akh-en-Aton. Maya was a high Egyptian official at the court of the latter, then acting as commander of the Egyptian forces in Palestine. Peya bears an Egyptian name, in spite of the Canaanite name of his mother(?), and he was probably a minor Egyptian officer.

[2] Yapakhu was prince of Gezer after the death of Milkilu. By *Sutu* is meant the nomadic tribesmen of Semitic origin who were in Egyptian service, as we know from other documents.

Further: I have become like an empty bronze cauldron (because of) the debt (15) at the hands of the Sutu, but now I have heard the sweet breath of the king, and it goes out (20) to me, and my heart is very serene.

EA, No. 298

To the king, my lord, my pantheon, my Sun-god, the Sun-god of heaven. Thus Yapahu, the prince of (5) Gezer, the dirt (under) thy two feet, the groom of thy horse. At the two feet of the king, my lord (10) the Sun-god of heaven, seven times and seven times I fall, both prone and supine; and everything (15) which the king, my lord, commands me I hear very attentively. A servant of the king am I, and the dirt of thy two feet. (20) Let the king my lord know that my youngest brother is estranged from me, and has entered (25) Muhhazu, and has given his two hands to the chief of the 'Apiru. And now the [land of . . .]anna is hostile to me. (30) Have concern for thy land! Let my lord write to his commissioner concerning this deed.

EA, No. 320 [1]

To the king, my lord, my pantheon, my Sun-god, the Sun-god of heaven: Thus (5) Widia, the prince of Ashkelon, thy servant, the dirt (under) thy feet, the groom of thy horse. (10) At the feet of the king, my lord, seven times and seven times verily I fall, both prone and (15) supine.

Now I am guarding the place of the king which is with me, and whatever the king, my lord, has sent to me (20) I have heard very attentively. Who is the dog that does not hearken to the words of the king, his lord, (25) the son of the Sun-god?

Letter from Tell el-Hesi [2]

[To] the (Egyptian) officer say: [Thus P]a'pu. At thy feet I fall. Thou shouldst know that (5) Shipti-ba'lu

---

[1] Note the Indo-Aryan name of the prince of Ashkelon, whose servile words illustrate the impotence to which he was condemned by his nearness to the Egyptian residence at Gaza, as well as by the smallness of his territory.

[2] This letter vividly characterizes the atmosphere of mutual suspicion and treachery which prevailed in Palestine in the early part of Akh-en-Aton's reign. Zimreda was prince of Lachish (Tell ed-Duweir) and Shipti-Ba'lu was to succeed him in that capacity. As shown by his name, Pa'pu was an Egyptian official, perhaps the local commissioner at Lachish.

and Zimreda have plotted publicly and Shipti-ba'lu said
to Zimreda: ["The pr]ince of Yaramu wrote to me:
'Give me ⌐six⌐ bows, and three daggers, and three
swords. (15) Verily I am going out against the land
of the king, and thou art my ally!'" And yet he returns (the charge of) (20) lèse-majesté (saying): "The
one who plots against the king is Pa'pu! And send
him to (confront) me!" And [now] I have sent Rabi-ilu
(25) to bring him (to thee) [because of] this matter.

Shechem Letter

To Birashshena say: Thus Baniti-[. . .]. From three
years ago until now (5) thou hast caused me to be paid.
Is there no grain nor oil nor wine which thou canst
send? What is my offense that thou hast not paid me?
(10) The children who are with me continue to learn.
I am their father and their mother every day alike
[. . . (15) . . . .] Now [behold] whatever [there is]
beneath the feet [of my lord] let him [send] to me (20)
and let him infor[m me].

Taanach, No. 1[1]

To Rewashsha say: Thus Guli-Adad. Live well! (5)
May the gods take note of thy welfare, the welfare
of thy house, of thy children! Thou hast written to me
concerning silver (10) and behold I will give fifty
(shekels) of silver, truly I will do (so)!

Further, and if (20) there is a wizard of Asherah,   I Kings 18:19 ff.
let him *tell our fortunes* and let me hear *quickly*, and
the omen and the interpretation send to me. (25)

As for thy daughter who is in the town of Rubutu,
let me know concerning her welfare; and if she grows
up thou shalt give her to become *a singer*, (30) or to a
husband.

---

[1] This letter and the other letters found by Ernst Sellin at Taanach, five
miles southeast of Megiddo in northern Palestine, unquestionably belong
to the fifteenth century B.C., and they may be dated roughly about three
generations before the bulk of the Amarna Tablets. Rewashsha was the
prince of Taanach; his Egyptian name illustrates the extent of Egyptian
penetration about a century after the initial conquest. The word here
rendered "wizard" is Akkadian *ummanu*, which passed into Hebrew as
omman and into later Phoenician as *ammun*, always with the general
sense of "learned, skilled man, expert." The diviners of Asherah appear
in the time of Elijah as "prophets of Asherah": they also figure in the
Baal Epic of Ugarit.

Aramaic Letters

TRANSLATOR: H. L. GINSBERG

LETTERS OF THE JEWS IN ELEPHANTINE

"THE PASSOVER PAPYRUS"

A very defective strip of papyrus with writing on both sides. Text: Sachau, 6; Ungnad, 6; Cowley, 21. Date: 419 B.C.

[To] my [brethren Yedo]niah[1] and his colleagues the [J]ewish gar[rison], your brother Hanan[iah].[2] The welfare of my brothers may God [seek at all times]. Now, this year, the fifth year of King Darius, word was sent from the king to Arsa[mes[3] saying, "*Authorize a festival of unleavened bread for the* Jew]ish [garrison]." So do you count fou[rteen days of the month of Nisan and] obs[erve *the passover*],[4] and from the 15th to the 21st day of [Nisan observe the festival of unleavened bread]. Be (ritually) clean and take heed. [Do n]o work [on the 15th or the 21st day, no]r drink [beer,[5] nor eat] anything [in] which the[re is] leaven [from the 14th at] sundown until the 21st of Nis[an. For seven days it shall not be seen among you. Do not br]ing it into your dwellings but seal (it) up between these date[s. *By order of King Darius.* To] my brethren Yedoniah and the Jewish garrison, your brother Hanani[ah].

[1] A priest and head of the Jewish community (military colony) of Elephantine.　　[2] Apparently a secretary for Jewish affairs to Arsames.
[3] Satrap of Egypt from 455/4 to at least 407.
[4] The word *psh'* in two ostraca from Elephantine may mean "passover (offering)."
[5] This restoration is only correct if Hananiah's tradition, like rabbinic law, included under "leaven" fermented corn but not fermented fruit (wine). The Samaritans take a more rigorous view.

CONTRIBUTIONS TO THE CULT OF YAHO

A very broad sheet of papyrus with 7 columns of Aramaic; traces of palimpsest. Text: Sachau, 17-19; Ungnad, 19; Cowley, 22. Date: 419 or 400 B.C.[1] See the special study of U. Cassuto in *Kedem*, I, pp. 47-52.

On the 3rd of Phamenoth,[2] year 5. This is (*sic*!) the names of the Jewish garrison which (*sic*!) gave money to the God Yaho, [2 shekels] each.

(Lines 2-119, 126-135 name 123 contributors of both sexes.)

[1] Depending on whether the fifth year is that of Darius II or of the native Egyptian king Amyrtaeus.
[2] A month in the Egyptian calendar.

(120-125) Cash on hand with Yedoniah the son of Gemariah on the said day of the month of Phamenoth: 31 *karash*, 8 shekels. Comprising: for Yaho 12 *k*., 6 sh.;[1] for Ishumbethel[2] 7 *k*.; for Anathbethel[3] 12 *k*.

[1] Since 1 *karash* = 20 (light) shekels, this is the correct total for 123 contributions of 2 shekels each. The monies for the other two deities were doubtless contributed by non-Jews, Yedoniah (see n.1) acting as treasurer or banker for all the Arameans of Elephantine.

[2] Male divinity.   [3] Probably female divinity.

SETTLEMENT OF CLAIM BY OATH

Text: Sayce-Cowley, F; Cowley, 14. Date: 440 B.C.

The Jewess Mibtahiah (*Mbṭhyh*) had apparently married the Egyptian Pi' and then the marriage had been dissolved. The marriage had meant Mibtahiah's exit from the Jewish community and adoption into the Egyptian. Even its liquidation necessitated her swearing by an Egyptian deity. The witnesses to this document are neither Jewish nor Egyptian.

On the 14th of Ab, being the 19th day of Pahons, in the year 25 of King Artaxerxes, Pi' the son of Pahi (*Phy*), builder, of the fortress of Syene, said to Mibtahiah, daughter of Mahseiah the son of Yedoniah, an Aramean of Syene of the detachment of Varizata (as follows): In accordance with the action which we took at Syene, *let us make a division* of the silver, grain, raiment, bronze, iron, and all goods and possessions and marriage contract. Then an oath was imposed upon you, and you swore to me concerning them by the goddess Sati. I was satisfied with the oath which you took to me concerning your goods, and I renounce all claim on you from this day for ever.

PETITION FOR AUTHORIZATION
TO REBUILD THE TEMPLE OF YAHO

A well-preserved papyrus with writing on both sides, apparently a copy of one sent to Jerusalem. Text: Sachau, 1-2; Ungnad, 1; Cowley 30. Date: 407 B.C. (Another, defective copy, with some variants: Sachau, 3; Ungnad, 2; Cowley 31.)

To our lord Bagoas, governor of Judah, your servants Yedoniah and his colleagues, the priests who are in the fortress of Elephantine. May the God of Heaven seek after the welfare of our lord exceedingly at all times and give you favor before King Darius and the nobles a thousand times more than now. May you be happy and healthy at all times. Now, your servant Yedoniah and his colleagues depose as follows: In the month of

Tammuz in the 14th year of King Darius,[1] when Arsames (5) departed and went to the king, the priests of the god Khnub, who is in the fortress of Elephantine, conspired with Vidaranag, who was commander-in-chief here, to wipe out the temple of the god Yaho from the fortress of Elephantine. So that wretch Vidaranag sent to his son Nefayan, who was in command of the garrison of the fortress of Syene, this order, "The temple of the god Yaho in the fortress of Yeb is to be destroyed." Nefayan thereupon led the Egyptians with the other troops. Coming with their weapons to the fortress of Elephantine, they entered that temple and razed it to the ground. The stone pillars that were there they smashed. Five (10) "great" gateways built with hewn blocks of stone which were in that temple they demolished, but their doors *are standing*, and the hinges of those doors are of bronze; and *their* roof of cedarwood, all of it, with the ... and whatever else was there, everything they burnt with fire. As for the basins of gold and silver and other articles that were in that temple, they carried all of them off and made them their own.—Now, our forefathers built this temple in the fortress of Elephantine back in the days of the kingdom of Egypt, and when Cambyses came to Egypt he found it built. They knocked down all the temples of the gods of Egypt, but no one did any damage to this temple. (15) But when this happened, we and our wives and our children wore sackcloth, and fasted, and prayed to Yaho the Lord of Heaven, who has let us see our desire upon that Vidaranag. The dogs took the fetter out of his feet,[2] and any property he had gained was lost; and any men who have sought to do evil to this temple have all been killed and we have seen our desire upon them.—We have also sent a letter before now, when this evil was done to us, ⟨to⟩ our lord and to the high priest Johanan and his colleagues the priests in Jerusalem and to Ostanes the brother of Anani and the nobles of the Jews. Never a letter have they sent to us. Also, from the month of Tammuz, year 14 of King Darius, (20) to this day, we have been wearing sackcloth and fasting, making our wives as widows, not anointing ourselves with oil or drinking wine. Also, from then to now, in the year 17 of King Darius,[3] no meal-offering, in[cen]se, nor burnt offering

Neh. 12:22-23

I Chron. 3:24

---

[1] 410 B.C.   [2] Perhaps a mistake for "his feet out of the fetter."   [3] 407 B.C.

have been offered in this temple. Now your servants Yedoniah, and his colleagues, and the Jews, the citizens of Elephantine, all say thus: If it please our lord, take thought of this temple to rebuild it, since they do not let us rebuild it. Look to your well-wishers and friends here in Egypt. Let a letter be sent from you to them concerning the temple of the god Yaho (25) to build it in the fortress of Elephantine as it was built before; and the meal-offering, incense, and burnt offering will be offered in your name, and we shall pray for you at all times, we, and our wives, and our children, and the Jews who are here, all of them, if you do thus, so that that temple is rebuilt. And you shall have a merit before Yaho the God of Heaven more than a man who offers to him burnt offering and sacrifices worth a thousand talents of silver and (because of)   gold. Because of this we have written to inform you. We have also set the whole matter forth in a letter in our name to Delaiah and Shelemiah, the sons of Sanballat the governor of Samaria.   (30) Also, Arsames knew nothing of all that was done to us. On the 20th of Marheshwan, year 17 of King Darius.

Neh. 2:19

ADVICE OF THE GOVERNORS OF JUDAH
AND SAMARIA TO THE JEWS
OF ELEPHANTINE

Text: Sachau, 4; Ungnad, 3; Cowley, 32.

Memorandum of what Bagoas and Delaiah said to me: Let this be an instruction to you in Egypt to say before Arsames about the house of offering of the God of Heaven which had been in existence in the fortress of Elephantine (5) since ancient times, before Cambyses, and was destroyed by that wretch Vidaranag in the year 14 of King Darius: to rebuild it on its site as it was before, and the meal-offering and incense[1] to be made on (10) that altar as it used to be.

[1] The Mazdean Arsames was likely to react more favorably if no mention was made of burnt offering, since it involved the profaning of fire by contact with dead bodies.

PETITION BY ELEPHANTINE JEWS,
PERHAPS TO ARSAMES

Text: Sachau, 4; Ungnad, 4; Cowley, 33.

Your servants Yedoniah the son of Ge[mariah] by name 1, Ma'uzi the son of Nathan by name [1], Shemaiah the son of Haggai by name 1, Hosea the son of

Yatom by name 1, (5) Hosea the son of Nathun by name 1, 5 men in all, Syenians who [ho]ld proper[ty] in the fortress of Elephantine, say as follows: If your lordship is [favo]rable, and the temple of ou[r] God Yaho [is rebuilt] in the fortress of Elephantine as it was for[merly buil]t, (10) and n[o] *sheep*, ox, or goat are offered there as burnt offering,[21] but (only) incense, meal-offering, [and drink-offering], and (if) your lordship giv[es] orders [to that effect, then] we shall pay into your lordship's house the s[um of ... and] a thous[and] *ardabs* of barley.

INDEX TO BIBLICAL REFERENCES

NOTE: The numbers in italics refer to illustrations.

1. Statuettes of Sumerians which stood before the god of the Nintu Temple V at Khafajah early in the third millennium.

2. Ibsha, "the ruler of a foreign country," leads a caravan of "thirty-seven" Asiatics bringing eye-paint to Egypt; a tomb painting dating from about 1890 B.C. The bellows on each of the donkeys suggests traveling metalworkers (cf. Gen. 4:19-22).

3. Head of a Mede, with hair and beard elaborately curled, carved on a decorated stairway at Persepolis; from the time of Darius and Xerxes.

4. Bound Syrian captive on the head of a ceremonial walking stick of Tut-ankh-Amon found in his tomb at Thebes.

5. Syrian tribute bearers, bringing ointment horn, quiver, vessels, rhyton, and child; on a fragment of plaster from the wall of a fifteenth-century tomb at Thebes.

6. A beardless Hittite prisoner with a rope around his neck; on the wall of the great temple at Abu Simbel.

7. Prisoners of Ramses III from his campaign in Amor—Lybian, Syrian, Hittite, one of the Sea Peoples (perhaps a Philistine), Syrian; on wall of temple at Medinet Habu.

8. Kneeling Syrians and Negroes decorate the platform (footstool) of Amen-hotep III enthroned.

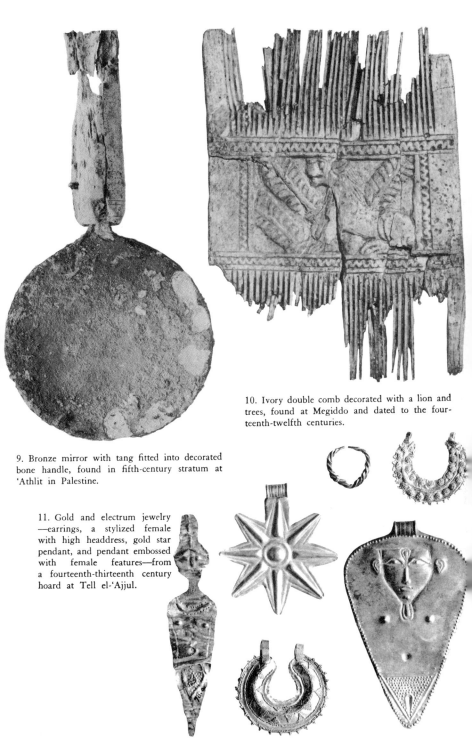

9. Bronze mirror with tang fitted into decorated bone handle, found in fifth-century stratum at 'Athlit in Palestine.

10. Ivory double comb decorated with a lion and trees, found at Megiddo and dated to the fourteenth-twelfth centuries.

11. Gold and electrum jewelry —earrings, a stylized female with high headdress, gold star pendant, and pendant embossed with female features—from a fourteenth-thirteenth century hoard at Tell el-'Ajjul.

12. An Egyptian barber dresses the hair of one of the recruits of Amen-hotep II; fifteenth century.

14. Egyptian woman holding mirror and applying paint to her lips with a brush; on a papyrus from the time of the New Kingdom.

13. Egyptian razor blade of bronze with holes for attaching to handle; possibly Eighteenth Dynasty.

15. Dairy scene on frieze from Tell el-Obeid: milking of cow, doorposts of the sacred precincts, and preparation of milk products; limestone figures set against a black shale background held within copper borders; middle of third millennium.

16. Wooden model of a man plowing with a two-handled wooden plow drawn by two yoked oxen; late third millennium.

17. Seed plow with drill on a basalt stela of Esarhaddon.

18. Traditional brickmaking in Egypt: workmen with hoes knead clay moistened with water, as laborers carry material to two brickmakers; from fifteenth-century tomb painting of Rekh-mi-Re at Thebes.

20. Mesopotamian god and worshiper drinking (beer?) through tubes.

21. Wooden model of a boat equipped with rudder, mast, sail, and cabin, in which sits Meket-Re with his son and a singer; Eleventh Dynasty.

19. Gathering grapes from an arbor, treading, and storage of wine in jars with stoppers; fifteenth century.

22. Clay figure bending over a trough kneading dough; from a cemetery of 900-600 B.C. at ez-Zib.

23. Limestone weight inscribed with *pym* from Tell en-Nasbeh (cf. I Samuel 13:21).

24. Clay weight with inscription found at Gibeon.

25. Weight in form of human head found at Ras Shamra; fourteenth-thirteenth century.

26. Model of potter's shop, in which one figure turns clay on a wheel as another tends a kiln; twenty-first century, from Sakkarah.

27. Profiles of characteristic pottery types from the principal archaeological periods in Palestine.

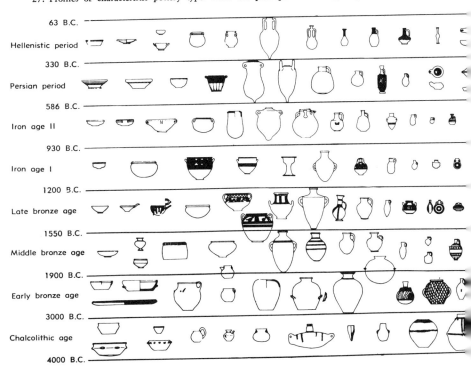

28. Woman's head framed by recessed window (cf. I Kings 6:4), carved from ivory for an inset in woodwork (cf. II Kings 9:30); from Nimrud, possibly first half of eighth century.

29. Box from one piece of ivory with sphinxes and lions carved in high relief; from Megiddo, 1350-1150 B.C.

30, 31. Ivory carving of nude woman; and ivory figurine with eyes of glass, of a woman holding staff, probably used as an inset for furniture (cf. Amos 6:4); from Megiddo, 1350-1150 B.C.

32. Painting of spinning and weaving scene on wall of Middle Kingdom tomb.

33. A dye plant consisting of two cylindrical stone vats and two rectangular basins, from eighth-century level at Tell Beit Mirsim.

34, 35. Gold helmet of Mes-kalam-dug (not the king), hammered out of one piece of metal, and gold dagger and sheath; twenty-fifth century tomb at Ur.

36. Coat of mail made of bronze plates laced together with thongs, from a level dated to the middle of the second millennium at Nuzi.

37. A pottery mold for casting implements with two axes or chisels in place; from Shechem, Middle Bronze Age.

38. Drawing of the reconstructed copper-smelting furnace found in the eleventh-century level at Tell Qasile; two clay crucibles containing remains of smelted copper were found nearby.

Copper

Clay crucible

Coal

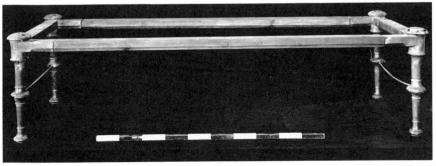

39. A bed of the Persian period reconstructed from bronze fittings and iron tie-rods found at Tell el-Far'ah (south).

40. Ashurnasirpal hunting lions, on a ninth-century bas-relief found at Nimrud.

41. Tut-ankh-Amon, standing in his chariot with drawn bow, charges a herd of gazelles and ostriches fleeing before the king's hounds; painting on the lid of a box found in the king's tomb at Thebes.

42. Wooden model of Egyptian soldiers arranged in four columns, armed with lances and shields; from Siut, Middle Kingdom.

43. Assyrian soldiers leading away prisoners of war and transporting women in a cart; from seventh-century palace of Ashurbanipal at Nineveh.

44. Reconstructed lyre with sound-box ending in a gold bull's head; found in a twenty-fifth century tomb at Ur.

45. Egyptian musicians: harpist, lutist, dancer, player of double pipe, lyrist; fifteenth-century tomb painting at Thebes.

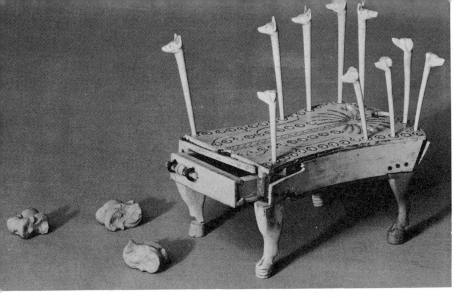

46. Game board of ivory and ebony veneer, ivory pins, and knucklebones, for playing "hounds and jackals"; from a Theban tomb.

47. Game board with ten playing pieces and an ivory teetotum pierced on four sides with varying number of holes; from Middle Bronze stratum at Tell Beit Mirsim.

48. An ivory game board with fifty-eight holes, from Megiddo, 1350-1150 B.C.

49. Plastered skull found in a Neolithic stratum at Jericho.

50. Fourth-century Jewish coin with bearded figure seated on a winged wheel.

51. Fourth-century coin from Beth-zur, inscribed with "Hezekiah" and "Judaea."

52. Seated scribes, equipped with sharpened rush pens and palettes; Fourth Dynasty.

53. Ink-wells of terra-cotta and bronze found in the remains of scriptorium at Qumran.

54. Scribes list the booty and the slain of a town captured by Sennacherib.

55. Restored writing equipment of an Egyptian scribe: rush pen, palette, and water jar.

56. Legal document in cuneiform from Cappadocia with its envelope.

57. Cylinder seals, varying in size and shape, carved with scenes which were impressed on wet clay for purposes of identification.

58. Cuneiform tablet with account of the conquest of Jerusalem by Nebuchadnezzar in 598 B.C.

60. Historical records of Esarhaddon on an octagonal prism.

61. Ancient clay map of the town of Nippur, showing locations of temple, walls, gates, and canals; found at Nippur.

59. The stela of Hammurabi inscribed with laws; from Susa.

68. Portion of the text of the legend of Aqhat on clay tablet from Ras Shamra.

69. Fragment of clay tablet from Nineveh inscribed with the Babylonian account of the flood.

70. Sheet of papyrus rolled, tied, and sealed with an impression on mud, containing, a marriage contract in Aramaic.

71. Section of the Theban recension of the "Book of the Dead," written on papyrus and illustrated with a vignette.

72. The Rosetta stone, inscribed in hieroglyphic, demotic, and Greek.

73. The Siloam inscription cut into the rock wall of the tunnel of Hezekiah south of the temple area in Jerusalem.

74. Inscription of Mesha, king of Moab, on a black basalt stela; carved about 840-820 B.C.

75. "Belonging to Shema, servant of Jeroboam"; eighth century, from Megiddo. 76. "Belonging to Jaazaniah, servant of the king" (cf. II Kings 25:23); from Tell en-Nasbeh, about 600 B.C. 77. Impression on a jar handle: "Belonging to Eliakim, steward of Joiachin"; from Tell Beit Mirsim, sixth century.

78. Jar handle stamped with a "royal stamp," inscribed "For the king, *mmšt*; from Gibeon. 79. Jar handle stamped with later "royal stamp," "For the king, Ziph"; from Gibeon.

80. Reverse of Ostracon IV from Tell ed-Duweir with mention of Lachish; early sixth century.

Ahiram Inscription 1

Yehimilk Inscription 2

Samaria Ivories 3

Gezer Calendar 4

Moabite Stone 5

Kilamuwa Inscription 6

Samaria Ostraca 7

Shema Seal 8

Bar Rakab Inscription 9

Siloam Inscription 10

Nerab Stelae 11

Pharaoh Letter 12

Lachish Ostraca 13

Jewish Seals 14

Meissner Papyrus 15

Leviticus Fragments 16

Elephantine Papyri 17

Eshmunazar Sarcophagus 18

81. Table of Semitic alphabets; outlined letters indicate carving; solid letters, writing with ink.

82. Portion of an Aramaic papyrus, dated 404 B.C., describing the gift of a house by Anani bar Azariah to his daughter.

83. Column of Isaiah manuscript from Dead Sea cave; contains Isaiah 33:1-24.

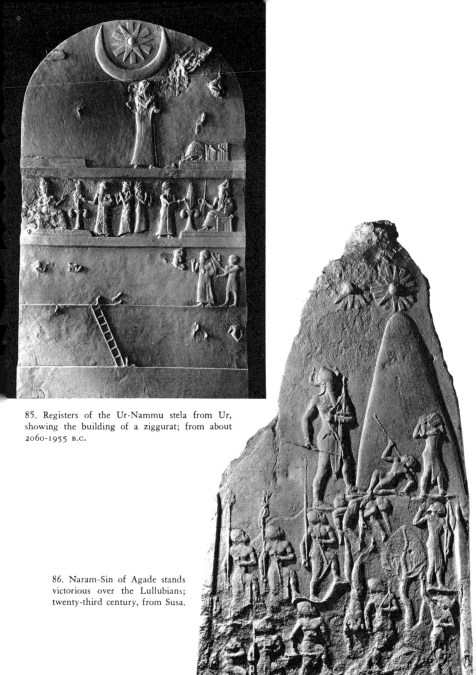

85. Registers of the Ur-Nammu stela from Ur, showing the building of a ziggurat; from about 2060-1955 B.C.

86. Naram-Sin of Agade stands victorious over the Lullubians; twenty-third century, from Susa.

87. The fortress of 'the town of the Canaan" under attack by Seti I; on wall at Karnak.

88. A portion of the list of the Asiatic conquests of Thut-mose III; from Karnak. Each name-ring is surmounted by the figure of a bound Asiatic.

89. Chiefs of Lebanon felling cedars and assuring an Egyptian officer of Seti I of their submission; at Karnak.

90. The Prince of Megiddo celebrates a victory with feasting and music and the procession of prisoners; he sits upon a cherub throne; from Megiddo, 1350-1150 B.C.

91. The fortress of Ashkelon being conquered by the forces of Ramses II; men on the tower raise their hands in a gesture of submission; at Karnak.

92. Ship of Ramses III engaged in battle with the Philistines and other Sea Peoples who wear feather crowns.

93. Counting and recording the hands of Hittites killed in battle with Ramses II (cf. I Samuel 18:25 ff.).

94. Part of the scene and list of conquests in Palestine by Sheshonk I (cf. I Kings 14:25-26; II Chron. 12:2-4).

95. Ramses III attacks a walled fortress in Amor manned by Syrian lancers, on a relief at Medinet Habu.

96. Detail of the name "Israel" from the stela of Mer-ne-Ptah, found at Thebes.

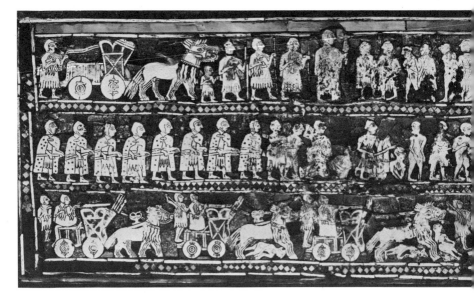

97. The "war panel" from a standard found at Ur, depicting the triumph of the king over his enemies; twenty-fifth century.

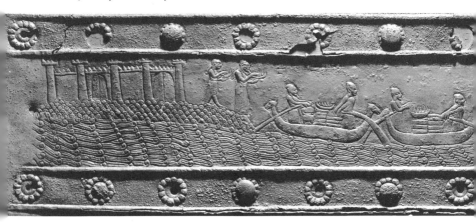

98. Bronze bands from Balawat: tribute taken from Tyre by Shalmaneser III (above); sacrifice prepared at the source of the Tigris (below).

99. Ramses II before Amon-Re, on a thirteenth-century stela found at Beth-shan.

100A. Scenes from the Black Obelisk of Shalmaneser III from Nimrud; in second register from top, "Jehu, son of Omri" presents his tribute to the king.

100B. Opposite side of the "Black Obelisk" depicting camels, an elephant, monkeys, and other tribute for Shalmaneser III.

101. Attack upon Lachish by siege-engines pushed up an incline and accompanied by archers who shoot from behind shields; archers, spearmen, and sling-throwers support the siege-engines; three nude figures impaled; relief of Sennacherib found at Nineveh.

102, *opposite*. Sennacherib seated on his throne receiving the booty taken from Lachish; inhabitants of the town kneel before him; from Nineveh.

103. Reliefs of Ramses II and Shalmaneser III (?) carved on the cliff at Nahr el-Kelb, near Beirut.

108. Akh-en-Aton, sun-worshiper and the first monotheistic king of Egypt, from Amarna.

109. Nefert-iti, queen of Akh-en-Aton.

110. Family scene of Akh-en-Aton, Nefert-iti, and their daughters, under the sun-disc with radiating arms; from Amarna.

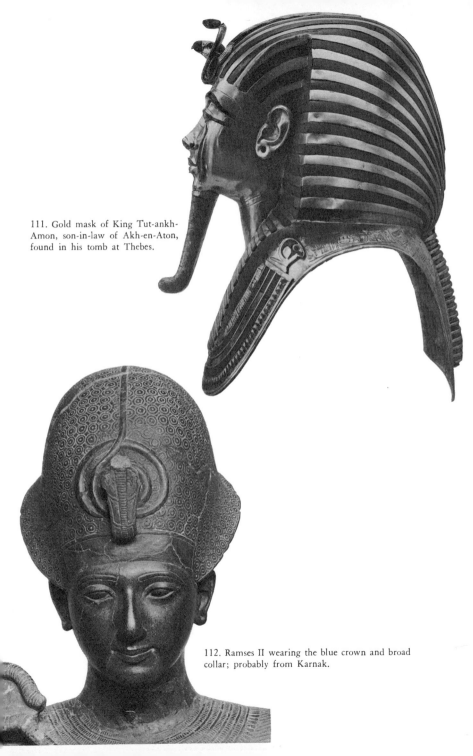

111. Gold mask of King Tut-ankh-Amon, son-in-law of Akh-en-Aton, found in his tomb at Thebes.

112. Ramses II wearing the blue crown and broad collar; probably from Karnak.

113. King Mer-ne-Ptah, from
Thebes.

114. Seti II sitting on throne
holding a small shrine.

115. Enannatum, king of Lagash, about
2500 B.C.

116. Lamgi-Mari, king of Mari, dedication
to Ishtar; middle of third millennium.

117. Gudea, e n s i of Lagash, dedication to Nin-
gizzida; from Tello, beginning of twenty-first
century.

119. King Tiglath-pileser III of Assyria (744-727 B.C.); from Nimrud.

118. Ashurnasirpal II; from Nimrud.

120. Sargon II of Assyria, from Khorsabad.

122. King Ashurbanipal banqueting in a garden with his queen, attended by servants and musicians, while an enemy's head hangs on a tree nearby.

123. King Darius seated on his throne, Crown Prince Xerxes behind him, with attendants; Persepolis.

124. Ashurbanipal carrying a basket for rebuilding of the temple of Esagila in Babylon.

125. King Merodach-baladan of Babylon (II Kings 20:12) making a grant to an official.

126. Ahiram, king of Byblos, seated on a cherub throne, before an offering table.

127. King Barrakab of Sam'al seated on his throne, with his scribe.

128. Nude female figurines, cultic objects of fertility worship, from 2000-600 B.C.

129. Nude goddess standing on a lion, flanked by a worshiper and the god Seth.

130. King Yehawmilk presents a libation to his goddess, the "Lady of Byblos."

131. The goddess with two horns, and a worshiper holding a lotus, on a thirteenth-century stela from Beth-shan.

132. Silver goddess with gold collar and skirt from Ras Shamra; 2000-1800 B.C.

133. Copper goddess from Ras Shamra; 1900-1600 B.C.

134. Bronze god overlaid with gold and silver; from Minet el-Beida, 1500-1300 B.C.

135. Nude goddess with a *was* scepter on a fourteenth-century gold pendant from Beth-shan.

137. God with headdress, from Ras Shamra, 2000-1800 B.C.

136. The "Baal of Lightning," 1900-1750 B.C., from Ras Shamra.

138. Presentation of offering to god "El," on a thirteenth-century stela from Ras Shamra.

140. Storm-god astride a bull, with lightning bolts in his hands; from Arslan Tash, eighth century.

141. The god Marduk on a piece of lapis lazuli; from Babylon, middle of ninth century.

139. The god Melqart on a dedicatory stela "which he vowed to him" (see Chapter IX), erected by Barhadad (Ben-Hadad), king of Aram about 860 B.C.

142. Boundary-stone of Nebuchadnezzar I, with symbols of various gods and goddesses; twelfth century.

143. Upper part of a statue of a goddess with flowing vase; from Mari, 2000-1500 B.C.

144. Shamash enthroned within his shrine, to whom Nabuaplaiddin is presented; from Abu Habbah, middle of ninth century.

145. Squads of Assyrian soldiers of Tiglath-pileser III carrying away the statues of the gods of a captured town; from Nimrud.

147. Bronze model of the ritual of the dawn, with representations of cultic objects; from Susa, twelfth century.

148. Horned incense altar from Megiddo; tenth-ninth century.

149. Bronze openwork stand from Megiddo; 1050-1000 B.C. (?).

150. Cylindrical cult object from Beth-shan, decorated with birds and serpents; eleventh century.

151, 152. Clay models of the liver. One inscribed with omens and magical formulae for use of diviners (cf. Ezek. 21:26), from about 1830-1530 B.C.; other uninscribed, from Megiddo, 1350-1150 B.C.

153. Clay figurine of a bound prisoner with a curse upon the enemies of Egypt written over the body; the figurine was broken in order to make the inscribed curse take effect (cf. Jer. 19:10-11); from Sakkarah, eighteenth century.

154. Sumerian priest with libation vase.

155. Shalmaneser III sacrificing to his gods, before his own royal image cut in the rock at Lake Van.

156. Ashurbanipal pouring a libation over dead lions before an offering table and incense stand, to the accompaniment of music; from Nineveh.

157. Ceremony of "opening the mouth" for giving the deceased a new body in the hereafter; New Kingdom.

158. Egyptian sky-goddess Nut, arched as the heavens, supported by the air-god Shu; at his feet, the earth-god Geb; a vignette in the "Book of the Dead" from Deir el-Bahri, tenth century.

160. The god Osiris.

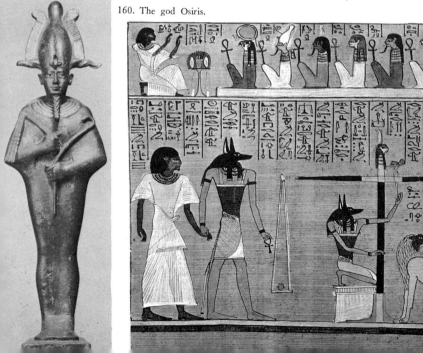

161. Gods of Egypt lead a soul in the land of the dead and weigh his heart.

159. The king as Amon.

162. The god Khnum fashions the prince Amen-hotep III and his *ka* on a potter's wheel, as the goddess Hathor extends the *ankh* sign, the emblem of life; at Luxor.

163. Winged lion of Ashurnasirpal.

164. Goat upright beside a tree; from "Great Death Pit" at Ur, twenty-fifth century.

165. Winged creature, from Carchemish.

166. Ivory sphinx in lotus thicket, inset for panel (cf. Ps. 45:8); from Samaria, ninth century.

167. Sun-god with Ea to his right; to the left, a "Flora" and Ninurta.

168. The sun-god before the enthroned Ea, god of wisdom; from Ur.

CYLINDER SEALS OF THE AKKADIAN ERA (2360-2180 B.C.)

169. Sun-god, holding a plow, travels in his boat.

170. Seven-headed fiery dragon attacked by two gods; from Tell Asmar.

171. Fighting gods and the building of a temple tower.

172. Massive tower of Neolithic Jericho, nine meters in diameter, a part of the city defenses; in its center is a stone staircase with twenty steps leading downward to a horizontal passage.

173. The east city-gate at Shechem.

174. Hazor: "House of Makhbiram" of eighth century (upper); pillared building of time of Ahab (center); Solomonic gate and casemate wall (below and left).

175. Ancient Megiddo.

ith century; cf. I Kings 9:15, 19, etc.

ay at Megiddo; cf. Ezek. 40:5-16.

f the chapel and palace at Tell
yria; eighth century; similar in
salem temple.

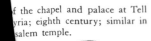

176. City wall and gate at Tell en-Nasbeh; with stone benches at the gate.

177. Foundation of city wall, near a gate of ninth-century Samaria.   178. Hellenistic tower at Samaria.

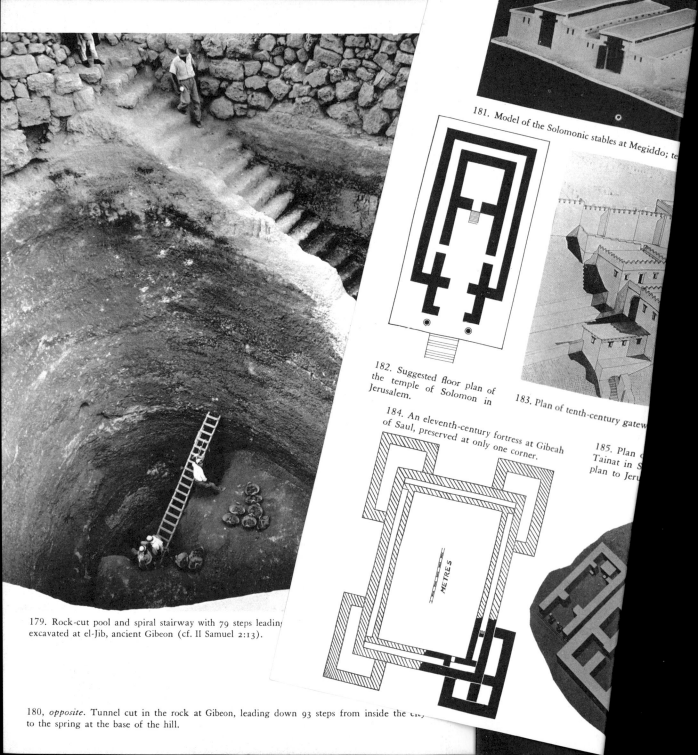

181. Model of the Solomonic stables at Megiddo; te

182. Suggested floor plan of the temple of Solomon in Jerusalem.

183. Plan of tenth-century gatew

184. An eleventh-century fortress at Gibeah of Saul, preserved at only one corner.

185. Plan o Tainat in S plan to Jeru

METRES

179. Rock-cut pool and spiral stairway with 79 steps leading excavated at el-Jib, ancient Gibeon (cf. II Samuel 2:13).

180, *opposite*. Tunnel cut in the rock at Gibeon, leading down 93 steps from inside the city to the spring at the base of the hill.

176. City wall and gate at Tell en-Nasbeh; with stone benches at the gate.

177. Foundation of city wall, near a gate of ninth-century Samaria.   178. Hellenistic tower at Samaria.

179. Rock-cut pool and spiral stairway with 79 steps leading to water 25 meters below the surface; excavated at el-Jib, ancient Gibeon (cf. II Samuel 2:13).

180, *opposite*. Tunnel cut in the rock at Gibeon, leading down 93 steps from inside the city wall to the spring at the base of the hill.

181. Model of the Solomonic stables at Megiddo; tenth century; cf. I Kings 9:15, 19, etc.

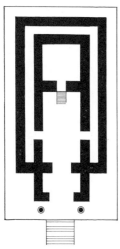

182. Suggested floor plan of the temple of Solomon in Jerusalem.

183. Plan of tenth-century gateway at Megiddo; cf. Ezek. 40:5-16.

184. An eleventh-century fortress at Gibeah of Saul, preserved at only one corner.

185. Plan of the chapel and palace at Tell Tainat in Syria; eighth century; similar in plan to Jerusalem temple.

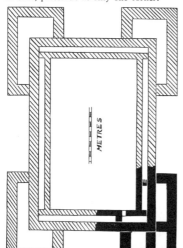

METRES

186. Shrine with a large altar; at Megiddo, about 3000 B.C.

187. Temple with mud-brick platform, altar, and benches for offerings, from the Late Bronze period at Lachish.

188. The temple tower, or ziggurat, at Ur; cf. the "tower" of Babel in Gen. 11:1-9.

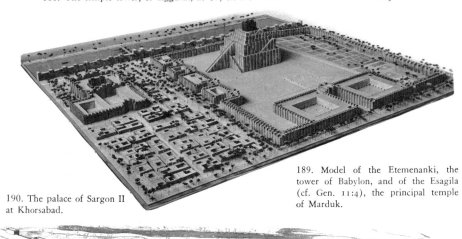

190. The palace of Sargon II at Khorsabad.

189. Model of the Etemenanki, the tower of Babylon, and of the Esagila (cf. Gen. 11:4), the principal temple of Marduk.

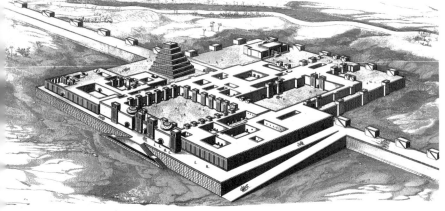

191. Tomb for King Djoser of the Third Dynasty, in the form of a step pyramid, at Sakkarah.

192. A sphinx with the head of King Khaf-Re guards the necropolis of Giza with its three great pyramids.

193. The Ishtar gate of Nebuchadnezzar II at Babylon.

194. Bound enemy carved on a door socket from Hierakonpolis.

195. The tomb of Cyrus at Pasargadae in Iran, erected about 529 B.C.

196. Tombs of Darius I, Artaxerxes I, and Darius II, cut in the rock at Naqsh-i-Rustam in Iran.

197. The apadana, or audience hall, of Darius and Xerxes at Persepolis.

INDEX AND GLOSSARY

NOTE: The numerals in italics refer to illustrations.